# THE EXTREME RIGHT IN INTERWAR FRANCE

# The Extreme Right in
# Interwar France
## The Faisceau and the Croix de Feu

SAMUEL KALMAN
*St Francis Xavier University, Canada*

**ASHGATE**

Published by
Ashgate Publishing Limited
Gower House
Croft Road
Aldershot
Hampshire GU11 3HR
England

Ashgate Publishing Company
Suite 420
101 Cherry Street
Burlington, VT 05401-4405
USA

Ashgate website: http://www.ashgate.com

**British Library Cataloguing in Publication Data**
Kalman, Samuel
   The extreme right in interwar France : the Faisceau and the Croix de feu
   1. Faisceau des combattants et des producteurs 2. Croix de feu (Organization : France)
   3. Right-wing extremists – France – History – 20th century
   4. Radicalism – France – History – 20th century
   I. Title
   320.5'33'0944'0941

**Library of Congress Data**
2007045482

ISBN 978-0-7546-6240-2

Printed and bound in Great Britain by MPG Books Ltd, Bodmin, Cornwall.

# Contents

# List of Tables

# Acknowledgements

This book could not have been written without the support of numerous individuals and organizations, all of whom assisted in its gestation and completion. This includes the financial support afforded by two Government of Ontario graduate scholarships and a Social Sciences and Humanities Research Council of Canada doctoral fellowship, which funded my Ph.D. studies at McMaster University, including preliminary research for this project in Canada and France. In addition, I benefited from McMaster's Richard Fuller Memorial Scholarship for History, which enabled research trips to Paris that provided the bulk of the archival material used in writing this book. Subsequent support from the University Council for Research at St. Francis Xavier University facilitated the collection of supplementary material in Aix-en-Provence.

My project has received encouragement from numerous mentors and colleagues over the years. I owe by far the largest debt of gratitude to Wayne Thorpe, who supervised my Ph.D. dissertation at McMaster, first suggested that I pursue this topic, and has consistently provided invaluable recommendations concerning subsequent undertakings. His guidance, intuition, and friendship inform every page of this effort. The members of my dissertation committee also deserve many thanks. Martin Horn, the late Robert Johnston, and especially William Irvine all left an indelible imprint upon my work. A large expression of gratitude is also due to Sean Kennedy, Sam Goodfellow, Laurent Kestel, Robert Soucy, Cheryl Koos, Will Sweet, Errol Clauss, and Jerry Pubantz for their readings of various sections of the manuscript, suggestions for its improvement, and/or advice concerning various aspects of the publication process. I am similarly grateful to my colleagues in the St. Francis Xavier Department of History for their encouragement. At Ashgate, Tom Gray, Ann Newell, Adam Richardson, and Anne Keirby proved equally supportive, nurturing the book to completion, their suggestions and ideas invariably improving the manuscript. The latter is equally true of the two anonymous readers, whose corrections and comments allowed me to avoid awkward errors, while positing new, valuable lines of enquiry.

Hearty thanks are also due to a variety of individuals and institutions in France and North America, whose assistance facilitated my research during each stage of the project. This includes Odile Gaultier-Voituriez at the Centre d'histoire de l'Europe de Vingtième-Siècle (now the Centre d'histoire de Sciences-Po) in Paris, Daniel Hick and the staff at the Archives d'Outre-Mer in Aix-en-Provence, and a variety of persons at the Archives Nationales, Bibliothèque Nationale, Archives of the Paris Prefecture of Police, and the Centre de documentation juive contemporaine. I am indebted to the late Gilles de la Rocque for permission to consult his father's papers at the AN and CHEVS, and to Jacques Nobécourt for useful suggestions concerning research at the latter institution. Further thanks are due to the inter-library loan personnel at St. Francis Xavier University, Salem College, and McMaster University, and particularly the late Susan Taylor at Salem, who tirelessly tracked down the most arcane materials with incredible ease.

I wish to further thank the editors of *Historical Reflections/Réflexions historiques* for graciously allowing me to reproduce material from my article "Parasites from all Civilizations: The Croix de Feu/Parti social français Confronts French Jewry", to Sage Publications for permission to republish material from my article "Faisceau Visions of Physical and Moral Transformation and the Cult of Youth in Interwar France", *European History Quarterly* 33 (2003): 343–366, to Oxford University Press for permitting me to reprint passages from my article "Reconsidering Fascist Anti-Semitism and Xenophobia in 1920s France: The Doctrinal Contribution of Georges Valois and the Faisceau", *French History*, 16 (2002): 345–365, and to the Western Society for French History for permission to republish portions of "Vers un ordre économique nouveau: Conflict Between the Modern and the Traditional in the Croix de Feu/Parti social français Economic Vision", *Proceedings of the Western Society for French History*, Vol. 27 (Greeley: University Press of Colorado, 2001).

Finally, I must offer profound thanks to friends and family for their unwavering support and enthusiasm at every stage of the project's development. Those who have patiently listened to me prattle on about the extreme right in interwar France include Neil Mayers, Peter Ferguson, Aaron Farrell, Milena Kras, Geoff Spurr, Derek Neal, Graeme Clyke, Laurie Lemmond, Rob Wickham, and Christie Lomore. I further owe a tremendous debt to my late mother Judith, father Calvin, and brother Ben for their consistent encouragement throughout my scholarly career. Last but certainly not least, I offer the greatest affection to my very best friends: my wife Brenda and son Josh, whose love and inspiration is more valuable than words can say. Without you, the successful completion of this project would be truly meaningless.

# List of Abbreviations

| | |
|---|---|
| ACJF | Association catholique de la Jeunesse française |
| AN | Archives nationales (Paris) |
| AOM | Archives d'Outre-Mer |
| AP | Archives privés (AN) |
| APP | Archives de la prefecture de police (Paris) |
| BN | Bibliothèque nationale (Paris) |
| CDF/PSF | Croix de Feu/Parti social français |
| CDJC | Centre de documentation juive contemporaine |
| CGPF | Confédération générale de la Production française |
| CGQJ | Commissariat générale aux Questions juives |
| CGT | Confédération générale du travail |
| CGTU | Confédération générale du travail unifié |
| CIPF | Confédération de l'intelligence et de la production française |
| FC | Faisceau des Corporations |
| FFCF | Fils et filles des Croix de Feu |
| FU | Faisceau universitaire |
| GP | Groupe patronale |
| JF | Jeunesses fascistes |
| JOC | Jeunesse ouvrière chrétienne |
| LICA | Ligue internationale contre l'antisémitisme |
| NS | Nouveau Siècle |
| PCF | Parti communiste français |
| PPF | Parti populaire français |
| SFIO | Section française de l'Internationale ouvrière |
| SFRN | Section feminine du Regroupement national |
| SPES | Société de préparation et d'éducation sportive |
| SPF | Syndicats professionels français |
| UCF | Union des Corporations françaises |
| UF | Union Fédérale |
| UNC | Union nationale des combatants |
| VN | Volontaires nationaux |

# Introduction

Historians of the French Third Republic often write of the *Guerre franco-française*, an intellectual and ideological conflict waged against parliamentary democracy and its supporters from the 1880s onwards. This was never more apparent than during the interwar period, when public discourse betrayed an increasing frustration with the political, economic, and social status quo, a fact reflected in the innumerable projects designed by various figures to renovate a government system perceived to be decadent, tottering, and beyond repair. Groups from across the political spectrum derided the republican administration, portrayed as weak, immoral, corrupt, and unstable. In its place, they proposed to remake the nation and state in their own doctrinal image.[1]

On the left, from the strike waves of 1919–1920 until the victory of the socialist-led Popular Front government in June 1936, a variety of militant working-class movements strove to transform the French political and economic landscape, either through revolutionary means (PCF, CGTU), or evolutionary and reformist ones (SFIO, CGT). Communists hoped to establish a Soviet-style government in France, Léon Blum sought to rebuild the socialist party – his *vieille maison* – in order to implement changes to both the nation and state, and syndicalists of all stripes presented ideas for a complete transformation of the production process and society at large. Influenced by both the gospel of rationalization preached by Frederick Winslow Taylor and Henry Ford in the United States, and the *planiste* Marxism of Hendrik de Man in Belgium, French leftists like Léon Jouhaux, Marcel Déat, and Blum himself argued for a radical redesign at once ultramodern and informed by the precepts of social justice.[2]

A similar tendency emerged on the political right, where a diverse aggregation of individuals and combinations generated a variety of technocratic proposals. For André

---

1    Throughout this work, the concept of the nation is used to denote both population and society within a fixed territorial boundary, and an idealized France from which undesirables are excluded. The state refers to the apparatus of government on all levels: local, regional, and national. It further includes those bodies outside politics, particularly in the realm of finance and economics, which are responsible for the determination of policy. Thus the reform of the nation discussed in this work focuses upon the roles of women, the family, youth, and undesirables, while the construction of the new state is limited to political change and the implementation of a new economic order.

2    These struggles have received considerable academic attention, and the various programs espoused by revolutionary and reformist syndicalism, socialism, anarchism, and communism, the subject of numerous monographs, are well-known. See, for example: Julian Jackson, *The Popular Front in France: Defending Democracy, 1934–1938* (Cambridge, 1988), especially pp. 52–85; Jeremy Jennings, *Syndicalism in France: A Study of Ideas* (New York, 1990); Richard F. Kuisel, *Capitalism and the State in Modern France* (Cambridge, 1981), chapters three and four.

Tardieu, Ernest Mercier, or the French automobile industrialists, national renovation hinged upon the adoption of corporatism and the rationalization of production. Envisioned as a gigantic factory, society and government operated according to new business principles.[3] Many of the so-called non-conformist intellectuals of the 1930s vigorously supported this platform as a defense against Bolshevism, American economic supremacy, and the weakness of the Third Republic at a critical juncture in French history.[4] They particularly lambasted traditional right-wing groups, such as the Alliance démocratique and Fédération républicaine, which remained content to work within the republican framework during the interwar period.

Yet for all of their opposition to the interwar Third Republic, the movements had little impact upon the prevailing system. Partisans either tacitly supported the Republic, like the socialists and the 'young Turks' of the Radical party whose reformism did not encompass the complete dismantling of parliamentary democracy, or were too few in number to radically alter French society and government. Even the Parti communiste français, so virulently hostile to the Chamber of Deputies and French liberal culture from its inception, remained weak until the 1930s, when it followed the Dimitrov line and collaborated in the Popular Front. Despite the crises of the era – the economic slump, widespread pacifist sentiment, and the strength of the opposition to established political parties – the Republic continued to command the allegiance of the majority. As William Irvine concludes, even those conservatives who berated the parliamentary regime throughout the interwar period lauded its virtues during wartime.[5]

Yet in looking back at the tumultuous prewar decade, Raymond Aron wrote that 'nothing existed other than the hatred of Frenchmen for each other'.[6] Robert Paxton similarly references 'the virtual civil war of the mid-1930s'.[7] How can the persistence of such opinions be explained? Given the evident failure of various attempts to remodel or topple the republic, are such theories mere exaggerations? The answer lies beyond moderate disapproval of republican weakness or a general social response to decadence and disorder. For the *Guerre franco-française* was not primarily the work of socialists or dissident Radicals, and even less so a purely conservative phenomenon. Historians principally associate the ongoing conflict with a strong xenophobic and nationalist tradition in France dating from the 1880s, a perpetual anti-

3     François Monnet, *Refaire la République* (Paris, 1993); Richard F. Kuisel, *Ernest Mercier: French Technocrat* (Berkeley, 1967); Patrick Fridenson, 'L'Idéologie des grands constructeurs dans l'entre-deux-guerres', *Mouvement social*, no. 81 (1972): 51–68.

4     Jean-Louis Loubet del Bayle, *Les non-conformistes des années 30: Une tentative de renouvellement de la pensée poltique française* (Paris, 2001); John Hellman, *The Communitarian Third Way: Alexandre Marc and Ordre Nouveau, 1930–2000* (Montreal, 2002).

5     William D. Irvine, 'Domestic Politics and the Fall of France in 1940', *Historical Reflections/Réflexions historiques* 22 (1996): 77–90.

6     Raymond Aron, *Le Spectateur éngagé*, quoted in Pierre Laborie, *L'Opinion française sous Vichy* (Paris, 1990), p. 69.

7     Robert O. Paxton, *Vichy France: Old Guard and New Order, 1940–1944* (New York, 1982), p. 243.

republicanism which continually pervaded extreme right-wing political discourse.[8] Variously characterized by the defense of traditional values and social order, ardent Catholicism, anti-Semitism and xenophobia, virulent nationalism, and support for authoritarian government, its leading movements frequently assailed the status quo, seeking to remove all vestiges of decadent and corrupt parliamentary democracy.[9] From the late nineteenth century onwards, French conservatism increasingly yielded political authority to extra-parliamentary mass-based organizations, which eclipsed the counter-revolutionary elite of the post-1789 era, whose royalist pretensions never commanded a popular audience.

Thus began a verbal, and often physical, conflict between the insurgent extreme-right and the Third Republic. Its chapters are well-known to any individual with a passing knowledge of modern French history: the Boulanger and Dreyfus affairs, the rise to prominence of the royalist Action française in newspaper columns and on the streets of the Latin Quarter, the tumult resulting from the election of the Cartel des Gauches in 1924 and the Popular Front 12 years later. One can add to this list the events of 6 February 1934, when the forces of the right took to the streets, coming perilously close to breaching the Chamber of Deputies and burying the republic. Evincing the same programmatic elements, from a defense of 'traditional' values to anti-Semitism, bellicose nationalism to unbridled authoritarianism, the extreme right-wing leagues further posed a genuine threat to the liberal regime.

At every historical turn, and particularly during the interwar era, the leagues pledged to overthrow the status quo, to reconstruct France according to various plans reflecting their specific doctrinal principles. They enjoyed far greater public support than left-wing, centrist, or even conservative opponents of the Third Republic, with hundreds of thousands of members and a vast press network. Far from being isolated intellectuals, like the non-conformists and technocrats of the 1930s, they created mass-based organizations, whose populism appealed to a wide swathe of the public. If the leagues never grew to encompass most French citizens, and were forced to co-exist with representatives of the centre and left, during the interwar era they nonetheless introduced their broad memberships to the very concepts which fuelled the triumph of authoritarianism in France after the defeat of June 1940 and the subsequent inauguration of the Vichy regime.

---

8    Pierre Milza and Michel Winock describe this development as a 'national populist' tradition dating from the Boulanger affair. See Pierre Milza, *Fascisme français: Passé et présent* (Paris, 1987), chapter eight, and Michel Winock, *Nationalisme, antisémitisme et fascisme en France* (Paris, 1990), chapter two. Although they prefer the term fascism, Robert Soucy, Zeev Sternhell, and William D. Irvine argue in the same vein, albeit with different definitions of the phenomenon and its origins. See Robert Soucy, *French Fascism: The First Wave, 1924–1933* (New Haven, 1986) and *French Fascism: The Second Wave, 1933–1939* (New Haven, 1995); Zeev Sternhell, *La Droite révolutionnaire* (Paris, 1997) and *Neither Right Nor Left: Fascist Ideology in France* (Princeton, 1996); William D. Irvine, *The Boulanger Affair Reconsidered: Royalism, Boulangism, and the Origins of the Radical Right in France* (Oxford, 1989), pp. 3–20.

9    Pierre Birnbaum, 'Affaire Dreyfus, culture catholique, et antisémitisme', in Michel Winock (ed.), *Histoire de l'extrême droite en France* (Paris, 1993), p. 122; Zeev Sternhell, *Neither Right Nor Left*, p. XXXV.

With the exception of the royalist Action française, little scholarly attention has been paid to these designs.[10] The doctrine of the so-called fascist intellectuals – Pierre Drieu la Rochelle, Robert Brasillach, Marcel Déat, and Gaston Bergery among others – has been extensively treated, primarily due to their collaborationist role following the German victory in June 1940.[11] The ideology and goals embodied in the proposals of the leagues, on the other hand, have rarely been subjected to close scrutiny. Historians continue to discuss at length their composition, membership, and organization, mainly to assess the degree to which they may warrant the label 'fascist'.[12] Yet their precise program for France, and visions of the reconstructed nation and state, are rarely deliberated. Nowhere is this more apparent than in the history of the largest extreme-rightist leagues in the nineteen-twenties and nineteen-thirties respectively: The Faisceau and the Croix de Feu/Parti social français.[13] In both cases, plans for the renovation of the French nation and the re-creation of the state became the primary goals. Both groups aspired to the conquest of power in order to implement their transformative program. In the process, they prepared a generation of right-wing French men and women to support an authoritarian state, creating a substantial clientele for the Vichy regime.

## II

Originally conceived as an unnamed veteran's organization, the Faisceau was founded on November 11, 1924 by Georges Valois, the economic affairs columnist of the royalist league Action française, and director of its Nouvelle Librairie

---

10    Books and articles on the subject of the Action française are too varied to list here. On the subject of the group's doctrine and program, see Edward Tannenbaum, *Action française* (New York, 1961); Eugen Weber, *Action française: Royalism and Reaction in Twentieth-Century France* (Stanford, 1962); Ernst Nolte, *Three Faces of Fascism* (London, 1965); Colette Capitan-Peter, *Charles Maurras et l'idéologie d'Action française* (Paris, 1972); Robert Soucy, *French Fascism: The First Wave, 1924–1933* (New Haven, 1986); Victor Nguyen, *Aux origines de l'Action française* (Paris, 1991).

11    See for example Philippe Burrin, *La Dérive fasciste* (Paris, 2003); Zeev Sternhell, *Neither Right Nor Left*; David Carroll, *Nationalism, Anti-Semitism, and the Ideology of Culture* (Princeton, 1995).

12    Again, the list is too extensive to include here. See, for example: J. Plumyène and R. Lasierra, *Les Fascismes françaises, 1923–1963* (Paris, 1963); Philippe Machefer, *Ligues et fascismes en France, 1919–1939* (Paris, 1974); Philippe Burrin, *La Dérive fasciste*; Robert Soucy, *French Fascism: The First Wave, 1924–1933* and *French Fascism: The Second Wave, 1933–1939*; Pierre Milza, *Fascismes français: passé et présent*; Winock (ed.), *Histoire de l'extrême droite en France*. Their activities during the interwar period are described in detail, but the groups are far too often consigned to the role of mere political forces within the Republic. Ideology is usually absent, or presented solely to demonstrate their fascist qualities.

13    Although the doctrine of Faisceau leader Georges Valois is noted by certain historians (discussed below), his colleagues in the group are resoundingly ignored. In addition, the ideological portrayal of Valois himself is often erroneous and incomplete, hence the group's inclusion among the ranks of the unexamined. Similarly, assessments of the CDF/PSF doctrinal program are incorrect or incomplete at best, again as noted below.

Nationale publishing house. Attracting luminaries on the left (Communist mayor of Périgueux Marcel Delagrange and ex-union leader Pierre Dumas) and the right (noted academic Hubert Bourgin, ex-royalist Jacques Arthuys, and author Philippe Barrès, son of the arch-nationalist luminary Maurice), the group published a daily newspaper – *Nouveau Siècle* – from February 1925 onwards. Following his split with the royalists that October, Valois proclaimed the group fascist at an armistice day rally attended by 4,000 supporters, and named it the Faisceau for the first time. Until its decline in late 1927 the group was the largest and most influential of the extreme-rightist leagues, boasting 40–60,000 members and a major publishing house. Throughout this period, Valois and his collaborators consistently agitated in favour of a *Révolution nationale* when the paramilitary *Légions,* a corps of battle-hardened *anciens combattants*, would obliterate republican democracy and establish the *État Combattant*: a new political, economic, and social order.

Despite their prioritization of national renovation, historians of the Faisceau have paid them little attention. Furthermore, most treat the group as monolithic, equating Valois's thought with that of the group as a whole, and virtually ignoring his confreres. The earliest treatments label the Faisceau a small link in Valois's intellectual progression, presenting an economic critic or revolutionary syndicalist.[14] More recent scholars similarly omit the Faisceau, and are rather selective in their interpretation of Valois himself. Zeev Sternhell, in his much-debated *Neither Right Nor Left*, portrays the group as an organization dedicated to the eradication of nineteenth-century liberalism. Simultaneously anti-bourgeois and nationalist, Sternhell's Valois sought an ideological third way between capitalism and Marxian socialism, courting the worker while assembling a youthful modernizing elite drawn from the trenches. However, the *État combattant* is relegated to the background as the author attempts to prove that the group represented but one facet of a larger project: Fascism as the anti-materialist revision of Marxism.[15] Rejecting Sternhell's

---

14. Yves Guchet, *Georges Valois: L'Action française, le Faisceau, la République syndicale* (Paris, 1975); Jules Levey, 'The Sorellian Syndicalists: Édouard Berth, Georges Valois, and Hubert Lagardelle', Ph.D. Dissertation, Columbia University, 1967. Levey's subsequent article on Valois merely encapsulates the group's history, paying attention to the Faisceau solely in terms of membership and organization. See Jules Levey, 'Georges Valois and the Faisceau: The Making and Breaking of a Fascist', *French Historical Studies* 8 (1973): 279–304. Articles on the subject of Valois and the Faisceau by Clarence Tingley and Jerzy Eisler come to the same conclusions. Tingley echoes Levey's argument concerning Valois as a 'Sorellian syndicalist', while Eisler concludes that Valois was a 'left-fascist'. Both works centre on Valois rather than the Faisceau, and neither delves into the group's plans for the new nation and state. See Clarence D. Tingley, 'Georges Valois and the Faisceau: Apocalyptic Politics in Twentieth-Century France', *Proceedings of the Annual Meeting of the Western Society for French History*, 1976; Jerzy Eisler, 'Georges Valois et une idéologie des combattants', *Acta Poloniae Historica* 48 (1983): 133–163.

15. Zeev Sternhell, *Neither Right Nor Left*. See also 'The Anti-Materialist Revision of Marxism as an Aspect of the Rise of Fascist Ideology', *Journal of Contemporary History*, 22 (July 1987): 379–400. Sternhell's thesis has been the subject of fierce debate since its appearance in 1983. See Michel Winock, 'Fascisme à la française ou fascisme introuvable', *Le Debat*, no. 25 (May 1983): 35–44; Jacques Julliard, 'Sur une fascisme imaginaire: à propos

thesis, other scholars instead emphasize Valois's technocratic leanings, omitting his more conservative social thought and aligning his entire oeuvre with Taylorist economics.[16] Taking this argument to its logical conclusion, one Valois biographer claims that he was a 'utopian modernizer', reducing group ideology largely to Valoissian monetary theory, and regarding the project for a new nation and state as a type of St.-Simonian social engineering.[17]

The characterization of the Faisceau as exponents of left fascism has been contested by several authors who place the group at the opposite end of the political spectrum. Yet they similarly portray the Faisceau as ideologically monolithic, their doctrine the product of Valois alone. Thus Robert Soucy emphasizes that they were 'frankly imitative of Mussolini's blackshirts', and that Valois represented 'economically progressive conservatism'. Supported by bourgeois interests, the group proposed a dictatorship dedicated to the destruction of liberalism and socialism.[18]

Regardless of their respective positions, none of the historians who discuss Valois and the Faisceau sufficiently concentrate on plans for the transformation of the nation and state according to group principles. All focus primarily upon the group as a political actor within the Third Republic, and its organization and membership. That they were monolithic, a product of Valois's thought and design, is taken for granted, and there is little mention of other leading Faisceau luminaries. This situation is mirrored in discussions of the largest extreme-rightist league of the 1930s, the Croix de Feu/Parti social français. Although group leader Colonel François de la Rocque and his colleagues continuously emphasized initiatives to transform France according to group principles, frequently alluding to changes 'when our ideas take power', historians primarily discuss their organization and contemporary activities, neglecting programmatic elements within CDF/PSF discourse.[19] When the subject of doctrine is raised, they are inevitably

---

d'un livre de Zeev Sternhell', *Annales*, no. 4 (July–August 1984): 84–94; Serge Berstein, 'La France des années trente allergiques au fascisme: à propos d'un livre de Zeev Sternhell', *Vingtième siècle*, no. 2 (April 1984): 83–94; Antonio Costa-Pinto, 'Fascist Ideology Revisited: Zeev Sternhell and his Critics', *European History Quarterly*, 16 (1986): 465–483; Robert Wohl, 'French Fascism, Both Right and Left: Reflections on the Sternhell Controversy', *Journal of Modern History*, 63 (1991): 91–98.

16     Alfredo Salsano, 'Georges Valois e lo Stato Tecnico. Il Corporativismo Tecnocrato tra Fascismo e Antifascismo', *Studi Storici*, 34 (1993): 571–624. Salsano owes a small debt to an earlier work on the relationship between fascism and technocracy: Klaus-Jürgen Müller, 'French Fascism and Modernization', *Journal of Contemporary History*, 11 (1976): 75–107.

17     Allen Douglas, *From Fascism to Libertarian Communism: Georges Valois Against the Third Republic* (Berkeley, 1992). See also 'Fascist Violence in France: The Case of the Faisceau', *Journal of Contemporary History*, 19 (1984): 689–712.

18     Robert Soucy, *French Fascism: The First Wave, 1924–1933*. Using essentially the same sources, right-wing historian Jean-Maurice Duval concludes that Valois and the Faisceau were Gaullist rather than fascist. His biography is an exercise in rehabilitation, however, lacking Soucy's scholarly and objective approach. See Jean-Maurice Duval, *Le Faisceau de Georges Valois* (Paris, 1979).

19     It is significant that La Rocque refers to the group's ideas rather than the CDF/ PSF itself. Such phrasing indicates the importance which CDF/PSF leaders attached to their transformative program.

portrayed as homogeneous, much like the Faisceau, with La Rocque as the ideologue whose convictions the rank and file followed without question.

Such claims are even more difficult to believe in the case of the CDF/PSF because of its size and breadth. Like the Faisceau, the Croix de Feu initially emerged as a veterans' organization, founded by Maurice Hanot dit d'Hartoy in 1927 with membership restricted to those who had fought during the Great War. Funded by François Coty, the extreme-rightist perfume magnate, both the group's 5000 members and its newspaper *Le Flambeau des ançiens combattants de l'avant* remained largely commemorative. This changed dramatically in 1931, with the ascension of Colonel de la Rocque to the Presidency. Under his guidance, the group severed its ties to Coty and entered the turbulent realm of French politics, playing a leading role in the infamous 6 February 1934 riots. They grew dramatically in the insurgency's aftermath, and by the summer of 1936 counted well over 500,000 members. Dissolved by the Popular Front government that June, along with other extreme-rightist leagues, the group renamed itself the Parti social français and nominally accepted electoral politics. The PSF remained among the largest political party in France until the Second World War, with over one million members by 1938, an expansion interrupted only by the defeat in June 1940 and the subsequent emergence of the Vichy regime. Moreover, the CDF/PSF never hid their ultimate ambition: The conquest of the nation and state, in order to implement the authoritarian *État social français*.[20]

However, historians choose to view the group as a political entity devoid of substantial ideological foundation. The earliest academic treatments of the movement claimed that the CDF/PSF were free of doctrine altogether. René Rémond concluded that the group represented nothing more than 'political boy-scouting for grown-ups and civilian war games', neither a genuine political movement nor extreme-rightist, and therefore unequipped with a systematic doctrine.[21] Likewise, Philippe Machefer proclaims the CDF/PSF Catholic and conservative, rejecting the reconstruction of France advocated by the extreme-rightist leagues, and hence developed no comprehensive plans for the nation and state.[22] Following Machefer's lead, various

---

20    Although certain differences emerged with the formation of the PSF, largely resulting from newfound populism due to increased membership, the CDF organization and doctrine remained mostly unchanged throughout the 1930s. As a result, the term CDF/PSF is used throughout this work.

21    René Rémond, *The French Right: From 1815 to De Gaulle* (Philadelphia, 1971). The original French version appeared in 1954.

22    The bulk of Machefer's work appeared in article form: 'Autour du problème algérien en 1936–1938: la doctrine algérienne du PSF: le PSF et le projet Blum-Violette', *Revue d'histoire moderne et contemporaine* 10 (1963): 147–156; 'Sur quelques aspects de l'activité du Colonel de La Rocque et du Progrès social français pendant la Seconde Guerre Mondiale', *Revue d'histoire de la Deuxième Guerre Mondiale*, 57 (1965): 35–56; 'L'Union des droites: le PSF et le Front de la liberté, 1936–37', *Revue d'histoire moderne et contemporaine* 17 (1970): 112–136; 'Les Croix de Feu', *L'Information historique* 34 (1972): 28–34; 'Le Parti social français', *L'information historique* 34 (1972): 74–80; 'Tardieu et La Rocque', *Bulletin de la Société d'histoire moderne*, 15 (1973): 11–21; 'Presse et politique dans les années trente: le cas du Petit journal', *Revue d'histoire moderne et contemporaine*, 23 (1975): 13–45; 'Le Parti social français', in René Remond and Janine Bourdin (eds), *La France et les*

French works on the CDF/PSF have emphasized their political legalism, social Catholic and conservative doctrine, and lack of a transformative program.[23] Thus Jacques Nobecourt's weighty and meticulously researched 1996 biography of La Rocque, despite its size and scholarship, gives the reader little information regarding the group's purpose. Nobecourt presents the CDF/PSF and their leader as a synthesis of Maréchal Lyautey, Count René de la Tour du Pin, and papal encyclicals *Rerum Novarum* and *Quadregisimo Anno*. They desired only to instill Christian principles into the Republic, proffering a 'fourth way' between communism, fascism, and liberal democracy.[24] Similarly, Albert Kéchichian portrays La Rocque and the CDF/PSF as aristocratic in orientation, the product of social Catholicism and a chivalric 'code of honour'. Conservative rather than totalitarian, La Rocque dominated the group, initially attempting to recreate the *Union sacrée* of 1914 by authoritarian means, but by 1935 accepting parliamentary liberalism.[25]

Recent scholarship has tended to oppose the vision of La Rocque and the CDF/PSF as political actors loyal to the Republic, devoted to a social Catholic and conservative program. William Irvine and Robert Soucy deem the group fascist, yet their description of the projected renovation of the nation and state is highly selective, perhaps due to the brevity of their treatments.[26] More promisingly, current scholarship resists the fascist/non-fascist debate, instead utilizing material from the French archives to study the group from both a regional and national perspective. Yet historians such as Kevin Passmore and Sean Kennedy, although they certainly help dispel the myth that the CDF/PSF was La Rocque's one-man show, at least from an organizational perspective, continue to focus primarily on the group's history and structure rather than plans for a new nation and state.[27]

---

*Français en 1938–1939* (Paris, 1978), pp. 307–326; 'L'Action française et le PSF', *Études Maurrassiennes*, 4 (1980): 125–133; 'Les Croix de Feu devant l'Allemagne', in *La France et l'Allemagne, 1932–1936* (Paris, 1980); 'La Rocque et la problème antisémite', in *La France et la question juive* (Paris, 1981); 'Le Parti social français et la petite enterprise', unpublished paper in CHEVS/60; 'Les Syndicats professionnels français (1936–1939)', *Mouvement social*, no. 119 (1982): 91–112. Machefer also edited a collection entitled *Ligues et fascismes en France, 1919–1939* (Paris, 1974). His doctoral thesis, left unfinished at the time of his death, is held in the Fonds La Rocque at the CHEVS archives.

23     Weng Ting-Lung, 'L'Historique et la doctrine des Parti social français', Thèse de droit, Université de Nice, 1970.

24     Jacques Nobecourt, *Le colonel de La Rocque, 1885–1946 ou les pièges du nationalisme chrétien* (Paris, 1996). This view is seconded by Pierre Milza in *Fascismes français*, pp. 133–142.

25     Albert Kéchichian, *Les Croix de Feu à l'âge des fascismes* (Paris, 2006).

26     Robert Soucy, *French Fascism: The Second Wave, 1933–1939*. See also 'French Fascism and the Croix de Feu: A Dissenting Interpretation', *Journal of Contemporary History* 26 (1991): 159–188.

27     Sean Michael Kennedy, 'Reconciling the Nation Against Democracy: The Croix de Feu, The Parti social français and French Politics, 1927–1945', Ph.D. Dissertation, York University, 1998 and *Reconciling France Against Democracy: The Croix de Feu and the Parti social français, 1927–1945* (Montréal and Kingston, 2007). Although it contains brief sections concerning the group's doctrine, Kennedy's work is primarily a comprehensive analysis of the group as a socio-political actor within interwar France. Passmore's major work is a study

**III**

This book provides a new interpretation of the Faisceau and the CDF/PSF, linking the interwar extreme right with antecedents from the Dreyfus Affair onwards, and its subsequent climax during the Vichy era. It is a comparative study, and as such reveals the continuities and ruptures inherent in interwar extreme right-wing discourse. As such, the effort also examines the growth and development of such organizations and their doctrines. It aims to study what others have not: Attempts by both groups to develop comprehensive plans for an extensive transformation of the French nation and state. For the Faisceau and the CDF/PSF actively advocated the overthrow of the Third Republic in order to install a new regime, continually referring to the renovation of existing institutions and demanding their replacement with the *État Combattant* and *État social français*. To this end, they re-examined every facet of the nation and state, from politics and economics to gender, youth, and the politics of exclusion.

Moreover, this work contests the view that both were doctrinally monolithic. The conventional approach, in which the program of the leagues emanated from a leader, and filtered down through the party ranks, who accepted it without question, fails to account for the proliferation of distinctive opinions within the Faisceau and CDF/PSF. Despite the major contributions made by Hubert Bourgin, Jacques Arthuys, Philippe Barrès and numerous others to Faisceau plans for the nation and state, historians have viewed the group doctrine as the exclusive product of Georges Valois. Not only did these figures write and speak extensively on the topic, they often promoted a vision of the *État combatant* quite antithetical to that of the Faisceau leader. This conservative faction challenged Valois's modernizing left-fascism at every turn, from the definition of an authoritarian state to the role of women, family, and youth in France following the *Révolution Nationale*.[28]

---

of the right in the Rhône province, in which the CDF/PSF appears only in the latter stages. Kevin Passmore, *From Liberalism to Fascism: The Right in a French Province, 1928–1939* (Cambridge, 1997); '"Planting the Tricolore in the Citadels of Communism": Women's Social Action in the Croix de Feu and Parti social français', *Journal of Modern History*, 71 (1999): 814–851. Passmore has most recently turned his eye to the issue of women in the CDF/PSF, but again from the perspective of organization and gender-roles within the group. Mary Jean Green has also studied the position of women within the CDF/PSF, drawing primarily upon the group newspaper and the *Bouboule* novels of T. Trilby. See 'Gender, Fascism, and the Croix de Feu: The "Women's Pages" of *Le Flambeau*', *French Cultural Studies*, 8 (1997): 229–239; 'The *Bouboule* Novels: Constructing a French Fascist Woman', in Melanie Hawthorn and Richard J. Golson (eds), *Gender and Fascism in Modern France* (Hanover, 1997). Passmore has also written several articles on the issue of fascism and the CDF/PSF: 'The French Third Republic: Stalemate Society or Cradle of Fascism?', *French History*, 7 (1993): 417–449; 'The Croix de Feu: Bonapartism, national Populism or Fascism?', *French History* 9 (1995): 93–123; 'Boy Scouting for Grown-ups? Paramilitarism in the Croix de Feu/Parti social français', *French Historical Studies*, 19 (1995): 527–557.

28    I employ the terms 'traditionalist' and 'modernizer' in this work to denote two conflicting tendencies within the Faisceau and the CDF/PSF. The traditionalists espouse more conservative arguments, from social Catholic economic principles to conventional right wing views concerning gender, education, and political culture among others. Modernizers within each group eschew staid ideas in favour of innovation, from Taylorism and *Planisme*

A proliferation of differing views was equally apparent within the CDF/PSF, where many of the group's members openly advocated far more radical views than those held by the conservative La Rocque. Technocrats objected to the traditionalist and social Catholic economic discourse of the CDF/PSF leadership, and rabid anti-Semites believed La Rocque to be far too moderate regarding the politics of exclusion. Conservatives, modernizers, and even geneticists vigorously debated the place of youth within the *État social français*. When consensus was achieved within either group, special circumstances alone permitted an agreement. Valois's new economic order, for instance, was unanimously accepted because he alone possessed expertise in the field.

Such doctrinal decentralization, however, in no way diminishes its central importance to the Faisceau and CDF/PSF. To be sure, there existed no common set of beliefs in either group; apart from ardent nationalism and anti-communism, the various factions agreed on little. But in spite of their differences, all believed that the transformation of the nation and state was absolutely necessary, to replace the weak and corrupt Third Republic. For the expected metamorphosis was predicated upon the attainment of power, impossible to achieve without a sufficiently large organization. Thus the various factions put aside their differences because the appearance of unity alone enabled membership growth and public recognition. Each agreed with the populist tactics of their leaders in order to seize political control of France, after which they hoped for the triumph of their own unique program.

Furthermore, the factionalization of each group, and the ideas espoused by each clique, bear distinct similarity to the authoritarian Vichy regime. The culmination of 55 years of extreme right-wing activity against the Third Republic, from the Boulanger and Dreyfus affairs at the end of the nineteenth century onwards, the wartime administration represented such ideas in power. Yet its inner dynamic mirrored the internecine quarrels of the Faisceau and CDF/PSF. Vichy represented what Stanley Hoffman terms a 'pluralist dictatorship'.[29] As Robert Paxton has noted in this regard, 'Vichy was not a Bloc', but instead grouped together various 'sets of alternatives', pitting Catholic moralists against the paganism of prewar fascism, proponents of federalism against advocates of a centralized authoritarian

---

in political and economic terms to forward-looking proscriptions concerning the position of women and the role and function of youth in society. Although modernizers and traditionalists occasionally shared terminology – the notions of hierarchy, authoritarianism, or order, for example – these concepts are defined in a very different manner by each camp, in the service of their respective agendas. Thus for Valois, hierarchy reinforces the productivism inherent in his desired new economic order. Yet Hubert Bourgin instead proffered traditional elitism based upon social class rather than economic utility. Clearly the traditionalist and modernizing positions overlapped in certain cases, most notably in their espousal of xenophobia, but the differences are clear enough to warrant the categorization.

29     Stanley Hoffmann, *Decline or Renewal: France since the 1930s* (New York, 1974), p. 4. I am here referring to Vichy in doctrinal terms, to the wishes of various figures and factions during the *années noires*. However, as Gérard Noiriel remarks, much of the legislative and bureaucratic framework of the Republic remained in evidence after June 1940. See *Les origines républicaines de Vichy* (Paris, 1999).

state, and economic modernists against agrarian lobbyists.[30] Its various factions mirrored identical conflicts within the Faisceau and CDF/PSF, which engaged economic modernizers against artisanal and agrarian conservatives, proponents of a youthful new order against old-fashioned Catholic moralists, and eugenicists against pronatalists among others.

It is therefore unsurprising that the Vichy regime found supporters in France after the German victory in June 1940. Far from being a 'divine surprise', Pétain and his cohorts finally achieved a longstanding goal, gaining the social and political control required to negate the Republic.[31] To be sure, the extreme-right were not the only political faction keenly interested in renovating France, and Vichy attracted numerous luminaries from the centre and left, including members of the Radical party, ex-socialists, and parliamentary conservatives, in addition to partisans of the leagues.[32] It must also be noted that the population as a whole did not actively collaborate. In fact, the initial enthusiasm dwindled by 1942, as the regime failed to maintain French sovereignty and the German occupation government assumed control over the southern zone.[33] Nevertheless, a significant portion of the right found itself applauding the new authoritarianism and government attempts to institute a new order, and in almost every case their platforms bear a clear resemblance to similar initiatives proposed by members of the Faisceau and CDF/PSF. It is thus no coincidence that many members gravitated to the new government, assuming leadership positions within various ministries and organizations. What else did Vichy represent but the long awaited opportunity to construct their ideal politics and society?

Neither is this a purely historical issue. On April 21, 2002, shocked French citizens were informed that the extreme right-wing National Front had gained 17 per cent of the vote in the first round of Presidential elections. For the first time in its thirty year history, group leader Jean-Marie Le Pen, who once called the gas chambers at Auschwitz-Birkenau a 'minor detail in history', mounted a serious challenge to the democratic Fifth Republic. Although trounced in the second round by Jacques Chirac, Le Pen and the National Front successfully courted nearly 20 per cent of the electorate with an anti-immigrant, authoritarian and illiberal political program.[34] Faced with contemporary echoes of a seemingly buried past, newspapers

---

30    Robert Paxton, *Vichy France: Old Guard and New Order*, p. 139. This argument has been largely accepted by many historians of the Vichy era. See, for example, Pierre Laborie, *L'Opinion française sous Vichy* (Paris, 1990), p. 81; Julian Jackson, *France: The Dark Years, 1940–1944* (Oxford, 2001), part one.

31    This is the view espoused by Robert Paxton in *Vichy France: Old Guard and New Order* and Jean-Pierre Azéma in his chapter on Vichy in Michel Winock (ed.), *Histoire de l'extrême droite en France*.

32    Paxton, *Vichy France: Old Guard and New Order*, chapter three.

33    On the French withdrawal from Vichy, see Jackson, p. 278. Various studies have demonstrated that active collaboration was frequently quite limited. See, for example, John F. Sweets, *Choices in Vichy France* (Oxford, 1986).

34    For the election results and editorial coverage, see *Le Monde*, 23 April and 7 May 2002. Far from diminishing, Le Pen's popularity has steadily grown since the Front National's overwhelming defeat in the second round of the 2002 elections. When asked in a December 2003 survey if they approved of a *Frontiste* government, 22 per cent of French respondents

and television commentators invoked Vichy. Mobilizing a program similar to the agenda of the contemporary extreme-right, Marshall Philippe Pétain and his fellow leaders in unoccupied France enacted legislation against Jews and immigrants, rejected republican democracy in favour of an authoritarian government, and praised 'traditional' French values. Le Pen himself evoked this connection, lauding the Vichy maxim *travail, famille, patrie* during the 2002 electoral campaign.[35] Although the FN's vote tally faltered somewhat in May–June 2007 presidential and legislative elections, clearly the *Guerre franco-française* has not yet ended, and its progenitors assume a chilling contemporary relevance today.

---

endorsed the party. See *Le Monde*, 10 December 2003. The FLN has run under the slogan 'one million unemployed is one million immigrants too many', while Le Pen advocates 'a France indissolubly tied to our blood, our soil, and our memory'. He claims that other races are biologically inferior, and that millions of immigrants have destroyed French racial purity. In *Le Monde: Dossiers et Documents*, June 2002.

35    'Front National', *Le Monde*, 9 April 2002.

# Chapter One

# *Vers un ordre politique nouveau*: Renovating State and Government

'France is gravely stricken by deep infected wounds', wrote Lucien Rebatet in his 1942 work *Les Décombrés*. 'Those who attempt to disguise this fact, for whatever reason, are criminals.'[1] A collaborator in Nazi-occupied France, Rebatet expresses an oft-repeated sentiment prevalent on the extreme right during the Third Republic years. The conviction that parliamentary democracy had bled the nation to death, and that republicans were crooks out to murder the true France, had been repeated *ad nauseam* by the far right since the 1880s. For men like Rebatet, there was but one solution to the electoral malaise: An authoritarian governing system which restored tradition, hierarchy, and elitism to the political sphere. This project attracted both doyens and plebeians to the wartime Vichy regime and Nazi European order, regarded as the embodiment of the social and political principles for which they had fought so fervently in the preceding decades. Yet if Vichy was the first success of its kind for the French extreme right, it was by no means the only attempt to create, by force if necessary, a new anti-democratic political order.

From its beginnings the Third Republic was beset by accusations of corrupt practices and ineptitude, charges that emanated from both the right and the left. The arch-conservative Robert de Jouvenel quipped famously before the Great War that 'there is less difference between two deputies, when one is revolutionary and the other is not, then between two revolutionaries, when one is a deputy and the other is not'. Simultaneously on the centre-left, Anatole France dedicated a section of his *Île des Pingouins* to the corruption endemic in the Chamber of Deputies and the capitalist system which it served. Anti-parliamentarism was in vogue by the turn of the century, appearing seemingly everywhere. Cartoons, popular novels, and cabarets often mocked the opportunism, buffoonery, and incompetence of parliamentarians.[2]

For all their complaints, most citizens actively expressed their exasperation in light-hearted satire, or more earnest sarcasm at the expense of the government; few of them actively contemplated the eradication of the Republic. The extreme-right, however, went far beyond mere jest. Maurice Barrès, the prominent author whose works on Alsace-Lorraine and Gallic deracination schooled a generation of young Frenchmen in the redemptive concepts of the soil and the dead, claimed that the deputy had no redeeming qualities. His only concern was the satisfaction of constituent electoral committees, Barrès jeered, which were deemed of greater

---

1    Lucien Rebatet, *Les Décombrés* (Paris, 1942), p. 13.

2    Jean Estèbe, 'Le Parlementarisme', in Jean-François Sirinelli (ed.), *Histoire des droites en France: Vol. 3, Sensibilités* (Paris, 1992), pp. 336, 340.

importance than public service.[3] Worse still, claimed Charles Maurras, leader of the royalist Action française, the Republic itself – *le pays légal* – contradicted the will of the people – *le pays réel*. Maurras viewed parliamentary democracy as a conspiracy against the common good, 'the regime of windbags', and a malignant affliction that would destroy France if untreated. 'There is only one way to improve democracy', seethed the *vieux maître royaliste*: 'to destroy it'.[4]

Barrès and Maurras wrote during a time of weakness for the right, and especially the extreme-right. The defeat of Boulanger, the acquittal of Dreyfus, and the staunchly anti-Catholic policies of the Waldeck-Rousseau and Combes ministries left conservatives in disarray before the Great War. Although they rejected laicism and despised the Radical Party, often referring to the Republic as *la gueuse* and the left-centre bloc as its pimp, even die-hard traditionalists like Albert de Mun and Jacques Piou rallied to the status quo. Furthermore after the 1903–1904 separation of church and state, and the landslide radical victory in 1906 elections, only the extreme-rightist Action française embraced anti-republicanism. Lacking a broad electoral base in a nation where only 25 per cent of the populace supported a right wing, Catholic agenda, newer conservative voices like Raymond Poincaré accepted the status quo and pledged to work within the framework of democracy and the Chamber of Deputies.[5]

However, their fortunes improved dramatically in the interwar period. The right enjoyed a postwar political resurgence, electing a Bloc national majority from 1919–1924 in the *Chambre Bleu-Horizon*, and again from 1926–1932 under Poincaré and André Tardieu. Such electoral popularity effectively rehabilitated right-wing antiparliamentary sentiment. The success of the left, first apparent in the strike wave in 1919–1920, and again with the election of the Cartel des Gauches government in 1924, led both conservatives and the extreme-right to believe that a Bolshevik coup was possible in France. On the traditional right André Thibaudet warned that a new leftist political class, groomed exclusively at the École normale supérieure, desired to create a *République des professeurs*. Others were far more blunt: The title of Camille Aymard's best-selling 1926 treatise *Bolchévisme ou fascisme, Français il faut choisir* became a rallying cry for right-wing anti-republicans during the remainder of the interwar period.[6]

In the 1930s the right grew still more restless, as the depression struck France, the Hanau, Oustric, and Stavisky banking scandals publicly revealed governmental corruption at the highest levels, and Hitler loomed menacingly across the Rhine. With the rise of the French Popular Front and its 1936 electoral victory, right-wing anti-democratic sentiment became even more widespread. Faced with wildcat strikes

---

3    Michael Curtis, *Three Against the Third Republic: Sorel, Barrès, and Maurras* (Princeton, 1959), p. 79.

4    Quoted in Ernst Nolte, *Three Faces of Fascism* (London, 1965), pp. 107–108. See also Charles Maurras, *Kiel et Tanger* (Versailles, 1928), p. 199; Charles Maurras, *Enquête sur la monarchie et la classe ouvrière* (Paris, 1924), p. 139. These works were written in 1899 and 1900 respectively.

5    James F. McMillan, *Dreyfus to De Gaulle: Politics and Society in France, 1898–1969* (London, 1985), pp. 30–37.

6    Estèbe, 'le parliamentarisme', pp. 342–345; Jean-Luc Pinol, '1919–1958: Le temps des droites?', in Sirinelli, *Histoire des droites en France: Vol. 1, Politique* (Paris, 1992), p. 291.

and factory occupations across the country, conservatives watched in horror as Léon Blum's socialist government negotiated the Matignon Accords, granting labour the eight hour day, paid vacations, and participation in management. Believing the 'Sovietization of France' to be imminent, Victor Perret of the Republican Federation called for the elimination of the Chamber, because 'the great majority of all Frenchmen today condemn parliamentarism'.[7] Far greater threats to the stability of the Republic were the extreme-rightist leagues, whose hundreds of thousands of members and ominous street presence directly challenged the existing order. The 6 February 1934 riots, in which the leagues, together with veterans associations and the royalist Action française, marched on the Chamber of Deputies, shook the French populace. Initially gathered in protest against real and imagined revelations of corruption arising from the Stavisky Affair, the increasingly menacing crowd turned violent, forcing the resignation of Premier Edouard Daladier. The next two years were marked by street battles with communists and mass meetings denouncing democracy. The banning of the leagues in June 1936 had little effect; most simply transformed themselves into political parties and continued their anti-parliamentary agitation, attracting hundreds of thousands of new members. Given the relative strength of the interwar extreme-right, Jean Estèbe relates, 'the transformation of summer-fall 1940, where a democratic nation seemed to instantly accept a counter-revolutionary and racist dictatorship, was prepared well in advance'.[8]

The largest extreme-rightist leagues in 1920s and 1930s France respectively were the Faisceau and the Croix de Feu/Parti social français. Like their *liguer* confreres, both groups prioritized the revitalization of French politics, predicated upon the transformation of the feeble and corrupt Republic into a robust authoritarian state. For the Faisceau this meant the installation of an *État combattant*, directed by a new elite composed of war veterans. Defending Catholic morality and French tradition while enforcing social justice and enshrining economic modernity, their reinvigorated state aimed to eliminate materialism, restoring the values of family, church, and nationalism to France.

Despite a prevailing agreement on these general principles, two opposing sets of expectations existed within the Faisceau. For group leader Georges Valois, the new political order preserved French tradition and identity, while simultaneously acting as a hyper-modern agent of governmental and economic efficiency. The state would be run by an elite drawn from all classes, working ceaselessly to rejuvenate the nation. Hence Valois's fascist dictatorship was a transitory one, necessary only to create favourable conditions for the renovation of government. He certainly employed much of the rhetoric of the contemporary extreme-right, espousing corporatism, referring to the nation as an organic whole, and praising nationalism and Catholic virtue as essential components of any French renaissance. Valois further invoked the experience of the Great War to lend legitimacy to his project, often speaking of the need to recreate the fraternity and mentality of the trenches within the new fascist state. Yet he idolized Georges Sorel, Le Corbusier, and Henry Ford as much as Maurras and Barrès, and his proposals were dominated by a *planiste* spirit more commonly

7    William D. Irvine, *French Conservatism in Crisis* (Baton Rouge, 1979), pp. 81–88, 101.
8    Estèbe, 'le parliamentarisme', p. 345.

associated with the left than the extreme-right. Far from reactionary, his *combattant* elite was expected to make France suitable for the 'age of electricity'.[9] Valois's arguments thus rejected many programmatic elements common to the extreme-right during the Third Republic, including the notion that any new regime exclusively imposed Catholic values and French tradition, and a wariness of progressive ideas, which were associated with the anticlerical and socialist Cartel des Gauches.

Valois's progressive bent was not shared by many of his Faisceau colleagues. The modernism of Sorel and Le Corbusier meant nothing to Hubert Bourgin, Jacques Arthuys, or Philippe Barrès, Faisceau leaders whose politics emphasized the inculcation of tradition, hierarchy, discipline, and order. Valois was brought up in a working-class milieu, beginning his political trajectory on the anarcho-syndicalist left before joining the Action française in 1906. Although they were his closest confidantes within the group, Arthuys and Barrès both came from traditional right-wing backgrounds, born into conservative, privileged families. The son of a career army officer, Arthuys was a lawyer and highly decorated war veteran, owner of a Roubaix-Tourcoing industrial concern, and a supporter of the Action française. Barrès's father was the extreme-rightist author and deputy Maurice Barrès, veteran of Boulangism and staunch anti-Dreyfussard. The son wrote for several conservative newspapers and in 1921 authored a nationalist book about the Great War, entitled *La Guerre à vingt ans*. Bourgin graduated from the École normale supérieure, a docteur ès lettres, and a veteran of the Ligue des patriotes and the Action française. These three men were joined in the conservative faction of the Faisceau by founding members Maurice de Barral and Marcel Bucard, the decorated war veteran and future leader of the fascist Francistes movement.

Apart from the obvious differences in social and political background, the conservative faction expected the Faisceau to follow the pattern of the established extreme-rightist leagues. Their fascism consisted of the conquest of state by the paramilitary Légions, followed by the construction of an authoritarian regime, the living embodiment of the national will. Employing social Darwinist rhetoric, they favoured bellicose nationalism to restore French predominance. Thus a meritocracy represented heroism, patriotism, and discipline; far from constructing a new world, its mission was to preserve the old one. Faisceau conservatives thus dismissed the rationalization of politics and espoused order, hierarchy, and the preservation of the past, rejecting fascist 'revolution' in favour of a moral and physical cleansing of the masses.[10]

No such divisions existed within the ranks of the CDF/PSF, whose political plan straddled the traditional and extreme-right, and bore no resemblance to Valois's modernizing bent. Like the Faisceau, the CDF/PSF composed a program for state

---

9    The French term *combattant* is used throughout this work in place of the English 'war veterans'. In the parlance of the French extreme right, the *combattant* is more than a mere soldier of the Great War, endowed with the moral authority to lead France, and dedicated to a neo-authoritarian replication of the politics of the trenches in civil society.

10    In a 1972 interview with right wing historian Jean-Maurice Duval, Barrès stated that he joined the Faisceau expecting it to be a group of elite *combattants* dedicated to bringing the spirit of the trenches into politics, with the further goal of restoring French greatness and tradition. See Jean-Maurice Duval, *Le Faisceau de Georges Valois* (Paris, 1979), p. 74.

and government, to be implemented once the group had either seized or been elected to power. Yet their model exclusively resembled that proposed by Faisceau conservatives, an authoritarian construct in the service of French tradition. Despite their frequent public proclamations to the contrary, the group was rabidly anti-parliamentary, deriding the Republic and its officials as corrupt, immoral, and self-centred. They thus demanded the institution of discipline and trumpeted the primacy of the national over individual interest. If the CDF/PSF rejected fascism, they were far from republican; even as they sent deputies into the chamber after June 1936, the group championed authoritarianism, characterized by the restoration of strong central authority to combat parliamentary 'excess' and restraints on 'anarchic' liberty.

During the Croix de Feu years this vision of the new state was linked to the *esprit combattant* of the Great War. References to the fraternity of the trenches abounded in various tracts and the group newspaper, which continually claimed that their sacrifice granted veterans the moral authority to lead France. However, after their 1936 transformation into the parliamentary Parti social français, their emphasis shifted to social Catholicism and nationalism, in the vein of La Tour du Pin and Maurice Barrès respectively. As the leader of a mass party of over one million members by 1938, La Rocque increasingly called for socio-political reconciliation and the 'equality of souls' in an opportunistic bid to seize power and transform French politics.

# I

On July 23, 1926 the chief press organ of Mussolini's Italy, *Il Popolo d'Italia*, dedicated its front page to a new French political phenomenon – fascism. It reprinted in full an article by Faisceau leader Georges Valois, entitled 'La Révolution nationale est en marche', alongside the seven resolutions from the group's June conference in Reims. Accompanied by photos and sympathetic commentary, the generous attention devoted to the group led members to believe that French fascism had gained official recognition and invaluable support from their Italian counterparts. The Faisceau coveted such attention, regarding the Duce as the herald of a new Europe in which fascism would invariably replace liberalism and parliamentarism, and devoted numerous articles in their newspaper to the Italian phenomenon and its leaders.[11]

Such a quest for the official approval of Italian fascism seems to indicate that the Faisceau had adopted the political vision of Mussolini and his advisors, that the group was but a pale copy of its Italian counterpart. Yet in a 1928 autobiographical work published mere months after the splintering of the Faisceau, Valois boldly claimed that they 'never had any connection with Italian fascism, directly or indirectly'. The group's doctrine and vision were their own, he insisted; if anything, they had been adopted by many Italians. Yet the fascism espoused by the Faisceau was no longer practiced in Italy. Valois had admired the revolutionary movement of the march on Rome, but

---

11    'La Presse italienne et le fascisme français', *Nouveau Siècle* (hereafter *NS*), 24 July 1926. Articles praising Italian fascism were omnipresent in the pages of *Nouveau Siècle*. See, for example, 'Une interview avec M. Mussolini', *NS*, 2 July 1926; Philippe Lamour, 'Visite à L'Italie vivante', *NS*, 20 Sept. 1926.

six years later abhorred the reactionary imitation into which it had evolved.[12] As the Faisceau experiment disintegrated, he proclaimed his loyalty to the Republic, stating that he had always been so inclined, seeking only to install a 'syndicalist' parliament and enable working-class participation in both the nation and state.[13]

Faisceau political plans tell a different story. During the group's existence, Valois and his colleagues were not supporters of republican government, despite his post-mortem statements to the contrary. Instead they advanced designs for an authoritarian corporative state, in which representative assemblies of families and producers advised an all-powerful dictator on political, economic, and social needs and desires. Taken at face value, this framework resembled the Italian model. Yet the Faisceau's proposed fascist state, while sharing certain assumptions and beliefs with Mussolini and his confreres, was in fact *sui generis*. Valois's fascism assimilated ideas drawn from both left and right, a program that the Italians rhetorically accepted, but ignored in practice.

From the very beginning, while still a member of the royalist Action française, Valois perceived Italian fascism to be a revolutionary movement whose goals mirrored those of the left, even if its political means did not. In his preface to the French edition of Pietro Gorgolini's work *La Révolution fasciste*, he claimed that the movement's raison d'être was to defeat bourgeois democracy and capitalism, and the plutocrats who exclusively benefited from those systems. Liberalism served only the cause of capital, while fascism – an alliance of intellectuals, war veterans, workers, and peasants – laboured for the greatness of the nation. Mussolini's dictatorship was dedicated to public service in place of class-based interests, forging a corporative political and economic system with the aid of an elite composed almost exclusively of workers. Having weakened the nation through ineffective government, the bourgeoisie were replaced by 'the spiritual, moral, and economic forces of Italy ... coordinated and aimed towards one national goal: Italian greatness'. To this end, royalists, republicans, conservatives, and even ex-communists joined the fascist party in a united effort to replace the rule of the *lira* with new heroic values. Old political forms were destroyed root and branch, replacing the liberal plutocratic order of the nineteenth century.[14]

To be sure, the rejection of liberalism and the pursuit of national greatness were fundamental principles of Italian fascism. Yet Valois's vision of a revolutionary working class elite ignored Italian reality. Mussolini's Partito Nazionale Fascista contained 780,000 members by the end of 1923, of whom few supported the extension of power to Italian labour and many rejected revolutionary change in any form. The views espoused by the small faction which promoted a syndico-corporativist state, led by Edmondo Rossoni, Sergio Pannunzio, and A.O. Olivetti, certainly resembled Valoissian fascism, as did the extreme-left populism of Curzio Malaparte, albeit

---

12    Georges Valois, *L'Homme contre l'argent* (Paris, 1928), pp. 264–265.

13    Georges Valois, 'À la recherche d'un parti nouveau', *NS*, 5 June 1927. That the concept of electoral politics was anathematic to syndicalists did not stop Valois from frequently using the term to describe political projects.

14    Georges Valois, preface to Pietro Gorgolini, *La Révolution fasciste* (Paris, 1924), pp. VII–XII. Gorgolini was a leading Turin fascist in the early 1920s.

to a lesser extent. Rossoni's Unione Italiana del Lavoro and the Olivetti-penned Manifesto dei Sindicalisti attracted the support of various Italian intellectuals, but enjoyed little success among the working class. Viewing Mussolinian fascism as reactionary, both men argued instead for neo-syndicalism, in which politics became the domain of producers from all sectors of society. A strong state would replace weak and decisive parliamentary government, serving the collective good rather than the individual.[15] Similarly, Malaparte's soldier-producers rejected antiquated liberalism in favour of fascism, because the latter best served the modern world. As he fought for the nation during the Great War, the veteran engaged in the battle for production in its aftermath.[16]

But various cliques resolutely opposed these ideas, including the moderate revisionists led by Massimo Rocca – who proposed the incorporation of fascist principles within the pre-existing political system, the authoritarian and imperialist *squadristi* – for whom violence and empire would transform Italy, and the promoters of fascism as a cultural revolution led by Giovanni Gentile. Much to Rossoni and Olivetti's dismay, it was the arch-conservative Alfredo Rocco whose proposals gained official approval during the so-called 'Napoleonic Year' of 1926, formalizing fascist governing institutions in a decidedly reactionary fashion. There was little legal or administrative change: PNF membership and leadership remained overwhelmingly middle-class (only 15 per cent of its members were workers), and the oldest partisans bitterly denounced the *embourgeoisement* of the party. Labour remained in the factories under Mussolini's regime, while government and the civil service continued to exist as the exclusive preserve of the educated elite.[17]

Yet Valois's opinion of Italian fascism did not change. Moved by the rhetoric of the regime rather than its actions, he continued to champion a fascism of the left upon abandoning royalism in late 1924. By 1926 Valois, now the leader of the Faisceau and seemingly unaware of the newfound Italian conservatism, announced that fascism openly opposed the right, fulfilling the needs of the people and defending their interests against the ruling class. While Rocco consolidated the fascist system of government with the full participation of the middle class, effecting few concrete changes and steering political discourse and practice to the right, Valois proclaimed that fascism represented the logical conclusion of 1789, when French revolutionary forces attempted to create the first modern state. He theorized that the feudal *ançien regime*, epitomized by old elites who fought only to preserve material gain, had been relegated to the dustbin of history, unable to meet the challenges of a new era. Yet those who succeeded the aristocracy, whether republican, royal, or imperial in nature, failed to construct a just and efficient state, resulting in a century of unparalleled bourgeois decadence that rivaled the worst excesses of the old monarchy. The true legacies of 1789, patriotic nationalism and a socialism devoid of class conflict, were buried in an avalanche of crass materialism. Fascism aimed to restore both ideals in

---

15    David D. Roberts, *The Syndicalist Tradition and Italian Fascism* (Chapel Hill, 1979), pp. 177–185, 256–259.

16    Alexander de Grand, 'Curzio Malaparte: The Illusion of the Fascist Revolution', *Journal of Contemporary History* 7/1–2 (1972), 77–81.

17    Stanley G. Payne, *A History of Fascism, 1914–1945* (Madison, 1995), pp. 110–121.

a modern political context. A movement for all classes, it unified the people through the inculcation of a genuine national consciousness, under the direction of a great leader who guaranteed liberty. Thus to Valois, this system best expressed 'the state of the industrial age'.[18] Fascism represented for twentieth century Europe what liberalism and parliamentarism had evoked in 1789: a universal political, economic, and social structure exemplifying the avant-garde of modernity. The latter would be replaced by a syndical, corporative, and familial system of political representation.

For all Valois's talk of fascism originating on the left, however, his political doctrine displayed an equal sympathy for the ideology of the French extreme-right, specifically its unique brand of 'national-socialism', and particularly the Barrèssian variant. Maurice Barrès and other turn of the century rightists posited that the working class, farmers, and small businessmen, fell victim to the capitalist bourgeoisie, exploited by wealthy interests. Yet they defined social justice in rather nebulous terms, through initiatives ranging from taxes on foreign workers to protectionist legislation designed to benefit shopkeepers. Barrès and his confreres rejected Marx and 'German-Jewish' internationalist socialism in favour of the nation as a revolutionary vehicle, with the state defending its weaker subjects against a shady consortium of international financiers and rich industrialists.[19] Hence Valois wrote that the fascist state mobilized a socialism freed from the German conception of internationalism (i.e. Marxism), combined with a state-sponsored nationalism that specifically defended the interests of the working-class. Where socialism provided the state with its sense of social justice, fascism added the national discipline of individual (i.e. bourgeois) initiative.

Thus Valois willingly accepted the political platform of the right, with its emphasis on national order and authority, yet only if the causes of the left (primarily its advocacy of social justice) were maintained. Here his political doctrine fused Barrèssian national-socialism with the syndicalism of Georges Sorel, whose 'proletarian vigour' had inspired fascism to aid the working class in toppling the 'decadent' bourgeois Republic. One of the intellectual founders of French revolutionary syndicalism, Sorel espoused a Proudhonian socialism not dissimilar to Valois's own. The Faisceau leader first came into contact with the author of *Reflections on Violence* in 1910, when Sorel responded to the *Enquête sur la monarchie et la classe ouvrière*, a survey examining labour's view of monarchism undertaken during Valois's time as labour expert for the Action française. Although the *vieux maître* abruptly abandoned royalism in 1911, somewhat embarrassed by the reactionary discourse of Maurras and his followers, Valois continued to lionize Sorel during the Faisceau years, honouring him as a key progenitor of French fascism.[20]

18    Georges Valois, 'Le Fascisme: conclusion du mouvement de 1789', *NS*, 14 July 1926.

19    On Barrès, early national socialism, and a critique of decadent modernity, see Michel Winock, *Nationalisme, antisémitisme, et fascisme en France* (Paris, 1990), pp. 19–21, 43–45, 250–51; Zeev Sternhell, *Maurice Barrès et le nationalisme français* (Paris, 1985), pp. 155–160, 203–207, 224–232.

20    See, for example, Georges Valois, 'Origines françaises du fascisme', *NS*, 27 April 1926.

In particular, Valois admired *Reflections on Violence* and *The Illusion of Progress*, works that probed the social roles of the bourgeoisie, the working class, and the state. To Sorel, proletarian myths and violence alone possessed the power to physically and morally transform society. The liberal notion of progress was a lie, a political tool used during the nineteenth century to justify middle-class power. But bourgeois hegemony protected a system based upon corruption and exploitation, the very opposite of the syndicalist 'cult of work'. Only a revolutionary society of producers could reorganize France according to the 'primacy of production', abandoning capitalism in favour of a vitalist spirit alone capable of regenerating both the proletariat and bourgeoisie. The latter faced a choice: Adopt a proletarian mentality or succumb to the violence of the revolutionary worker.[21]

Valois appropriated Sorel's position as his own during the Faisceau years, arguing that the new fascist state replaced the age of empty talk with the 'age of construction', when the working class revived the dormant creative energy of the bourgeoisie, those who had built railroads, canals, roads, and factories in the previous century.[22] On this point he was quite clear: Although the bourgeoisie were not useless, they were nevertheless unequipped to lead the nation. This opinion, first formulated in the 1924 work *La Révolution nationale* while Valois was still a member of the Action française, remained unchanged throughout his political career, even after he abandoned fascism. That the middle class would direct enterprise was a given, their cardinal virtues of savings and industry left untouched by the state. Yet they were incapable of governing, having managed the state as a business, run according to the rules of commerce to allow financiers and industrialists the greatest potential earnings. Such a system made the bourgeoisie lazy and greedy, and generated class conflict. Fascism, in contrast, worked the rich, imposing discipline and obliging the bourgeoisie to labour for the good of the people and the greatness of the nation:

> Take away from the bourgeoisie the authority which they are incapable of exercising, in order to place the power in the hands of a national leader ... who will keep the bourgeoisie at their posts, obliging them to leave behind the economic anarchy in which they situate themselves, and to fulfill all of their duties concerning the people.[23]

Not all Faisceau members viewed the fascist political project in the same manner as Valois, instead envisioning the movement as a vehicle for traditional right-wing demands without the concomitant socio-economic platform. For Hubert Bourgin, formerly a member of the ultra-conservative Ligue des patriotes and publisher of the *Chronique des ligues nationales*, fascist political doctrine was essentially conservative in nature. Despite paying lip service to the coming 'revolution', he posited that the political form of the state embodied continuity, duration, and conservation, the

21    Jack J. Roth, *The Cult of Violence: Sorel and the Sorelians* (Berkeley, 1980), pp. 34–39, 50–61, 91.

22    See variously: Georges Valois, 'Nationalisme et socialisme', *NS*, 25–26 Jan. 1926; F/7/13211, Tract – 'Le Faisceau des combattants, des chefs de famille, et des producteurs' (Paris, 1926), p. 4; Georges Valois, *1er Assemblée des combattants, des producteurs et des chefs de famille* (Paris, 1926); Georges Valois, 'Origines françaises du fascisme', *NS*, 27 April 1926.

23    Georges Valois, *La Révolution nationale* (Paris, 1924), pp. 62–80, 153–158.

eternal principles and profound human truths that composed the 'Latin genius'. To Bourgin, Mussolini's inspiration came from ancient Rome, and not the contemporary syndicalism or national socialism that fascinated Valois. Rather, the Duce represented order, discipline, and hard work: The roots of all progress and greatness. In addition, Italian fascism destroyed the corrupt plutocracy, which ruined Europe by fomenting political and economic anarchy for personal gain. Although the ex-*liguer* accepted the notion that fascist politics went beyond class-based interests, he insisted that Mussolini's fascism at heart represented a voluntary and organized service of elites within military and corporativist forms, which both intensified industrial production and engaged in the moral and physical cleansing of the masses. This included the propagation of bellicose patriotism, with which the state severely punished any degradation of *la Patrie*. As a result, a successful fascist regime liquidated national enemies, classified as deputies, speculators, merchants, and the decadent.[24]

If Valois's fascism synthesized Sorel and Barrès, Bourgin's lauded Charles Maurras and La Tour du Pin. Nor did he alone view fascism as reactionary. To Jacques Arthuys, the lawyer and industrialist from Roubaix-Tourcoing who assisted Valois in the formation of both the Estates-General campaign of 1923 and the Faisceau, fascism could not simply abandon the past. The fundamental tenets of the fascist state merely regenerated French civilization and tradition into new forms, but left intact the traditional political values and socio-economic hierarchies.[25] This seemingly unbridgable chasm between Valois's left-fascism and the cult of tradition and patriotism espoused by Bourgin and Arthuys prevented the establishment of any consensus regarding the new political order.

Yet if they proved unable to agree upon the details of a new political order, Faisceau members of all stripes were unanimous in condemning communism, liberalism, and parliamentarism. Here both Valois and the conservatives found common ground, much like the Italian fascists, who similarly accepted these points from the expansion of the Fasci di Combatimento in 1920–1921 onwards.[26] But Faisceau anti-parliamentarism and anti-communism were not servile imitations of their Italian counterparts. In arguing that the new state would be based upon an unbending opposition to communism and parliamentary democracy, Valois and his colleagues reacted to developments in France as much as they adhered to fascist doctrine.

Although the Russian Revolution did much to demonize Bolshevism in France, a massive strike wave among transportation and industrial workers in 1920 brought anti-communism to public attention. Articles about the 'barbaric' Soviet Union abounded in the French press across the political spectrum. Portrayed as the polar

24    Hubert Bourgin, 'Le Discours de Pérouse et la doctrine fasciste', *NS*, 1 Oct. 1926; Hubert Bourgin, 'A qui nous aime, à qui nous hait', *NS*, 22 Oct. 1925.
25    Jacques Arthuys, 'Vers un nouveau siècle', *NS*, 24 April, 1927.
26    On Mussolini's anti-communism/liberalism/parliamentarism, see Benito Mussolini, 'The Political and Social Doctrine of Fascism', *International Conciliation*, no. 306, Jan. 1935, pp. 8–12. The latter is an English reprint, in extenso, of Gentile and Mussolini's definition from the *Encyclopedia Italiano*. See also Payne, pp. 95–98; Alexander de Grand, *Italian Fascism: Its Origins & Development* (Lincoln, 1989), pp. 144–145. For the anti-communist/liberal views of the fascist left, see Edmondo Rossoni, 'La Corporazione Fascista', in Francesco Perfetti (ed.), *Il Sindicalismo Fascista* (Rome, 1988), pp. 270–271.

opposite of the Gallic temperament and doctrine, communism was variously blamed for aiding German militarism, plotting to Sovietize the French working class and state, and actively supporting the 1925 Rif Rebellion, during which Abd el Krim's forces rose up against French colonial rule in Morocco. Such sentiments were equally apparent in the Chamber of Deputies, where various Bloc National representatives spoke in vociferous terms about eliminating the Soviet menace. Outside the chamber, conservative movements like General de Castelnau's *Fédération national Catholique* threatened mass action should the government fail to contain the communist threat.[27]

Yet the May 1924 electoral victory of the Cartel des Gauches acted as the catalyst for the Faisceau and other extreme-rightist groups, who viewed the new ministry as a precursor to communist triumph in France. Although not as loathsome to the right as Blum's Popular Front a decade later, the radical and socialist-led Cartel nonetheless angered conservatives by demanding the entry of the Soviet Union into the League of Nations and proposing progressive legislation which evoked the socialization of France. That new radical-socialist premier Edouard Herriot had visited the Soviet Union a year earlier, proclaiming admiration for its success, did little to alter this perception. Nor were rightist worries allayed by the November internment of SFIO founder Jean Jaurès's ashes in the Pantheon, which attracted a 100,000-strong communist demonstration on the streets of Paris, or the February 1925 decision to recall the French ambassador from the Vatican. The Catholic extreme-right, represented in the Faisceau ranks by Valois, Bourgin, and Philippe Barrès among others, found the latter action particularly odious.[28]

By 1926 the communist party made inroads at the ballot box, and groups like the Faisceau were increasingly wary of a potential socialist or Bolshevik ministry. Having gained 8 per cent of the vote in the 1924 general election, coming close to 10 per cent two years later, the Parti communiste français supplemented parliamentary forays with demonstrations and street battles. Their actions received lengthy coverage in the Faisceau press, which portrayed the PCF as a foreign menace attempting to subjugate France.[29] Valois referred to communism in apocalyptic language, as a dire threat to French security: 'A tremendous duel has begun between Barbarism and Civilization, between the Horde and the *Cité*, between the Asiatic world and the European world. European nations, on pain of death, must inaugurate institutions with which they will be victorious in this struggle.'[30] In his 1924 work *La Révolution nationale*, he contrasted the pillaging communist with the benevolent fascist, at once the defender of European civilization and the rights of the worker:

The Slavic Bolshevik is the Northern warrior leading the Asiatic and Scythic horde, for whom doctrine furnishes a justification to go forth and pillage the Roman world which

---

27    Jean-Jacques Becker and Serge Berstein, *Histoire de l'anticommunisme en France* (Paris, 1987), pp. 44–62, 85–86, 117–126, 170–182. The accusations appeared in a wide variety of French newspapers, from *Le Temps* and *L'Oeuvre* to *L'Ami du peuple* and *Action française*.

28    Ibid, p. 186.

29    Faisceau articles on communist activities are far too numerous to list here. For daily examples, see Valois's column 'La Horde'.

30    Georges Valois, 'Appel aux producteurs, aux épargnants, aux combattants', *NS*, 2 July 1925. See also Georges Valois, *La Politique de la victoire* (Paris, 1925), pp. 76–77.

he terms capitalist. The Latin fascist is the veteran from the Midi, who wants to tear the State away from the feeble hands of the bourgeois administrator, protect labour against big money, and stiffen the defense of a civilization abandoned by profiteers and lawyers incapable of bearing arms.[31]

Communism thus became the tool of the plutocracy and its parliamentary allies, who used leftist organizations to keep working class dissent visible and controlled. Only fascism could truly defend labour, because the Faisceau strove for heroism and peace, protecting the worker from the Bolshevik and the *usurier*. Realizing the devious nature of the movement, Europe had 'vomited up communism', with the exception of France, where gullible workers continued to believe Marxist promises.[32]

Valois's critique of communism went beyond obloquy, however. The French leftist was not 'the man with the knife between his teeth', he admitted. Communism and fascism were *frères ennemis*, both inherently anti-parliamentary/liberal/ plutocratic in nature, proposing socio-economic reform through the renovation of existing political institutions and the installation of a dictatorship.[33] That communism worked to defeat capitalism and the bourgeoisie proved similarly compatible with fascist aspirations. Only the communist insistence upon class war in place of fascist national unity raised serious objections. The results in Russia spoke for themselves, Valois argued, including the cessation of production, famine and death, and state-sanctioned violence against any perceived ally of the bourgeoisie. Ignoring improved French economic prospects in the mid-1920s, in March 1926 Valois claimed that communism flourished in France solely as a result of economic instability due to the fall of the franc, unemployment, and poverty. The fascist state, which aimed to eliminate the immiseration of the worker through improved production methods and organization, while granting a political voice to labour, removed the need for such extreme solutions.[34]

Although the Faisceau unanimously rejected communism as unsuitable for France, to be driven from the nation by fascist dynamism and violence, various members were even more hostile to democracy and parliamentarism. Again Valois set the tone, this time arguing that the precipitous fall of the franc provided an opportunity to demonstrate the ruinous consequences of liberal democracy in action. French

31    Georges Valois, *La Révolution nationale* (Paris, 1924), p. 151.
32    'La Nouvelle activité communiste', *NS*, 24 Sept. 1926. Other Faisceau members were no less virulent. See, for example, Hubert Bourgin, 'La Verité sur le regime Bolchevique telle qu'elle se dégage des documents officiels Soviétiques', *NS*, 15 March 1926.
33    Georges Valois, 'Fascisme ou communisme', *NS*, 3 Dec. 1925.
34    F/7/13211, tract – 'La Conquête de l'avenir'; Georges Valois, 'Communistes', *NS*, 19 March 1925; Georges Valois, 'Elimination du communisme par la création économique', *NS*, 20 March 1926. Valois's gloomy assessment, that poverty and unemployment led to communist success, did not accurately reflect the French economy in the mid-1920s. Despite the fall of the franc, only 243,000 workers were unemployed in 1926, down from 537,000 five years earlier. Furthermore, the industrial production index rose from 55 in January 1919 to 111 in January 1925, reaching 130 in August 1926. Similarly, workers' purchase power, indexed at 394 in February 1921, rose to 464 by October 1925, and 570 a year later. In Alfred Sauvy, *Histoire économique de la France entre les deux guerres: T.1, de l'armistice à la dévaluation de la livre* (Paris, 1965), pp. 218–219, 465, 505.

fiscal problems first emerged in 1919, when wartime currency exchange controls were removed at the insistence of the United States and Great Britain. Assuming that reparations payments would bolster the sagging franc, postwar ministries relied upon bond issues and the currency reserves of the Banque de France to meet the nation's financial obligations. With the coming of the Ruhr crisis in January 1923, the currency dovetailed precipitously, the victim of foreign speculation and governmental refusal to levy a sufficient income tax. Although somewhat soothed in 1924 by the Dawes reparations settlement and loans tendered by New York banking house J.P. Morgan, the currency again fell steadily throughout late 1925 and early 1926, bottoming out at 243 per pound in the summer.[35] *Nouveau Siècle* ran daily broadsides accusing successive Cartel finance ministers Louis Loucheur, Raoul Péret, Joseph Caillaux, and Anatole de Monzie of incompetence. Caillaux was particularly reviled by the right, with various conservative deputies threatening him with canes and revolvers, and the Faisceau joined in the chorus of denunciation. Attacks continued in *Nouveau Siècle* and the chamber upon the return of Poincaré to power in July 1926, until the devaluation of the franc in June 1928, which effectively ended the monetary crisis.[36]

Poincaré's return certainly reconciled parliamentary conservatives with the Republic, but did little to assuage more extreme voices. Writing in the pages of *Nouveau Siècle*, Philippe Barrès crudely referred to the Chamber of Deputies as the place 'where they distill an incapacitating morphine which leads the country to its death', while longtime Valois associate René Johannet announced that it was time for the surgeon to operate, to remove the parliamentary 'sickness' from France.[37] Valois himself was no less dramatic. 'You know full well that we vomit on parliamentarism', he jeered, 'the electoral regime favoured by gossips, second-raters, and the rich'. While the *combattants* had fought at the front during the Great War, he charged, deputies sold the nation to the 'King of Petrol'.[38]

---

35    For a detailed overview of the postwar fiscal debacle, see Stephen A. Schuker, *The End of French Predominance in Europe: The Financial Crisis of 1924 and the Coming of the Dawes Plan* (Chapel Hill, 1976).

36    Philippe Bernard and Henri Dubief, *The Decline of the Third Republic, 1914–1938* (Cambridge, 1986), pp. 97–98, 155. For the right-wing response to Caillaux, see Édouard Bonnefous, *Histoire politique de la Troisième Republique: Vol. 4, Cartel de Gauches et Union Nationale (1924–1929)* (Paris, 1960). Faisceau attacks on Caillaux and de Monzie were a daily occurrence in *Nouveau Siècle*. See, for example: Jacques Arthuys, 'Et voici: Le Franc-Caillaux', *NS*, 11 June 1925; Georges Valois, 'Pour sauver le franc', *NS*, 9 July, 1925; 'La Révolution en marche', *NS*, 6 July 1926; Georges Valois, 'Contre l'inflation', *NS*, 19 July 1926. In each case, Valois's own 'national solution' – the reinstitution of the gold franc – was contrasted with the 'ruinous' fiscal policies of the left. For attacks on Poincaré's financial acumen, see: Georges Valois, 'Observations techniques sue le discours de M. Raymond Poincaré', *NS*, 12 Dec. 1926.

37    Philippe Barrès, 'Le Sens du pèlerinage', *NS*, 21 Feb. 1926; René Johannet, 'Le Chirurgien et son heure', *NS*, 21 June 1926.

38    Georges Valois, 'La Révolution nationale', *NS*, 20 Aug. 1925. See also 'Décrépitude', *NS*, 9 Dec. 1925.

Beyond mere insults, the Faisceau critique of parliamentary democracy pointed to its ubiquitous corruption and inefficiency. To Hubert Bourgin, fraud, intrigue, and party interests were rife within the Chamber and its back rooms, impeding effective government. Echoing Maurice Barrès's complaint, Bourgin charged that deputies were concerned solely with re-election, while powerful moneyed interests and ambitious prefects intervened behind the scenes, and the lords of industry, banks, and steel imposed their will upon greedy elected representatives. Popular government remained a hollow myth, Bourgin wrote, masking the reality of utter disorder, electoral victories bought with dirty money, influence peddling, and broken promises. His critique was not entirely groundless: Rampant speculation followed the acceptance of the Dawes plan and resulting currency stabilization, and many elected officials participated in a variety of banking and investment syndicates.[39]

Others voiced concerns over the weakness of the government, and its obsession with sectarianism. The political parties, representatives of the older generation, had failed to win the peace in the manner that the *combattants* – the generation of 1914 – won the war. Valois unhesitatingly blamed the divisive parliamentary system. Exclusively concerned with deriding the opposition, deputies ignored the security and prosperity of France.[40] Fascism presented the nation with a 'new team', for whom power was a responsibility and not a profit scheme: 'Left-wing parties, right-wing parties, all that belongs to the language of parliamentarians. We know only the French and the anti-French, men who want greatness for France and the French, and those who fear greatness and live in pettiness: war veterans and shirkers, victors and defeatists'.[41] He left no doubt as to which category best described the politician.

## II

Although the political doctrine of the Faisceau shared certain affinities with Italian fascism, the group's proposed state was unique, combining elements of both national-syndicalism and conservative authoritarianism. Yet individual members remained far from unanimous regarding its ideological bent. The disagreements between Valois, Bourgin, and Arthuys became increasingly visible when discussions turned towards the actual construction of a new political order.

In keeping with his adoption of Sorel and Barrès as the ancestors of fascism, and his belief in the 'age of electricity', Valois's proposed state was at once hyper-modern and traditional. The Barrèssian cult of the soil and the dead – the very identity of France – would be preserved within the family, whose representation before the state guaranteed familial interests and preserved tradition. They would be joined by the producers, who strove to remake the French economy, society, and aesthetic, bringing

39    Hubert Bourgin, 'Pourquoi nous sommes antiparlementaires', *NS*, 23 Dec. 1925; Hubert Bourgin, *Cinquante ans d'expérience démocratique* (Paris, 1925), pp. 235–236. The most visible example of the industrialist-politician during the twenties was Louis Loucheur, confidante of Aristide Briand and baron of heavy industry.

40    'Discours prononcée le 11 Novembre', *NS*, 12 Nov. 1925; Georges Valois, 'La Forme nouvelle de l'Etat', *NS*, 30 Jan. 1926.

41    Georges Valois, *La Politique de la victoire*, pp. 10–12.

France into the modern world, where industrial values predominated. Valois's vision placed him in clear conflict with most prominent group members, who prioritized a conservative agenda. Any modernizing impulse present in their discourse and ideas was drawn exclusively from the trench experience during the Great War. Where Valois saw the war years as a rude awakening for backwards France, a chance to bring the nation into the age of electricity, Faisceau conservatives perceived the conflict as a reaffirmation of the need to preserve French tradition at all costs, reinforced by a hierarchical dictatorship which resembled the command structure of the trenches. Yet both sides understood that elections were absurd, that the necessary dictum 'agir en équipe, avec un chef' could not be voted upon. The *État Combattant* elided the entire republican apparatus, including elected representatives.

Valois and Arthuys first developed plans for political reform during the Estates-General campaign of 1923–1924, joining various right-wing luminaries in demanding their reconvention to save France from economic and political ruin. These Estates little resembled their antecedents, the representative assemblies of the aristocracy, clergy, and commoners convened to voice their opinions to the king. Launched in December 1922, the campaign published a monthly journal, the *Cahiers des États-Généraux*, and received substantial financial backing from prominent right-wing industrialists. By October 1923, the group attracted 646 'notables' to Estates president Eugène Mathon's meeting at the Salles des ingénieurs civils, primarily businessmen, wealthy farmers, and independent professionals. Many were members of the Action française, including both Arthuys and Valois, who directed the Nouvelle Librairie Nationale, the group's publishing house, and wrote regular columns on economic affairs for their daily newspaper. Given their intellectual pedigree, members of the Estates plotted the eradication of the parliamentary system. In its place they envisioned a corporativist state in which permanent assemblies of families and producers counseled an authoritarian leader and his ministers.[42]

As described by Arthuys in the April–May 1924 edition of the *Cahiers des Etats-Généraux*, the new Estates-General consulted with the state on the drafting of laws, bringing the needs and desires of the populace to the attention of the leader. In place of the three estates of the ançien regime, Arthuys proposed two general assemblies, for families and producers. Delegates to these assemblies included fathers in the first case, and both owners and non-communist/socialist workers from various economic corporations in the second. Legations from each assembly came together in the Conseil supérieur des Etats-Généraux, through which families and producers communicated with the state. The council met once a month to debate questions of national import, but any problem meriting further guidance could be brought to the general assembly – the entire Estates-General – for discussion.[43] Although the state alone administered the armed forces and diplomatic corps, the police, and the civil service, it answered to the Estates (its 'financial conscience') in commercial matters.

---

42    Yves Guchet, *Georges Valois: L'Action française, le Faisceau, la République syndicale* (Paris, 1975), p. 129, Allen Douglas, *From Fascism to Libertarian Communism: Georges Valois Against the Third Republic* (Berkeley, 1992), pp. 55–58.

43    Jacques Arthuys, 'Une manière de concevoir les Etats-généraux', *CEG*, April–May 1924, pp. 532–533, 537–543.

Taken by itself, such a scheme seems hardly appropriate for a fascist state. Yet Valois added certain details that prefigured his later discourse during the Faisceau years. Although the resolutions of the general assembly were binding, the state alone rendered the final decision. The Estates possessed no legislative power, providing only information and consultation necessary for the creation of various laws. It was the responsibility of the state, for example, to ensure that industry functioned according to strict guidelines, did not exploit the worker, and took only its fair share of necessary resources. Although open to arguments about other facets of industrial production, these precepts were non-negotiable; the corporations obeyed without discussion. Although Valois described the final product as a 'collective effort' of the Estates and leadership, there were clearly severe limits to any collaboration.[44]

Nor did Valois share the rationale of Mathon and others, that the Estates-General should be a vehicle for a conservative political agenda and the hegemony of bourgeois industrial power. In an October 1923 article in the *Cahiers des Etats-Généraux*, he used Barrèssian terminology, referring to the state as the head of France, the family as the heart, and the nation as the body, integral nationalist sentiments far removed from the pragmatic goals of the Northern industrialists and Western farmers who answered Mathon's call, wishing only to foment regionalism and conservative government. Rather than supporting the traditional right, Valois's assembly rested above politics entirely, rejecting the sterile regime of parties and plutocrats: 'The Estates-General will be an assembly where there is neither left nor right, nor centre ... None of its members will represent a party name or political doctrine. Only the representatives of social, intellectual, or economic duties will be deputies'.[45] Furthermore, this national elite came from all sectors of society. It reflected the permanent realities of the nation, and hence the state called upon families (moral and regional representatives) and producers (workers and owners) to present themselves. The emphasis upon a state above partisan politics, continual references to the national interest and collective duty, and the rejection of class-based concerns were common themes in fascist Italy at the time, but quite foreign to the French *haute bourgeoisie*, for whom the Estates project was inseparable from individual interest.[46]

Although the Estates-General campaign wound down in 1924, riven apart by internal ideological bickering, such ideas brought Valois and Arthuys to the threshold of fascism, effectively terminating their adherence to the royalist doctrine of Charles Maurras and the Action française.[47] Valois had been a member of the group since 1906, serving for years as the group's economics expert and director

---

44    See variously Georges Valois, 'Réponse au *Provençal* et à quelques contradicteurs de Paris et de Province', *CEG*, May 1923, pp. 149–150; Georges Valois, 'La Coordination des forces nationales', *CEG*, Oct. 1923, pp. 138–140, 148–150; 'Avant-propos', *CEG*, April 1923, 5–7; 'La Réforme de la représentation national devant l'Etat', *CEG*, April 1923, p. 19; Jacques Arthuys, 'Une manière de concevoir les Etats-généraux', *CEG*, April–May 1924, 543; Georges Valois, *La Révolution nationale*, p. 176.

45    Georges Valois, 'La Coordination des forces nationales', *CEG*, Oct. 1923, pp. 132, 151.

46    Georges Valois, *L'Economie nouvelle* (Paris, 1919), pp. 180–181; 'La Réforme de la représentation national devant l'Etat', *CEG*, April 1923, pp. 12–15; Georges Valois, 'Origines de la campagne pour les Etats-généraux', *CEG*, April 1923, p. 85.

47    On the collapse of the campaign, see Douglas, pp. 58–60.

of the Nouvelle Libriarie Nationale publishing house. Arthuys too had been a loyal postwar member of Maurras's organization. Yet neither mentioned the pretender in their presentations, and Valois questioned the utility of royalism in his 1924 work *La Révolution nationale*. Rejecting any reactionary return to pre-1789 politics, he asserted that 'to form the national State: that is one of the first acts of the national revolution, and it is an essentially revolutionary act'. Although he shared the royalist goal of destroying nineteenth-century liberalism and parliamentarism in France, Valois's new elite moved beyond the aristocracy. Instead the best and brightest from each class would rule, akin to the *combattants* of 1914, who fought shoulder to shoulder in the collaborative environment of the trenches.[48]

The authoritarian tone of Valois's discourse heightened after the formation of the Faisceau. Having fully embraced fascism, he openly espoused a seizure of power, with the goal of forcing the abdication of parliament, and the installation of a fascist *État Combattant* in its place by the Légions, those Faisceau members who had served during the Great War. Contrary to the dictum of the Estates-General campaigners, there would be no democratic debate in representative assemblies concerning the fate of the Republic. The Faisceau were dedicated to the spirit of 1914, wrote Valois, composed of war veterans rather than the royalists and industrialists who surrounded Mathon's project. Thus it represented the national unity and greatness for which one-and-a-half million soldiers died during the Great War, a recreation of the classless fraternity of the trenches, which rejected sectarian politics. This experience allowed the Faisceau to speak on behalf of the entire nation, which Valois believed to be both anti-parliamentary a priori and receptive to a national dictatorship dedicated to the suppression of the plutocracy, immorality, and individualism.[49]

The form of state was also significantly altered. During the Estates-General campaign, Valois and Arthuys advocated the re-organization of France along corporative, regional, and familial lines. Although this basic framework remained intact three years later, additional detail was added. The assemblies of families and producers (Valois continued to refer to them as the Estates-General) now encompassed local, regional, and national political organizations. Producers from local corporations were charged with providing generally elected delegates to regional bodies, which themselves sent representatives to the national assembly, to advise the leader on all economic matters.[50]

This assembly of producers included both workers and owners, and rested alongside an assembly of families, which represented the 'spiritual, intellectual, and moral forces of France'. Here Valois abandoned modern discourse, instead echoing

---

48     Georges Valois, *La Révolution nationale*, pp. 50–53.

49     CHEVS/V 45, 'Manuel de délégué', Aug. 1926, pp. 1–4; 'La Révolution nationale', *NS*, 20 Aug. 1925. See also Philippe Lamour, 'La Conception fasciste de la législation', *NS*, 28 March 1926.

50     F/7/13209, tract – 'Faisceau des combattants et des producteurs'; *1er Assemblée des combattants, des producteurs, et des chefs de famille* (Paris, 1926), p. 95; Georges Valois, 'L'Assemblée des producteurs', *NS*, 3 Feb. 1926. In the hands of Valois and Pierre Dumas, former CGT member and head of the Faisceau des corporations, plans were developed for productivist and technocratic 'syndico-corporations' to enact this program. These plans are discussed in chapter two.

sentiments expressed by Maurice Barrès in the late nineteenth century, and by his one-time mentor Charles Maurras. The values of the family mirrored those of the state, he wrote in a 1926 *Nouveau Siècle* article addressing the issue of national representation, because 'the father is like the sovereign State, but he does not make a final decision without consulting the mother, who is the home, and represents the foundation of society: stability, prudence, order, and savings'. To Valois, the family represented the cell of the nation in the natural and divine order. Where the producers symbolized modern innovation in the postwar era, the family symbolized tradition, keepers of the modest home and the soil of France. In balancing the modern and the traditional, Valois concluded, an equilibrium of national forces could be maintained, advancing the interests of all sectors of society.[51] This included religion; in the fascist state, Christian principles governed work, commerce, and communities through the assembly of families. This effectively dissipated nineteenth-century immorality, which reduced the family to a mere societal footnote, while allowing social injustice to take root in French communities.[52] Hence the state and assembly of families worked together to regulate national morality, clean unhygienic cities, and create conditions of stability for the worker and struggling French farmer.[53]

Regionalism and corporativist political organization were not particularly original concepts in postwar France. On the surface, Valois's fascist corporations recalled an ideal promoted by various contemporary social Catholic intellectuals. Influenced by the papal encyclical *Rerum Novarum*, which condemned the immiseration of the working class and its socialist response in equal measure, Albert de Mun and René de la Tour du Pin both demanded a corporative reorganization of society characterized by class conciliation. To La Tour du Pin, the decentralization of government along local and provincial lines, with the collaboration of workers and ownership, allowed a true representation of interests and professions.[54] Similarly for Eugène Duthoit, postwar president of the Semaines sociales Catholiques de France, the state was a mere superstructure, arbitrating amongst competing familial, professional, local, and regional institutions. These self-governing bodies, termed the infrastructure, actually governed the people. By the 1920s such ideas were common currency in the Republic, so much so that Laurent-Thiésy, Radical senator of Belfort, called for the adoption of regional assemblies in the pages of *L'Ère nouvelle*.[55]

---

51    Georges Valois, 'La Représentation nationale devant l'Etat', *NS*, 2 Feb. 1926; Georges Valois, 'Appel aux producteurs, aux épargnants, aux combattants', *NS*, 2 July 1925.

52    Georges Valois, *La Politique de la victoire*, pp. 54–55, 59–60; Georges Valois, 'Aux sources de la vie: la vie spirituelle', *NS*, 9 Feb. 1926; Georges Valois, 'La vie spirituelle: les Catholiques du Faisceau', *NS*, 10 Feb. 1926; F/7/13211, tract – 'La Conquête de l'avenir'.

53    Georges Valois, 'La Représentation nationale devant l'Etat', *NS*, 2 Feb. 1926; Georges Valois, 'Appel aux producteurs, aux épargnants, aux combattants', *NS*, 2 July 1925.

54    Jean-Marie Mayeur, *Catholicisme sociale et démocratie chrétienne* (Paris, 1986), pp. 55–59, 226.

55    On Duthoit, see Philippe Lécrivain, 'Les Semaines sociales de France', in Denis Maugenest (ed.), *Le Mouvement social Catholique en France au XXe siècle* (Paris, 1990), pp. 153–58; Mayeur, pp. 227–229. Founded in 1904, the Semaines sociales attracted a variety of Catholic luminaries, from Duthoit to Maurice Blondel. Maurice Barrès also argued for federative regional assemblies which outwardly resembled those proposed by the Faisceau,

Valois was not proposing federalism, however, but fascism, in which power was retained exclusively by the state, which represented the 'living will' of the nation. For the Faisceau leader, the duality of the all-powerful *chef* and state on one side, and the purely consultative associations of families and producers on the other, mirrored the fascist conceptions of authority and liberty. It was the duty of the state to ensure that liberty existed independently of the anarchy prevalent in parliamentary democracy. To Valois, false liberty – the anarchic absolute freedom of the Third Republic – represented decadence and societal weakness. Any true freedom would be possible only through the acceptance of discipline and responsibility, mobilized by the fascist state to maintain the structure of society. Hence the representative assemblies symbolized political liberty, but they accepted without question the duties and demands imposed upon them by the state. But Valois never advocated fascist government in the style of Mussolini, where the state reigned supreme, above reproach or question. The 'surgical operation' of the Légions, by which parliamentary government would be removed, installed a transitory dictatorial state charged with the formation of the assemblies of families and producers.[56] Once the system became self-sufficient, the dictatorship itself – the cornerstone of fascist politics – would no longer be necessary.

Valois's belief in the temporary nature of the state stemmed from his 'left fascism'. His leader spoke for the nation and was vested with absolute power, but like Edmondo Rossoni he believed that the corporative assemblies, and not an autocracy, provided the driving force behind the creation of a new nation and state, suitable for the age of electricity. He therefore frequently spoke of elites instead of a dictatorship. Once the corporativist system became self-sufficient, new teams composed primarily of war veterans would direct the nation, their experience in defending France lending them the necessary moral authority to lead. Young and ardent, these men represented the antithesis of the tired republican elites, the politicians and financiers incapable of meeting modern challenges. Taken from all factions and classes across the political spectrum solely according to talent, the new team worked to rejuvenate France, demolishing the old and decrepit system where leaders of the left (Édouard Herriot) and right (Raymond Poincaré) were pawns of shady financiers like Horace Finaly and Robert Pinot. Once the fascist 'revolution' succeeded, with the new elites installed in positions of power, the dictator became redundant.[57]

Yet there was another reason for Valois's insistence upon the transitional nature of any fascist dictatorship in France. At the first Faisceau conference in November 1925, he demanded an efficient government, in keeping with the rational principles governing the modern world. The group eschewed arty politics, with its endless

---

referring to the region as the true 'laboratory' of social and political transformation. On Barrès and Laurent-Thiésy, see Guy Rossi-Landi, 'La Région', in Jean-Paul Sirinelli (ed.), *Histoire des droites en France, Vol. 1-Politique* (Paris, 1992), pp. 84, 91.

56    Georges Valois, 'L'Autorité et la liberté, ou la souveraineté et la représentation', *NS*, 1 Feb. 1926.

57    Finaly was the director of the Banque de Paris et Pays-Bas; Pinot headed the Comité des Forges. Georges Valois, 'Le Fascisme: la dictature et les dictateurs', *NS*, 3 Sept. 1926; Georges Valois, 'La Conquête de l'État', *NS*, 30 July 1925; F/7/13211, tract 5-'La Conquête de l'avenir', pp. 3–4, 13–14.

bickering. Termed the 'organ of progress' engaged in the creation of a new world, fascism protected the populace against greedy speculators and foreign enemies. Yet it also faced an internal enemy: Inefficiency, which necessitated formation of a 'modern state, endowed with indispensable economic instruments, and capable of meting out national and social discipline to the industrial forces of the modern world, rendering them wholly beneficial'.[58] In keeping with his theoretical left-fascism, Valois here went far beyond the beliefs of Mussolini and the Faisceau conservatives, leaving behind discipline, will, heroism, and moralism. In their place, he proffered politics that, more closely resembling the discourse of Premier André Tardieu later in the decade, insisted that the state be run according to the Taylorist mentality prevalent in the emergent modern industrial sector.[59]

## III

Valois's vision of political and economic modernity clashed with the traditionalist faction, which demanded the strong, capable leadership of a staunchly nationalist autocrat. Faisceau conservatives had questioned the theoretical foundations of Valois's fascism, embracing extreme-nationalism, moral cleansing, and the cult of tradition, and they similarly rejected his conception of a post-dictatorial fascist state. Figures such as Maurice de Barral contended that either a dictator or a directorate would be a permanent feature of the new regime. Barral's leader, described in his *Dialogues sur le Faisceau*, was a warrior, possessing courage, the taste for responsibility, decisiveness, and ardent nationalism. He embodied a living synthesis of all castes and classes, much like the Italian fascist state.[60] Hence, Barral's projected state, devoid of the modernist sentiment that permeated the Faisceau leader's political discourse, was far less ambitious. Prioritizing internal and external security, his France confronted a social Darwinist world in which hostile neighbours threatened her destruction. As a result, he demanded the strengthening of the armed forces, critical to the restoration of French global predominance. He further insisted upon the creation of a rigorous justice system, protecting the state from internal enemies. Although he did not directly challenge the leader on this point, Barral dismissed the spirit of solidarity engendered by the corporations as an inadequate half-measure, unable to deliver social peace.[61]

This version of the future fascist state differed greatly from Valois's because it was based upon an incongruous set of principles. For Faisceau members like Arthuys,

---

58     Valois speech in *1re Assemblé nationale des combattants, des producteurs et des chefs de famille*; 'Discours prononcée le 11 Novembre', *NS*, 12 Nov. 1925.

59     Georges Valois, *Le Fascisme* (Paris, 1927), p. 15. A discussion of Tardieu's plans can be found in chapter two.

60     Maurice de Barral, *Dialogues sur le Faisceau: Ses origines, sa doctrine* (Paris, 1926), pp. 17–20.

61     Ibid. This is not to imply that Valois ignored foreign policy – he too believed in the necessity of a strong France, to repel hostile neighbouring countries. But Valois did not prioritize diplomatic matters, instead concentrating upon the modernization of the French economy and politics.

Barral, Bourgin, Barrès, and Marcel Bucard, fascism represented the opportunity to forge what historian Antoine Prost calls the 'combatant's nation', the notion held by many returning soldiers of a fraternal France undivided by partisan politics and sterile class conflict. This disposition was by no means unique during the interwar era. Groups such as the Union nationale des combattants and the Union fédérale, claiming 1.7 million members between them, clearly distinguished between the generation of the defeat and the men of 1914, believing that the trench experience created new leaders, their mission to bring the *esprit combattant* into civil society. As a result, veterans groups demanded a union of the political left and right, the demolition of parliament in its current form, and the replacement of material values with moral and spiritual ones.[62] Various Faisceau members lauded extreme variants of these sentiments, advocating a reactionary dictatorship based upon the experience of the trenches and the Barrèsian notion of 'the soil and the dead'.

'We are the new men', declared Philippe Barrès in the 1 January 1926 edition of *Nouveau Siècle*, referring to French *combattants* as an 'elite of commanding officers' who directed the masses. The *combattant* (the *type des lignes*) possessed moral and intellectual superiority as a result of his wartime experience, which imbued him with the leadership qualities lacking in the deputy (the *type d'arrière*).[63] Having paid in blood for four years, Arthuys thundered in 1926 to a crowd in San Quentin, veterans had earned their leadership positions, replacing the traitors and parliamentarians who waited out the war in the neighborhood café or bar. As the class system did not exist in the trenches, for all castes had sacrificed equally and displayed comparable heroism, each *combattant* was superior regardless of social rank.[64] This was not Valois's technocratic elite, which mobilized youthful talent to manage France. Instead Arthuys anteriorized patriotism: Veterans were neither left nor right, he claimed, but French.[65] His *combattants* conserved the past, the 'immaterial capital' of glory, virtue, and memory that comprised the tradition and strength of past centuries, and commanded obedience based upon moral authority and action.[66]

In keeping with their conservative rhetoric, Arthuys's faction inextricably linked prosperity and greatness with the preservation of tradition. To Hubert Bourgin, the state imbued all citizens with the cult of *la patrie*, the notion of suffering and sacrifice for France. This meant an active promotion of maternity, the soil, and a defense of French Catholicism, all of which comprised the political impetus of the fascist regime. Only absolute order and hierarchy guaranteed the perpetuation of the race, he wrote in his 1926 work *Les Pierres de la maison*, and ensured the security and development of French intellectual and moral forces.[67] Alongside his traditionalist confreres, Bourgin's vision of the new state embodied the politics

---

62    Antoine Prost, *Les Anciens combattants et la société française, 1914–1939, Mentalités et idéologies* (3 vols. Paris, 1978), vol. 3, pp. 128–148.

63    Philippe Barrès, 'Notre voeu', *NS*, 1 Jan. 1926; Philippe Barrès, 'Avant Verdun', *NS*, 14 Feb. 1926.

64    F/7/13209, Commissaire Central de Police de San Quentin to Minister of the Interior, 21 Nov. 1925.

65    Jacques Arthuys, *Les Combattants* (Paris, 1925), pp. 108–109, 198.

66    Ibid, pp. 200–215.

67    Hubert Bourgin, *Les Pierres de la maison* (Paris. 1926), pp. 14–20, 56–59.

of what Maurice Barrès termed the soil and the dead, the two eternal facts which defined France: 'Our earth gives us discipline, and we are the continuation of our dead ... The soil speaks to us and collaborates with our national conscience'.[68] Thus the preservation of ancestral tradition was far more important than any economic or technological advances, and rather than looking to the future, as Valois's elite would do, Barrès's Frenchman is bound to the past as a culmination of his race, nation, family, and history. Every act reflects the thoughts and influence of one's ancestors, the eternal laws that govern life. The lessons of the dead – heroism, acceptance of the supremacy of French Catholicism and the church – form teachings from which no true Frenchman can deviate.[69]

Omnipresent in the speeches and writings of Faisceau conservatives, the doctrine of the soil and the dead informed the experience of the *combattant* during the Great War. Valois's vision of Barrès retained only the synthesis of nationalism and socialism, with the soil and the dead providing a profoundly Catholic spiritual example for the French family to emulate. Other members adopted Barrèssian thought in the service of bellicose nationalism and the authoritarian state. Marcel Bucard told a Faisceau gathering at Verdun on 21 February 1926 to remember forever the sacredness of the dead, 'the immortal soul of those killed in action for France'. The infinite beauty of sacrifice was the lesson to be learned from the meeting, he concluded.[70] Elsewhere Bucard wrote of the 'motherland of the earth' as representative of the entire French nation. Those who died for its survival, he asserted, 'give their blood when she is thirsty and their entrails when she is hungry'. The *patrie* was an extension and enlargement of France as a whole, found in communes and villages, and the defense of national tradition.[71]

Faisceau members like Arthuys, Bourgin, Bucard, and Philippe Barrès wed these ideas to the experience of the *combattant*, arguing that the values of the soil and the dead formed the basis for the fascist state. Echoing his father's words, Philippe Barrès told a crowd in the Meuse in 1926 that the vision of the combattant was the *sentiment Lorraine*, of a politics above class and party in the service of tradition. The government of the trenches, emphasizing hierarchy, leadership, and strict discipline would be imported into civic and political life.[72] For Hubert Bourgin, this meant the importance of will over doctrine. Where politicians theorized, the Faisceau acted, as they had done in the heat of battle, remaking France politically and spiritually. Bourgin's leader and administration mirrored the officers and *poilus*, committed to obedience, duty, and disciplined public power. This corps served the nation above all else, cleansing the state of economic and political parasites.[73]

---

68    Maurice Barrès, *Scènes et doctrines du nationalisme* (Paris, 1987), p. 50.

69    Ibid., pp. 67–69; Maurice Barrès, *Amori et dolori sacrum* (Paris, 1921), pp. 267–269; Maurice Barrès, *Colette Baudoche* (Paris, 1908), pp. 177–179, 194, 203–204; Pierre Barral, 'La Terre' in Jean-François Sirinelli (ed.), *Histoire des droites en France, Tome 3: Sensibilités* (Paris, 1992), 49–50.

70    Au marché couvert', *NS*, 28 Feb. 1928.

71    Marcel Bucard, 'Patrie', *NS*, 1 May 1927.

72    F/7/13209, Commissaire special to the Director of the Sûreté-Générale, 'Rapport sur une réunion privé organisée par le Faisceau à Slenay-Meuse', 6 June 1926.

73    Hubert Bourgin, 'Doctrine et volonté', *NS*, 6 Jan. 1926.

Valois agreed that the combattant sacrificed everything he owned, including his life, to rejuvenate the nation and bring the classless fraternity of the trenches into civil society.[74] But contrary to Arthuys's and Bourgin's standard-bearers of tradition, and Barral's and Barrès's defenders of race and nation before the onslaught of the enemy, Valois's soldiers 'lay the foundations of a new world', preserving whatever traditional elements were useful in the age of technology. For this purpose, the law of the trenches – a national fraternity, animated by the spirit of heroism, under the command of authority – became the basis for fascist civil society:

> The combatant, the authentic combatant, is a man who has the national interest in his blood, in his flesh, because during four years all of his deeds and thoughts served the nation. And he has been branded in this fashion for his entire life. It is why he is and will be the great worker transforming the State.[75]

Yet Valois's heroic spirit of the trenches was but one part of a larger project; the political and aesthetic modernization of the state: 'In short: the democratic spirit + nationalism + socialism = fascism. Fascism = the foundation of the modern state, for a new economic era, for national greatness and social justice'. His young *combattants* invented the forms of the new world 'and put the rest in a museum', redesigning every city, town, and factory.[76] Convinced that the state should be restructured as much as indoctrinated, Valois and like-minded Faisceau members drafted plans to rebuild France, and especially Paris, to suit the needs of the modern economy and family. This entailed the rational creation of working-class stability, through a coordinated effort by workers and owners to fight poverty and misery, accompanied by state initiatives in architecture and city planning. The new French city, inhabited by a multitude of large happy families, symbolized both the modern rationalizing impulse inherent in Valois's political thought, and his belief in organic nationalism, that the family was the cell of the nation. The physical reconstruction of France became a major Faisceau project: Dozens of articles by numerous writers discussed the issue, and Valois frequently asserted its centrality to the fascist modernization of French politics, economy, and society.

Valois's scheme was directly influenced by the modernism of Le Corbusier and various contemporary American urban/industrial development schemes. Le Corbusier's rationalist architecture and avant-garde urban planning probably caught his eye at the Exposition des Arts Decoratifs in 1925, where the flamboyant Swiss

---

74    See variously Georges Valois, *D'un siècle à l'autre* (Paris, 1924), p. 267; F/7/13209, tract – 'La Conquête de l'avenir', pp. 1–2; Georges Valois, 'La Conquête de l'avenir', *NS*, 16 July 1925, Georges Valois, *La Politique de la victoire*, pp. 80–83; Georges Valois, 'L'Esprit du combattant', *NS*, 13 Feb. 1927; Douglas, 16.

75    CHEVS/V 44, tract – *Le Faisceau des combattants, des chefs de familles, et des producteurs* (Paris, 1926), p. 8; Georges Valois, 'L'Année du légionnaire', *NS*, 1 Jan. 1926; F/7/13209, tract – 'Les Légions: appel aux Combattants'; Georges Valois, *La Politique de la Victoire*, pp. 19–21.

76    F/7/13211, tract – 'Le Faisceau des combattants, des chefs de famille, et des producteurs', p. 3; Georges Valois, 'Vétéran ou organisateur du futur?', *NS*, 24 April 1927.

displayed his *Plan Voisin* in the Esprit Nouveau pavilion.[77] As Stanislas von Moos attests, the designer's *Plan* presented the architecture of the Fordist age, rationally planned and utilitarian, 'a closed form, complete in itself, a work of art in the service of technocracy'.[78] A member of Ernest Mercier's Redressement français, he advocated many of the same concepts as Valois: An American-style economy, Taylorism, the rejection of tradition ('the detritus of dead epochs'), and the notion of society as an organic, living whole.[79]

Valois and his colleagues took from Le Corbusier only those elements which corresponded to their own doctrine. But they did not have far to look within his oeuvre. In his 1925 text *L'Urbanisme*, the architect berated the modern city as a palace of chaos. Strict order, the precursor to any truly civilized society, was absent in the contemporary urban setting, he complained. Only construction which harnessed the totality of modern industrial and social power could cure this disease, resulting in a new era of humanity. If for Valois the family was the cell of the nation, to Le Corbusier it was the home, whose current form failed to address the needs of modern industrial civilization. Using Valois-style terminology, he claimed that his new city would banish the law of least effort from France. Greater emphasis would be placed on speed and technology, and the new city outfitted with an abundance of wider roads and airports.[80]

The Faisceau press openly lauded both the architect and his plans. Le Corbusier was named an *animateur* of the group in January 1927, designated as 'one of our most outstanding architects', whose genius and rejection of tradition created 'the dazzling light of the city of the future'.[81] Mere months later, after a meeting between Faisceau members and the Swiss icon, Valois claimed that his concepts expressed the goals of the fascist revolution. He singled out Le Corbusier's emphasis on discipline and the rationalization of all facets of national life, and reprinted the *Plan Voisin* in the pages of *Nouveau Siècle*, complete with its monumental artwork.[82]

Like Le Corbusier, Valois blamed the modern city for a host of problems, including working-class misery and the subsequent deterioration of the French family, consequences of rapid population growth and insufficient planning and organization. Working class suburbs spilled out haphazardly into the countryside, composed of shoddy houses more often than not built by the workers themselves. In the words of Georges Ondard, whose article on urban renewal was published in *Nouveau Siècle* in May 1926: 'Can you imagine teams of masons positioned on the four corners of a field, building the exact same house, each according to his

---

77    Gerald Monnier, *Le Corbusier* (Lyon, 1986), pp. 33–34.

78    Stanislas von Moos, 'Ville et Monument: à propos du Plan Voisin', in *Le Corbusier: la ville, l'urbanisme* (Paris, 1995), pp. 84–85.

79    Mark Antliff, 'La Cité française: Georges Valois, Le Corbusier, and Fascist Theories of Urbanism', in Matthew Affron and Mark Antliff (eds.), *Fascist Visions* (Princeton, 1997), pp. 134, 137, 152; Le Corbusier, *Urbanisme* (Paris, 1966), p. 233. Despite his fascism, Antliff notes, Valois ignored the Italian aesthetic and *planiste* example, praising its modernity but insisting on the redesigning of nation and state according to specifically French conceptions.

80    Le Corbusier, *L'Urbanisme*, pp. V, 24, 37, 65–70, 79, 84, 87, 92–95, 109–110.

81    'Les Animateurs: Le Corbusier', *NS*, 9 Jan. 1927.

82    'Le Plan Voisin', *NS*, 1 May 1927; Georges Valois, 'La Nouvelle étape du fascisme', *NS*, 29 May 1927. See also Paul-Charles Biver, 'L'Esprit Nouveau', *NS*, 20 March 1927.

whim, and without the least idea of what the finished building will look like? That is exactly what has happened in the *département de la Seine*'. As a result workers lived in hovels and private companies rarely built promised new housing because they insisted that the lots be pre-sold.[83] Faisceau authors thus deemed modern cities unconducive to family life. In a *Nouveau Siècle* piece contributed by Le Corbusier's close friend Pierre Winter, they were lambasted as dirty, over-crowded, and rapidly deteriorating. They possessed neither aesthetic unity nor proper light, fresh air, and hygiene. Constantly at risk, the worker and his family required space, greenery, and a healthy home environment. Winter further demanded the construction of suburban housing and the inauguration of a national health program.[84]

Various Faisceau members advanced proposals for a new type of city corresponding to Winter's criteria. Echoing Le Corbusier, Valois supported the construction of a *Grand Paris*, with factories and offices in the city centre, and homes on the periphery or in the suburbs. Working-class neighbourhoods were deemed especially important, and he demanded the construction of public gardens, proper housing, and sports fields, to replace industrial grime and pre-empt communist grievances. In conjunction with the industrial corporations and municipal assembly, a Direction de la région Parisienne would transform the capital section by section. A new Palais des corporations et des régions would be constructed for the assemblies of families and producers, surrounded by corporative houses for each profession and region. Every industry concentrated in a specific quarter, regulating training and working conditions, with housing beautified street by street, administered in each sector by a Bureau d'habitation. Then and only then, claimed Valois, would 'France and Europe possess economic material and a complete economic organization where the builders of the New World will come and take lessons.[85]

The final product mirrored the emerging model of suburban and industrial America. In its 12 May 1926 edition, *Nouveau Siècle* prominently displayed a drawing of the ideal workers' family and home. The husband stands with his arm around his wife, her hands clasped in awe as she stares at their large home complete with pristine automobile in the driveway. Surrounded by trees and a spacious garden, with his children joyously playing at his feet, the man and his family resemble the American dream, a fact emphasized by the caption of the picture: 'It is no longer just a dream ... it will be a reality'.[86] Various group members openly espoused the American model, and articles in the group newspaper frequently lauded New York and modern architecture. Valois emphasized the need for roads and airports, adopting the Fordist dictum that high salaries were necessary for labour, and that the new suburban homes and cars

---

83    Georges Ondard, 'Pour une organisation rationnelle de la banlieue', *NS*, May 12, 1926.

84    Dr. P. Winter, 'La Ville moderne', *NS*, 16 May 1926. A statement of approval by the Faisceau Corporation medicale was appended to Winter's article.

85    Georges Valois, 'Le Grand Paris doit être une unité administrative, économique et sociale, pourvue d'un direction propre', *NS*, 12 May 1926; Georges Valois, 'Notre campagne de banlieue et notre mobilisation financière', *NS*, 3 April 1926; quotation from Georges Valois, *Le Fascisme* (Paris, 1927), p. 92. This vision was essentially that of Le Corbusier. See *L'Urbanisme*, pp. 158–168, 191–194, 263.

86    *NS*, 12 May 1926.

bought by the workers required highways and rapid transportation. The Faisceau were midwives to the new century, he stated boldly, making French men and women the masters of machines, a nation of healthy and strong builders.[87]

By the summer of 1927, Valois's preoccupation with modernization and rationalization effectuated a complete transformation of the purpose and discourse of the Faisceau. He had previously disagreed with various group members concerning the content, and to a lesser degree the form of the state, eschewing the *État combattant* of Bourgin, Arthuys, Barrès, and Barral, based exclusively on nationalism, the cult of tradition, and the trench experience. Common ground could still be found, however, in the need for corporatism, and the infusion of discipline, order, and hierarchy within a renewed organic nation. Yet in June and July 1927 articles, concerning the formation of a *parti nouveau*, Valois proclaimed himself in favour of a republic.[88] While Bourgin claimed that the syndical state was an anti-communist vehicle dedicated to toppling parliament and its *anarchie sterilisante*, mobilizing the united will of the organic nation, the Faisceau leader fell completely to the left.[89] His notion of a provisional dictatorship remained, enacted through a 'small vacation from legality', but the final product was a syndical state in which *combattants*, producers, and families participated in a 'syndicalist democracy animated by active minorities'. Although he continued to claim that the state acted above party and class, in the hands of a leader and a legislative council, constant communication between government and the assemblies became fundamental to the decision-making process. Thus in November, Valois for the first time openly rejected Italian fascism as a political model. By January 1928, he jettisoned the idea of a 'Boulangist dictator', calling for a *République des combattants et des producteurs*, and officially ended the Faisceau experiment.[90] Valois went on to form several neo-syndicalist and libertarian communist groups in the 1930s, while many of his former Faisceau colleagues, most notably Bucard, Barrès, and Bourgin, continued to promote fascism or returned to the conservative right.

## IV

In the final analysis, the Faisceau's outward unity served to mask simmering disagreements concerning the shape and purpose of the fascist state. No similar

---

87    *NS*, 31 March 1926; F/7/13211, tract – 'Le Faisceau des combattants, des chefs de famille et des producteurs', 6; Georges Valois, 'Le Faisceau en action', *NS*, 22 Sept. 1926; Georges Valois, 'Le Grand Paris doit être une unité administrative, économique et sociale, pourvue d'un direction propre', *NS*, 3 April 1926. On New York and American architecture, see Yvan Noé, 'New York et l'architecture moderne', *NS*, 2 March 1926. Valois was perhaps prescient: He posited that society could only be fully transformed by 1950. See 'Vétéran or organisateur du futur', *NS*, 24 April 1927.

88    Georges Valois, 'Le Parti nouveau: la discussion', *NS*, 26 June 1927; Georges Valois, 'Les Nouvelles formes de l'État et de la vie économique et sociale', *NS*, 17 July 1927.

89    Hubert Bourgin, 'L'État syndicale', *NS*, 29 Feb. 1928.

90    Georges Valois, 'L'Avenir de la civilisation', *NS*, 27 Nov. 1927; Georges Valois, 'Au-délà des vieilles limites', *NS*, 10 Jan. 1928.

factionalization existed within the CDF/PSF, where leadership and rank and file alike supported group leader Colonel François de la Rocque's call for a thorough renovation of the French political system. Although they publicly accepted republicanism and constitutional democracy, the group actually envisioned an authoritarian state instilled with hierarchy, discipline, renewed central authority, and order, run by battle-hardened elites. Concomitantly, La Rocque portrayed the coming *État social français* as the antithesis of the weak, divided, and corrupt Republic, whose elected representatives were more concerned with material gain than public service.

On the surface, such rhetoric appears similar to the beliefs of the Faisceau traditionalists. But unlike Bourgin or Arthuys, La Rocque and the CDF/PSF claimed to be ardent republicans. During his appearance before the parliamentary committee investigating the role of the Croix de Feu in the 6 February 1934 riots, in which the group led the massive right-wing protest to the Chamber of Deputies, forcing the resignation of premier Edouard Daladier, La Rocque voiced their displeasure with the current government, but steadfastly rejected any comparisons with either Mussolini or Hitler. Contemporary French problems could not compare to the perpetual crises of Giolitti's Italy or Weimar Germany, he claimed, and totalitarian solutions were therefore out of the question. The *tricolore* was the only CDF/PSF standard: 'We are loyal to current institutions and we believe that you cannot build the future of our country without the current constitutional basis.'[91] That March La Rocque reaffirmed his 'profound republicanism' during an interview for the radical newspaper *Marianne*, claiming that 'le progrès est a gauche'.[92]

Nor did membership in the CDF/PSF preclude participation in electoral politics. A municipal elections circular in 1935 vigorously promoted electoral participation. Although leaders in the Croix de Feu and Volontaires Nationaux (the group's civilian/ youth wing) were forbidden from running for office to maintain their neutrality, the rank and file could participate if they agreed not to mention the CDF/PSF.[93] The following year, La Rocque abandoned the notion of non-participation altogether, bowing to public and legislative opposition to the extreme-right. For on 13 February 1936, several Camelots du Roi, members of the Action française youth wing, attacked socialist party leader Léon Blum at the funeral service for historian Jacques Bainville. As Joel Colton notes, both the left and centrist wings of the newly formed Popular Front perceived the assault to be a direct challenge to the Republic itself. Hence upon their election in June 1936, the government promptly banned the extreme-rightist leagues, including the Croix de Feu.[94] Having been labeled fascist and effectively barred from the public sphere, La Rocque transformed the group into the parliamentary Parti social français, whose press continually emphasized that the group would take power by legal means

91    APP/Ba 1857, Extracts from the Report of the Parliamentary Commission into the events of 6 February 1934, pp. 1607–1612.

92    Philippe Boegner, 'L'Heure des ligues? Les Croix de Feu', *Marianne*, March 1934.

93    AP/451/81, 'Circulaire préparatoire à la période des élections municipales', 14 March 1935.

94    Joel Colton, 'The Formation of the French Popular Front', in Martin S. Alexander and Helen Graham (eds), *The French and Spanish Popular Fronts* (Cambridge, 1989), p. 20.

or not at all. The new party immediately announced its intention to run a full slate of candidates in municipal and state electoral campaigns.[95]

However, the group's favourable public stance towards the republican system of government obscured opposing sentiments frequently expressed by various CDF/PSF leaders and members. They unleashed a torrent of anti-republican abuse in both newspaper articles and speeches during the Croix de Feu years, assailing weak, inefficient, and unnecessarily divisive parliamentary democracy, a trend equally apparent after their transformation into the Parti social français. In a July 1933 article, La Rocque bemoaned the artificial division of France into political parties, declaiming the parliamentary system as a virus, poisoning the nation at the expense of the national interest. He variously blamed political parties for state fiscal woes, the splintering of the national collective, and the corruption inherent in French politics. Then during a 1935 interview with Georges Suarez in the right-wing tabloid *Le Document*, he bluntly referred to the government as an enemy of the state, 'the agent of moral and administrative disorder'.[96]

Group members often mentioned the Stavisky affair as an example of republican frailty and official corruption. De rigueur in the interwar era, banking scandals attracted public attention and not infrequently entangled government ministers. Both the Hanau and Oustric imbroglios in 1928 and 1930 respectively implicated deputies and financiers, including André Tardieu's justice minister Raoul Péret.[97] But the Stavisky Affair in late 1933 trumped its predecessors. Named after a con artist caught selling faulty bonds from the Crédit Municipal de Bayonne, the affair toppled the Chautemps government, whose colonial minister Dalimier had supported the bond issue. As outrage emanated from both the left and right, the CDF/PSF membership declaimed the scandals as proof that the government was rotten to the core. When asked for a response to the Stavisky affair during an interview with the staunchly conservative *Pétit journal*, La Rocque bluntly proposed to 'disinfect parliament', a maneuver seemingly realized during the events of 6 February 1934 in which the CDF/PSF played a leading role.[98]

Naturally the group reserved its most extreme malice for the deputies themselves. One group tract in April 1936 called them profiteers, serving the nation exclusively

---

95    Expressions of the group's electoralism were common in their daily newspaper and speeches. See for example, F/7/12966, 'Réunion organisée par la Fédération Est de l'Île de France du Parti social français', 20 Feb. 1937. M. Lecocq, the local CDF/PSF propaganda delegate, explained the group's electoral strategy to the crowd.

96    CDLR, 'Professions du foi', *Le Flambeau*, July 1933; Georges Suarez, 'Une entrevue avec Colonel de la Rocque', *Le Document*, June 1935. See also CDLR, 'Commentaires', *Le Flambeau*, 11 Nov. 1932; Habib, 'Fin des partis', *Le Flambeau*, 2 March 1935; Un Normalien, 'Contre la nation', *Le Flambeau*, 18 Jan. 1936.

97    Claude Bellanger, *Histoire générale de la presse française* (2 vols, Paris, 1972), vol. 1, p. 497.

98    CDLR, 'PSF et suffrage universel', *Pétit Journal*, 23 Feb. 1934. For similar arguments, see 'À la Salle Wagram', *Le Flambeau*, Feb. 1934. Despite their transformation into the parliamentary PSF in 1936, the group continued to argue in much the same fashion. See CHEVS/LR 38, 'Déclaration du Lt.-Colonel de la Rocque, radiodiffusés le 24 avril 1936'; P.L., 'Pourquoi nous sommes pas "comme les autres"', *Volonté du Centre*, 11 March 1939.

for salaries and benefits frequently paid by Germany and the Soviet Union. The Croix de Feu aimed to purify the government and administration through their patriotic and social mystique, and the inculcation of discipline.[99] In a similar vein, La Rocque dismissed deputies as the masters of chatter 'from the lounge and cabaret, snobby gossips who come from the [Masonic] lodge and the noisy kitchen table'. In focusing on action and rejecting the empty words of the chamber's false electoral promises, the CDF/PSF possessed the moral authority necessary to lead France.[100] Similarly harsh critiques of parliamentarians continued to appear during the PSF years. For instance, one Le Poulennec leader encouraged local members to purchase guns and ammunition with their hunting licenses, in preparation for an assault against 'scumbag' politicians and gendarmes.[101]

Of course, such criticism was not particularly novel during the interwar period. Various extreme-rightist organizations evinced similar attitudes, from the royalist Action française to ex-communist Jacques Doriot's Parti populaire français. Yet much like the Faisceau a decade earlier, the CDF/PSF distinguished themselves through the formulation of a unique political program, which eclipsed mere critical parlance. First composed in 1931 and relatively unchanged thereafter, this platform provided the basis for the group's political engagement with the republic throughout the 1930s.[102] Nor did the group experience a programmatic shift after the formation of the Parti social français. Combining a radical restructuring of parliamentary government with distinctly authoritarian principles throughout their history, CDF/PSF proposals for the state eschewed fascism while nonetheless adopting certain features more common to a Faisceau-style dictatorship than democracy.

To begin with, although the group viewed the parliamentary system as the necessary legal means to attain power, leadership and rank and file alike rejected its continued operation under a CDF/PSF government. La Rocque frequently spoke of the time 'when our ideas will seize power', and group circulars often emphasized (with Valoissian flourish) a re-establishment of discipline, the creation of a new order, and the building of new institutions better suited to the modern world. Electoral victory was necessary, read one such bulletin in 1936, because 'illegal activity is not popular in France'. The tract thus rejected any *coup de force romantique*, while reminding the reader that Mussolini and Hitler had been elected by the people,

---

99 APP/Ba 1853, tract – 'Autour des élections', April 1936, pp. 7–9, 14–15.

100 CDLR, 'Sang-froid', *Le Flambeau*, July 1934; CHEVS/LR 34, CDLR, 'Le Chef parle', *Bulletin des associations Croix de Feu du Département d'Alger*, 15 June 1935. See also *Le Flambeau* supplement, 'Pour le peuple, par le peuple', 11 April 1936.

101 F/7/14817, Inspecteurs Paux de Police Mobile Le Poulennec et Douasbin to the Prefect du Département des Côtes-du-Nord. For similar statements during the PSF years, see variously F/7/12966, 'Réunion organisé par la Fédération de l'Île de France du Parti social français', 20 Feb. 1937; CHEVS/LR 22, Colonel de la Rocque, *Paix ou guerre* (Paris, 1939), p. 23; CHEVS/LR 46, 'Conférence faites par Ybarnégaray', Limoges – 3 April 1938, in which PSF deputy Jean Ybarnégaray told a party gathering that a *grand nettoyage* would be necessary to remove corrupt men and excessive behaviour from the political realm.

102 This argument is best demonstrated by Sean Kennedy in 'Reconciling the Nation Against Democracy: The Croix de Feu, the Parti social français, and French Politics, 1927–1945', Ph.D. dissertation, York University, 1998, p. 23.

invested with legal means to transform their nations without popular resistance. That the CDF/PSF was inherently anti-parliamentary, with many members displaying a 'veritable repugnance for elections', therefore presented no cause for concern.[103]

Unlike Valois and the Faisceau, however, the group firmly rejected fascism, both publicly and privately. The CDF/PSF program of 1936 derided the 'religion of the state' practiced in fascist Italy and Nazi Germany, in which the government controlled the people without consulting them. While Valois and his colleagues proffered a dictatorship, the CDF/PSF spoke of the government as an independent arbitrator. La Rocque envisioned an authoritarian elite driven by the *mystique nationale*, embodying the doctrine 'he who serves best will lead', but its main purpose was protective rather than transformative. The mission of the state, he wrote in his 1934 work *Service public*, involved the coordination of interests within the *Cité*, organizing public services and adapting them to collective needs, while ensuring civil peace and external security. The state protected and guided, wielding 'the harsh authority indispensable to the execution of its task', but the social body remained sovereign in economic and social matters.[104] Speaking to the 1936 CDF/PSF national congress, group deputy for Maine-et-Loire François de Polignac made this point abundantly clear, stating that 'the first duty of the state is to protect the lives of citizens and defend the nation against external enemies, while enshrining the rule of law within its borders'.[105]

A Faisceau-style assembly of families and producers was never discussed. Instead, the CDF/PSF called for a renovation of existing republican institutions. The group first formulated ideas for the reform of government in 1931, gradually adding additional detail throughout the decade, culminating in a comprehensive platform in spring 1936, which foreshadowed the group's parliamentary turn that summer. Published in the 1931 Remembrance Day edition of *Le Flambeau*, the first CDF/PSF political plan envisioned a new French ruling elite united by a desire for political order. In keeping with this goal, its architects demanded continuity in public affairs. Under the *État social français*, the president formed the government, reformed parliamentary work methods, and conducted legislative work in conjunction with the constituent elements of French production.[106] In a May 1934 interview in the right-wing newspaper *L'Ordre*, La Rocque further suggested a streamlined government with fewer ministers and deputies, lessening the opportunity for corrupt practices: 'The attainment of political power not by makeshift conspirators, but energetic, competent, and hard-working leaders, freed from the grip of partisan struggles, unfamiliar with scandals and the errors and weaknesses of the postwar era'. The new leaders were to be patriotic men, ethically sound, and dedicated to the reconciliation of all citizens

---

103    CHEVS/LR 38, CDLR, 'Les 'Croix de Feu' devant le problème des élections'; F.R., 'Réflexions', *Flambeau du Sud-Est*, June 1936; CHEVS/LR 13 1 A 4, 'Principes généraux d'organisation, de propagande et du coordination', n.d. [PSF].

104    APP/Ba 1980, tract – 'Programmes', March 1936; Lt.-Colonel de la Rocque, *Service public* (Paris, 1934), pp. 197–198, 202.

105    François de Polignac, 'L'Éducation nationale', in *Le Parti social français devant les problèmes de l'heure* (Paris, 1936).

106    'Nos motifs', *Le Flambeau*, 11 Nov. 1931.

of goodwill on the right and the left. Their primary duty comprised the cleansing of government and administration, rooting out mismanagement and inculcating the state with the virtues of public service.[107] Serious constitutional reform was the first step towards the achievement of moral and managerial renewal, reflecting the principles of discipline, talent-based hierarchy and authority, anti-communism, and collective needs above individual desires. At a January 1935 meeting in Paris, La Rocque stated that such reforms were necessary to cure 'legislative power, which has the flu'.[108]

Although these statements suited the needs of the extra-parliamentary Croix de Feu, they lacked genuine depth, merely interspersing various broad political ideas with economic and social demands. This shortcoming became readily apparent after the inauguration of the Popular Front, which presented a rejuvenated republicanism and non-chauvinist nationalism, and enjoyed broad public appeal. Little more than a year after the riotous events of 6 February 1934, in which the CDF/PSF contingent played a leading role, Léon Blum, communist party leader Maurice Thorez, and radical luminary Edouard Daladier addressed a massive July 1935 gathering at Buffalo stadium in Paris. Demonstrating solidarity against the extreme-right, the three linked arms, sang the Marseillaise and the Internationale, and took a solemn oath 'to defend the democratic liberties conquered by the people of France'. The three parties subsequently formed an electoral coalition to fight fascism in France, represented in frontist publications by leagues like the CDF/PSF, and stunned the right in June 1936 by winning handily with 5.42 million votes.[109]

Perhaps more disturbing to the CDF/PSF than the prospect of Léon Blum as premier of France, the revolutionary Parti communiste français captured 72 seats after campaigning vigorously against the extreme-rightist leagues. For despite his internationalism, Thorez mobilized conservative rhetoric in a direct attempt to attract La Rocque's partisans: 'We stretch our hand out to you, Catholic worker, employee, artisan ... We stretch out our hand to you, volunteer in the service of the nation, you, war veteran of the Croix de Feu, because you are a son of the people.'[110] Left with little choice by the tactics of the Popular Front, the group abandoned outward extremism and presented its first comprehensive political plan in April 1936, in various tracts designed to appeal to potential voters, while simultaneously eroding support for the Popular Front. With the subsequent formation of the Parti social français, group publications systematized previous ideas and provided a coherent political schema that they continued to espouse until the Second World War.

The new platform expanded upon earlier variations. Although it endorsed recommendations for fewer ministers and deputies and proportional representation, La Rocque now added an age limit for all parliamentary representatives, and

---

107   CDLR, 'Redressement', *L'Ordre*, 1 May 1934; La Rocque, *Service public*, p. 222.

108   F/7/13320, 'Meetings organisées par 'L'Association des Croix de Feu et Briscards', le 25 janvier', 29 Jan. 1935. See also APP/Ba 1980, '90 per cent des français et des françaises sont de notre avis', n.d. [1935]; AP/451/121, CDLR, Typed responses to interview questions from the *Gazette du Lausanne*, n.d. [1935]; CHEVS/LR 41, 'Déclaration du parti', n.d. [1936].

109   Julian Jackson, *The Popular Front in France: Defending Democracy, 1934–1938* (Cambridge, 1990), pp. 5–10, 41; Colton, p. 14–22.

110   Colton, p. 21.

proclaimed that none could hold a private or state appointment outside the Chamber. A reasonable stipend was offered to replace lost income, and absenteeism or abstention from voting would be severely punished. The Chamber would further be stripped of its control of expenses, a proposition championed by La Rocque from the outset of his group presidency as a measure to eliminate corruption. For the same reason, the *Président du Conseil* concurrently served as President of the Republic, bringing deputies to heel.[111] These harsh administrative provisions were wedded to electoral reforms designed to eliminate opposition at the ballot box, particularly from the Popular Front, whose electoral success came at the expense of right-wing political parties. Thus the 1936 plan called for the *vote familial*, including permission for women to cast ballots in municipal elections.[112] Although the group's rationale included language concerning the family as a moral entity, fervently opposed to unethical candidates and practices, CDF/PSF leaders clearly believed that women would vote against socialist or communist politicians, effectively preventing another successful Popular Front electoral campaign. Finally, the plan advocated control of the press to ensure that newspapers were not funded by hostile elements (i.e. the left), which worked against the nation. Parties and publications that agitated against the civic and patriotic duty of each citizen would face stiff censorship.[113]

Taken at face value, the PSF parliamentary plan seemingly jettisoned violent rhetoric while signaling acceptance of parliamentarism. If anything, the 1936 plan resembled the conservative platform advocated by traditional parties like the Republican Federation. Led by right-wing notable Louis Marin, the Federation garnered 80–100 deputies throughout the interwar era, and the financial support of influential steel magnates François de Wendel and Édouard de Warren. Marin's party adamantly supported a program of order, social and political hierarchy, and an end to parliamentary corruption. Buoyed by ultra-nationalist members like Xavier Vallat and Philippe Henriot, both veterans of the Faisceau, the federation initially viewed the Croix de Feu as a useful ally. Like the CDF/PSF, they called for the reduction by half of the number of deputies in the Chamber, the vote for women and the heads of families, and an end to the introduction of financial bills by parliament. Federation leaders themselves believed the group to be a kindred spirit. In the words of Vice-President Henriot, the Croix de Feu 'was a useful barrier of resolute men against the threatening violence of revolutionary forces'. Thus the two organizations forged a tactical alliance from late 1934 until the transformation of the Croix de Feu into the parliamentary PSF, which the Federation viewed as unwanted competition.[114]

Although they flirted with the authoritarian and fascist right during the 1930s, however, the *modérés* held fast to their belief that liberal democracy provided the

---

111   CDLR, 'Pour le peuple, par le peuple', supplement to *Le Flambeau*, 11 April 1936.

112   This portion of the CDF/PSF platform was hardly original, and the *vote familial* became a staple of interwar French conservatism. See Jean-Yves Le Naour, *La Famille doit voter: le suffrage familial contre le vote individuel* (Paris, 2005), chapter five.

113   APP/Ba 1980, tract – 'Programmes', March 1936, CDLR, 'Pour le peuple, par le peuple'. For a further discussion of the CDF/PSF and the *vote familiale*, see chapter three.

114   Kevin Passmore, 'Catholicism and Nationalism: The Fédération Républicaine, 1927–1939', in Kay Chadwick (ed.), *Catholicism, Politics and Society in Twentieth-Century France* (Liverpool, 2000), pp. 48–49, 61; Irvine, pp. 100–101, 119–126, 131–134.

means with which their agenda could best be implemented. The CDF/PSF ideal, in contrast, was far from parliamentary, and the group's future state went far beyond the reforms discussed by Marin and his cohorts.[115] To begin with, their program was opportunistic in nature. Although certain details were added after the transformation into the PSF, none of the main points were altered, and the 1936 plan formed the basis of their electoral platform. Its goal was to secure victory for the group, at which time the transformation of the state would begin. Hence the public facade of reform masked decidedly undemocratic language and concepts. For instance, the group championed a rigid political hierarchy and the elimination of 'parasitism'.[116]

Moreover, the CDF/PSF exhibited a marked tendency towards authoritarianism, supporting the formation of a non-parliamentary government even as its deputies sat in the chamber from 1936 onwards. Various members frequently spoke of the restoration of authority, an indispensable component of the reform of state, termed the 'sole guarantee of personal liberty'. As late as 1938, PSF political bureau director Edouard Barrachin told a national congress that the party needed to create a *choc psychologique* through the restoration of authority, to morally cleanse the government, facilitate parliamentary practice, remove agitators paid by foreign countries (i.e. the left) from French soil, and remake national and regional administrations. Nor were such statements mere political posturing.[117] One writer in the *Ralliment du Nord* earnestly intoned that man needed authority to protect society from the dangers of absolute liberty, which lead only to anarchy and weakness.[118]

Clearly the group envisioned more than a simple reform of parliamentary composition and practice. Although he rejected the 'quasi-religious' cult of the state in fascist Italy, often suggesting a polycratic leadership structure for the *État social français*, La Rocque nevertheless maintained that collective discipline and strong centralized authority were necessary to guard against excess in government: 'Before building a new edifice, to shore up the foundations, we first want authority to vigorously reestablish order in homes, administrations, our cities, and the justice system.'[119] This implied an agenda that eclipsed constitutional democracy. In fact, the CDF/PSF actively promoted authoritarian-style leadership throughout their history, even as they spoke of parliamentary reform. In *Service public*, La Rocque described a leader more compatible with the traditional concepts of the French extreme-right than the Chamber of Deputies: 'When the interests of the *Cité* are at stake, individuals do not count: They step aside. Government leaders must distinguish themselves, not

---

115  Irvine, pp. 65, 112–115, 125–126, 152.

116  AP/451/102, tract – *Le Parti social français: un mouvement, une programme* (Paris, 1936).

117  AP/451/117, 'Extraits du rapport de M. Edouard Barrachin, Directeur de Bureau politique, sur la politique générale', Third PSF National Congress, 3 Dec. 1938. See also Anon., *Pourquoi nous sommes devenus Croix de Feu* (Paris, n.d. [1934]), p. 5; Jean Debay, *Remise du fanion à la sous-section Blida-Mitidja* (1934), pp. 16–17.

118  Diagoras, 'L'Homme, cet inconnu!', *Ralliment du Nord,* 17 July 1937.

119  La Rocque, *Service public,* pp. 256–257. See also *Le Flambeau,* 2 May 1936; Ybarnégaray speech in *Flambeau du Sud-Ouest,* 3 July 1937; F/7/12965, M. Kiffer in steno of 18 March 1936; F/7/14817, Inspecteur Paux de Police Mobile Le Poulennec et Douasbin to Prefect of Côtes du Nord, 23 Oct. 1936.

in popularity, the daughter of demagogy, but through their active and responsible personality'.[120] The leader existed to impose discipline on state and society, he added in *Le Flambeau* in May 1935, acting for the collective good while pushing citizens to do the same.[121] Neither Maurras nor Mussolini would have disagreed. For the CDF/PSF action and will, alongside discipline and obedience, were the cornerstones of the new state. Such pronouncements did not cease with the banning of the Croix de Feu, repeated ad nauseam in print and speeches during the PSF years. Although La Rocque refused the role of dictator-in-waiting, clearly a renovated parliament was not the group's only card to play.[122]

## V

Although the CDF/PSF prioritized the renovation of government, it represented but one piece of a larger political puzzle. For La Rocque and various group leaders and members the renovation of the state was both a physical and an ideological project, in which the introduction of authoritarian principles in government hinged upon a modification of the national *mentalité*. During the Croix de Feu years, this meant the introduction of the authority, hierarchy, and discipline of the trenches. As the living representatives of those who fought for France, the group believed itself to be in sole possession of the moral superiority necessary to transform the state, ushering in a government of national renewal. Once they mutated into the parliamentary PSF, however, their calls for an *État combattant* ceased abruptly, replaced by a social Catholic political program. Throughout the PSF years the group called for the restoration of Christian values in France, combined with the creation of an idyllic national community based upon social harmony and government-imposed hierarchy and discipline.

Like many veterans groups in France, including the Faisceau, the Croix de Feu adopted the trenches as a political model, inspired by the nationalist cult of the dead. In this regard, they were not dissimilar from a multitude of interwar organizations. Rejecting social class and partisan politics alike, groups like the Union fédérale (UF) and the Union nationale des combattants (UNC) trumpeted the myth of an absolute fraternity of the trenches. Founded in 1919, the UF attracted 900,000 members by 1932, enjoying particular success in the Rhône, Pas-de-Calais, and Alsace-Lorraine. Formed immediately following the armistice, the UNC also wielded considerable clout, with 860,000 members by the early 1930s, most notably in the Nord, Picardy, Normandy, and Paris. Unlike the radical Fédération nationale des combattants or the left-wing Association républicaine des anciens combattants, both groups rejected politics as corrupt, believing themselves to be a moral elite qualified to lead France

---

120   La Rocque, *Service public*, p. 86.

121   CDLR, 'Des Chefs', *Le Flambeau*, 18 May 1935. For similar pronouncements from other group members, see Un Normalien, 'Retour à la franchise', *Le Flambeau*, 13 April 1935; Habib, 'Volonté', *Le Flambeau*, Nov. 1933.

122   See CHEVS/LR 46, 'Extraits du discours prononcée par le Colonel de la Rocque, à Jocelyn (Morbihan), le 11 décembre 1938'; BN/tract – Edouard Barrachin, *Le PSF devant le pays*, n.d. For La Rocque's refusal, see AP/451/101, 'Pourquoi La Rocque n'est-il pas candidat?', *Bulletin d'Informations* 16, 26 Jan. 1937.

because of their 'baptism by fire'. In bringing the *esprit combattant* into the political realm, the rude lessons of 1914 replaced inefficient parliamentary democracy. Moral and spiritual values, especially nationalism and Catholicism, family and profession, were placed in staunch opposition to noxious materialism, which had led France to decadence and ruin. The latter was embodied in the deputy, a 'prostitute' who infested parliament with his *vomissements*. Greedy and individualist, he had little in common with the *combattant* fraternity born during the Great War. Unsurprisingly, by the 1930s both organizations tended to oppose republican initiatives, and the UNC in particular joined the extreme-rightist leagues during the 6 February riots, while its members tended to speak admiringly about Hitler and Mussolini.[123]

Both the UF and UNC augured the programmatic tone of Marshall Philippe Pétain and the authoritarian Vichy regime that came to power after the fall of France in June 1940. Yet as Antoine Prost has argued, their vision of the trenches was a myth, far removed from the horrors of war and the fatalistic attitude adopted out of necessity by the average *poilu*, whose comrades-in-arms seldom lasted very long. Furthermore, few veterans associations abandoned parliamentarism altogether, instead arguing for the infusion of nationalism and the principles of the trenches into republican government. Nor did the UF and UCF genuinely represent French war veterans, who numbered 5.5 million in 1935. Yet despite its romantic overtones, the myth nevertheless formed the backbone of the postwar politics of the *combattant*. For example, the UNC extolled Catholic nationalism, an end to the tyranny of political parties, and a conservative familial, social and economic agenda, much like the traditionalist faction of the Faisceau.[124]

La Rocque's band likewise commemorated the *mystique Croix de Feu*, a spirit that motivated French soldiers from Joan of Arc to the heroic troops at the 1916 battle of Verdun.[125] According to the CDF/PSF leader, the group alone embodied this tradition, a fact regularly parroted at a variety of group military parades in Paris and the provinces.[126] Hence only the postwar spirit of the victory, through which France had re-discovered its authentic heritage, provided the *élan* of effective government. As the living representatives of the war generation, the CDF/PSF possessed the moral authority to act in the national interest, recreating the politics of fraternal unity that guided the war effort.[127] By destroying the fruits of the victory paid for by the blood and sacrifice of the *combattants*, stated one member of the group's Comité directeur in March 1936, republican politicians placed themselves in opposition to the morally sound 'generation of war veterans possessing a special understanding forged by four

---

123 Antoine Prost, *Les Anciens combattants et la société française, 1914–1939, Mentalités et idéologies* (3 vols, Paris, 1978), vol. 3, pp. 26–32, 128–148, 168–173; Antoine Prost, *Les Anciens combattants* (Paris, 1977), pp. 60–71, 168–176, 203–209. Although Prost himself denies the extreme character of the UF and UNC, the quotations and documentation provided (including entire group manifestos) paints a decidedly different picture.

124 Antoine Prost, *Les Anciens combattants*, pp. 73–76, 223–228.

125 Hébert, 'Patrie', *Flambeau des Vosges*, July 1939; La Rocque, *Service public*, p. 28.

126 F. de Hautclocque, *Grandeur et décadence des Croix de Feu* (Paris, 1937), pp. 17–20; CHEVS/LR VI A 2, Prugniaux, 'Harmonie', *Bulletin mensuel du mouvement Croix de Feu (51e et 100e sections)*, 1 March 1936.

127 CDLR, 'Esprit Croix de Feu', *Le Flambeau*, 4 July 1936.

years of war'. Joined by youth who never knew the horrors of war but nevertheless shared the group's ideals, the CDF/PSF would remake France in its own image.[128] Hence La Rocque prophesied the defeat of the generation of 1900, the complacent bourgeoisie concerned solely with materialism, and the rise of the self-disciplined and decisive generation of 1914.[129]

The group thus adopted the mythical version of the trenches so dear to the UF and UNC, a political composite of an idealized future France:

> With us, it is not a question of rank, social distinction, wealth, or poverty, because at H hour we go over the top, certain that on our left and our right we will have a friend ready to help when the need arises, no matter what the number, colour, metal, or wool on the stripes sewn on our sleeves.[130]

As class and social status were irrelevant at the front, they would be similarly ignored in the state, with the government treating its subjects as a collective whole. Because the Croix de Feu were a *combattant* elite which understood these central truths, they possessed the power to speak and act for France, to renovate the French collective and its institutions independently of corrupt, self-serving politicians. To buttress their argument, CDF/PSF publications contrasted the honourable sacrifice of the soldier with the greed and corruption endemic in the parliamentary world. One May 1934 cartoon in *Le Flambeau* showed a deputy/banker with portfolio in tow being grabbed by a skeleton replete with troop fatigues, a caption on the chamber/bourse in the background reading 'closed for disinfection'.[131]

The CDF/PSF further joined the moral authority and sacrifice of the *combattant* to the Barrèssian notion of the cult of the soil and the dead. La Rocque dedicated *Service public* to the commands and ideas of the dead, claiming that the Croix de Feu message – of fraternity, will, effort, and sacrifice – transmitted the lesson of fallen comrades to future generations. The Barrèssian theory that each French family was but a continuation of their ancestors, he argued, mirrored the experience of the *combattant*, who fought to preserve centuries of Gallic tradition. As the soldier gave his life for eternal France, the state defended and valorized the national heritage. Writing in *Le Flambeau* in November 1935, his France resembled Barrès's pastoral Lorraine: 'She is gentle. In her soil, she contains the seed of that which delights the eyes, reconciles souls, calms suffering, enriches homes, feeds the hungry, controls wealth, and tempers antagonisms'.[132]

Although it retained the use of Barrèssian imagery and values after the transformation of the group into the parliamentary PSF, the doctrine became linked

---

128   F/7/12965, 'Réunion privée organisée par la 10e section du Mouvement social français des Croix de Feu', 18 March 1936.

129   La Rocque, *Service public*, pp. 49–55.

130   'Ordre et bon sens', *Le Flambeau*, May 1932.

131   AP/451/104, 'Note du President-Général', 2 Jan. 1933; CDLR, 'Et nous?', *Le Flambeau*, May 1932; 'Le Soldat inconnu ou soluable connu', *Le Flambeau*, 1 May 1934.

132   Lt.-Colonel de la Rocque, *Service public*, pp. 244–245; CHEVS/LR 38, 'Note du Président-Général', 2 Jan. 1936; CDLR, 'La France', *Le Flambeau*, 30 Nov. 1935. For a remarkably similar passage from Barrès's writings, see *Colette Baudoche*, pp. 112–113.

to a specific brand of social Catholic politics, which replaced the concept of an *État combattant* in group parlance from mid-1936 onwards. The restoration of a nation based upon Christian values, whose absence in the Third Republic was bemoaned by CDF/PSF members, became an increasingly important priority as the decade progressed. Where Croix de Feu writings referred to the moral right and duty of the *combattant* to lead, various PSF members, including La Rocque himself, spoke of French politics in increasingly evangelical tones. Fewer references were made to the trenches, while religious themes became a daily topic for discussion in various articles, tracts, and speeches. That this change occurred after the left-wing Popular Front government banned the Croix de Feu cannot be ignored, but it hardly tells the whole story. La Rocque wished to transform the Parti social français into a genuine mass party, bringing together elements of all classes and political constituencies. Such an organization could hardly confine itself to veterans' politics and calls for the recreation of the trenches. From 1936 onwards, subtlety proved to be the best policy; just as the group promoted electoralism for opportunistic purposes, so too did it disguise the desire for an authoritarian state in social Catholic rhetoric.

On the surface, social Catholicism seemed tailor-made for a disbanded league attempting to exude republican legitimacy. Throughout the interwar era the movement drew Catholics back to the republican fold, and particularly youth, through organizations like the Association catholique de la jeunesse française and the Jeunesses ouvrière chrétienne. Inspired by the social teachings of the church, young Catholics sought solutions to the economic and social problems wrought by the modern industrial world, under the guidance of Pope Pius XI, who enjoyed warm relations with liberal, secular governments. The progeny of prewar Ralliment leaders like Marc Sagnier and the Sillon, they gained great popularity in the Nord, and in working-class neighbourhoods in Lyon and Paris, eclipsing the ultra-conservative Catholicism of the late nineteenth century.[133]

However, the social Catholicism that attracted La Rocque and the CDF/PSF was not the electoral Christian democracy of the new *ralliés*. The group instead admired the arch-conservative political views of certain traditional and extreme right-wing figures from the fin-de-siècle period. In claiming to support the reconciliation of diverse social forces, La Rocque and various group members borrowed from conservative social Catholic thinkers La Tour du Pin and the pre-*Ralliment* Albert de Mun. They were also heavily influenced by the papal encyclicals *Rerum Novarum* and *Quadragesimo Anno*, which proposed a traditionalist third way between liberal capitalism and socialism, including paternalist corporatism and the injection of Catholic values into contemporary society. The CDF/PSF thus rejected individualism, liberalism, and socialism in equal measure, as the destroyers of natural social fraternity, turning to an

---

133 Mayeur, pp. 9–13, René Rémond, 'Pensée sociale de l'église et mouvements catholiques', *Revue du Nord* 73 (290–91), pp. 472–473. On the Sillon and prewar social Catholicism, see Jeanne Caron, *Le Sillon et la démocratie chrétienne, 1984–1910* (Paris, 1967); Paul Cohen, 'Heroes and Dilettantes: The Action Française, Le Sillon, and the Generation of 1905–14', *French Historical Studies* 15 (1988): 673–687.

organic model of society, in which the state functioned as a family.[134] Like La Tour du Pin, La Rocque and his coevals believed that family and church were the pillars of social order, and that the state assembled all facets of the nation to work in the collective interest. The state ensured that the general good was always followed, while defending the welfare and morality of its members. As their highest political goal the group chose the defense of the 'natural' Christian social order, a realization of La Tour du Pin's dictum that 'every social order corresponds more or less to a religious concept'.[135] As Jérome Regnier correctly notes, such precepts directly inspired Vichy-era legislation, including charters for labour and agriculture.[136]

To be sure, the use of such arguments on the French right was not confined to the CDF/PSF in the 1930s. Both General de Castelnau's Fédération nationale catholique and the Republican Federation utilized 'Catholic nationalism', combining social Catholic principles with antipathy to the Republican state, the repository of laicism, feminism, and anti-church political practices. As Kevin Passmore notes:

> Far from being pushed into the background by the class struggles of the 1930s, anti-clericalism had been given a new lease on life by the growth of civil service trade unions, for these were the most modern arm of the struggle against Catholicism and the social order.[137]

Yet in the final analysis, neither the FNC nor the RF proposed the dismantling of the Republic and the complete rejection of 'modern' politics, and De Castelnau and Marin were never portrayed in Christ-like terms, as the spiritual saviours of France. CDF/PSF arguments for the injection of social Catholic principles inevitably invoked both themes, from the Croix de Feu years onwards. 'Travail, Famille, Patrie', the slogan which appeared on the front page of the Croix de Feu newspaper *Le Flambeau* and became the official slogan of Vichy, unabashedly paid homage to La Tour du Pin and turn-of-the-century social Catholicism. Furthermore, in *Service public* La Rocque wrote of 'the primacy of the spiritual in human affairs', claiming that 'the men of the Croix de Feu movement have become prophets and apostles'. French reconciliation became the instrument of group success, which in CDF parlance meant the unification of the diverse political factions in France, 'the association of classes, religions, and origins in a collective effort to save the country'. Replacing the moral supremacy of the *combattant* with Catholic virtue in an article published

---

134   On *Rerum Novarum* and *Quadragesimo Anno*, see Mayeur, pp. 20–23, 35, 55–59, Jérome Régnier, 'Diffusion et interprétation de *Quadragesimo Anno*', and Philippe Levillain, '*Rerum Novarum* et *Quadragesimo Anno*: Une même question? Une même réponse?', *Revue du Nord* 73 (1991): 349–355.

135   René de la Tour du Pin, *Vers un ordre social chretien* (Paris, 1987), p. 134. See also Sean Kennedy, *Reconciling France Against Democracy: The Croix de Feu and the Parti social français, 1927–1945* (Kingston and Montréal, 2007), p. 61; Matthew Elbow, *French Corporative Theory, 1789–1948* (New York, 1953), pp. 47–51, 63–69, 75–79.

136   Regnier, 'Diffusion et interprétation', p. 358.

137   Passmore in Kay Chadwick, *Catholicism, Politics, and Society*, pp. 50–60.

in *Le Mois* in fall 1935, La Rocque now referred to the 'vague salvatrice et pure du mouvement Croix de Feu', who alone possessed 'la formule de régénération'.[138]

The appearance of religious themes heightened dramatically after the transformation of the Croix de Feu into the parliamentary PSF. Group sympathizer and prominent social Catholic François Veuillot, the nephew of ultramontane Catholic journalist Louis Veuillot, portrayed La Rocque and the CDF/PSF as the embodiment of church doctrine, advocating a patriotic and social reconciliation of all men.[139] Various group members also adopted an outright evangelical tone. At the 1938 PSF national congress, La Rocque lauded the faithful, 'the Croix de Feu apostolate who await the spirit capable of resuscitating their faith and brotherhood'. The leader himself was frequently portrayed as a Christ-figure by various CDF/PSF authors. Writing in *L'Heure française* in May 1938, one called La Rocque 'a man who has suffered for us, the members of the PSF and beyond us for France'. His speeches were likened to spiritual experiences, the words of the wise father who gave the PSF family a new reason to believe.[140]

Such talk attempted to persuade the public that the extreme-rightist Croix de Feu had been reborn as a traditional conservative political party. No longer a demagogue-in-waiting banned by the Popular Front, La Rocque became the leader of a movement dedicated to moral and spiritual renewal through electoral means. Yet neither the group nor the leader had converted to republicanism. Speaking to a gathering of CDF/PSF students in May 1938, La Rocque detailed their mission to construct a new man, a transformation enabled by the Christianization of all facets of society through which every government decision would be informed by Catholic morality. The new state would be established upon the tenet that 'all souls are equal', irrespective of class, the opposite of liberal materialism and Marxist economic determinism.[141] In this regard, CDF/PSF articles frequently repeated La Rocque's phrase 'aimez-vous les uns les autres', referring to both social peace and political virtue.[142] To François Veuillot, this meant the popular inculcation of the lessons of the evangelicals, that all French men, women, and children served spiritual forces, in a nation and state governed by the *paix chrétienne*. All were equal in the eyes of God, and would be viewed similarly by the state.[143] Hierarchy and authority, however, were to be maintained at all times. In an article on the CDF/PSF in the Catholic journal

---

138  La Rocque, *Service public*, pp. 108, 224, 244–245; CDLR, 'Ou vont les Croix de Feu?', *Le Mois*, Sept.–Oct. 1935.

139  François Veuillot, *La Rocque et son parti* (Paris, 1938), p. 55. On Louis and François Veuillot, see Mayeur, pp. 29–30.

140  AP/451/117, 'Déclaration du PSF, présentée par le Président du parti', steno of third national party congress, 4 Dec. 1938; Marcel Vigo, 'Impressions d'audience', *L'Heure française*, 21 May 1938. See also Charles Vallin, *Aux femmes du Parti social français* (Paris, 1937), p. 8.

141  CHEVS/LR 41, 'Déclaration de la Rocque aux étudiants', 11 May 1938. On a similar note, see Raymond Gricourt, 'Social et socialisme', *La Flamme*, 13 May 1938; CDLR, 'Coopération', *Flambeau de Flandres-Artois-Picardie*, 9 Jan. 1938.

142  AP/451/102, *Le Parti social français: un mouvement, une programme*, p. 5; R. Yvon, 'L'Ordre nouveau par le PSF', *Espoir Lorrain*, 5 June 1937.

143  Veuillot, *La Rocque et son parti*, pp. 64–68.

*Orientations*, group sympathizer Jacques Daujat emphasized that although all souls were equal, social hierarchy was a *fait accompli*.[144]

Hence despite the group's rhetoric, the *grand famille PSF* did not herald true equality, instead proffering a 'fusion spirituelle des classes'. La Rocque derided the notion of class as un-Christian, claiming that the new CDF/PSF state represented: 'The community of patriotic ideals, a permanent pursuit of social progress, no matter how audacious, a desire to cure the obligatory inequality of circumstances through the absolute equality of souls, the worship of meritocracy, and contempt for hierarchy without merit'. The commandments of Christian civilization demanded the return of elites, taken from all classes, who recognized the supremacy of collectivity and tradition (from the 'house of our fathers') rather than money. Opportunity would be open to all classes, he wrote in May 1936, as part of the 'perfection of civic and professional conditions'.[145]

# VI

Thus apart from linguistic nuances, there was little difference between the Croix de Feu *État combattant* and the PSF inculcation of a Christian hierarchy and elitism into French political culture. La Rocque and his followers merely substituted the phrase 'commandments of Christian civilization' for 'experience of the trenches', a more proper turn of phrase for the mass-based Parti social français, proving particularly attractive to the moderate and conservative right.[146] In both cases they evinced organic nationalism, according to which the state was duty-bound to restore civic peace, and mobilized hierarchy and elitism within an authoritarian political system. Talk of fraternity and reconciliation also obscured a more sinister component of their political plans. For the proposed state could only function if its political enemies were expunged. Like the more conservative elements within the Faisceau, the CDF/PSF situated this threat squarely on the left, arguing that socialism and communism could not be reconciled with the new system. The group's thought was purely Manichean on this point: Either the CDF/PSF enacted the proposed renovation, or the Godless communist hordes would raze France to the ground, as they had previously done in Stalin's Soviet Union and Spain under the Popular Front.

Unlike the Faisceau, they were unanimous in this belief. Valois wrote of a potential rapprochement with leftist forces, arguing that the communist was not the man with the knife between his teeth, in opposition to conservative members who opposed leniency of any kind towards Marxism. His benevolence stemmed partially from his belief

---

144   CHEVS/LR 11, Jacques Daujat, 'Chronique: les catholiques et la poilitique: les Croix de Feu', *Orientations*, March–April 1936.

145   CDLR, 'Thèmes de propagande', *Le Flambeau*, 21 Aug. 1937; CDLR, 'Sous l'invocation de Jeanne d'Arc', *Le Flambeau*, 16 May 1936.

146   As William Irvine and Kevin Passmore note, members of the Republican Federation, PDP, and even centrist social Catholics in groups like the JAC evinced great interest in the PSF's new program. In Irvine, *French Conservatism in Crisis*, pp. 100–134; Passmore in Chadwick, *Catholicism, Politics, and Society*, p. 68 and *From Liberalism to Fascism*, pp. 241–243.

that certain left-wing doctrines (revolutionary syndicalism, for example), informed the Faisceau creed. But the weakness of socialism and communism during the 1920s facilitated his gesture. The scission at the Congress of Tours in December 1920, when the communist majority voted to join the Third International, left Blum's organization politically moribund. Maurice Thorez's fledgling PCF, which attracted only 900,000 votes (8 per cent of the total) in the 1924 elections which vaulted the leftist Cartel des Gauches to power, packed little punch in the chamber or on the street. Léon Blum and the socialist SFIO gained 101 seats in the Chamber in 1924, but only through an alliance with the centrist Radical party, on whom they were dependent for any genuine electoral success. A similar split quickly emerged at the Lille congress of the CGT in June 1921, leading to the formation of the communist-dominated CGTU shortly thereafter. Left with a minority of the rank and file, CGT leader Léon Jouhaux spent the remainder of the decade fighting for the formation of a national economic council, and promoting a reformist agenda, comprised mainly of scientific management and increased wages for the workers. Only in 1936, following the rapprochement between the socialist and communist parties, did the CGT and CGTU reunite. Clearly Valois spoke from a perceived position of strength, and could afford to be charitable.[147]

By 1934, when the Croix de Feu first came to national prominence as a serious political force, the situation differed dramatically. Following the massive street actions provoked by the Stavisky affair at the Palais Bourbon on the night of 6 February 1934, which led to the resignation of Premier Edouard Daladier, and created fears of an extreme-rightist coup d'état, the left found renewed vigour. By summer 1934, following the adoption by the Soviet CPSU of the 'Dimitrov line' on left-wing unity, the socialist and communist parties banded together to form the Common Front, pledging to collaborate in the fight against fascism and the extreme-right in France. They also gained electoral momentum, bringing the Radical party into a rechristened Popular Front in July 1935. The following June, the alliance won 334 seats in the chamber, and Léon Blum became the first socialist premier in French history.

Worse still, the arch-nemesis of the extreme-right – the French Communist Party – enjoyed tremendous success by the mid-thirties, aided by the late emergence of the Great Depression in France in 1932. A disheveled mess a decade earlier, with only 60,000 members in 1924, French communism lacked doctrinal unity and working-class support.[148] Despite the reservations of the Faisceau, the party never managed to obtain even 10 per cent of the popular vote. Yet by 1937, during the heyday of the Popular Front, its membership ballooned to 300,000, while the communist daily newspaper *L'Humanité* handily outsold right-wing standards like *Le Temps* and *Le Figaro*, not to mention the PSF daily *Le Petit Journal*. Having abandoned their revolutionary rhetoric in favour of an ardent defense of French republican values, the PCF also found themselves staunchly allied with former enemies, both radical and socialist. Such support was unthinkable during the Faisceau years.[149]

---

147   Bernard and Dubief, pp. 152–156.

148   M. Adereth, *The French Communist Party: A Critical History (1920–84)* (Manchester, 1984), pp. 33–35.

149   Serge Wolikow, 'Le PCF au temps du front populaire', *Cahiers d'histoire de l'Institut des Recherches Marxistes*, 36 (1989), 6–13; Becker and Berstein, 243. According

To La Rocque and the CDF/PSF communist prominence symbolized the first step towards a Soviet-style regime. Nor were they reassured by the massive wildcat strikes that greeted Blum's entry into the Matignon in May 1936, during which two million workers occupied factories across France, demanding concessions from ownership. At the Renault works in Baillancourt, strikers carried out mock funerals for workers suspected of sympathizing with the CDF/PSF.[150] Unsurprisingly, the group did not *tendre la main* as had Valois, but instead launched an all-out verbal and written assault against the left, both warning the country of the perceived threat and occasionally acting with tragic results. In late 1936, for example, hundreds of CDF/PSF demonstrators engaged in protracted street battles with communists outside a left-wing rally at Parc-aux-Princes stadium in northern Paris, in which dozens were wounded on both sides.[151]

Yet for the most part the group's assault was verbal, and CDF/PSF authors rarely distinguished between communism, socialism, and the trade unions, all jumbled together into one category: the political enemy. Writing in *Le Flambeau* in June 1936, just as the Blum's government settled into the Matignon, La Rocque unleashed a thinly disguised torrent of abuse:

> But reconciliation will encounter enemies; it would be illusory to hide this fact. It will eliminate harmful forces. It will drive out the beneficiaries of corrupt regimes. It will discard the servants, imitators, and hired hands of foreign countries, banning their clandestine or avowed influence on the destiny of our race.[152]

Communist and socialist party members were frequently denounced in the CDF/PSF press as 'nos ennemis – les hommes du drapeau rouge', traitors sent to France by the Soviet Union to start a civil war.[153]

The group also issued apocalyptic statements concerning communism and the Popular Front, describing the consequences of a Soviet victory in France. Mere months before Blum's victory, *Le Flambeau* ordered readers to: 'Remain calm. Remain steady. Safeguard each house, each home through our vigilant, fraternal, and protective presence. Unmask the criminal machinations of instigators. Ridicule the false idols'. Voicing concern about governmental inactivity in the face of the calamity, La Rocque complained of revolutionary action, a daily occurrence under the Popular Front:

> Each Sunday, processions blanket cities, villages, and countryside behind a foreign flag, behind placards laden with hateful slogans, parodies of religion and the military ridiculing what we believe in, honour, and serve. Everywhere groups of youths decorated in red insult innocent passers-by, bully the pleasant customers on the terraces, and attack newspaper vendors.

---

to Claude Bellanger, *L'Humanité* outsold the three competitors combined by a margin of 358,000 to 327,000. In Bellanger, p. 511.

150   Jackson, pp. 103–104.

151   Maurice Larkin, *France Since the Popular Front* (Oxford, 1988), pp. 50–52.

152   CDLR, 'Pour et contre', *Le Flambeau*, 6 June 1936.

153   CDLR, 'Programmes', *Le Flambeau*, April 1934; 'Congrès régional du Sud-Ouest'; *Flambeau du Sud-Ouest*, 3 July 1937; AP/451/103, tract – *Qu'est-ce que le PSF*, Dec. 1936, pp. 11–12.

As late as January 1938 he assured members that the CDF/PSF had 'now set up on every street, in every house, in each village'. The choice was simple: Either the CDF/PSF would renovate the state, barring the road to communism, or the Marxist nightmare would consume France.[154]

Thus the group undertook various propaganda initiatives in order to combat the left, while simultaneously attempting to persuade the French population that a CDF/PSF government was far more appealing than the Popular Front. From the early 1930s onwards, the group established an extensive press network, including the daily *Le Flambeau* and over 50 local bulletins and broadsheets delivering party news and editorials, along with announcements of meetings and activities. This effort culminated in the June 1937 purchase of the *Petit Journal*, one of the largest daily newspapers in France. Although far from successful in the fiscal sense, losing over 500,000 francs per month in 1938 alone, the initiative provided the CDF/PSF with a national platform. The paper attracted a variety of right-wing luminaries, including Henri Daniel-Rops, Edmond Jaloux, André Maurois, and Gabriel Marcel, countering the republicanism of the Popular Front with the gospel of social reconciliation and virulent anti-communism.[155]

Yet by the 1930s, newspapers were somewhat old-fashioned. The Popular Front owed its success to the utilization of new communicative forms, including mass meetings, radio, film, and photography. For frontist intellectuals betrayed a keen interest in 'the power behind those narrative forms that seemed to mobilize a mass audience'. Most importantly for the CDF/PSF, they harnessed such techniques against the French extreme-right, consistently mocking such organizations in the left-wing and radical media.[156] Fighting fire with fire, La Rocque took to the airwaves in 1936, attempting to reach the three million registered listeners in France, and the group held regular mass meetings throughout the metropole and colonies, with extensive press coverage and propagandistic pageantry.[157]

The group also experimented with less traditional forms of media-based propaganda. One such attempt, a comic strip entitled 'Francoeur et Labusé', portrays both the dangers of communism and its antidote – the CDF/PSF. Francoeur is a noble artisan, unemployed upon returning from the trenches because foreign revolutionaries have taken his place at the factory. He ends up in a CDF/PSF soup kitchen, where he meets 'real men' and feeds his family. Upon coming into contact

154   'Trêve du peuple', *Le Flambeau*, 14 March 1936; CDLR, 'Formules', *Le Flambeau*, 5 Sept. 1936; CDLR, 'Le PSF dans la cité', *Flambeau de Flandres-Artois-Picardie*, 23 Jan. 1938, Jean Ybarnégaray in *L'Espoir de l'Est*, 13 Nov. 1937. See also F/7/12966, note of 24 Feb. 1937; AP/451/101, 'Schema de conférence #1-le communisme', supplement to *Bulletin d'information* 20, 23 Feb. 1937. See also 'L'Emouvante et noble discours de La Rocque', *La Flamme*, 16 July 1937.

155   Fred Kupferman and Philippe Machefer, 'Presse et politique dans les années trentes: Le Cas du *Petit Journal*', *Revue d'Histoire Moderne et Contemporaine* 22 (1975): 7–51; Bellanger, pp. 511, 518.

156   Martin Stanton, 'French Intellectual Groups and the Popular Front: Traditional and Innovative Uses of the Media', in Alexander and Grahem, pp. 257–258, 267.

157   CHEVS/LR 38, 'Déclaration du Lt.-Colonel de la Rocque, radiodiffusés le 24 avril 1936'.

with 'these honest and simple men', Francoeur rediscovers the fraternity of the front and becomes a member, finding a good job and a stable home. Labusé, his former comrade-in-arms, falls under the spell of Legras, a leftist deputy. He becomes an extremist, surrounded by *étrangers* in 'foreign organizations'. By chance, he meets Franceour at a street demonstration, is saved from certain imprisonment, and takes up the service of France. The moral message was clear: Although the left claimed that their political solution would lead the worker to happiness, it represented a prescription for illegality and nothing more, while the CDF/PSF provided a healthy environment for French labour, a fact reflected in its political program.[158]

Group authors and speakers also used negative propaganda, attempting to wean the populace away from communism, socialism, and the Popular Front by describing the disastrous effects of leftist governments throughout Europe. Akin to many of their extreme-rightist confreres, the CDF/PSF singled out republican Spain as a manifestation of the left-wing threat in Europe. Elected by a wide margin in February 1936, the Spanish Popular Front seemingly resembled its French counterpart, linking centrist parties with socialists, communists, and anarcho-syndicalists. Yet where French workers occupied factories, Spanish labour attacked landlords, businessmen, and the clergy, practicing intimidation and revolutionary violence against their former oppressors. When conservatives and the armed forces fought back in July, the Spanish Civil War summarily began, provoking an intellectual corollary across Europe between loyalist sympathizers and right-wing supporters of the rebellion. From Doriot's PPF to the Action française, the French extreme-right unleashed a torrent of abuse towards the Spanish Popular Front, detailing the assassination of priests, the violation of nuns, and similarly nefarious deeds. In each case, General Francisco Franco and the nationalist rebels were portrayed as defenders of Christianity against Godless Marxism and its savage followers. According to groups like the CDF/PSF, French aid to Franco could only be used to fund Bolshevism. As a result, despite the existence of a legal commercial treaty with Spain, Blum's government ceased shipments to the loyalists after various right-wing newspapers revealed the delivery of military planes and equipment across the Pyrenees.[159]

However, the CDF/PSF was not satisfied with French non-intervention in the Spanish conflict. To La Rocque, the Iberian Popular Front served as a warning to other nations, and particularly France. Various members lauded Franco's nationalist troops, supporting war against the socialist 'desecration' of Spain. The General had the *droit de belligérence*, wrote one author in the *Flamme Tourangelle*, championing his defense of Christian virtue against the treasonous Marxist cowards in government, and recommending the firing squad as the best means of their disposal.[160] Warning that a similar fate awaited France should the Popular Front triumph in Spain, CDF/PSF writers often listed the 'crimes' of the loyalist side, from the killing of priests to the suppression of patriotic newspapers. Claiming that a loss for Franco or the CDF/PSF could mean the defeat of Western civilization, La Rocque painted a graphically violent portrait of Popular Front activities in Spain: 'The violation of cemeteries,

---

158  AP/451/82, Comic strip – 'Francoeur et Labusé'.
159  Jackson, pp. 202–206; Becker and Bernstein, pp. 303–309.
160  René Pierumet, 'De quoi s'agit-il?', *Flamme Tourangelle*, 25 Feb. 1939.

pillage of churches, and sacrifice of women, children, and peasants carried out by conscripted "regulars" leaves no doubt: Bolshevism has unleashed its wave of assault across the Iberian Peninsula.'[161]

Group activities reinforced the image of the CDF/PSF as the saviour of France against the left, with the Spanish experience often serving as a case study. In the CDF/PSF film *La France est à nous*, an educational piece about the 'tragic history of the Spanish revolution', Asiatic Bolsheviks are shown marching through Spain. The program guide instructs the viewer that 'leaders in the pay of Moscow go everywhere desseminating hatred, appealing to the vilest sentiments, and abusing the masses who they paint in glowing terms, under the fallacious guise of the "Soviet paradise"'. The film itself is a documentary portraying anarchic false liberty (France), and Marxism corroding all that it touches (Spain). The guide continues: 'Anguished, we witness the systematic destruction of civilization: Deportations, buildings torn apart, treasures pillaged and ransacked, churches violated, fleeing priests gunned down, and the assassination of women and children.' Spain is shown terrorized by a bloody Soviet dictatorship, with Franco portrayed as the national liberator, triumphant in the second part of the feature. That the film constituted political propaganda for the CDF/PSF is made clear in the guide, which offers a warning to the French populace that the forces of evil in France remain unchecked, and lauding 'La Rocque, the apostle of reconciliation', whose person unites France and rejects the Marxist conception of class war.[162]

Group publications also contained frequent mentions of the Soviet case, cast as a further example of the Marxist destruction of a people. The information bulletin devoted a November 1936 article to André Gide's exposé *Retour de l'URSS*, detailing the author's condemnations of Soviet society. Similarly, a November 1938 article in the *Flamme Tourangelle* argued that Soviet Marxism had created a new and brutal bureaucratic aristocracy in Russia, fueled by statism and tyranny far worse than the old Tsarist regime.[163] Group authors left no stone unturned in 'unmasking' the evils of Soviet oppression, comparing them unfavourably with the traditional French politics of the CDF/PSF. For example, La Rocque bombarded his audience with bloody imagery during a speech discussing the Marxist system of government at a Provençal regional congress in June 1937:

> I hear all around me the threatening rumblings of communists who want to enslave us to Moscow. The Soviet regime, which in other countries is exemplified by the most noxious propaganda, an absolutism equal to that of the Tsars, the massacre of millions of *moujiks*, the tyranny of a few individuals over the enormous lifeless masses, who possess neither

---

161   CDLR, 'Repères', *Le Flambeau*, 15 Aug. 1936. See also 'Fascisme rouge: hypocrite et barbare', *Le Flambeau*, 2 May 1936.

162   AP/451/103, programme for 'Ciné-PSF propagande'.

163   AP/451/101, 'L'URSS jugée par un de ses amis', *Bulletins d'Informations* no. 7, 24 Nov. 1936; 'Notre programme sociale', *La Flamme Tourangelle*, 26 Nov. 1938. On Gide's disenchantment with communism, see Herbert R. Lottman, 'André Gide's Return: A Case Study in Left-Bank Politics', *Encounter* 58 (1982): 18–27.

personalities nor civil rights, will not ... exercise the least influence on the internal life of the French nation.[164]

Exemplars of discipline, the CDF/PSF combated this hatred and disarray.

## VII

Faisceau and CDF/PSF plans for the new state represented political trends apparent throughout the Third Republic years. In opposing liberal democracy, socialism, and communism, both groups sought a political third way apart from the Republic they detested, and the rule of the left which they abhorred all the more. For the Faisceau, the answer was both modern, in the case of Georges Valois, and anti-modern for the conservative faction of Bourgin, Arthuys, Barrès, and de Barral. Lacking the divisiveness which characterized Faisceau political schemes, the CDF/PSF were united in choosing the latter option. Although they promoted different means, adopting authoritarianism in place of fascism, the political ends of the CDF/PSF and the conservative faction of the Faisceau were one and the same: A hierarchical, disciplined, and organic state, in which authority in the service of tradition, morality, and patriotism predominated. In so choosing, both became the heirs of the traditional extreme-right, from the Bonapartists and Boulangists to Barrès and Maurras. They also prefigured the political doctrine and dynamics of the wartime Vichy regime, which used similar arguments to justify authoritarian rule.[165] Yet unlike the Faisceau, whose political impact proved negligible, the CDF/PSF grew from a league into a mass organization with over one million members by 1938. Given the chance to attain power and realize their program, and concerned with the success of the Popular Front, La Rocque and the CDF/PSF became cautious, concealing their authoritarian program behind a veil of conciliatory social Catholicism.

Valois's theorizing also betrayed the influence of Maurras and Barrès, but he chose a different path, wedding social conservatism to political and economic modernism. This is not to imply that he abandoned the extreme-right: After all, Vichy attracted technocrats alongside social Catholic conservatives and xenophobes. But from the beginning Valois expounded 'left fascism', a composite of the syndicalist and *planiste* left on one hand, and Barrèssian nationalism and the doctrine of the trenches on the other. Although he fused corporatism, the organic nation, and the primacy of family and religion into his new state, the Faisceau leader insisted that the government be run according to the principles of scientific management, that the

---

164   CHEVS/LR 46, excerpts from CDLR speech at the PSF regional congress in Provence, 6 June 1937.

165   On Vichy's political doctrine and actions, see Julian Jackson, *France: The Dark Years, 1940–44* (New York, 2001), chapters 7, 14; Robert O. Paxton, *Vichy France: Old Guard and New Order, 1940–1944* (New York 1972), chapters 2–3. Almost every component of the Faisceau and CDF/PSF political platforms reemerged under Vichy, expounded by a variety of factions. Most notoriously, the regime commandeered Valois's phrase 'the National Revolution', and La Rocque's 'Travaille, Famille, Patrie', making them the official slogans of the Vichy government and its auxiliaries.

state be transformed according to the aesthetic principles of Le Corbusier, and that the Sorellian syndicalist ethic of the primacy of production drive a constant effort towards political modernization and renewal.

He thus came into conflict with his more conservative colleagues, veterans of extreme-rightist groups who did not share his proclivity for hyper-modern solutions, much like Pierre Pucheu and the Vichy technocrats battled Pétain and like-minded ultra-conservatives. For Valois, fascism was revolutionary, auguring the complete transformation of France as a socio-political construct. His classless society of producers reproduced the bourgeois revolution of 1789 for the twentieth century, rejecting stale materialism and individualism in favour of collective construction in the age of electricity. Tradition and Catholicism, the Barrèssian notion of the soil and the dead, and organic nationalism would be preserved within the family, but the state itself represented the modern values of the industrial age, derived from the experience of the Great War. Valois's fascist dictatorship was but a means to an end, to demolish the old parliamentary system in favour of rationalized government, termed the organ of progress, and a corporatist structure animated by young and ardent elites.

As veterans of the Ligues des patriotes, Action française, and similar organizations, Faisceau conservatives like Bourgin, Arthuys, and Philippe Barrès rejected Valois's progressive plans for the new state, and instead sought the renewal of conservatism. Schooled by Maurras and Barrès, they displayed no interest in the ideas of Sorel and Le Corbusier, or the rationalization of government and society. While Valois sang the praises of modern France and the age of electricity, Faisceau conservatives promoted a political agenda envisioned by the older extreme-right: The imposition of discipline, hierarchy, order, and authority, and the fight against communism and immorality. Their political fascism was a revolution of form and not content, calling upon renewed elites instilled with voluntarism to accomplish old-fashioned ends.

Their fascism, like that of Valois, reflected preconceived notions rather than Italian realities. True, their concept of the leader as a living synthesis of the will of the people did not differ greatly from the conception proposed by the Duce. Similarly, the notion that the *combattant* possessed the moral right to lead, and the values ascribed to them – patriotism, obedience, discipline, and a social Darwinist world view, were present in Mussolini's creed. Yet the politics of the Faisceau conservatives were identical to those of the French extreme-right from Dreyfus to Vichy. Their ideal state functioned according to the dictum of the soil and the dead, exalting the traditions of the French ancestors, the cult of the fallen hero, social Catholicism, and extreme nationalism.

Taken at face value, the CDF/PSF resembled the conservative faction of the Faisceau. Both the leadership and rank and file unanimously heralded a new political order informed by conservative authoritarianism, social Catholicism, and the primacy of the *combattant*. Yet La Rocque and the CDF/PSF leadership were consummate opportunists. Faced with the constant threat of a government ban of the leagues, even after the formation of the Parti social français, they proclaimed ardent republicanism. Neither did the group wish to be associated with fascism, for unlike Faisceau conservatives they did not believe that such a system provided a suitable vehicle for the political transformation of France.

Yet their public reformist discourse was a facade. Much like their fellow *liguers*, the CDF/PSF completely disapproved of the parliamentary system, and of liberal democracy in general. Rejecting the fascist concept of a state religion, the group nevertheless proposed an authoritarian regime in which discipline and hierarchy prevailed, and a government run by elites dedicated to the suppression of 'excessive' liberty. Much like the Faisceau, their restoration of authority, and insistence upon the primacy of the collective good over individual and material desires, echoed ideas prevalent among the extreme-rightist leagues throughout the Third Republic, culminating in their legislative actualization under Vichy. Nor did the transformation of the group into the parliamentary PSF change their political program or conception of the state. The CDF/PSF continued to advocate authoritarian solutions well into the war years.

The same was true of their doctrinal basis for the new state. Here again La Rocque was opportunistic, changing the group's tone to suit a wider audience once the mass-based PSF was formed. Croix de Feu members called for the creation of an *État combattant*, because the *combattant* alone was morally fit to lead. La Rocque and his followers firmly believed in the myth of the trench experience, that the fraternity, hierarchy, and order of the troops could be implemented in the political sphere. Like the Faisceau and other extreme-rightist leagues, however, the CDF/PSF existed solely to transform the French nation and state according to group principles. However, with only 40–60,000 members, numerous for an extreme-rightist group in the nineteen-twenties, but minute in practical political terms, the Faisceau never abandoned its position to reach a wider audience, because the possibility of success was slight at best. Conversely by July 1936, the CDF/PSF had become a mass organization with hundreds of thousands of adherents, and as such their public stance reflected a perceived potential to attain power and achieve their ultimate objective. By summer 1936, the goals of their proposed state – nationalism, Catholicism, family, and profession – were couched in the reconciliatory language of social Catholicism, complemented by the tenets of Maurice Barrès. More palatable to a mass audience, the credo that 'all souls are equal' and the defense of Christian civilization against Godless Marxism allowed the group to proclaim itself the sole protectors of French tradition.

# Chapter Two

## *Vers un ordre économique nouveau*: The Traditional and the Modern in the New Economy

The interwar period in France was indelibly marked by internal conflict. From the armistice of November 1918, which ended the Great War, until the renewal of hostilities in the fall of 1939, various factions within government, industry, and society debated every facet of national policy. Proponents of hawkish militarism clashed with cautious appeasers over the terms of the Versailles settlement, the wisdom of the Ruhr action in 1923, and the methods for containing both Hitler and Stalin a decade later. Domestic politics were no less volatile, from the battles between the Bloc National and the Cartel des Gauches in the 1920s, to the conflicts in the Chamber of Deputies and the streets a decade later, as the Popular Front government and exponents of the communist, socialist, and syndicalist left clashed with supporters of the moderate and extreme-right. These stormy debates left no stone unturned. A seemingly harmless subject, such as educational reform, became a partisan issue, less a discussion of the future of French youth than a stream of accusations.

One of the crucial battles of the interwar period took place in more staid surroundings: in the boardroom, the pages of the financial press, and the committee meeting. Although it has received less scholarly attention, the issue of economic modernization was one of the most prominent of its kind within the Third Republic. Lacking the violence and intensity of skirmishes between the left and right, discussions of the relative merits of scientific management, Taylorism, and the rational organization of production were nevertheless volatile, pitting traditionalists utterly opposed to any radical alteration of the national economy against modernists who acclaimed the new methods as the saviours of increasingly moribund French industry. In the nineteen-twenties, this battle was rather lop-sided. Most owners refused any significant change, at most adopting a diluted corporatism in furtherance of a platform historian Charles Maier calls 'bourgeois defense', a tactic designed to rebuild the pre-1914 social order and defend the traditional small shop. Modern industries employed full-blown corporatism, but they were few and far between: The Entente Internationale de l'Acier in November 1925 adopted production quotas, and Louis Renault and several colleagues in the automobile industry proselytized at length on the virtues of American business practices. Thus while corporatist solutions and industrial concentration figured prominently in the plans of German heavy industry, few owners in postwar France shared the opinion of André Citroën that 'a ministry of national industry must be created to force industrialists to specialize'. Working-class organizations also hesitated; the reformist faction of the syndicalist

Confédération générale du travail (CGT) espoused productivism, but many on the left agreed with the editors of *L'Humanité*, who lauded May 1926 strikes against 'the Americanization of production'.[1] Although the decade ended with the ascension of neocapitalist André Tardieu to the premiership, the fierce opposition of the Radical party in the Chamber denied him the majority needed to implement modern state-planning and industrial organization.

The playing-field leveled dramatically by the mid-1930s. Caution prevailed during the first half of the decade, as the depression engendered both a return to liberal economic doctrine and the more conservative monetary policy of deflation. But by 1936, productivist solutions resurfaced in the form of the economic plan, and certain authors even attempted to bridge the traditional and modern positions, albeit without much public acclaim. Adopted by the CGT, various socialist and radical bureaucrats within the Popular Front government, and rightist organizations like X-Crise, *planisme* proposed state-sponsored solutions to industrial malaise.[2] Yet while these factions agreed wholeheartedly upon the *planiste* form, they were far from unanimous regarding content. Figures like Marcel Déat, Bertrand de Jouvenel, and Léon Jouhaux advocated Americanization and the adoption of scientific management, while more conservative elements preferred the social Catholic corporatism of Albert de Mun and René de la Tour du Pin. Hence despite support from both the left and the right, economic planning and modern industrial techniques were not universally accepted until the end of the Second World War.[3]

Both the Faisceau and the Croix de Feu/Parti social français evinced interest in re-shaping the French economy during the interwar period, forging plans for a new economic order which were crucial to their projected reconstruction of the nation and state. However, their experiences in this regard were remarkably different. The Faisceau economic program was essentially that of Georges Valois. When other members broached economic matters, they inevitably referred to his arguments, often restating positions from his postwar book *L'Économie nouvelle* and articles in *Nouveau Siècle*. Moreover Valois's new economic order prescribed strict productivism, and he advocated solutions in which all social organization served the needs of industry. Like the technocratic clique in the 1920s, he espoused corporatism as a vehicle to modernize the French economy through the implementation of Taylorism and scientific management. Although Valois retained the cause of social justice from a prewar infatuation with La Tour du Pin, he severed all ties with social Catholic doctrine by 1924, a process directly related to his wartime experiences and an increasing belief that the future of the national economy depended upon the French adoption of American industrial techniques. Although he professed admiration for

---

1    Maier, *Recasting Bourgeois Europe* (Princeton, 1975), pp. 6, 8–15, 530–531, 540–545; Patrick Fridenson, 'L'Idéologie des grands constructeurs dans l'entre-deux-guerres', *Mouvement social*, no. 81 (1972), pp. 53–54, 64.

2    The term productivism is here taken to mean the primacy of industrial production over profit, and a commitment to modern economic methods such as Taylorism and Fordism.

3    See chapter four of Richard F. Kuisel, *Capitalism and the State in Modern France* (Cambridge, 1983). On those who adopted the middle ground, see Jackie Clarke, 'Imagined Productice Communities: Industrial Rationalization and Cultural Crisis in 1930s France', *Modern and Contemporary France* 8 (2000), pp. 345–357.

the accomplishments of fascist Italy, Valois's program of high salaries, low prices, and the worker-as-consumer came from Detroit rather than Rome. The Faisceau were thus among a minute faction arguing for modernization at a time when most owners looked approvingly to the prewar laissez-faire model for inspiration.

The situation was quite different for the CDF/PSF a decade later. Little conflict between traditionalists and modernizers existed in the 1920s, because the latter had no true voice. At that time, representatives of supposedly modern industries, such as Robert Pinot of the Comité des Forges, denounced American practices. But by the 1930s, as the *planiste* vogue bloomed, the conflict which erupted between conservatives and progressives took root in the CDF/PSF. La Rocque and various traditionalists within the group championed a social Catholic corporatist economy, at once anti-liberal and anti-capitalist, to protect the artisan, shopkeeper, and farmer. In their view, Taylorism and scientific management were anathematic to French business practices, which emphasized the small shop and enabled the reconciliation of labour and ownership in the workplace. A modern faction, more akin to Valois than La Rocque, instead adopted *planisme*, technocracy, and the rational organization of production. Arguing against the artisanal tradition as a relic from the past, figures such as Bertrand de Maud'huy, Luc Touron, and Marcel Canat de Chizy instead adopted the American model so dear to Valois, a new economic order based upon Taylorism and Fordism, to preserve French economic competitiveness.

Both groups were thus embroiled in a nation-wide debate concerning the nature and future shape of the French economy, representative of opposing sides in a conflict which continued throughout the interwar period, culminating in the implementation of state-planning in France after the Second World War. Far from embodying the economic doctrine of the extreme-right, Valois, the Faisceau, and the CDF/PSF modernists shared their vision of a modern, highly organized, and technocratic French economy with left-wing luminaries such as Jouhaux and Henri de Man, centrists within the radical party and the automobile industry, and right-wing partisans like André Tardieu and Ernest Mercier. Although they were proponents of social Catholic corporatism, hierarchy and discipline in the workplace, and anti-Taylorism – opinions habitually shared by the extreme-right – La Rocque and the CDF/PSF traditionalists were equally contemporary. Their defense of small business and its practices, and their calls for worker-owner reconciliation seconded similar views held by members of the CGPF, the Comité des Forges, and the majority of French businesses, 99 per cent of which employed fewer than 100 workers in 1936.[4]

# I

On March 18, 1928 Georges Valois signaled the end to the Faisceau experiment by publishing a 'Premier manifeste pour la République syndicale'. Although the political framework of the piece differed substantially from the authoritarian

---

4     Statistics taken from Alfred Sauvy, *Histoire économique de la France entre les deux guerres: T. 2, De Pierre Laval à Paul Reynaud* (Paris, 1967), p. 486. It is worth noting that 82.84 per cent of businesses in 1936 employed *five workers or fewer*. Hence La Rocque's views were far from abnormal in 1930s France.

solutions espoused by the Faisceau, signaling a return to the syndicalism that he had abandoned two-and-a-half decades earlier, Valois's economic doctrine remained virtually intact. The message was unchanged: It was the duty of the productive classes to contribute the greatest possible effort in order to preserve France's pre-eminence on the world stage.[5]

Valois had long been active in this regard, seeking to create a syndico-corporativist state in the modern economic mold. As a young Action française activist before the war, he took the lead in several royalist attempts at economic organization, culminating in the Cité française declaration of 1910 undertaken with his revolutionary syndicalist mentor Georges Sorel, and the December 1911 formation of the Cercle Proudhon study group with the young Edouard Berth. More critical than substantive, both initiatives lambasted the French bourgeoisie and the Republic without offering concrete alternatives, reflecting Valois's prewar devotion to La Tour du Pin-style social Catholicism and the anti-republican side of Sorellian thought. This world-view was abruptly transformed in August 1914, however. Like so many of his generation, the experience of modern warfare alerted him to hitherto unimagined human potential. Valois admired the systematic organization of the trenches, emphasizing discipline, teamwork, and sacrifice, in which individual interest was subordinated to the common good. In 1919, he discovered the economic corollary to this sentiment, which remained central to his thought throughout his postwar career: Taylorism, combined with a technocratic corporative structure of economic organization, which he adopted as the scientific basis of his proposed economy.

Valois's early beliefs parroted the doctrine of the royalist Action française, which he joined in 1906. An ex-revolutionary syndicalist who had organized fellow workers at the Armand-Colin publishing house, he was chosen by group leader Charles Maurras to lead a campaign designed to woo labour to the royalist cause. Maurras initiated the program in July 1908, siding with striking workers in the Villeneuve-Saint-Georges district. Alongside the socialist daily *L'Humanité* and the syndicalist CGT, the group's newspaper attacked Premier Georges Clemenceau's decision to use force against the agitators, bemoaning the exploitation of labour by bourgeois owners and liberal capitalism. Simultaneously, Valois unveiled an 'Enquête sur la monarchie et la classe ouvrière' in the *Revue critique des idées et des livres*, inviting a variety of syndicalist and labour leaders to comment upon the monarchy as a feasible working-class alternative to socialism and the Republic.[6] Designed as an updated version of Maurras's royalist tract *Enquête sur la monarchie*, its young editor hoped to initiate dialogue with labour organizations, widening the appeal of the Action française.

Yet Valois's effort failed to attract any tangible support. Only those syndicalists sympathetic to the right responded to the royalist call, figures like philosopher Georges Sorel and his disciples Edouard Berth and Hubert Lagardelle. As Paul Mazgaj notes, the group's reactionary royalism won few converts in the increasingly

---

5     Georges Valois, 'Premier manifeste pour la République syndicale', *NS*, 18 March 1928.

6     Paul Mazgaj, *The Action française and Revolutionary Syndicalism* (Chapel Hill, 1979), pp. 71–78. Valois's *enquête* was later published in book form as *La Monarchie et la classe ouvrière*.

volatile world of organized labour: 'For Maurras ... workers were interesting only as they might be of service in restoring the king'.[7] Similar problems beset Valois's 1910 project for the *Cité française* journal. A collaborative effort with Sorel, the review faltered before a single issue appeared due to the latter's demand that ardent syndicalist Jean Variot join the editorial board. In December 1911, Valois and Henri Lagrange, a member of the Action française youth auxiliary the Camelots du Roi, finally succeeded in founding a group dedicated to the question of labour – the Cercle Proudhon. But neither revolutionary syndicalists nor labour representatives were invited to join, with the exception of Berth and Albert Vincent, recently converted to the royalist cause. As a result, both the circle and its journal, the *Cahiers du Cercle Proudhon*, which appeared until the outbreak of war in 1914, grouped together right-wing intellectuals, and its connection to the worker remained tenuous. Nor did it prove to be a great success – fewer than 1,000 copies of each issue were printed.[8]

True to the Action française agenda, Valois's prewar arguments for a new economic order were vague at best, anti-Semitic and anti-capitalist rants which delineated problems rather than proposing solutions. Speaking to a royalist gathering in February 1910, at the beginning of the group's campaign to attract working-class supporters, he bemoaned the lack of help available to the struggling labourer, blaming the mutual hostility of workers and owners for the problem. Neither revolution nor exploitative capitalism were viable, Valois stated, because they benefited only 'men with Jewish names', who dominated both socialism and the laissez-faire economy. Yet at the time he elaborated no third way, content to offer scathing criticisms without presenting viable alternatives to prewar liberal economic principles.[9] Two years later, in the pages of the *Cahiers du Cercle Proudhon*, he provided a rudimentary Proudhonian antidote to both systems: The destruction of the modern capitalist economy, substituting a genuinely national variant for the subordination of all human values to the law of gold. But Valois continued to reject precise planning for his new economic order, on the grounds that such proposals were inevitably construed as utopias, offering false hopes to the masses in the manner of socialism. All that one could do was support the monarchy, which would destroy the rule of the Jewish capitalist plutocrats and organize the economy according to the principles of social justice.[10]

Such theorizing betrayed the influence of social Catholicism, and particularly the ideals of Albert de Mun and René de la Tour du Pin. Having founded the Cercles Catholiques d'Ouvriers in 1871, in an attempt to bring together workers and ownership under the rubric of collaboration rather than class conflict, the two men became highly influential on the burgeoning French right. Five years later, they began publication of *L'Association Catholique*, a journal promoting 'the devotion

---

7 Ibid, p. 221.

8 Allen Douglas, *From Fascism to Libertarian Communism: Georges Valois Against the Third Republic* (Berkeley, 1992), pp. 24–30. The Cercle took its name from nineteenth century anarchist philosopher Pierre-Joseph Proudhon.

9 F/7/13195, 'Conférence royaliste de MM. Arnal et G. Valois', *Le Nouvelliste*, 7 Feb. 1910.

10 Georges Valois, 'Sorel et l'architecture sociale', *Cahiers du Cercle Proudhon*, April–May 1912, 111; Georges Valois, 'Notre première année', *Cahiers du Cercle Proudhon*, April–May 1912, pp. 158–161.

of the directing class to the working class', and in 1886 De Mun founded the Association Catholique de la jeunesse française to convert university students to social Catholicism.[11] However, De Mun heeded the call of the *Ralliement* in 1892, turning to mainstream conservative politics. In contrast, his former colleague La Tour du Pin remained a staunch reactionary. His 1907 work *Vers un ordre sociale chrétien* proved particularly welcome in royalist circles, and both Charles Maurras and the young Valois professed admiration for his doctrine, a favour repaid when the social Catholic icon joined the Action française in 1905.

In *Vers un ordre social chrétien*, La Tour du Pin argued for an injection of religious principles into the modern economy. The family represented the cell of the nation, and thus required protection. This meant a fair deal for the worker, including a just salary and social insurance, enshrined in collective contracts negotiated between owners and workers. Capitalism fomented chaos, an economic anarchy in which money and profit ruined labour. In their place, La Tour du Pin proposed a reconstruction of the corporations of the ancien regime, associations of producers that engendered class collaboration, the antidote to socialism and class war. Firmly inculcated with Christian values, such a system would eradicate liberal individualism in favour of a moral economy.[12]

Combining the social Catholic writings of La Tour du Pin with the regenerative prescriptions of Maurrassian monarchism, Valois's new economy mirrored traditional French society, in which work provided the focal point of men's lives, 'the most precious activity of man'. The specialized guild system, which he posited as the ideal form of commercial activity, served the material and moral interests of the worker and the nation as a whole. Man belonged to a family, corporation, and social class, but freely communicated with other classes, as part of a harmonious economy in which the worker and owner knew their rightful place. This Christian social order, defined by hierarchy and corporative discipline, had been destroyed by liberalism and its lust for gold, in which profit replaced dignity and social peace.[13] Only the mutual constraint of both sides, wrote Valois in his 1913 Catholic philosophical novel *Le Père*, could allow the restoration of this natural order. The rich used their gold and command of labour for the good of the *Cité*, while the poor received security and their daily bread in return, with the leader ensuring that both performed their duties and eschewed personal interest.[14]

Valois's prewar writings were thus an almost ver batim restatement of the arguments of La Tour du Pin and De Mun. Yet in August 1914, like the rest of his generation, he enlisted in the French army, serving at the front for two years until seriously wounded. The experience of modern warfare shook Valois's faith in social Catholicism. The concerted effort necessary in battle, the overarching organization,

---

11     Benjamin F. Martin, *Count Albert de Mun: Paladin of the Third Republic* (Chapel Hill, 1978), pp. 15–16, 63. The Cercles enjoyed immediate success, attracting 56,000 members by 1883.

12     René de la Tour du Pin, *Vers un ordre sociale chrétien* (Paris, 1987), pp. 22–41, 115–116, 126–127, 143–144.

13     Georges Valois, 'La Bourgeoisie capitaliste', *Cahiers du Cercle Proudhon*, Dec. 1912, pp. 220–221.

14     Georges Valois, *Le Père* (Paris, 1924), pp. 196–197.

and the classless fraternity of the trenches convinced him that the reconstitution of ancien-regime corporatism was both impossible and unproductive. Though the state socialism of the *union sacrée* had failed, he wrote in 1917, the war demonstrated the need to balance individual and collective interests. The government initially erred in directing the economy without proper organization and specialization, yet the collaboration of all classes led France to victory. Most importantly, such organization could not succeed while utilizing the mores of the small guild workshop. Where Valois had previously argued in favour of medieval corporatism, he now adopted productivism. In the modern, mechanized world the economy would be run by *Syndicats professionaux*, in which workers and owners collaborated for maximum production mobilizing competence, speed, and careful planning at the minimum possible cost. As in the trenches, trained and disciplined personnel should run the postwar economy, directed by specialists and a technically-able administration which constantly studied industrial problems.[15]

Such a transformation had seemingly begun in France well before 1914, when the hydroelectric and automobile industries took tentative steps towards modernizing production. Yet France remained far behind Germany and the United States in this regard, with above 40 per cent of its output confined to agriculture. Only 29.3 per cent of French goods were industrial or material in 1907, and the Gallic *patronat* rejected American-style standardization as incompatible with business needs. Where massive concerns with thousands of employees drove the German economy, France remained the nation of the small shop par excellence.[16] However, the experience of modern, mechanized warfare awoke ownership and government to the need for modernization. Armaments Minister Albert Thomas lauded American management techniques and the gospel of rationalization, that owners and workers could cooperate to dramatically raise production. His successors Étienne Clementel and Louis Loucheur were equally impressed with the modus operandi pioneered by Frederick Winslow Taylor and Henry Ford in the United States, implementing the new methods with impressive results, producing shells and weapons according to ever-increasing production targets and exceeding government expectations.[17]

Productivism had always been present in Valois's work. His 1905 treatise *L'Homme qui vient* introduced the theme central to both the technocratic plans of the Faisceau and Valois's lifelong work: 'the law of least effort.' According to this *loi eternelle*, those who exerted themselves to their full capacity survived and thrived, while those who existed solely for pleasure and exhibited decadent behaviour withered and died out. Man had a duty to produce, Valois proclaimed, rather than enjoy the fruits of his labour. Yet human nature inclined individuals to seek the exact opposite, the minimum effort required in order to survive. Such tendencies could only be defeated by the 'man with the whip', a figure whom Valois called the *chef de l'industrie*. Where man once exerted himself in war, expanding and conquering,

15  Georges Valois, *La Cheval de Troie* (Paris, 1918), pp. 249, 251–255.
16  Kuisel, *Capitalism and the State*, pp. 26–29. Well over 90 per cent of French businesses in 1906 employed fewer than 100 workers. See Sauvy, p. 460.
17  Kuisel, *Capitalism and the State*, pp. 36–41; Stephen D. Carls, *Louis Loucheur and the Shaping of Modern France, 1916–1931* (Baton Rouge, 1993), pp. 11–12.

the new captain of industry replaced the general, adapting the warrior effort to the modern battlefield: the factory.[18] After 1919, Valois added a technocratic edge to the law, arguing that it was the motor of all economic progress, continually pushing industrialists to improve the means of production. By refusing to submit to this maxim, the old-fashioned *patronat* and politicians condemned the French nation and economy to decadence through the use of outdated methods.[19]

Valois's first economic plan, revealed in his postwar effort *L'Économie nouvelle*, expanded upon the productivism of *L'Homme qui vient*. Critiquing the law of supply and demand, he claimed that the latter was constant, rather than flexible as the classical liberal economists believed. The Marxist concept of value was equally false in its assertion that quantity rather than quality of work was the determining factor. Valois disapproved of anti-capitalist reaction and conservative defender of artisanal virtue in equal measure. Instead he explained that the leadership of the owner and not the quality of the finished product determined value, manifested in rationally organized production methods. Value thus reflected human effort, combining the skills of the worker and the progress-minded owner. The new economy dispensed with the bourgeois fiction that taste determined value or price, with the state acting to inculcate the utilitarian value of commodities while keeping decadence at bay.[20]

The incentive for the owner was his profit, driving him continually to improve and innovate. But the *patronat*, which viewed material gain as its sole commercial raison d'être, lacked the necessary motivation to spur technical progress, believing it unnecessary to maximize earnings. Bereft of the ability to administer and enrich the nation, conservative owners needed to embrace rationalization as a modern economic necessity. Specialized technicians acted as the motor force of such innovation. Charged with maintaining high skill and production levels, they encouraged the lazy *patronat*.

Valois further argued for the improved treatment of labour, equally important to the success of the modern economy. The worker would be paid according to production, assured of a wage sufficient to raise a family and proper living conditions. Although they maintained a rigid hierarchy in the factory, owners and employees exercised 'mutual constraint', their needs protected by the syndical organization of society. All facets of a business, from prices to wages, were to be enacted by corporative bodies: 'In this regime, everything will be syndicalist: sales, purchases, production, labour, the prices of all goods, working conditions, and wages, the conditions of production regulated by agreements between the syndicates concerned.' Although he revealed little precise detail, Valois clearly expected technical progress and the maximization of commercial activity to be assured by a respect for corporative discipline and hierarchy, and collective syndical accords. The spirit of the soldier at the front would be perpetuated by workers and owners, he proclaimed, giving the French factory the same prestige as her armed forces. The Marxist notion of the bourgeoisie and the

---

18    Georges Valois, *L'Homme qui vient: Philosophie de l'autorité* (Paris, 1906), pp. 145, 158–160. Although written in 1905, this work was published a year later, after Valois joined the Action française.

19    See Georges Valois, *L'Économie nouvelle* (Paris, 1919), pp. 126–134, 142–143; Georges Valois, 'À l'Union des corporations françaises', *Action française*, 4 Oct. 1925.

20    Valois, *L'Économie nouvelle*, pp. 78–85, 112–115, 145–147.

proletariat would be replaced by a new concept born of the trenches: The productive class, defined solely by *metier*.[21]

Despite his emphasis upon technology and productivism, the Valois of *L'Économie nouvelle* remained a slightly more modern version of La Tour du Pin. He continued to eschew capitalism in favour of social Catholic justice in the workplace. As late as 1923 Valois wrote that the capitalist economy (specifically supply and demand, and free trade) was inherently anti-Christian, and urged French Catholics to correct its abuses through the moral and religious discipline recommended in the papal encyclical *Rerum Novarum*.[22] Yet in 1924, he fully shed his reactionary economic views in favour of technocracy, epitomized by the rational organization of industry proposed by Taylor and Ford in the United States.[23] The Valois of the Faisceau years favoured a modern economic model, in which scientific management and the rule of experts prevailed, a natural corollary to his Le Corbusier-inspired utopian state.[24]

# II

Valois and the Faisceau remained faithful to one tenet of nineteenth-century social Catholic economic organization: Corporatism. Yet their corporations were not the medieval relics described by La Tour du Pin, emphasizing social harmony in the setting of the small workshop. To be sure, hierarchy, discipline, and worker-owner reconciliation were still heavily emphasized by Faisceau corporative planners, but Valois's corporations lent a new, distinctly modern content to the older social Catholic form. Indebted to revolutionary syndicalists like Georges Sorel, various Faisceau writers proposed a technocratic and productivist corporatism, in which the national good outweighed individual interest.

---

21    Ibid., pp. 156–158, 168–172, 181–183, 204, 245.

22    Valois, preface to Nel Aries, *L'Économie politique et la doctrine Catholique* (Paris, 1923), pp. X–XI. This work is a systematic attempt to demonstrate the compatibility of Valoissian economic thought with Catholic doctrine.

23    The definition of technocracy used here is that of Gerard Brun: A society whose principal goal is the direction of all social energy to production, in which politics is subordinate to economics. See *Technocrates et technocratie en France (1914–1945)* (Paris, 1985). For Valois's praise of Ernest Mercier and the Redressement français in this regard, see 'Notre politique ouvrière', *NS*, 1 May 1927. Discussions on collective action were held between the Faisceau and Mercier's group, but did not come to fruition. See Georges Valois, *L'Homme contre l'argent* (Paris, 1928), p. 239.

24    Certain authors have indeed placed Valois in the Action française camp even during the Faisceau years, arguing that he displayed the same 'socio-economic conservatism', and never deviated from his prewar philosophies. Thus to Robert Soucy, Valois proposed to defend upper-class status despite his anti-bourgeois rhetoric and his claim that 'Nationalism plus socialism equals fascism'. See Robert Soucy, *French Fascism: The First Wave* (New Haven, 1986), pp. 164–165. Similarly, Plumyène and Lasierra write that his combination of nationalism and socialism represented anti-capitalism severed from proletarian internationalism, and hence served the very bourgeoisie that he charged with complacency. In J. Plumyène and R. Lasierra, *Fascismes français, 1923–1963* (Paris, 1963), p. 39. While such statements are fair assessments of Valois's prewar and immediate postwar thought, they ignore his subsequent doctrinal evolution.

Sorellian syndicalism heavily influenced Valois's thinking in this regard. A staunch moralist who rejected the individualistic pleasure-seeking bourgeois in favour of the family as a natural social cell, Sorel proclaimed that man could be reified through technical progress and labour. Motivated by production alone, the worker would master nature and cleanse society. Such sentiments led him to briefly collaborate with the Action française from 1908–1910, until it became clear that Charles Maurras was interested in syndicalism solely as a royalist recruitment vehicle.[25] Yet Sorellian doctrine was embedded in Valois's postwar oeuvre. As Sorel had done, he argued for an organized productivism, in which the worker would re-energize and spur the flaccid bourgeois to participate in a collective effort of national construction. Infused with this theory, La Tour du Pin's corporations became modern economic vehicles for ever-greater production. Termed the syndico-corporative state, the new economy would be rationally planned, dividing industry and the nation by profession, rather than class or party. National, regional and local corporations replaced the existing economic structure, encouraging production in the service of the nation and eschewing the divisive tactics of socialism and parliamentary democracy.

Immediately following the war, Valois attempted to realize this program, but lacked the standing necessary to attract the French economic elite. His first effort, the Confédération nationale de la production, an attempt to gather together the nation's industrial leaders under the banner of a renewed national economy, proved unsuccessful. Established in May 1918, the initiative received scant attention, failing to attract more than a handful of minor engineers, bankers, and industrialists. The group was quickly overshadowed by the rival Confédération générale de la production française (CGPF), founded by such luminaries as Etienne Clémentel and André Tardieu. Where Valois and the royalists preached conservatism, the CGPF (and especially its ultramodern branch, the Société d'études et d'informations économiques) appealed to specialists and technicians rather than old bourgeois money. Undaunted, Valois tried again in March 1920, initiating the Confédération de l'intelligence et de la production française (CIPF), this time with the full backing of his royalist colleagues in the Action française. But again his success was severely limited. While his other organizational effort, the Semaines économiques, attracted experts to trade conferences in various metiers (currency and publishing were the most notable) and enjoyed a high public profile, the CIPF languished in obscurity, prompting the Paris police to call it an 'organization on paper only', able to form small delegations in the capital or the provinces, each containing a smattering of members. In 1923, Valois changed its name to the Union des corporations françaises (UCF), simultaneously introducing the principles of hierarchy and rigid leadership, and proposed a reconvention of the Estates-General, in the modern guise of an economic parliament to represent producers and the heads of families. To the UCF fell the task of organizing the economy for the pursuit of the national interest instead of individual profit, divided by profession along corporatist lines with inter-corporative accords determining prices, salaries, and benefits.[26]

---

25    Mazgaj, pp. 28–31, 126–127.
26    Douglas, pp. 46–48; Brun, pp. 17–19; F/7/13211, report of April 1926.

Although the Estates-General campaign attracted attention from prominent royalists and non-royalists alike before splintering in 1924, the UCF suffered the same fate as the CIPF, attracting little support while going virtually unnoticed by the French industrial world. Frédéric François-Marsal, former Minister of Finance, director of the Banque de l'Union Parisienne, and chair of the Semaine de la Monnaie wrote for the *Cahiers des États-Généraux*, as did Eugène Mathon, the social Catholic baron of industry from Lille-Roubaix-Tourcoing. No such recognizable figures entered the UCF, and Valois left the project behind upon exiting the Action française.[27]

As a result, by 1923 Valois evinced an interest in American scientific management, and his emphasis upon old-fashioned corporatism withered. In any case the modern industrialists with whom he sought to join forces had appropriated corporative thinking, previously the exclusive preserve of reactionary forces. Where corporatism once meant the acceptance by the worker of an inferior position in return for stability granted by the small-shop conservative owner, budding technocrats used the same arguments to press for economic rule by those most educated and technically able. It was this concept which drove Clementel's plans for the CGPF: That collective effort and industrial concentration directed by a national economic council were necessary to restore French economic predominance. Employers and owners would work together for the national economic good in a centrally planned and rationally organized modern economy. For this reason, postwar Minister of Industrial Reconstruction Louis Loucheur demanded syndicates of iron and steel producers, working together according to 'a single hymn, the hymn of production'. Although rejected by leading industrialists such as Robert Pinot, the head of the powerful Comité des Forges, who held to traditional paternalist doctrine, even the most reactionary recognized that production methods could not remain static.[28]

Valois was among those interested in the new corporatism. Although he kept intact the basic corporative framework discussed in *L'Économie nouvelle*, he quickly abandoned most of its social Catholic underpinnings. By 1923, UCF pamphlets referred to France as a collective industrial entity, where individual prosperity depended upon national economic performance. Corporatism now meant the concentration of production and Valois's theory of mutual constraint replaced the concept of irreconcilable economic classes. Henceforth, workers provided maximum effort for maximum production in return for higher wages and the eight-hour day. All conflict between different categories of producer (owners/management, technicians, employees, workers) would be resolved within the corporations, which defended the common interest of their adherents. The President of the corporation alone made all decisions, however, after consulting with the corporative executive committee.[29]

---

27    F/7/13211, report of April 1926; Douglas, pp. 46, 49, 53–60. The notions of hierarchy, discipline, and state protection of the worker actually predated *L'Économie nouvelle*, first discussed – albeit briefly – in an October 1918 speech given at the Cercle commerciale et industriel du France. See Georges Valois, *La Réforme économique et sociale* (Paris, 1918), pp. 39–40.

28    Georges Valois, *L'Économie nouvelle*, pp. 269–272, 279, 281–283; Matthew Elbow, *French Corporative Theory, 1789–1948* (New York, 1953), pp. 63–75; Jennings, pp. 22–23; Carls, pp. 129–130; Maier, pp. 21, 33, 75, 82–83.

29    F/7/13209, Pamphlet – 'Union des corporations françaises', 1923.

These two central UCF tenets, authoritarianism and syndicalism, formed the basis for Faisceau economic planning. Combined with an emphasis on Taylorism and the rationalization of production, they were mobilized in the Faisceau des corporations (FC), the foundation of the group's new economic order.

Many UCF members left to join Valois in the Faisceau, mostly veterans eager to build the *État Combattant*. Although some were workers, the defectors mainly comprised representatives of emergent modern professions: Engineers, factory managers, and owners of technologically advanced industrial concerns. Valois moved quickly to organize the contingent. Formed as a successor to the Action française-dominated UCF, the FC emerged in December 1925 with Valois as President, Pierre Dumas – the ex-CGT activist and Faisceau expert on syndicalism – as Vice-President, and René de la Porte – ex-socialist and junior bank executive – as Secretary-General. Like the UCF, the FC formulated an economic plan to combat 'disorder and ruin' in the French economy, the result of decadent commercial and industrial institutions. It had considerably more success, however, attracting up to 9,000 members by October 1926, many of whom represented the technocratic elite long courted by Valois. Out of 2,500 Paris FC members in April 1926, over 1,000 came from industrial or high commercial professions.[30]

The structure and platform of the FC reflected its technocratic bent. At bottom, the organization mirrored Valois's plans for the state, wherein the Assembly of Families functioned as a representative body for political purposes, and the corporative Association of Producers expressed the needs and goals of the national economy. Both associations chiefly aimed to implant the Faisceau's *Révolution nationale* on French soil. Each advised the national leader on political, social, economic, and moral matters, voicing their concerns and desires. In the case of the Association of Producers, which gathered together representatives of owners, workers, employees, technicians, and farmers, the role was purely economic: Consulting the state on the renovation of the existing socio-economic order, to be replaced with a more modern and benevolent model in order to restore French predominance. In this way syndico-corporatism symbolized the industrial age and the spirit of the trenches, claimed Valois, anathematic to liberal economic doctrine.[31] For this reason, Faisceau authors took pains to emphasize that their corporative system bore no relation to similarly-named bodies proposed by La Tour du Pin, which flourished under the ancien regime. Writing in *Nouveau Siècle* in February 1926, for example, Antoine Fouroux called such corporations impractical in the modern world. Only their spirit of fraternity, discipline, and social justice remained, while the form had been updated to serve the needs of the age of electricity.[32]

---

30    F/7/13208, report of 12 Dec. 1925; F/7/13211, report of April 1926; Pierre Dumas, 'Chronique des corporations', *NS*, 20 Dec. 1925; F/7/13208, report of 13 Oct. 1926; F/7/13210, report – 'Effectifs du Faisceau', Oct. 1926.

31    F/7/13211, Tract – Georges Valois, *Le Faisceau des combattants, des chefs de famille, et des producteurs* (Paris, 1926), 9; 'Notre but', *Faisceau Bellifontain*, April 1926. See also CHEVS/V 45, 'Manuel de délégué', Aug. 1926.

32    Antoine Fouroux, 'L'Ingénieur dans l'organisation corporative', *NS*, 21 Feb. 1926.

Corporations were established in 1926–1927 in many professions, with priority given to modern concerns. By April 1926, 22 had been formed, ten of them in commerce and heavy industry, reflecting Valois's belief in scientific management and modern production, including 'Machines, Electricity, Automobiles, and Aeronautics', 'Engineers', and 'Banking and Stock Exchange'. These were joined by various *Corporations de métiers*, comprising liberal and intellectual professions such as medicine and the arts. All were sub-divided into Unions professionnelles of workers, technicians, employees and ownership/management, representing the various facets of the production process. Thus the Corporation du bâtiment, for example, contained unions of architects, painters, civil engineers, and many others.[33] Each was also given a mandate based upon the needs of the profession. The Corporation de la banque et de la bourse grouped together technicians and workers from the bank and stock exchange, financial publicists, and bank executives. They wished to standardize banking practices and regulations to allow better service, while organizing each bank more rationally and efficiently.[34]

The group's Conseil technique, which included Dumas as its President, Valois, Jacques Arthuys, Hubert Bourgin, Philippe Barrès and representatives from the various FC branches, developed plans for a reorganization of the entire French economy along similar corporative lines.[35] Dumas sketched out the precise details using Valois's rudimentary scheme from *L'Économie nouvelle* as a blueprint. Local corporations administered the affairs of a prescribed area (Town/Canton/City district), grouping together owners, managers, technicians, and workers, each of whom was given a specific role. Owners were responsible for primary materials, the organization of credit, import/export flow, tariffs, and the rationalization of production. Technical matters were left to the technicians, the engineers and directors achieving the maximum benefit from human and material resources. For salaried workers and employees, the professional union afforded the opportunity to participate in the regulation of the workday, wages, workplace health and safety, and the organization of apprenticeship. Social insurance (for accidents, illness, and death), family allowances, and pensions would also be regulated, subsidized by employee and ownership contributions. Finally, the unions informed the local corporation of their specific needs. In this way tailors, whose methods were slower and more meticulous, would not be expected to produce like clothing factories, which possessed new machinery and adopted Taylorist principles.[36]

Atop the local bodies were regional corporations, composed of delegates elected by the former. Charged with the administration of each geographic *département*, they determined policy and allocated resources to the local corporations, relaying

---

33    F/7/13211, report of April 1926; 'Les Corporations', *NS*, 24 July 1926; APP/Ba 1894, report – 'Faisceau des corporations', 27 July 1926.

34    Paul Duman, 'La Corporation de la banque et de la bourse', *NS*, 1 March 1926. Duman was the President of the banking corporation.

35    APP/Ba 1894, 'Faisceau des corporations, direction technique'.

36    Pierre Dumas, 'Vers une organisation totale et rapide', *NS*, 12 Sept. 1926; Pierre Dumas, 'La Corporation moderne', *NS*, 23 May 1926; Pierre Dumas, 'La Corporation moderne', *NS*, 6 June 1926/20 June 1926/ 4 July 1926. See also Lusignac, 'Je vous présente les corporations en action', *NS*, 1 Aug. 1926.

the needs and concerns of the smaller districts to the state. Each regional corporation also maintained inter-corporative ties with other, related professions. This complex web was managed by the FC (the national corporation), composed of delegates from the various regional bodies, whose tasks included the formulation of national economic policy and the arbitration of inter-corporative disputes.[37]

Above the corporative bodies lay the state. Although business was conducted solely by the corporations, the state would be empowered to collaborate in the management of the economy. According to Valois, its delegates worked with the corporations to determine commercial policy, ensuring that mutual constraint, high salaries, low prices, and fair treatment of the worker were maintained. Although forbidden from direct intervention in local or regional economic affairs, the state ensured suitably high production levels. In this regard, authorities kept national project logs, enabling forecasts regarding future exports and domestic market shares. Finally, on the international level, the state negotiated accords to import primary materials and export finished products.[38]

This complex organization aimed to shake the French bourgeoisie out of their complacency while simultaneously addressing the issue of class conflict. For the Faisceau retained one facet of social Catholic economic doctrine from his prewar years: The concept of social justice. The liberal economy, admonished the authors of a July 1926 economic plan in *Nouveau Siècle*, existed only to enrich the bourgeoisie, atomizing and immiserating the working class in the process. The former had succumbed to decadence, the shell of an elite for whom the organization of production proved anathematic. Worse still, the law of least effort combined with greed led the modern French middle class to deride all but profit.[39]

To Valois, the bourgeois republican status quo mirrored the situation in 1789, with one social class reserving power exclusively for itself. The liberal capitalist economy had emptied the soil of men, herding them into industrial cities where they existed as an impoverished, deracinated proletariat. The modern worker became a nomad, wandering from one menial job to another, a victim of alcoholism and misery. It was thus necessary to impose discipline upon the bourgeoisie, claimed Valois, ending the reign of individual interest. Profit, the motor of activity and spirit of invention, would be retained, but the new corporate system eliminated the exploitation of the workers.[40]

---

37    Pierre Dumas, 'La Corporation moderne', *NS*, 4 July 1926; Pierre Dumas, 'Nos créations nouvelles', *NS*, 15 Aug. 1926.

38    'Discours prononcée le 11 Novembre', *NS*, 12 Nov. 1925; CHEVS/V 21, Tract – Georges Valois, *La Politique économique et sociale du Faisceau* (Paris, 1926), pp. 18–19, 28. For an older, less developed version, see Georges Valois, 'La Coordination des forces nationales', *Cahiers des États-Généraux*, Oct. 1923, 141–144.

39    'Le Fascisme économique', *NS*, 29 July 1926. This plan was repeated ver batim in F/7/13211, *Le Faisceau des combattants, des chefs de famille, et des producteurs*; CHEVS/ V 21, Tract – *La Politique économique et sociale du Faisceau*, 9–10; Georges Valois, *Le Fascisme* (Paris, 1927), p. 34; Georges Valois, 'Notre politique ouvrière', *NS*, 2 April, 1926.

40    Georges Valois, 'Aux républicains', *NS*, 21 June 1926; Georges Valois, 'À L'Union des corporations françaises', *Action française*, 20 Sept., 1925; Georges Valois, 'Le Fascisme économique', *NS*, 29 July 1926.

Such conditions enabled the worker to live with stability and dignity, and to raise a family, the basis of all national life. According to Marcel Delagrange, the former mayor of Périgueux and ex-communist who joined the group in 1926, French labour had earned such security in the mud and blood of the trenches and the sweat and grime of the factories during the Great War. The worker had nothing to defend in 1914 except his country and a superior civilization; he now demanded the fruits of human progress, including fair wages and an education for his children.[41] Continuing in this vein, Valois claimed that the modern worker, unlike his nineteenth-century counterpart, did not owe his entire life to the owner. The *patron* provided leadership in the workplace, but outside the factory walls the labourer was his own man, the head of a family and an equal member of society.[42]

Syndico-corporatism thus provided the vehicle for both the defense of the worker and the advancement of his interests. Valois's ideal French labourer actively participated in corporative life, becoming initiated into the complexities of modern production. Within the new industrial *Cités*, the worker received a large representation at all levels save the state, which existed above parties and classes. To ensure that class conflict remained dormant, owners and labour representatives formulated collective contracts in tandem, balancing the need for social justice with the interests of the *patronat*. Owners who neglected their workers would be answerable to the state, which demanded fair and reciprocal treatment within the corporations.[43]

Valois and other Faisceau members predicted the victory of communism should France fail to adopt a syndico-corporatist system of economic organization. The French worker did not follow Marxist doctrinaires willingly, Valois argued, but they were left with no clear alternative because of their socio-economic victimization, battered by the mercantile Republic and the dictatorship of moneyed interests.[44] Nor was revolutionary syndicalism an alternative, wrote Dumas. The CGT attempted to attain power by supporting electoral candidates and reaching a modus vivendi with the bourgeoisie. Yet this strategy compromised their primary goal: Ensuring better wages and benefits for the worker. The CGTU acted no differently, a pawn of communists in Moscow which argued for the Marxist solution of unremitting class war.[45]

## III

The syndicates and corporations described by Valois and Dumas administered justice through a confrontation of interests between owners' and workers' representatives. Valois's theory of mutual constraint remained, as the Faisceau plan demanded the

---

41    Marcel Delagrange, 'La Classe ouvrière et les leçons du passé', *NS*, 17 July 1927.

42    CHEVS/V 21, Tract – Georges Valois, *La Politique économique et sociale du Faisceau*, pp. 9–10; Georges Valois, 'La Bel ouvrage et l'honneur ouvrier', *NS*, 2 Oct., 1926.

43    F/7/13209, 'Appel aux travailleurs français', n.d.; Georges Valois, *Le Fascisme*, 117–119; Georges Valois, 'La Politique économique', *NS*, 27 Dec. 1925.

44    Georges Valois, 'Premier Mai', *NS*, 30 April 1925.

45    Pierre Dumas, 'Le Travailleur français, dupé par la CGT', *NS*, 28 Feb. 1926; Pierre Dumas, 'Le Problème ouvrier ou Faisceau des Corporations', *NS*, 12 May 1926; Pierre Dumas, 'Le Parti communiste et le mouvement ouvrier', *NS*, 10 Jan. 1926.

maximum possible output. Yet his older visions of the owner and worker, labouring for the good of the nation, were here replaced by their American industrial counterparts. Owners improved the means and methods of production, while according high salaries and a multitude of fringe benefits to the worker, with concomitant low prices to increase consumption. To be sure, La Tour du Pin would not have approved of such a plan. But Valois had learned the power of modern techniques and the true human capacity for effort during the Great War. The fascist economy, he declared, used the principles of the trenches and technology to fight a new economic conflict. In this way French industry, stagnant because it adhered to the nineteenth-century precepts of liberalism, would awaken. A new economic order symbolizing the new century enabled the reconstitution of prewar commercial power, and then moved beyond it, incrementally increasing future capacity.[46]

In Valois's view, corporatism remained useless without a renewed commitment to production *en-soi*. Throwing off the yoke of social Catholicism, in 1924 he adopted the technocratic position that economic forces induced all change in the modern world. Machines facilitated massive production growth, while oil and electricity exponentially increased transportation capacity. Capitalizing on these advances, the new fascist economy would create an 'industrial *Cité* for the century of electricity', mobilizing the combined forces of French production to transform the national economic landscape, from factories to roads and housing. This work would be accomplished by a 'great economic team' composed of bankers, industrialists, technicians, workers, and farmers, a renovation on par with the era of Louis XIV or the nineteenth-century infrastructure creation program.[47]

Valois chose American scientific management as his vehicle for success. While still enamored of the theories of Maurras and La Tour du Pin, he moved towards Taylorism, promoting rationalized production in a series of 1919 *Action française* articles describing its successful application in American factories. Lauding increased production and efficiency, he advocated the use of the system within the new corporative economic order: 'At last, in the new economy, the company manager will no longer be free to accept or refuse technical progress. Whether or not it satisfies his ambition, he must rapidly effect the necessary changes.'[48]

As such, the principles of scientific management and an openly technocratic discourse permeated the economic plans of the Faisceau. Rejecting the corporative system of the ancien regime, the laissez-faire freedom of the nineteenth-century, and the communist redistribution of wealth, in 1925 Valois argued that higher

---

46     CHEVS/V 21, Tract – *La Politique économique et sociale du Faisceau*, p. 8. For Valois's comments on the subject while still at the front, see *Le Cheval de Troie*, p. 133.

47     Georges Valois, 'Ce que nous sommes', *NS*, 7 Dec. 1925; Georges Valois, *Le Fascisme*, pp. 84, 87–88; 'La Paix', *NS*, 30 Aug. 1926; Georges Valois, 'L'Equipe des grands producteurs', *NS*, 21 March 1926; F/7/13211, *Le Faisceau des combattants*.

48     Georges Valois, 'La Méthodisation de la production', *Action française*, 14 April 1919; Georges Valois, 'L'Économie de temp et d'effort', *Action française*, 28 May 1919; Georges Valois, *L'Économie nouvelle*, p. 193. Any remaining doubts disappeared by 1924, when he published the Taylorist manual *L'Organisation scientifique des usines* by French technocrat Émile Nusbaumer, who successfully implemented Taylorism in French munitions plants during the Great War. See E. Nusbaumer, *L'Organisation scientifique des usines* (Paris, 1924).

production alone raised the status of the worker while maintaining private property. When combined with a political voice for labour in the new fascist national and communal assemblies, the association of property with productive function, and the rule of competence in place of class-based roles in the workplace, productivism also eliminated class conflict. Furthermore, owners unable to properly direct their concerns could either acquire the necessary skills in engineering and management, or cede their businesses to those more able. No longer, Valois thundered, would bourgeois egoism and ancient commercial institutions be allowed to impede progress.[49]

The impetus clearly lay with ownership, viewed by the Faisceau as the directors of commercial policy, the only force capable of enacting changes which the government, possessing a vested interest in the status quo, would never effect. Taking up this strand of thought, industrialist and *Nouveau Siècle* columnist Paul-Charles Biver bemoaned the lack of interest displayed in new management methods and production techniques by ownership. The war had forced French industry to seek out new and innovative means of production, yet aside from isolated individuals such as Ernest Mercier, few of the notoriously conservative owners accepted renewal and modernization. This stance was at odds with the war generation, he asserted, who received a veritable education in management and technique in the trenches. The troops of Verdun and the Marne expected economic victory a decade later, and thus demanded owners and managers who were engineers and creative administrators rather than profiteering reactionaries.[50]

The Faisceau enthusiastically took up the American capitalist mantle with a St-Simonian flourish. It was no accident that Biver named Ernest Mercier, the staunch proponent of American production techniques in 1920s France. A graduate of the prestigious École Polytechnique, Mercier worked for armaments minister Louis Loucheur as a technical advisor during the war, and became the managing director of the Union d'Électricité at conflict's end. He was converted to Taylorism and Fordism after a 1925 tour of General Electric in the United States.[51] To this end, he formed the Redressement français (RF) in December 1925, gathering together right-wing technocrats in the service of industrial modernization: 'One law brings all nations under its discipline, the law of production.' Standardization and mass production, with concomitant high wages and low prices, had already been successfully copied by industrial cartels in Germany. Its age-old enemy so armed, France could either perish or modernize, Mercier claimed, eliminating the inefficient small shop in favour of corporations utilizing uniform production methods. By suppressing individualism, owners increased profits while workers became consumers, their increased wages further aiding market growth while the rule of experts replaced partisan politics.[52]

---

49    Georges Valois, 'Notre politique ouvrière', *NS*, 1 May 1927.

50    Paul-Charles Biver, 'L'Education du patronat', *NS*, 1 May 1927. Biver was also the head of the Paris branch of the Faisceau des corporations.

51    Richard F. Kuisel, *Ernest Mercier: French Technocrat* (Berkeley, 1967), pp. 3–9, 47–49.

52    Ibid, pp. 49–71.

Mercier and the RF succeeded in the 1920s, attracting 10,000 dues-paying members by 1927.[53] Nor did they exist in a vacuum. In the prewar era, only automobile manufacturers tentatively implemented American production methods, yet by the end of the conflict even the syndicalist CGT approvingly lauded such positive contributions to the workplace, particularly the eight hour day, one of the central planks of their November 1918 Minimum Program. But this success masked a more staid reality. Rejecting the experimental propositions of Mercier or the French automobile magnates, the postwar Bloc National government restored a Gallic variation of prewar laissez-faire liberalism. Hence rather than implementing scientific management or modern production techniques, French industrialists forged trusts to corner their markets, while lobbying for higher tariffs to keep out foreign competition.[54]

Even the election of the left-centre Cartel des Gauches in May 1924 did little to change business attitudes. Prime Minister Edouard Herriot proposed a quasi-technocratic National Economic Council grouping together workers, owners, and consumer delegates, including CGT leader Léon Jouhaux, Comité des Forges director Robert Pinot, and the noted economist Charles Gide. But industrialists simply ignored the initiative. For the technocrats were a 'ginger group', as economic historian Richard Kuisel notes, in no way indicative of the doctrinal norm. Most French owners followed the dictum of René Duchemin, the President of the national employers' federation, the Confédération générale de la production française, that traditional French methods were more than adequate for modern business needs. Rejecting any servile imitation of American practices, Duchemin defended the traditional modus operandi of the French family firm, arguing that industrial concentration or rationalization of production would ruin the French economy.[55] Only a fraction of the *patronat*, such as the Comité national de l'organisation française (CNOF), a small technocratic lobbying group founded in 1926, or Mercier and the RF, opposed the prevailing orthodoxy. Despite the unceasing efforts of such groups to promote rationalization, and their disgust with the inefficiency of state-run enterprises (such as the PTT), endorsements of productivism and scientific management went unheeded by most owners.[56]

Like Mercier and the CNOF, Valois and company recognized what the CGPF did not: That American firms were in a far stronger position than their French counterparts. France would either adapt to the new system, or fall prey to cheaper and better-produced American goods. The Faisceau leader continued fervently to argue for high wages and low prices, to stimulate consumerism and increase production, and voiced his approval for Mercier and Henry Ford, taking the latter's methodology as his model for the new economic order.[57] Ford was named an *animateur* of the group in the pages of *Nouveau Siècle*, which boasted that his workers were the highest

---

53    Ibid, p. 122.

54    Ibid, p. 18; Kuisel, *Capitalism and the State*, pp. 62–65. On the CGT and the eight-hour day, see Gary Cross, *A Quest for Time: The Reduction of Work in Britain and France, 1840–1940* (Berkeley, 1989), p. 131–160.

55    Kuisel, *Capitalism and the State*, p. 83–92; Carls, pp. 246–248.

56    Brun, pp. 17–19.

57    Valois, *Le Fascisme*, p. 154.

paid in the world and the company's sales the greatest of any global auto-maker.[58] Speaking at the Salle Wagram in May 1926, Valois contrasted the Ford wages of six dollars per day, and the low 15,000 franc price-tag of the model T, with the paltry salaries and exorbitant prices offered by Renault and Citroën. It was this system, he argued, that provided the antidote to socialist class war by allowing the worker to participate in company profits. Praise was equally forthcoming for the assembly-line production system.[59] One *Nouveau Siècle* columnist lauded the company's 'perfection de transport dans l'usine', marveling that a motor was finished in a mere 97 minutes, a technique that, if adopted by the Gallic *patron*, would allow France to conquer the European automotive industry.[60]

Valois also tied the Fordist methodology to his law of least effort. Mirroring the description of the human impulse to idleness in *L'Homme qui vient*, he applied the concept to business ownership, stating that the same natural law inspired some *patrons* to seek the largest possible profit for the least work. This phenomenon encouraged ownership to ceaselessly drive their workers, in order to maintain ever-greater production targets using primitive machines for the least possible pay. That the worker balked at this arrangement was understandable, he concluded, for his family was impoverished as a result. However labour's response, the socialist goal of collectivization of property, was equally deficient, suppressing economic activity due to a lack of initiative. Ford's five-day work week and high salaries provided the impetus for increased productivity without jeopardizing the profit motive, essential to securing the concerted effort of ownership.

It was the owner's responsibility to invest in the necessary technology, machines to save as much time as possible, and to remunerate labour accordingly as production levels rose. Workers who delivered maximum productivity through maximum effort would be rewarded, benefiting from guaranteed promotions based on demonstrated ability. To Valois, the true owner provided leadership, regarding the workers as valuable employees, and in turn commanding their respect.[61] Although hierarchy in the workplace should be maintained, he had as much responsibility as the worker or technician, charged with instilling energy and creative fervour into the workplace: 'The essential task is to always invent work and find new methods, so that harmony can be established through continuous creation.'[62] Thus Valois also wished to move beyond the nineteenth-century vision of the worker as a slave to the machine, breaking his back in its operation:

For the working-class, fascism wants the strongest possible general education, and the highest technical instruction, so that economic progress can be rapidly applied, a man's

---

58    'Les Animateurs: Henry Ford', *NS*, 13 March 1926.

59    CHEVS/V 21, *La Politique économique et sociale du Faisceau*, pp. 6–8, 10–14.

60    Mercure, 'Notre industrie automobile et l'exemple de Ford', *NS*, 14 Feb. 1926.

61    Georges Valois, 'La Politique des hauts salaires', *NS*, 30 Sept. 1926; Mercure, 'Les Hauts salaires en France', *NS*, 6 June 1926; J.B., 'La Politique des hauts salaires aux États-Unis', *NS*, 17 April 1927.

62    CHEVS/V 21, tract – Georges Valois, *La Politique économique et sociale du Faisceau*, pp. 6–8, 10–14.

arms can be increasingly replaced by the machine, and the worker more often becomes the intelligent manager of machines, the servants of man.

Addressing French labour in May 1926, Valois wrote in *Nouveau Siècle* that elites should display a dedication to industrial production, exhorting the captains of industry to ever-greater levels of invention and technical progress. The state removed those owners who resisted the new methods, parasites with no socio-economic value.[63]

Valois originally used this philosophy to counter the Marxist suppression of the profit motive. But by the mid-1920s, his position increasingly resembled that of the CGT, an ironic twist considering the group's fervent criticism of France's largest syndicalist organization. Valois promoted Léon Jouhaux's espousal of Taylorism, frequently repeating his slogan 'maximum production in minimum time for maximum salary'. Like the syndicalists, the Faisceau also supported the eight-hour day, a necessity in the new factory, where workers performed simpler and ever-more rapid tasks, and longer days inevitably resulted in accidents and fatigue.[64]

Broadening these themes, Biver demonstrated the potential of rationalized production for labour in *Nouveau Siècle* in January 1927, urging its adoption for the new economic order. The old back-breaking and mind-numbing schedule would be rendered obsolete, he hypothesized. With a minimum of effort and corporate expense, the new worker could produce and earn more, while the workday lessened. Nor would profit diminish, because standardization automatically lowered prices and reduced costs while facilitating exports. New markets were thus established, which required the subsequent rationalization of all national production and the science of the market – specialized advertising and publicity.[65]

Labour actively aided ownership, restoring the lost creative fervour of the French bourgeoisie. Like his mentor Sorel, Valois believed that the worker was inherently productivist, constantly pressuring the middle class to construct the *Cité* of the future. As the ancient Greeks had awakened the slumbering world to modern culture and creativity, he wrote in the 1927 work *Le Fascisme*, the proletariat shook the idling bourgeoisie: 'Working-class pressure exercises a civilizing influence, which will play a considerable role in the state of tomorrow.' Spurred by the fraternal experience of the trenches during the Great War, the worker demanded modern production methods, higher wages, and better working conditions suitable to the age of electricity. Like the great team of St-Simonian constructors of the nineteenth-

---

63    Georges Valois, 'Aux travailleurs français', *NS*, 1 May 1926.

64    For Valois's comments on Jouhaux see, for example 'L'Illusion révolutionnaire', *Action française*, 29 Sept. 1919; Georges Valois, *La Réforme économique et sociale*, pp. 26–33; Pierre Dumas, 'Les Huit heures', *NS*, 21 Aug. 1926; F/7/13209, Prefect of the Marne to the Minister of the Interior, Report of 21 June 1926 on a Faisceau meeting in Eparney. For the syndicalist program, see Jeremy Jennings, *Syndicalism in France: A Study in Ideas* (New York, 1990), pp. 158–160; Georges Valois, *La Politique de la victoire* (Paris, 1925), pp. 65–68. Valois acknowledged his debt to revolutionary syndicalism, specifically Pelloutier, Delesalle, and Sorel in *D'un siècle à l'autre: Chronique d'un génération* (Paris, 1924), pp. 108–114, 134–135.

65    Paul-Charles Biver, 'La Crise de la chômage condamnent l'État Parlementaire', *NS*, 9 Jan. 1927.

century, who built railroads and factories, the postwar labourer demanded the fabrication of automobiles. Above the fray, but sympathetic to the worker's demands, the state imposed national discipline on the bourgeoisie, maintaining the hierarchy desired by the middle-class while simultaneously restraining capitalist excess in granting security to the worker.[66]

This was the essence of Valois's fascism, a definition which he claimed to have received from the example of Mussolini. The Duce, he frequently opined, acted similarly to the monarchs of the ançien regime. He sponsored the construction of modern factories and engendered an Italian economic resurgence, while raising the working class standard of living and forging an alliance between state and people. Others within the group agreed wholeheartedly, praising Mussolini's corporatism, technocratic beliefs, and his benevolence to the Italian worker in *Nouveau Siècle*. To Jacques Boulanger, Mussolini had wiped out the deficit while creating new economic sectors such as hydroelectricity, and applying modern production techniques to the automobile industry and agriculture. In a 1926 tract, Valois also presented a technocratic Duce, seemingly closer to Ernest Mercier or Louis Renault than Italian fascist reality.[67]

Influenced as he was by Sorel, Taylorism, the experience of 1914, and the social Catholic concept of justice for the worker, the Duce that Valois imagined in 1925–1926 was decidedly left-fascist in orientation and creed. Articles in the Faisceau press continually described Italian fascism in this manner, emphasizing its syndico-corporatism and the benefits accorded to the worker. In an article lauding the creation of the General Confederation of Industry and the fascist corporations, Antoine Fouroux enthusiastically proclaimed that Italian class collaboration crushed the anarchistic practices of liberal capitalism and revolutionary dissent on the left, giving security to the worker and putting the middle-class to work for the nation. The suppression of communism institutionalized discipline, used by the state to safeguard the rights and interest of all sectors of Italian society, but did not necessitate the death of social justice.[68]

Such a plan was in fact present in early Italian fascist doctrine, embodied in the person of Edmondo Rossoni, the ex-revolutionary syndicalist who headed the Fascist Labour Confederation until his dismissal in 1928. The Faisceau press continually lauded Rossoni as an exemplar of the fascist economic ideal, the prophet of class collaboration and corporative organization.[69] Valois and Arthuys met the fascist union leader in Italy in September 1926, and were suitably impressed, hatching plans for an international conference on fascism and corporatism, to be held in Geneva.[70] Like the Faisceau, Rossoni argued against both socialism and liberalism, writing that

66 CHEVS/V 21, Tract – Georges Valois, *La Politique économique et sociale du Faisceau*, pp. 25, 55–60; Georges Valois, *Le Fascisme*, pp. 7–9, 14, 17–19.

67 Jacques Boulanger, 'L'Oeuvre de fascisme en Italie', *NS*, 12 April 1926; CHEVS/V 21, Tract – Georges Valois, *La Politique économique et sociale du Faisceau*, p. 22.

68 Antoine Fouroux, 'La Doctrine économique et sociale du fascisme', *NS*, 7 May 1925; Antoine Fouroux, 'La Révolution fasciste', *NS*, 22 Oct. 1925.

69 See, for example, 'Les Ouvriers Italiens contre la lutte des classes', *NS*, 4 June 1925; 'La Révolution fasciste est antilibérale', *NS*, 22 Oct. 1925.

70 Douglas, pp. 127–128.

capitalism must serve the nation rather than the individual. Collaboration replaced class conflict under fascism, with the bourgeoisie striving to perfect the means of production, while the state ensured a just repartition of benefits. Hierarchy would be maintained, but both workers and owners served the general interest by rationally increasing production: 'Syndicalism must be above all a productive discipline, that is to say a rational system of organization which serves to perfect production, and in the final analysis increases the wealth of a community, naturally delineated by a nation's borders'. The corporatist system ensured that all of the necessary preconditions – social justice, productivism, the nation above the individual, discipline and hierarchy – existed in the new economic order.[71]

But there existed a clear difference between theoretical fascism and its practical application, a reality unrecognized by Valois and his colleagues. The revolutionary ideals of the original movement, which envisioned the construction of a modern and revolutionary state, predominated before Mussolini seized power in 1925, uniting a conglomeration of syndicalists, Corradinian nationalists, squadristi, and fascist technocrats like Giuseppe Bottai. The economic corollary of such a plan, Rossoni's syndico-corporatism, came into conflict with political necessity following the seizure of power.[72] Mussolini, for whom the conquest of power was the primary goal of the fascist enterprise, sided with big business, prepared to offer its support in return for the suppression of labour's revolutionary potential.

In the economic sphere, the ambitions of Rossoni, Bianchi and other syndico-corporatists were thus squelched in the same manner as those of the violent and revolutionary squadristi, which were disbanded in 1923. The Duce compromised the position of the syndicalist faction that November, when the Palazzo Chigi agreement recognized Confindustria as the sole representative of Italian industry while rejecting the fascist unions. Dependent upon the state for any real power, the aspirations of Rossoni and his confreres to establish their proposed new economic order were moribund by 1924.[73] Alfredo Rocco became the ultimate architect of the fascist labour charter, breaking the unions while concurrently implementing regulations that favoured ownership. Syndico-corporatism never came to fruition; the corporations created throughout the thirties, administrative tools rather than representatives of *interclassimo*, bore no resemblance to those proposed by Rossoni.[74]

Valois eventually recognized the souring of the fascist revolution in Italy. During their visit in September 1926, he and Arthuys openly argued with Italian experts (including Arnaldo Mussolini, Benito's brother) about the future direction of the

---

71    Francesco Perfetti (ed.), *Il Sindicalismo Fascista: Vol. 1, Dalle Origini dello Stato Corporativo (1919–1930)* (Rome, 1988), pp. 270–281, 283.

72    See Roland Sarti, 'Fascist Modernization in Italy: Traditional or Revolutionary?', *American Historical Review* 75 (1970): 1029–1045; R.J.B. Bosworth, *Mussolini* (London, 2002), pp. 223–225.

73    Martin Blinkhorn, *Mussolini and Fascist Italy* (New York, 1984), pp. 18–19, 23–24; Alistair Hamilton, *The Appeal of Fascism* (London, 1971), p. 40; Maier, pp. 428–429, 547, 553, 557–577.

74    Blinkhorn, p. 24, De Felice, pp. 33–37. For an account of the failure of economic modernization in fascist Italy, see Roland Sarti, 'Fascist Modernization in Italy: Traditional or Revolutionary?'.

Italian economy.[75] Undeterred, Valois hosted an international meeting that November in Paris supporting the formation of a fascist Latin Bloc, where speakers included the aging futurist Filippo Marinetti. Yet Marinetti was no fascist reactionary, and Valois's break with the Duce came the following year. Disapproving of hesitation over the implementation of an elected corporative chamber, the Faisceau leader publicly criticized Italian fascism for the first time in July 1927. That December, the floodgates opened, with Valois clamoring that 'Italy made a revolution in order to solve the problem, but it seems now to have been halted by the intervention of reactionary elements'. By 1928, Valois jettisoned fascist terminology altogether, adopting the *République syndicale*, a construct wholly immersed in scientific management and the primacy of technology.[76]

## IV

Plans for a new economic order were equally common within the ranks of the Croix de Feu/Parti social français. Their leadership and rank and file prioritized commerce and industry, unsurprising for a group whose membership drew heavily upon workers, employees, and businessmen. The case of the CDF/PSF was quite distinct from that of the Faisceau, however. Where Faisceau leaders and membership unanimously accepted Valois's economic theories as authoritative, proponents of scientific management openly challenged La Rocque's social Catholicism with Taylorism and *planisme*. Far from being unified, CDF/PSF leaders and the rank and file devised plans of a diametrically opposite nature for the new economic order.

These positions corresponded to conflicting views concerning the nature and direction of the interwar French economy, present since the heyday of the Faisceau. New business leaders in emergent modern sectors, such as oil, electricity, and automotive production argued for the acceptance of rationalization and the principles of scientific management, along Taylorist and Fordist lines, as the guiding organizational principles for postwar industry. Industrialists like Louis Renault sought to make French products more competitive on the world market in this way, ending the protectionist mentality that had long been present in both government and the national popular consciousness. Such views encountered serious resistance from most French employers and bankers, who saw no reason to change the beneficial status quo. This reaction reflected the French economic landscape of the period, in which the small family firm and the medium-sized concern predominated. In 1931, for example, 80.32 per cent of French firms employed five or fewer workers, while only 6.44 per cent employed greater than twenty, trends apparent throughout the interwar period.[77]

Some progress was made after November 1929 by the government of André Tardieu, a technocrat who had served as High Commissioner to the United States during the Great War. Attracted by Fordism and Taylorism, which he believed to be

75 Douglas, pp. 127–128.
76 'La Réunion de 2 Novembre à Cirque du Paris', *NS*, 7 Nov. 1926; Georges Valois, 'Les Nouvelles formes de l'état et de la vie économique et sociale', *NS*, 17 July 1927; Georges Valois, 'Un Nouvel age de l'humanité', *NS*, 31 Dec. 1927.
77 Sauvy, p. 486.

the keys to American industrial dynamism, Tardieu was subsequently named Minister of Public Works in Poincaré's 1926 administration. By 1929, he became a dedicated St.-Simonian, convinced that state intervention could engender a complete modernization of the French economy. In tandem with Under-Secretary for the National Economy André François-Poncet, an avid proponent of industrial modernization, Tardieu initiated an overhaul of the French hydroelectric industry. But his government fell in December 1930, a victim of the Oustric banking scandal, in which leading politicians were accused of influence-peddling. Mere months later the depression buffeted France for the first time, providing additional justification for the avoidance of industrial rationalization. The first in France to incorporate Taylorist and Fordist ideas in the 1920s, production in the automobile sector plummeted, and Tardieu's successors turned to deflation and protectionism in an effort to soften the fiscal blow.[78]

Only in the mid-1930s did the technocrats of Valois's time, obsessed with the implantation of Taylorism and Fordism on French soil, gain a certain measure of popularity in business and political circles. Faced with the seeming failure of both unbridled capitalism and more conservative government policies, productivists shifted their emphasis, from the application of rational organization and Taylorist principles in French industry to a reform of state and society. Groups like Plans and the neo-socialists believed that the state should be run by administrative experts or managers: 'Political Engineers' in the words of Marcel Déat, a new St-Simonian ruling elite for modern times. A proliferation of economic plans appeared espousing such positions, rejecting liberalism and parliamentary government as a failure. To be sure, not all of the authors agreed on the specific *planiste* details, and some supposed modernizers remained closely linked to French traditions, specifically rejecting full-blown Americanization. Certain figures even attempted to bridge the two positions, proposing schemes at once in favour of more traditional modes of production and business organization, yet simultaneously recognizing the need for scientific management in the French economy. However, they failed to gain a substantial following. Rather, throughout the 1930s two distinct economic doctrines continued to clash, presaging a specifically French path to modernization that only came to fruition following the conclusion of World War Two. Neocapitalists such as Mercier or Tardieu, along with left-wing *planistes* like Belgian socialist Hendrik de Man and various members of the CGT, offered modern solutions that accepted the need for rationalization and technical progress. They proposed a national economic council to rule in place of parliament, and a syndico-corporative economy in much the same vein as that tendered by Valois and the Faisceau. According to the neocapitalists and *planistes*, high salaries and low prices would de-proletarianize the workers, making them consumers. This American-style arrangement was predicated upon the acceptance by the working class of hierarchy, discipline, and productivism. Taking the opposite approach, corporative theorists rejected a progressive and modernized economy in favour of tradition. Rather than Taylor and Ford, they continued to champion paternalistic French tradition and the small workshop as the model

---

78    Kuisel, *Capitalism and the State*, pp. 91–95; François Monnet, *Refaire la République* (Paris, 1993), pp. 138–139. On the effects of the depressioon upon even strident industrial modernizers, see Jackie Clarke, 'Imagined Productive Communities', pp. 347–349.

economic unit. This division was replicated within the CDF/PSF, with La Rocque and the traditionalist faction proffering a conservative social Catholic economy, while exponents of modern solutions voiced approval for neocapitalism.[79]

As in the Faisceau, representatives of modern concerns flourished within the ranks of the CDF/PSF. Pierre Milza has estimated that 25 per cent of the group's membership in mid-1934 came from the bourgeoisie and the elite cadres, as opposed to 16 per cent from the petit bourgeoisie. By October 1936, after the group's transformation into the parliamentary PSF, the representation of the former stood at 24 per cent, and remained above 20 per cent throughout the decade. These trends were equally apparent in the provinces, with managers and employees comprising 23.8 per cent of CDF/PSF membership in the Midi, 21 per cent in the Nord, 14.4 per cent in Vernon, 46 per cent in Prébendes, and approximately 20 per cent in the Rhône.[80] By 1938, 84 of the 202 members of the group's Comité directeur were drawn from engineering, industry, or banking, as were many of the group's parliamentary contingent. Two deputies – Fernand Robbe (Seine-et-Oise) and Jacques Bounin (Nice) – were engineers, Eugène Pebellier (Haute-Loire) was a graduate of the École des Mines, Marcel Deschaseux (Vosges) the director of the Compagnie des Thermes in Plombières, Paul Creyssel a lawyer specializing in political economy, and Charles Vallin a bank executive.[81] Ernest Mercier, La Rocque's employer in the late 1920s, was a dues-paying member until the summer of 1935, when his growing sympathy for the Soviet Union impelled the CDF/PSF to sever ties with him. Industrial magnate François de Wendel also displayed interest in the group, and in the early 1930s the CDF/PSF leadership attempted to

---

79    Klaus-Jürgen Müller, 'French Fascism and Modernization', *Journal of Contemporary History*, 11 (1976), p. 83; Fridenson, pp. 53–68; Kuisel, pp. X, 98–119; CHEVS/LR 60, Philippe Machefer, 'Le Parti social français et la petite entreprise', unpublished paper, 1981, pp. 12–15, Brun, pp. 69–78, 81, 117–130, 137–139. Jackie Clarke astutely points out that 'the ideological waters of the 1930s were rather more muddied'; clearly, not all *planistes* were either budding technocrats or die-hard conservatives. Yet her contention that such moderate figures represented the norm goes against the grain of existing scholarship. She is quite correct, however, to contend that Vichy proved every bit as interested in economic modernization as the movements discussed here. In 'Imagined Productive communities', pp. 345–357. On the specifically French path to economic modernity, see Richard Kuisel, *Seducing the French: The Dilemma of Americanization* (Berkeley, 1993); Kristin Ross, *Fast Cars, Clean Bodies: Decolonization and the Reordering of French Culture* (Cambridge, 1995), and Jackie Clarke, 'France, America, and the Metanarrative of Modernization: From Postwar Social Science to the New Culturalism', *Contemporary French and Francophone Studies* 8 (2004): 365–377.

80    Pierre Milza, *Fascisme français: Passé et présent* (Paris, 1987), p. 138; Machefer, 'Le Parti social français et la petite entreprise', p. 4.; Weng Ting-Lung, 'L'Historique et la doctrine du Parti social français', Thèse de droit, Université de Nice, 1971, pp. 104–106; Christine Jaubertho, 'Des Croix de Feu au Parti social français, la dérive vers la république', Mémoire de maîtrise, Université de Toulouse, 1993, p. 139; Sean Kennedy, *Reconciling France Against Democracy: The Croix de Feu and the Parti social français, 1927–1945* (Kingston and Montréal, 2007), p. 196; Passmore, p. 275.

81    Kennedy, p. 198.

curry the favour of André Tardieu.[82] Furthermore, the group viewed large industrial concerns such as Renault as primary targets for recruitment.[83]

Despite the abundant ties to heavy industry and commercial concerns within the ranks of the CDF/PSF, many within the group openly opposed modern industrial methods. Unlike Valois and his colleagues during the Faisceau years, group leader Colonel de la Rocque and like-minded members followed the tenets of social Catholic corporatism, envisioning the new order as a return to tradition, and utterly opposing Taylorism, Fordism, and state economic planning. To group sympathizer François Veuillot, La Rocque's proposed economy, termed the *profession organisée*, represented the views of the Catholic church as expressed in the papal encyclicals *Rerum Novarum* and *Quadragesimo Anno*, and the social Catholic doctrine of De Mun, La Tour du Pin, and the Semaines sociales des Catholiques de France.[84] La Rocque himself was suitably vague, writing in his 1934 book *Service public* that the *profession organisée* presented a corporative construct aimed at preventing the abuse of the working class while simultaneously defending the position of business owners. The state would be divided into different categories of producers, from diverse economic regions, which governed themselves on the local, regional, and national levels. Like La Tour du Pin, he rejected any political role for the corporations, in which hierarchy and collaboration replaced the current 'Bolshevik-republican' syndicalism of class conflict.[85] The main function of La Rocque's corporations was moral: The elimination of the frenzy for material gain in which rampant speculation and false materialism rather than the national interest held sway. In the *État social français*, La Rocque proclaimed, personal interest became subordinated to the general good. Thus the CDF/PSF leader enthusiastically adopted the social Catholicism which Valois left behind by 1923 as the basis for the group's proposed national economy.[86]

---

82    APP/Ba 1857, Excerpts from the Report of the Parliamentary Commission into the Events of 6 February 1934, pp. 1603–1604; Interview with Gilles de la Rocque and Jacques Nobecourt, June 1997; Jean-Noël Jeanneney, *François de Wendel en République: l'argent et le pouvoir, 1914–1940* (Paris, 1976), pp. 567–568.

83    F/7/13241, note of 18 June 1935; CHEVS/LR 38, 'Déclaration du Colonel de la Rocque, radiodiffusée le 24 Avril 1936'; 'Congrès régional du Sud-Ouest', *Flambeau du Sud-Ouest*, 22 May 1937; 'Notre activité', *L'Ouvrier libre*, 27 April 1937. This publication was the newspaper of the CDF/PSF worker. See also Philippe Rudaux, *Les Croix de Feu et le PSF* (Paris, 1967), p. 193.

84    Jacques Daujat, 'Chronique: Les Catholiques et la politique', *Orientations*, March–April 1936; François Veuillot, *La Rocque et son parti* (Paris, 1938), pp. 70/78. La Rocque's anti-capitalist and anti-rationalization both clearly betray the influence of La Tour du Pin and De Mun. See Elbow, pp. 69–79, 88–93; La Tour du Pin, pp. 22–24, 31–32, 37–41, 108–111, 117–120, 126. That the *profession organisée* was inspired by social Catholicism was plainly stated by Charles Vallin, who wrote that it derived from *l'école sociale Catholique* and papal encyclicals. See 'La Profession organisée et le corporatisme', *Petit journal*, 21 Jan. 1938.

85    La Rocque, 'Intérêts limités', *Le Flambeau*, 28 Nov. 1936. La Rocque's use of *profession organisée*, a term originated by La Tour du Pin, should not be confused with its meaning to 1930s technocrats, for whom it signified a planned, ultra-modern economy and society. See Brun, pp. 110–111.

86    Lt.-Colonel de la Rocque, *Service public* (Paris, 1934), pp. 141–145, 238–240.

Following La Rocque's lead, various members designed plans for the organization of the new economic order in the tradition of La Tour du Pin and De Mun. Despite proclamations in the group's program and elsewhere that the CDF/PSF *profession organisée* rejected corporatism, intended to separate their economic model from that of fascist Italy, the proposed economic bodies were indeed corporations. Yet unlike the Italian Ministry of Corporations under Giuseppe Bottai, and the model espoused by the Faisceau a decade earlier, CDF/PSF corporations were never envisioned as a political apparatus directed by the state.[87] Rather, the group imagined a model steeped in nineteenth-century social Catholicism, similar to that proposed by 1930s conservatives, such as the Institut d'études corporatives et sociales.[88] The syndicate was to be the basis of all economic activity, devoid of any political sentiment and dedicated to renewed worker-owner collaboration. A Conseil régional économique managed them, and the Conseil nationale économique coordinated the regional branches. All were to be self-regulating, directed by a state that acted solely as an arbitrator. Furthermore, unlike the Faisceau des corporations, the *Conseils* were not vehicles for industrial concentration, but merely represented French financial and economic interests, from artisans to industrialists.[89]

Traditionalists in the group believed the creation of a labour charter to be the necessary first step towards the establishment of the *profession organisée*. According to the CDF/PSF published program, the charter would establish and prepare collective contracts for each profession, operating tribunals to arbitrate conflicts between owners and workers. It would also regulate the length of the workday, establish paid holidays, a minimum wage, and social insurance and pension schemes.[90] Unlike the similar initiatives of the Popular Front, particularly the Matignon Accords, the CDF/PSF document proposed a ban on strikes and workplace dissent, the former permitted only when owners ignored contract arbitration rulings.[91] The latter would

---

87　On the corporative initiative in fascist Italy, see Alexander de Grand, *Italian Fascism: its Origins and Development* (Lincoln, 1989), pp. 79–82. The version implemented by Bottai and his successors existed as an economic parliament, tied to the state, with the active participation of government ministers under the authority of Mussolini himself.

88　Led by La Tour du Pin acolyte Maurice Bouvier-Ajam, the IECS argued from 1935 onwards in favour of social justice and class collaboration, frequently citing *Rerum Novarum* and *Quadragesimo Anno*. Like the CDF/PSF, they demanded self-regulating corporations, to determine production, prices, and wages, while instituting apprenticeship and social insurance programs. In this way, Bouvier-Ajam argued, liberalism ('qui condamne chacun à la lutte pour la vie') and leftist class-conflict could be circumvented by traditional French ideas. See Steven L. Kaplan, 'Un laboratoire de la doctrine corporatiste sous le régime de Vichy: l'Institut d'études corporatives et sociales', *Mouvement Sociale*, no. 195 (2001): 38–56.

89　André Maurois, 'Les Besoins de l'État moderne', *Le Flambeau*, June 1934; 'Pour le peuple, par le peuple', special supplement to *Le Flambeau*, 11 April 1936; *Le Parti social français: une mystique, un programme* (Paris, 1936), 19–21; Charles Vallin, 'La Profession organisée et le corporatisme', *Petit journal*, 21 Jan. 1938.

90　*Le Parti social français: une Mystique, un programme*, pp. 17–18, 21–22; AP/451/124 – 'Projet de décret-loi sur l'organisation professionnelle', 30 June 1938.

91　'A la vieille de la grève générale', *L'Ouvrier libre*, Dec. 1938; AP/451/117, 'Etudes sur la grève', *1er Congrès du groupe patronale*, 19–20 May 1939, 25–29; AP/451/117, 'Extraits du rapport de M. Pierre Forest sur le syndicalisme', from the Third PSF national

be effected through an eight-man 'Tribunel administratif des professions' (composed of government figures, legal advisors, and trade specialists), which enforced the final decision of an intersyndical conciliation committee if the owners and workers failed to reach an agreement.

No such social restrictions were placed upon owners, but they too were to be bound by economic restraints enforced by the state. Owners would be responsible for the reeducation of unemployed workers, the establishment of *caisses de compensation* to deliver pensions, social insurance payments (for illness, and work-related injury or death), and a family allowance to ensure that mothers stayed at home and raised large families in keeping with the group's pronatalist bent.[92] The corporation further cared for the worker and his family throughout his life, La Rocque told his audience at the first annual PSF national conference, from the first day in the factory through old age.[93] The group's information bulletin similarly reminded readers that any owner who did not meet this obligation betrayed both workers and the party itself, and that the penalty was a disciplinary committee hearing and possible expulsion from the group.[94]

Owners, commented Pierre Kula, the head of the CDF/PSF *Groupe patronale*, were to take an active interest in the welfare of their employees: 'They must banish scourge and anguish in workers' families; the impression of neglect.' Echoing sentiments expressed 50 years earlier by La Tour du Pin, Kula proposed the creation of a social Catholic economy, an established hierarchy in which each worker understood his role and acted with discipline, in return for the promise of fair treatment and the co-operation of ownership with labour. The worker, artisan, and owner would thus become conscious of their specific social roles, enabling them to 'work with pleasure'.[95]

Nor did the CDF/PSF conception of hierarchy in the workplace aim to disempower the worker on the job. A report on the 'Fonctions et droits respectifs du travail et du capital' referred to the standard business as a 'Société à participation mixte du travail et du capital', in which business viewed workers as co-owners rather than menial labourers.[96] La Rocque agreed, calling for the promotion of all sufficiently talented workers to higher positions for the good of the French economy, and telling a crowd at the Vélodrome d'Hiver in 1937 that the new economic elite included all who demonstrated an advanced aptitude, regardless of their background.[97] Traditionalists within the group firmly rejected the standard minimum wage, however. In its place, they proposed the *salaire réel*, sufficient to maintain a family and a home, but pegged

---

congress, 1 Dec. 1938. Forest decreed that strikes would be redundant in the new *État social français*, because the corporative system generously benefited both parties.

92    AP/451/124, 'Projet du décret-loi sur l'organisation professionnelle', 30 June 1938. For a discussion of CDF/PSF pronatalism, see chapter three.

93    'Le Discours de la Rocque', *Le Flambeau*, 26 Dec. 1936.

94    AP/451/101, *Bulletin d'information #83*, 28 July 1938.

95    AP/451/125, Pierre Kula, 'Contribution à l'étude de la profession organisée'. This argument was frequently repeated in CDF/PSF workers publications. See, for example, Jusot, 'Réconciliation sociale', *L'Ouvrier libre*, Feb. 1939.

96    AP/451/124, 'Fonctions et droits respectifs du travail et du capital', pp. 8–10.

97    *Petit journal*, 18 Dec., 1937. See also AP/451/102, Tract – *Le Parti social français: une mystique, un programme*, p. 15.

to the cost of living in each region, allowing the corporations (rather than the owner) to determine the necessary remuneration.[98]

Such attitudes reflected the traditionalist use of the small shop rather than modern heavy industry as their preferred economic model. This led the group in 1937 to establish a Confédération générale des commerçants, artisans et pétits industriels, affiliated with the PSF Bureau politique, to act as the foundation for the future defense of small businesses and craftsmen.[99] To La Rocque, the prosperity of France depended upon the stability of the artisan and shopkeeper: 'We all wish to preserve essential liberties, but we must understand that these freedoms, which enable French happiness and honour, are linked to the preservation of the modest shop, to small business and the artisanate'. The traditional practices of the artisan and shopkeeper, emphasizing apprenticeship and owner-worker collaboration, were destroyed by rationalization and standardization. Quantity had replaced quality of work, La Rocque complained, as French business slavishly copied American methods, rejecting pride in workmanship and Gallic tradition.[100]

The traditionalists frequently designated the artisan and shopkeeper as the true middle class, a sentiment which reflected both the preponderance of the small shop in France and the support for the group demonstrated by those in the traditional professions.[101] For the CDF/PSF this meant the skilled worker who owned a little house earned by the sweat of his labour, or the small manufacturer who directed his own workshop. The bourgeoisie were never seriously considered by the group, blamed for both the capitalist system and the decline of small business in France, which could not compete with the larger, richer trusts. In the words of one columnist writing in the *Volontaire 36*, the group's Lyon newspaper, the bourgeoisie would rediscover the 'basic qualities of the race' in the *État social français*, through the adoption of artisanal principles.[102]

In their defense of the workshop over the factory, the traditionalists actively sought to transform industry by infusing it with small-shop values. Lauding the continual contact between workers and owners in smaller concerns, and noting the respect shown by such *patrons* for their employees, in May 1939 the Commission

---

98     A. Langlade, 'Pouvoir d'achat', *Le Flambeau*, 13 June 1936; APP/Ba 1902, 'Les Croix de feu et la grève', 6 June 1936. See also AP/451/102, tract – *Le Parti social français: une mystique, un programme*, pp. 13–14.

99     CHEVS/LR 41, 'Instructions à donner aux Présidents de Fédération au sujet de la Confédération générale des commerçants, artisans et petits industriels'.

100     *Petit journal*, 26 June 1939; La Rocque, 'Achèvements', *Le Flambeau*, 18 Jan. 1936. This same argument appears in Pierre Murat, 'La France? ... Enfin une tradition et un idéal', *La France sera sauvée par le PSF* (Colour magazine/supplement to *Petit journal*), Oct. 1937. See also AP/451/117, 'Motion votée à la suite du rapport sur le commerce', 2 Dec. 1938.

101     Sauvy, p. 487.

102     *Volontaire 36*, 6 May 1938. See also CDLR, 'Classes moyennes', *Le Flambeau*, 20 March 1937; André Roche, 'Bourgeois, mon frère', *Flambeau de Sud-Ouest*, 3 July 1937. For criticism of bourgeois opportunism see: L. Cleri, 'Grandeur et misère des petites entreprises', *Le Flambeau*, 27 June 1936; Louis Recoules, 'Qualité', *Le Flambeau*, 11 Jan. 1936; AP/451/117, 'Extraits du rapport sur le commerce et l'industrie présenté par M. Eugene Pebellier, Député de la Haute Loire', 2 Dec. 1938.

d'études sociales of the PSF Groupe patronale urged medium and large concerns to adopt a similar pattern. As social benefactors to the worker, owners were instructed to frequently visit their businesses in order to establish a personal relationship with the employees. No longer a faceless demagogue, the CDF/PSF *patron* donated his time for meetings with workers and management, and provided the mandatory social assistance. The commission further decreed that mixed worker and management committees were to be established in each concern, to maintain standards and improve conditions in such areas as hygiene, apprenticeship, and leisure.[103]

The group's moral emphasis further extended to trade itself. The liberal economic system had failed, argued a 1938 group report on the *profession organisée*, revealing the dangers of unfettered free trade, which had led France into economic anarchy, leaving low salaries, high taxes, and decadence in its wake. In order to rebuild French prestige, businesses would become extensions of family and community, acting for collective rather than personal profit. Management would also be collective, with key decisions made by committees comprised of owners, managers, and workers delegates. Regional corporations set prices and salaries at acceptable levels, controlled the quality of the product, and trained labour in apprenticeship schools. Working with the government, the Conseil nationale économique ensured the good faith of business leaders and managers, fining corporations or removing corrupt and self-serving owners as necessary.[104] State control was to be severely limited, however. The Commission d'études sociales recommended self-regulation as the best corporative strategy, with the state as guarantor rather than executor of industrial ententes and regulations.[105]

Not surprisingly then, the group also vilified the capitalist system, blamed for both the misery of the French worker and the weakness of the nation's economy. 'Are we anti-capitalist?' asked Charles Vallin at a CDF/PSF meeting in Mortagne. His response betrayed a clear bias towards traditional values, particularly those of the artisanal class: 'Almost! We want to defend familial capital, that product of labour, slowly accumulated and increased through savings, which capitalism attacks, and which we must permit to be preserved and passed on.' The laissez-faire system proved necessary during the nineteenth century, having led to the technical and financial progress. But 'the remedy became poisonous', Vallin claimed, as free trade turned the world into an economic jungle where only the strong (those possessing sufficient

---

103    AP/451/117, Commission d'études sociales, 'Les Conditions de rencontre entre les syndicats ouvriers et patronaux', in *1er Congrès du groupe patronale*, May 1939, pp. 16–21. This argument was frequently repeated in the CDF/PSF press throughout the group's history. See for example 'Pour une action', *Le Flambeau*, Oct. 1931; 'Le Droit de remontrance et la marche des entreprises', *Temps nouveaux*, 5 Dec. 1936; François Derval, 'Critique et l'éloge du patronat', *l'Espoir Lorraine*, 20 March 1937.

104    AP/451/124, 'La Profession organisée', 25 April 1938.

105    AP/451/117, Commission d'études économiques, 'Le PSF et les ententes professionnelles' in *1er congrès du groupe patronale*, May 1939. Others argued for more extreme solutions. One group member called for the immediate suppression of all derelict or anonymous businesses and their owners, to be replaced by responsible men. See AP/451/124, Pierre d'Izarny Garafas, 'Etude sur un ordre économique nouveau', May 25, 1936. Report submitted by the author to CDF/PSF leadership.

capital) survived.[106] In his 1934 work *Service public*, La Rocque similarly referred to capitalism as irresponsible and parasitic, responsible for horrid working conditions, demoralized workers, and immoral materialism, as well as the Marxist menace – the reaction to its practices. Industry must be put to work for the nation, he wrote, and run according to the principle of discipline rather than covert banking interests.[107] Yet the group did not envision the destruction of capitalism pace Marxism. Rather liberalism itself was to be jettisoned, with the capitalist system simply modified, and infused with traditional morality.[108]

The CDF/PSF critique of capitalism also encompassed modern industrial doctrine and techniques. But rather than linking productivism and the depression, as did many of their conservative contemporaries, the traditionalists rejected its utility on moral grounds. Blaming industry for the deracination of the worker, recently torn from the natural surroundings of rural France, La Rocque claimed that the modern factory was as dangerous as alcoholism to the health of the labouring masses. Taylorism represented nothing more than misery and impoverishment for the worker, forced to endure unhygienic and back-breaking conditions. Higher wages and the eight-hour day, following the American example, were not viable solutions, because such initiatives merely papered over the growing gap between technical progress on one hand and moral or spiritual progress on the other. Echoing La Tour du Pin and De Mun, La Rocque claimed that the worker needed only a salary sufficient to raise a family and a healthy working environment, supplemented by protection from the whims of the financial oligarchy represented by large anonymous trusts. Man should not become a mere consumer as in America, he continued, for this aided the cause of parasitic monopolies and the cancer of intensified production which had led the world to the economic impasse of overproduction and depression.[109] La Rocque also rejected the American standard of living, which encouraged 'Malthusian individualism', while neglecting quality in favour of mass production and robotic factory workers:

> We will restrain everyone's appetites in keeping with the two-fold obligation to prosperity and children's safety. For the latter, we reject the introduction of mediocre, mass-produced food; we will instead provide the healthy and delightful nourishment of our soil. We wish to transform our country neither into an immense workshop full of robots, nor the standardized clientele of huge department stores.[110]

The CDF/PSF critique of modern production techniques, and especially their blatant anti-Americanism, echoed similar pronouncements made by right-wing opponents

---

106    *Volontaire de l'Ouest*, Oct. 1936.

107    La Rocque, *Service public*, pp. 139–140; CHEVS/LR 38, La Rocque speech in *Bulletin du liaison du mouvement Croix de Feu en Algérie*, 15 May 1938.

108    BN, Tract – *Le Parti social français devant les problèmes de l'heure*, pp. 37–40.

109    Such talk appears throughout La Rocque's oeuvre. See variously La Rocque, *Service public*, pp. 231–232; CHEVS/LR 38, 'Déclaration du Lt.-Colonel de la Rocque, radiodiffusée le 24 Avril 1936'; La Rocque, 'Ou vont les Croix de Feu?', *Le Mois*, Sept.–Oct. 1935. On the negative consequences of industrial labour and the emptying of the countryside, see Tract-Parti social français, *1er Congrès agricole* (Saint Brieuc, 1939), pp. 14–15.

110    *Volontaire 36*, 3 March 1939.

of technocracy throughout the 1930s. Various critics, most notably the journal *Ordre Nouveau*, derided American-style industrialization as tantamount to colonialism. Just as La Rocque berated French business for its lack of moral rectitude, editors Robert Aron and Arnaud Dandieu accused men like Ernest Mercier and André Tardieu of selling France's soul for material gain, idolizing Taylor and Ford while neglecting the duties of the Gallic *patronat*. In works like *Le Cancer américain* and *La Révolution necessaire*, they countered with social Catholic justice for the worker, 'an economy which serves man', akin to CDF/PSF demands for corporative co-operation between labour and ownership.[111]

Despite such rhetoric, however, Aron and Dandieu recognized the futility of merely returning to the past and erasing economic modernity. The CDF/PSF, on the other hand, joined their social Catholic and corporativist framework to a Barrèssian appeal on behalf of the family farm, idealizing preindustrial life and values. Various members decried the depopulation of the countryside, a phenomenon which they linked specifically to the preponderance of modern industry in France and governmental acquiescence in the elimination of the *paysan*. Although this stance seemed hopelessly outdated in the 1930s, such sentiments were shared by certain right-wing figures, notably André Tardieu and Henry Dorgères. Most commonly associated with technocracy during his years as Prime Minister after November 1929, Tardieu's rejection of laissez-faire economics instead stemmed from conservative beliefs. A staunch proponent of various technocratic ideas, including state-supported productivism, he proclaimed that the *paysan* could only be saved through agrarian modernization. This meant rural electrification and mechanized farming, stemming the exodus to the cities by providing employment and prosperity in the village.[112]

But this was not the rhetoric of La Rocque and the CDF/PSF traditionalists. Their arguments more closely resembled the doctrine of Dorgères and his Greenshirts, and Jacques le Roy Ladurie's Union des syndicats agricoles. Formed in response to the devastation effectuated by the depression in the countryside, Dorgères's Comités de défense paysanne proclaimed the moral and physical superiority of the French farmer. In the movement's newspaper *Haute les Fourches*, he wrote that the state had abandoned agriculture in favour of modern industrial production. Invoking similar arguments, the arch-conservative Ladurie demanded corporatism as the antidote to liberal capitalism, to preserve the vanishing agrarian way of life, a repository of French morality and greatness. Like the CDF/PSF, both placed the blame squarely on the Third Republic. As Dorgères candidly stated, his movement would 'throw the deputies in the outhouse'.[113]

---

111    Jean-Louis Loubet del Bayle, 'Une tentative de renouvellement de la pensée politique française', *Nouvelle Revue des Deux-Mondes* 5 (1975): 323–331; Marc Simard, 'Intellectuels, fascisme, et antimodernité dans la France des années trentes', *Vingtième Siècle* 18 (1988), pp. 63–65.

112    Monnet, pp. 149–151. Tardieu served as Minister of Agriculture in Pierre Laval's 1931 government.

113    Robert O. Paxton, *French Peasant Fascism: Henry Dorgères's Greenshirts and the Crisis of French Agriculture, 1929–1939* (Oxford, 1997), pp. 33–39, 55–64, 130–131. It is worth noting that Dorgères's speeches were frequently attended by the CDF/PSF Dispos,

Battered by the collapse of wheat and wine prices, worried about the exodus of tens of thousands from farms to cities each year, and frightened by the massive agrarian strike wave that greeted the 1936 election of Blum and the Popular Front, farmers responded positively to the rhetoric of the extreme-right. Given that fewer than 10 per cent of the CDF/PSF membership were rural denizens in 1936, it is unsurprising that La Rocque and his fellow traditionalists promoted their defense, proclaiming the virtues of agrarian life and promising them a place in the *État social français*. Clearly the countryside contained a vast reservoir of untapped potential support.[114] Thus CDF/PSF newspapers and tracts continuously stressed agrarian themes. To one author in the *Flambeau des Vosges*, machinism ravaged the countryside, emptying a multitude of French villages. The *paysan déraciné* and the local artisan had been lumped in with the working masses, breaking their ties to tradition and family. The PSF, he claimed, had but one solution to the problem: 'The machine must be suppressed'. The labourer should be returned to his human and Christian rhythm of life, looking as fondly upon his workplace as his ancestors gazed upon the family farm.[115]

According to the traditionalists, the *paysan* represented the unity of the French people, crucial to the national identity. To Gilles Marguerin, agricultural affairs columnist for the *Petit journal*, the French farmer was the guardian of the soil, the lifeblood of France: 'Journey through our countryside, enter the village cemetery. You will find few places where the pious living have not erected a monument in memory of those lost in the last battle, restoring an eternal unity'. The love of the earth represented a crucial component of the CDF/PSF spirit, he claimed, embodied by La Rocque and those members who understood 'the call of the soil'. Such Barrèssian imagery abounded in group newspapers, portraying rural life as pure and natural, in stark contrast to the factory and industrial *cité*. One example in the *Flambeau de Sud-Ouest* linked Catholicism and the countryside in a moral critique of technocracy:

> There are still some natural *paysans* in this country, peasants who in their souls, without devaluing the legitimate rights of progress, have remained integrally and profoundly attached to their native soil, and who wish that the bell which chimed to announce their baptism will also be the knell accompanying them into the hereafter.[116]

The CDF/PSF remedy for the woes of the French farmer resembled its prescription for the artisanate and shopkeeper: The *profession organisée*. The 'Marxist nationalization of agriculture' embodied by the Office de Blé of the Popular Front was to be avoided at

---

who provided security at Greenshirt meetings until the 1936 dispersion of the leagues by the Popular Front.

114   Sean Michael Kennedy, 'Reconciling the Nation Against Democracy: The Croix de Feu, the Parti social français and French Politics, 1927–1945', Ph.D. Dissertation, York University, 1998, pp. 181–182.

115   'Travail', *Flambeau des Vosges*, Feb. 1939.

116   Gilles Marguerin, 'Salut aux terres françaises', *Petit journal*, 2 Jan. 1939; Jean Desguerets, 'Esprit rural et esprit Croix de Feu', *Le Flambeau*, 12 Oct. 1935; CDLR, 'Aux agriculteurs', *Petit journal*, 19 Dec. 1937; Edouard Gourdet, 'La Terre nous parle', *Flambeau de Sud-Ouest*, 15 Jan. 1938.

all costs. Instead agricultural loans, at low rates, would finance a moratorium on rural debt, which the group blamed on governmental and industrial neglect of the farmer, refertilization of the soil, and improvements in tools and production. This *assurances paysannes* allowed farms to retain agricultural workers, stemming the exodus to the factories. The creation of a rural stock exchange and trade police further suppressed parasitic middlemen and trusts, while professional organizations stabilized the market and prices. Regional bodies also set price limits, raising wages to compete with industry, and administering *caisses de compensations* identical to their urban counterparts. Finally, a national agricultural council would create tariffs to protect the farmer until rural recovery was complete. These organizations were to be run by those who understood the needs of agriculture, the farmers themselves, rather than city-dwelling bureaucrats (termed 'the cosmopolitan intellectuals of the Hotel Matignon').[117]

The traditionalist vision of the new economic order plainly proposed a return to the past. Although various members of the faction claimed that their program did not reject economic modernity, the unceasing defense of artisans, shopkeepers, and farmers, and the 'French' way of life which these professions symbolized, paints a different picture. Hatred of Taylorism, disdain for scientific management, and professed anti-capitalism were a far cry from Valois's productivism. La Rocque and others of his ilk designed a corporatist system with the professed aim of halting 'harmful' progress. These plans represented more than utopian projections; they were put into action after the 1936 transformation of the group into the PSF in two distinct but related forms: The Syndicats professionnels français for workers, and a Groupe patronale directed at ownership.

## V

Much like Valois and the Faisceau, La Rocque and the CDF/PSF leadership believed that the implantation of a new economic order could begin even before the attainment of power. Once the worker and owner reconciled, adapted to the harmony and social Catholic virtue of the corporations, the support needed to establish the *État social français* would materialize. Thus beginning in the summer of 1936, the CDF/PSF

---

117    AP/451/82, Tract – 'Cultivateurs'; AP/451/102, Tract – *Le Paysan sauvera la France avec le PSF*, n.a., n.d., pp. 27–38; Tract – Parti social français, *1er Congrès agricole*, 16–17 Feb. 1939 (Saint-Brieuc, 1939), pp. 5–11, 16–19, 25–28, 45–47, 52, 60–62. Such sentiments directly presage the doctrine of the Vichy regime. See Robert O. Paxton, *Vichy France: Old Guard and New Order, 1940–1944* (New York, 1972), pp. 200–210; Richard F. Kuisel, 'Vichy et les origines de la planification économique (1940–1946)', *Mouvement social*, no. 98 (Janvier–Mars 1977), pp. 83–86. On the urban-rural dichotomy, see CDLR, 'Agriculteurs', *Le Flambeau*, 8 June 1935; A. Guérault, 'Sauvons la profession agricole', *Rénovation républicaine*, Aug. 1939; Pierre Lecerf, 'Avec nous, le paysannerie', *Le Flambeau*, 24 April 1937. Others attempted to counter the 'false' image of the big city prevalent among rural denizens, that the lights and glamour were worth the abandonment of the *pays natal*. Urban leisure pursuits and jobs were unhealthy while farm life, unblemished by modern industry, was far more hygienic: 'One frequently sees poor young girls, pale and thin, returning from the city to die on the family farm'. See 'La Terre et vos enfants', *Volonté Bretonne*, 5 Dec. 1938.

sponsored initiatives aimed at re-educating the worker and owner, and creating patriotic economic cadres dedicated to social justice. Yet La Rocque's indoctrination process was quite different from Valois's. As a productivist, the Faisceau leader eagerly promoted rational organization by immediately gathering ownership and labour under the same roof in the Faisceau des corporations. La Rocque, by contrast, ignored the gospel of production, in favour of altering economic attitudes, and therefore formed two groups – the Confédération des syndicats professionnels français in June 1936 for the worker and the Groupe patronale in March 1939 for ownership (technicians were never considered, in keeping with his anti-Taylorism), to convert both sides to the group's economic doctrine. Various members referred to these initiatives as CDF/PSF syndicalism.

The group minimized the adherence of workers to the program of corporatism and reconciliation, the segment of society whose support was crucial to the success of the new order by virtue of their growing demographic predominance. La Rocque and his colleagues thus presented their syndicalism as an alternative to the doctrine and program of the CGT.[118] This tactic also arose in response to the events of May and June 1936. The election that summer of the socialist-led Popular Front government precipitated wildcat strikes and factory occupations on a hitherto unimagined scale: 12,142 strikes involving 1.8 million workers in June alone, dwarfing the previous annual high of 1.3 million during the postwar wave of 1920. Throughout France factories were occupied, including 1144 in the Nord and all major works in Le Havre by 9 June.[119] One day later came the Matignon agreements, the inaugural act of Léon Blum as France's first socialist Premier, in which ownership ceded the 40-hour week, paid vacations, mandatory collective bargaining, and a pay raise which averaged 12 per cent.[120]

As scandalized as the *patronat* were, the horrified French right believed that socialism had triumphed in France. Describing the scene a posteriori, fascist intellectual Robert Brasillach wrote that 'the windows were covered with red flags, decorated with hammers and sickles, stars, or even condescending tricolor badges'.[121] During the wildcat strikes an irate Louis Marin, leader of the conservative Fédération républicaine, asked if France was still ruled by a 'legal regime', shouting that 'there was ... an

---

118 Although Philippe Machefer claims that La Rocque and his coevals were influenced by the ideas of Auguste Detoeuf, who advocated an apolitical conception of syndico-corporatism within a profession organisée, such a link is rather tenuous. La Rocque never referred to Detoeuf in his writings, and while the CDF/PSF leader would most certainly have agreed with his emphasis on social stability and the preservation of the French farm, there was a technocratic edge to the neo-liberal's writing that was incompatible with traditionalist doctrine. An advocate of industrial concentration and productivism, and the director-general of the mechanical engineering firm Thomson-Houston, Detoeuf was no defender of the artisinal economy. See CHEVS/LR 60, Philippe Machefer, 'Le Parti sociale français et la petite enterprise', unpublished paper, 1981. For an analysis of Detoeuf's neo-liberal and productivist beliefs, see Kuisel, *Capitalism and the State*, pp. 105–106.

119 Julian Jackson, *The Popular Front in France: Defending Democracy, 1934–1938* (Cambridge, 1990), pp. 85–88.

120 Maurice Larkin, *France Since the Popular Front* (Oxford, 1988), p. 55.

121 Robert Brasillach, *Une Génération dans l'orage* (Paris, 1968), p. 160.

unheard of moral damage; brutal force reigns over justice and law'.[122] La Rocque and the CDF/PSF agreed wholeheartedly. The front page of *Le Flambeau* on 20 June 1936 painted an apocalyptic picture of the new government and its partisans: 'In the city a sort of terror spread. Packs of youths – unknown, anonymous agitators – ordered store closings and the evacuation of construction sites. The police were nowhere to be found. Everywhere the red flag has replaced the *tricolore.*'[123] To La Rocque the choice was clear: Either convert the worker and begin construction of the new economic order at once, or face the implementation of a Marxist regime in France.

This situation differed remarkably from the one facing Valois and the Faisceau in the mid-1920s. The failure of postwar strike action led to the predominance of Léon Jouhaux and the reformist faction within the weakened CGT, leaving only the communist CGTU, whose members abandoned their colleagues after 1921, to pursue a revolutionary agenda throughout the decade. Worse still for the left, the scission at Tours in 1920, precipitated by the refusal of Blum and his minority to follow Maurice Thorez into the Soviet camp and accept Moscow's conditions for participation in the Third International, left the socialist party in tatters. During the Faisceau years, Blum attempted to rebuild the *vieille maison*, compromising with the Cartel des Gauches and presenting little threat to the stability of the Republic. Support for the communists, excluded as they were from governing coalitions, was slight when compared to that of their German brethren. Although he frequently warned readers of *Nouveau Siècle* about the dangers of the communist 'horde', Valois's adoption of the American worker-as-consumer model was motivated by the gospel of production rather than an imminent threat from the left.

The CDF/PSF, by contrast, needed French non-agrarian labour, which represented 38.3 per cent of the working population in 1936, in order to enact the *État social français.*[124] Although far less prevalent within the ranks of the group, comprising approximately 20 per cent of their supporters from 1936 onwards, these numbers were still significant, not least because the implementation of the new state necessitated the elimination of leftist rivals.[125] The CDF/PSF thus developed detailed plans for a new syndicalism to compete with both the CGT and the Popular Front, responding to the events of May and June 1936 by trying to wean the French working class away from the left.[126]

First and foremost, these proposals aimed to add a unique CDF/PSF brand of syndicalism to the corporative structure of the *État social français*. According to Pierre Forest, the group expert on syndicalism and labour, patriotism provided the first condition of working-class unity. The worker who received a fair share from the owner at the urging of the state and corporation possessed a stake in the nation. Hence social justice was predicated upon social order, opposing internationalism and the colonization of labour by communists and the CGT in favour of a *syndicalisme nouveau*. The notion of class war only succeeded where the immiseration of the

122   Louis Marin quoted in William D. Irvine, *French Conservatism in Crisis: The Republican Federation of France in the 1930s* (Baton Rouge, 1979), pp. 85–86.
123   'Des CDF a une action politique', *Le Flambeau*, 20 June 1936.
124   Larkin, p. 3.
125   Weng Ting-Lung, pp. 304–306.
126   CHEVS/LR 60, Machefer, 'Le Parti social français et la petite entreprise', p. 4.

worker remained unchecked, a problem easily resolved by the implementation of the *profession organisée*.[127]

In keeping with the social Catholic corporative system adopted by the traditionalist faction, each syndicate included representatives of ownership and labour, replacing the CGPF and the CGT with the doctrine of social reconciliation. They were to become cells 'with the goal of defending the common interests of [their] adherents', derived from the original Christian spirit that equated the notion of work with that of brotherhood, antithetical to the inhumanity of modern enterprise and its technical evolution. The syndical association of workers within the *profession organisée* would organize the technical instruction of labour, administer *caisses de compensation*, and elevate the status of the worker.[128]

Much like the Faisceau, the CDF/PSF also rejected the use of syndicates for political ends, claiming that such partisan aims were incompatible with the truly French syndicalism of Proudhon and Auguste Keufer, the positivist and anti-communist proponent of compromise within the CGT.[129] The group viewed revolutionary syndicalism as misguided because it adopted goals at odds with the professed desire to better the life of the worker. Writing in the *Liberté du Maine*, Michel Doumange called Jouhaux's organization 'a political party disguised as a trade union', whose aim was nothing less than the communist revolution in France, and whose leader served Moscow. Anti-national and anti-patriotic, the CGT faced dissolution under the *État social français*. Forest himself concluded that their support base was illusory: The worker voted for the correct factory representative because the union delegate stood next to him.[130]

A CDF/PSF syndical organization, called the Syndicats professionnels français (SPF), appeared in June 1936 in response to the perceived engagement of the CGT in the massive strike action that culminated in the Matignon agreements. La Rocque claimed that although he had personally founded the group, they were given complete freedom: As a CDF/PSF syndical organization, they were expected to be above politics, in direct contrast to the CGT. 'La Rocque is the father of the SPF', he told a crowd at the third PSF national congress in December 1938, 'but they are mature children. The [PSF] Federation Presidents have nothing to do with them'.[131] Yet La Rocque's position vis-à-vis the SPF was far from neutral. The socialist newspaper *Le Populaire* reproduced a group circular in September 1938 which proclaimed that

---

127  *Petit journal*, 4 April 1938; AP/451/102, Pierre Forest, *Le Parti social français et le syndicalisme: Rapport présenté au 2e congrès national du Parti social français* (Lyon, 1937), pp. 10/13/15; 'Union des classes', *Flambeau de Sud-Ouest*, 17 July 1937.

128  Pierre Forest, *Le Parti social français et le syndicalisme: Rapport présenté au 2e congrès national du Parti social français* (Lyon, 1937), pp. 10/13/15.

129  In March 1936, the reformist CGT and communist CGTU reunited as part of the Popular Front initiative in France.

130  Michel Domange, 'Du profession au politique', *Liberté du Maine*, Dec. 1938 (2e quinzaine); Pierre Forest, 'Syndicalisme professionnel', *Volonté Bretonne*, 5 Feb. 1939. See also AP/451/102, 'Fiche – Le Syndicalisme', April 1939; AP/451/102, Pierre Forest, 'Le Parti social français et le syndicalisme: Rapport présenté au 2e congrès national du Parti social français', Lyon, Dec. 1937, pp. 1–5, 20–22, 32–33, 42–45.

131  AP/451/117, 'Rapport Forest, intervention de la Rocque'.

Roger Vitrac, the SPF secretary-general, answered to La Rocque, a verdict shared by the Sureté de France.[132] Nor were these opinions unsubstantiated. Vitrac sat on the CDF/PSF Comité financiere, authored a regular column appearing in a variety of group newspapers, and wrote to La Rocque of the 'devotion' extended to the leader by all members of the SPF Bureau confédéral.[133] Finally, Jean Mermoz, La Rocque's good friend and right-hand man, belonged to the SPF aeronautique and often received praise in their numerous publications.[134]

The organization acted as the focal point of CDF/PSF labour recruitment activities. Like Valois's and La Rocque's corporations, the SPF included a local, regional, and national organization, with elected delegates at each level representing the interests of ownership and labour. Yet unlike the Faisceau des corporations, they succeeded in attracting a fair percentage of the French working-class. By June 15, 1936 the SPF claimed 2,000 cells throughout France, and one million members three years later. At their 1938 congress, Vitrac further stated that 41.9 per cent of all factory delegates were SPF in orientation. The *Petit journal* itself claimed that in the January 1939 factory elections, the SPF sponsored over one-third of the successful candidates, only ten fewer than the CGT. Although such numbers were artificially inflated, the new organization clearly achieved some success. SPF affiliates appeared across the country, from Paris, Lyon, and Lille to Marseilles, Alger, Montpelier, Mulhouse, and Bordeaux, in a wide variety of industries grouped into 16 regional bodies, each with its own press, service de placement, and collective contracts.[135]

Despite the anti-leftist slant within the union, and its success in attracting a segment of French labour, the SPF did not exclusively fight the CGT and CFTC. Like the Faisceau des corporations, it was to be the basis for the realization of the *profession organisée*, faithful to the principles of La Rocque's *Service public*. The union's goal echoed La Rocque and Kula's vision of class collaboration:

> Working with corresponding ownership syndicates to get to the heart of the matter – the proper means to guarantee a man, through his labour, living conditions corresponding to his potential, his professional abilities, his familial function in society ... to protect the profession and insure the defense of the material and moral interests of intellectual and manual labour.[136]

---

132   Jean-Maurice Herrmann, 'Les Syndicats professionnels français ne sont qu'un instrument politique', *Le Populaire*, 29 Sept. 1938; 4 MZ/67 (Archives Départementales des Yvelines), Chemise SPF.

133   CHEVS/LR 21, 'Comité Financier, séance du 17 Novembre 1938; CHEVS/LR 20 I R. Vitrac to La Rocque, 28 Oct. 1937.

134   *SPF de l'aéronautique*, Jan. 1937; CHEVS/LR 14 IV 2, 'Mermoz', 1 Aug. 1937. It is thus difficult to agree with Philippe Machefer's dictum that the SPF was merely 'inspired' by the CDF/PSF. See 'Les Syndicats professionnels français (1936–1939), *Mouvement sociale*, no. 119, Avril–Juin 1982, pp. 91–94.

135   CHEVS/LR 14 IV 2, 'SPF', 15 June 1937; 'Chez Renault', *SPF*, 15 Aug. 1938; 'Discours du Wisshaupt', *Automobile*, Mar. 1939; Pierre Forest, 'Les Travailleurs indiquent', *Petit journal*, 24 Jan. 1939; AP/451/125. Tract – 'CSPF: Travailleurs français, syndiquez-vous', undated [1936?]; *SPF de l'aéronautique*, Jan. 1937; *Banque et crédit*, May 1937.

136   AP/451/102, 'Fiche – Le Syndicalisme'.

Working in tandem with ownership, the SPF studied various economic problems and designed solutions, ensuring professional organization and effort on the regional and national levels. In keeping with La Rocque's defense of the artisanate, they also defended the French worker's family and implemented an apprenticeship system. Once put into place, Forest stated, this scheme aimed to destroy the communist *virus politique* which had infected labour through the CGT and communist party, a domination clearly demonstrated by the actions of May 1936.[137]

True to the traditionalist faction's dictum that French economic success required the collaboration of labour and ownership, the SPF embraced corporatism as the solution to the estrangement of the worker under the capitalist system. Echoing La Rocque, they lauded the corporations of the ancien regime, in which worker and owner toiled side-by-side, in constant personal contact. SPF leaders blamed industrial concentration for the alienation of labour, as it forced the worker to emigrate to a strange city where he slaved in an anonymous factory, chained to a machine and rejected when no longer of use. Owners exploited him, ignoring his need for proper housing, and denied him a wage sufficient to support them.[138]

This system could only be reversed by the suppression of trusts and monopolies, and the creation of professional ententes to regulate work. These contracts would be state-sanctioned, fixing working conditions and salaries. But as Armand Millot, secretary of the SPF Transport union, made clear, the syndicates bore no grudge against the owners, despite their past flagrant abuse of the worker: 'We do not consider our bosses as enemies, who must be cut down to size through pitiless struggle. We will co-operate in an intelligent manner, and not become loudmouths, making unreasonable protests which come to nothing because of their exaggeration.' The SPF defended working-class liberty 'to the last drop of blood', claimed Millot, but within predefined limits imposed by hierarchy, authority, and discipline.[139]

As such rhetoric clearly demonstrates, far from siding with labour, SPF leaders like Millot made few substantial demands. On the issue of wages, the SPF militants' handbook derided the concept of an equal salary for all workers accomplishing the same tasks in a given industry. In its place, the author proposed a *salaire sociale* for the married, contingent upon the size of the worker's family, and a *salaire économique* for the bachelor. Each consisted of the minimum needed to create a home, in material and moral comfort, continually adjusted to the cost of living. Where Valois and the Faisceau championed the worker as consumer, granted a high salary in return for the acceptance of rationalization, the SPF tied wages directly to labour productivity, the piece-work system of the artisanal workshop. Furthermore, where Valois's state constantly consulted the national corporations, acting as the final arbiter in cases of irreconcilable

---

137 Pierre Forest, 'La Confédération des syndicats professionnels français', *Petit journal*, 23 Dec. 1937.

138 AP/451/125, Tract – 'CSPF: Travailleurs français, syndiquez-vous', pp. 8–9, 13–15.

139 CHEVS/LR 14 IV 2, 'CSPF Cahier du militant', June 1939, pp. 50–57; Armand Millot, 'Nos idées, nos buts', *Les Professionnels de la S.T.A.*, April 1937.

differences between ownership and workers, the SPF handbook rejected all political intervention, arguing that syndical supervision sufficed to settle disputes.[140]

Following the CDF/PSF lead, the SPF prohibited strikes and rejected the 40-hour week. Examples of workers toiling ceaselessly above and beyond the legal limit abounded in SPF publications. In a 1936 article entitled 'Son de cloche', a group of workers at the M.J. Rooy typewriter workshop in Paris, presented with the sorry state of the company's finances, go behind the government's back and work 48 hours a week (the pre-Matignon norm) to save the factory. The paper condemned CGT workers for their non-participation, ending the article with the words 'Stakhanovism? Non! Collaboration!'[141] The SPF aeronautics newspaper also lambasted the forty-hour week and paid holidays, arguing that they resulted in a higher cost of living and a lessening of national productive capacity. Much more necessary, insisted the SPF handbook, were apprenticeship and professional orientation in schools. Worker re-education, the elimination of 'abusive' foreign labour, and a family allowance allowing women to remain in the home were deemed sufficient to complete the elimination of unemployment and recovery of the economy.[142]

The establishment of the *profession organisée* involved the co-operation of owners as well as workers, and consequently the CDF/PSF formed a Groupe patronale (GP) in March 1939 to mobilize ownership. Conceived as the basis for the new economic order alongside the SPF, the new association was most notable for its formation of an *idéologie du patronat*.[143] Like the SPF, the GP embodied the economic doctrine of the traditionalists, espousing corporatism and the defense of the artisanate while rejecting Taylorism. Under the guidance of Pierre Kula and Louis Escande the association amassed delegates from twenty-six industries, of which only eight represented heavy industry (chemicals, gas, electricity, and similarly large concerns), while twelve were artisanal in nature (small business, hairdressers, and clothing, for example).[144]

The closing resolutions of their first congress in May 1939 reveal a doctrine complementary to the wishes of La Rocque. The delegates passed motions in favour of the *profession organisée* and SPF-style syndicalism, supporting the amelioration of the state of the French working family, and the introduction of social peace and reconciliation into the economy. Escande, director of the group's Commission d'organisation et de propagande, championed a corporatist structure for the new economy, including local, regional, and national delegates, headed by a Comité

140   CHEVS/LR 14 IV 2, 'CSPF Cahier du militant', June 1939, pp. 26–29, 39–45; AP/451/125, tract – 'CSPF: Travailleurs français, syndiquez-vous', 16–18.

141   'Son de cloche', *L'Informateur du Syndicats professionnels français des industries chimiques et branches connexes*, Dec. 1936. The term Stakhanovism refers to a Soviet coal miner who broke production records, the authorities claimed, through Herculean effort and dedication to the communist cause.

142   A. Mahoux, 'La Danger des grèves', *CSPF de l'aéronautique*, Jan. 1937; CHEVS/LR 14 IV 2, 'CSPF Cahier du militant', June 1939, pp. 11–13, 15, 17–19; CHEVS/LR 20 K, 'Discours de clôture du 2me Congrès national de la CSPF, prononcé par Roger Vitrac.

143   Nobecourt, *Le colonel de la Rocque 1885–1946, ou les pièges du nationalisme chrétien* (Paris, 1996), p. 658.

144   'Réunion du 20 Mars au P.J.', March 1939.

directeur. Each owner would belong to the Chambre syndicale professionnelle in his industry, and a Chambre syndicale régionale which grouped his profession with analogous ones. The latter tackled labour issues, such as the application of laws and work regulations, and the negotiation of collective contracts. The national syndicate resolved larger technical questions, allocated resources and materials, and administered trade policies.[145]

Three permanent commissions were established to organize this transition, for social and economic studies, and organization/propaganda. Escande also called for the formation of Syndicats professionnels patronaux, composed of delegates from the Chambres syndicaux, to produce employers driven by *l'esprit social*, working alongside the SPF. These syndicates functioned as documentation centres, gathering statistical information about imports, exports, production, unemployment, and resources within the profession. In keeping with La Rocque's anti-Taylorist bent, they also kept a watchful eye on technical progress and its effects on the market.[146]

To Escande, this system guaranteed economic stability under the *État social français* while simultaneously providing representation on a national and regional basis. The GP itself symbolized *l'organisation professionnelle preparatoire*, foreshadowing economic regionalization by preparing personnel and adjusting business practices.[147] As such, both the SPF and GP represent the first attempts at actualizing the doctrine of La Rocque and the traditionalists, the means to enact the corporativization of the French economy. Their doctrines and concerns mirror those of La Rocque and Kula: Owner-worker reconciliation, the construction of a corporatist society, the defense of the artisanate and middle-class values, and non-Taylorist socio-economic organization. Production was a major concern, and neither the SPF nor the GP believed that economic modernity could be fully reversed, but both strove to restore the social Catholic order championed by La Rocque while combating the Marxist threat. Others within the group were not so convinced, however, and sought a progressive third way between liberal capitalism and Marxism, which they believed more appropriate to the industrial age.

## VI

Despite the clear bias towards La Tour du Pin-style corporatism and the defense of the artisanal class displayed by La Rocque, the GP, and other traditionalists within the CDF/PSF, a more modern stream of thought prevailed. Representative of forward-looking professions such as engineering and heavy industry, these progressive voices envisioned a new economic order similar to that proposed by Valois and the Faisceau,

---

145  AP/451/117, 'Patrons et professions', in *1er Congrès du Groupe patronale*, pp. 8–10. For a more technical version of this plan, with slightly different terminology, see AP/451/124, 'Charte patronale'.

146  AP/451/117, 'Patrons et professions', 'Rapport de la Commission d'organisation et de propagande' and 'Résolution de clôture', in *1er Congrès du Groupe patronale*, pp. 10–12, 64–68, 79.

147  AP/451/125, 'Réunion du 20 Mars au P.J.', March 1939; AP/451/124, 'Charte patronale'.

based upon the theories of Henry Ford and Frederick Taylor rather than De Mun or La Tour du Pin. Rejecting corporatist solutions that defended artisans and small business, these modernists regarded the transformation of the owner into a progress-minded industrialist as the key to prosperity within the *État social français*. Espousing *planisme* and technocracy, both of which were incompatible with La Rocque's social Catholic economic doctrine, they openly challenged traditionalists within the group.

Conflict first materialized in summer 1935, in what became known as the *Affaire des Maréchaux*, which resulted in the departure of a group of Volontaires nationaux disillusioned with the CDF/PSF's perceived lack of action or concrete plans, a dearth they blamed squarely on La Rocque. Included among the dissidents were Bertrand de Maud'huy and Pierre Pucheu, both of whom later joined Jacques Doriot's Parti populaire français and (in the case of Pucheu) the Vichy regime, and Claude Popelin, a rising young star of the 1930s extreme-right. Their resignation followed La Rocque's refusal to accept their plan, largely economic in nature, for the CDF/PSF state.[148]

La Rocque held faithfully to social Catholic corporatism, emphasizing co-operation, reconciliation, and the defense of the artisan, shopkeeper, and farmer against rationalization. Pucheu and Maudhuy, in contrast, found their inspiration in the Plan of July 9, 1934, the manifesto of a group of reform-minded syndicalists from across the political spectrum. Led by author Jules Romains, and including prominent members of technocratic organizations like X-Crise, the signatories argued for the replacement of liberal capitalism with a self-conscious economy, in which the state functioned as arbiter. True, social service and the joy of creation transcended the profit motive, yet production remained the primary goal. Maudhuy, who had participated in the drafting of Romains's initiative, increased its technocratic bent in the plan of the *maréchaux*, arguing for state control over the economy and the leadership of government-appointed experts in all commercial matters.[149] Published in *La République* on Sept. 21, 1935, the plan rejected La Rocque's tenet that the worker needed only a salary sufficient to raise a family, opting instead for a proto-American system in which the purchase power of the worker would be steadily raised and a maximum work week of 48 hours, instituted in order to end overproduction and high unemployment. National planning would thus replace laissez-faire liberalism, a new *économie organisée* in which the primary emphasis would clearly be placed upon heavy industry.[150]

---

148  The Volontaires nationaux was the section of the CDF/PSF reserved for members too young to have fought in the Great War. That the split was due to conflicting socio-economic doctrines was made clear by Pucheu in Bertrand de Jouvenel, 'Scission chez les Croix de Feu', *Vu*, 17 July 1935.

149  Despite the assertion of La Rocque's biographer Jacques Nobecourt that 'between *Service public* and the document of the *maréchaux* the words could be identical and the differences minimal', the division between the two sides is quite apparent. In Nobecourt, pp. 350–355. This view is also advanced by Sean Kennedy, who writes that the traditionalist and modern factions 'were certainly in keeping with one another', in Kennedy, 'Reconciling the Nation', p. 73. See also Philippe Machefer, *Ligues et fascismes en France* (Paris, 1974), p. 23. On the Plan de 9 juillet, see Brun, pp. 38–39; Kuisel, *Capitalism and the State*, pp. 100–101.

150  'Plan des volontaires nationaux qui ont quitté le mouvement', *La République*, 21 Sept. 1935. Various right-wing luminaries, including Bertrand de Jouvenel, Georges Suarez,

Nor were the *maréchaux* alone in their espousal of *planisme*, for economic plans were omnipresent in 1930s France. Although many simply poured old wine into new bottles, echoing past ideas without adding any novel element, *planistes* entered high-level government posts during the course of the decade, and organizations as diverse as the CGT, the CFTC, the neo-liberals, and various socialists and radicals in Léon Blum's Popular Front ministry formulated comprehensive versions.[151] Yet the majority of the newcomers adopted the Fordist and Taylorist mantle, long discarded by the movers and shakers of French industry like the Comité des Forges and the CGPF. Chief among them was X-Crise, the initiative of Gérard Bordet and André Loizillon, two young graduates of the École Polytechnique who favoured an *économie dirigée* as the solution to the depression in France. Founded in 1931, their group was quickly joined by *Plans*, a productivist journal which sold 5,000 copies per issue while lauding the Soviet five-year plan. By the mid-1930s, *Nouveaux Cahiers*, the newspaper edited by Auguste Deteouf, ex-member of the Redressement français and head of the Thomson-Houston engineering firm, proved equally popular with budding *dirigistes*.[152] Both right and left quickly followed suit. In November 1933 Marcel Déat and 30 neo-socialist deputies abandoned Blum and the SFIO over the issue of economic planning. Meanwhile, on the extreme-right, Jacques Doriot's Parti Populaire Français provided a haven for modernizers, attracting Bertrand de Jouvenel, Pierre Dominique, and Robert Loustau, along with CDF/PSF rebels Pucheu and de Maud'huy.[153]

Whatever their political beliefs, the planners shared a common program, influenced by the St-Simonian ethos: 'In place of the government of men, the administration of things.' They strongly believed that liberal capitalism had failed, the victim of depression and decadence. Only large-scale structural reform could salvage the French economy, involving management from above, directed by the state and syndico-corporatist organizations. Where liberalism preached the virtues of the free-market, and Marxism emphasized class conflict, *planistes* argued in favour of class collaboration in the service of industry: The maximization of human and technical effort to greatly increase production targets, with a modern and technocratic bent. In the words of leading *planiste* Sammy Beracha: 'Rationalization consists of the scientific organization of labour, the standardization of both materials and products, the simplification of procedures, as well as improvements in transport methods and sales'. To Beracha and others, such an agenda could only be achieved through national and regional economic bodies, combining workers, technicians,

---

and Pierre Drieu la Rochelle contributed regularly to this publication, which was edited by Pierre Dominique and Émile Roche.

151   Kuisel, *Capitalism and the State*, p. 98. For a comprehensive overview of various plans proposed throughout the decade, see chapter four of the same work. It should be noted, however, that CGT planning all but disappeared in 1936, a victim of the reunification with the communist CGTU, which disapproved of such an agenda.

152   Brun, pp. 31–55, 69–73; Richard Kuisel, *Ernest Mercier: French Technocrat*, pp. 138–139.

153   Kuisel, *Capitalism and the State*, p. 113; Brun, pp. 212–214.

and ownership in an *assemblée technique*, similar to the corporations proposed by Valois and the Faisceau.[154]

Given its popularity across the political spectrum during the 1930s, it is no surprise that *planisme* emerged within the CDF/PSF, despite clear opposition to any modernization of the French economy. Had not La Rocque and the traditionalists espoused corporatism, planners within the group argued, antiquated but nonetheless a socio-economic plan? But the CDF/PSF leader displayed little patience with economic planning. He lambasted the *planistes* for paying undue attention to economic matters at the expense of social issues: 'General anxiety has caused the proliferation of planning. Ask a "planner" to write a study on education, diplomacy, the art of war, music: He will talk about economics.'[155]

Certain corporatist tenets, such as the need for hierarchy and co-operation, were still present in the dissidents' plan. Nonetheless, by the time the group transformed itself into the Parti social français in the summer of 1936, the progressive faction completely severed any links to traditionalist doctrine. Members Luc Touron and Marcel Canat de Chizy followed the neocapitalist trend of the 1930s, rejecting corporatism in favour of technocracy. To the neocapitalists, the formation of large industrial combinations was seen as a necessary step towards economic prosperity. High wages and low prices alone could increase consumption. In exchange for his participation in scientifically managed production, the worker received job security, salary increases, less onerous work, and more leisure time along the lines of the emerging American model. Like Mercier or Tardieu, the modernist contingent of the CDF/PSF believed that Henry Ford provided the answer to the Marxist threat, and that small business, an antiquated concept, would inevitably give way to large integrated firms.[156]

The argument in favour of rationalization and the adoption of modern economic principles of trade and organization was fleshed out in a series of articles which appeared in the *Flambeau du Bourgogne* throughout 1937, written by engineer Luc Touron. To Touron, economic Darwinism rather than social Catholicism was the remedy for French business woes:

> The economic struggle continues daily between nations, or groups of nations, to satisfy the needs of their populations and to conquer world markets. The winning nations are those which have the freedom to develop their material and moral strength, the losers stagnate or disappear.

---

154   Kuisel, *Capitalism and the State*, pp. 98–99; Brun, pp. 82–86, 97 (Beracha quote), 118–119. Beracha was a contributor to Valois's post-Faisceau effort, the *Cahiers bleus*.

155   CHEVS/LR 43, La Rocque, 'Réconciliation sociale', *La France sera sauvée par le PSF*; La Rocque, 'Effort sociale', *Le Flambeau*, 5 Oct. 1935. For a similar argument, see Un Normalien, 'Nouvelle idole', *Le Flambeau*, Dec. 1934. For pro-*planiste* arguments within the CDF/PSF, see AP/451/125, 'Projet d'un discours sur le profession organisée', July 15, 1937; Jean-Pierre, 'Le 'Plan de travail' d'Henri de Man', *Le Flambeau*, 13 April, 1935; AP/451/125, 'Note sur le Profession organisée', n.a., n.d. (1937). *Planisme* also appears, in simplified form, in early newspaper articles. See, for example, 'Situation Économique', *Le Flambeau*, Jan. 1932.

156   Kuisel, *Capitalism and the State*, pp. 86–87, 89.

France would either encourage a highly modern and efficient economy, eliminating waste and maximizing production on a national level, or be swallowed by the competition and relegated to global second-class status. Production could only rise to necessary levels if the market and infrastructure – transportation capacity, for example – grew constantly, and capital served the national good. In order to obtain the maximum productive effort, economic liberty, the protection of property in all forms, and the rational organization of industry (including capital, labour, and resources) would need to be guaranteed by the state.[157] Although he paid lip service to La Rocque's theory of class collaboration and owner-worker reconciliation, Touron's message was clear: Modern economic realities demanded technocratic solutions. La Tour du Pin-style corporatism was both inefficient and unrealistic; a viable new economic order within the *État social français* above all depended upon technology and scientific management.

True, Touron declared, machinism robbed the worker of his initiative, skills, and sometimes his employment, condemning him to repetitive tasks, and weakening the artisanal class. Yet the traditionalist argument, that modern industry encouraged immorality, ignored the role played by rationalization in the progress of both the economy and humanity, and the truism that technical progress and production were a constant struggle. Far from enslaving the worker, the machine had liberated man from harsh labour, providing a safer working environment: 'driving impracticalities and dangers out of the factories, circulating air and light, allowing cleanliness and hygiene to prevail, and making work more joyous.' Nor could technology eradicate work, for men would always be required to operate the machines; by eliminating waste, it had merely reduced the workday and provided opportunities for greater leisure and higher wages.[158]

To prevent such excesses, Touron proposed a national economic plan, in which trade regulations and the distribution of materials would be preset, to co-ordinate the rationalization of the national economy, while simultaneously maintaining the independence of French business. High salaries and low prices would also be instituted to encourage increased consumption levels. In order to effectuate this transformation, owners and management would by necessity become specialists in the Taylorist mold, 'tied to professional selection, to studies of work schedules and overwork, factory hygiene, and fair wages'. Labour would also become specialized, emphasizing teamwork and specific professional skills.[159]

As a corollary to such measures, Touron emphasized mass production. He approvingly quoted Henry Ford, echoing the American liberal business ethic in complete opposition to La Rocque's corporatist mentality:

---

157   Luc Touron, 'L'Organisation politique de la production', *Flambeau du Bourgogne*, 14 March 1937.

158   Luc Touron, 'La Condition de l'ouvrier', *Flambeau de Bourgogne*, 15 Sept. 1937; Luc Touron, 'La Rationalisation et le progrès', *Flambeau de Bourgogne*, 1 May 1937.

159   Luc Touron, 'Qu'est-ce que la rationalisation', *Flambeau de Bourgogne*, 15 April 1937. Arguments for competency and specialization were not exclusive to Touron. See AP/451/124, anon., 'Fonctions et droits respectifs du travail et du capital'.

> We have built nothing for the pleasure of building. We have bought nothing for the pleasure of buying. We have manufactured nothing for the pleasure of manufacturing. All of our initiatives have always been undertaken in order to satisfy our clients and our employees.

The assembly-line method, involving the collaboration of all workers, technicians, and managers, would become the standard in France, as omnipresent in Michelin and Citroën as in American factories. Such production methods reduced prices and increased product availability, claimed Touron, and hence increased consumption and guaranteed prosperity.[160]

Like Touron, Marcel Canat presented a modern technocratic economic vision, in stark contrast to La Rocque's social Catholic corporatism. An engineer by trade, Canat was a columnist for the *Volontaire 36*, the CDF/PSF organ in Lyon.[161] Where Touron had been vague regarding details of the transformed economic state, Canat devised a complete blueprint for the future economic order. Like La Rocque, he argued for the creation of regional and national economic bodies to regulate French business. Yet unlike the CDF/PSF leader, the young engineer recognized the permanence and desirability of modern industrial organization and techniques.

To Canat, the basis for all economic organization were mixed *corps professionnels*, containing representatives of labour, technicians, management, and ownership, categories more applicable to heavy industry than the small workshop. Although their primary duties included the preparation of collective contracts and the arbitration of labour disputes, the Corps was also charged with regulating working conditions, fixing prices and quotas, organizing apprenticeship, and implementing social insurance. Class collaboration would be insured by the presence of an equal number of labour and ownership delegates, but Canat specifically rejected state monopolization along Italian fascist lines, arguing that true co-operation could not be achieved by coercion.[162] Unlike the corporate delegates proposed by the traditionalists, however, Canat's representatives, including the workers, were to be specialists in their fields, because modern rational organization demanded it. An improved education system increased the capacity of the worker, enabling him to adapt to new work environments by learning the required skills. Canat's worker was no automaton performing the same short and repetitive task at a machine for eight daily hours, but rather 'the colleagues of management and technical intelligence'.[163]

Above the Corps professionnels Canat placed the Conseils économiques régionaux (CER), directing the regional economy from above, and arbitrating commercial or labour disputes. The CER issued regional statistical reports and initiated studies of various local economic problems, legislating on a wide variety of issues, from pensions to commercial accords. Their role was to be strictly economic, replacing the CGT and Chambers of commerce and industry as the sole representative of the regional economic interest.[164] Atop this framework lay

---

160   Luc Touron, 'Notre économie politique', *Flambeau de Bourgogne*, 1 Nov. 1937.

161   Passmore, pp. 240, 272–273.

162   Canat, 'Les Corps professionnels', *Volontaire 36*, 14 May 1937; Canat, 'Syndicalisme', *Volontaire 36*, 30 April, 1937.

163   *Volontaire 36*, 18 March, 1938.

164   Canat, 'Les Conseils économiques régionaux', *Volontaire 36*, 7/14 Jan. 1938.

the Conseil nationale économique (CNE), protecting the rights of the worker while rationally organizing the French economy. The CNE approved and regulated all labour contracts and commercial accords, and initiated interprofessional and inter-regional ones on the national and international level. As a regulatory body, the CNE further ensured the equalization of supply and demand to deter overproduction and resulting unemployment, eliminated disputes over tariffs and prices, and organized a Comptoir nationale du Commerce éxtérieur to supervise international trade. The bridge between business and government, it guided and informed the adoption of trade and commerce policies, and consulted the state on all matters of production and distribution. Although the state had the power to impose its will should the need arise, Canat clearly leaned towards self-regulation for business. Composed of various corporate representatives, the CNE functioned as an economic parliament.[165]

That Canat considered the CNE to be primarily the tool of big business is most clearly seen in its proposed composition. Over half of the delegates were to be drawn from heavy industry and banking. Furthermore, eight of the 20 professional sections which he assigned to the CNE related to commerce or heavy industry, as opposed to five from agriculture, two for clothing, and two for the arts. In describing the role played by the CNE in the new order, Canat was even more specific, writing that the primary goals of the committee should be increased production and improved worker-owner relations, and placing special emphasis upon projects for industrial accords, production controls, and the trade balance.[166] The defense of small business and artisans was never discussed.

## VII

Professing themselves to be outside the Republic, both the Faisceau and the CDF/PSF demanded a radical reorganization of the nation and state that rejected liberalism, conservatism, and Marxism in equal measure. Their claims for a new economic order were no less bold, and both groups continually presented their plans as original, antithetical to the weak republican/capitalist system which had led France to the verge of economic collapse. Valois and his colleagues continually reminded *Nouveau Siècle* readers that they were the first fascist organization in France, that their economic alternative was fascist in nature, and hence quite novel. La Rocque and various CDF/PSF authors presented the *État social français* and the message of economic reconciliation as equally innovative, ideal solutions to French economic malaise. Yet their respective doctrines were surprisingly common, shared by many non-extreme-rightists who instead favoured the republican system of government, a rationally planned society, or a socialist/syndicalist state.

Such was the case of Valois, who by the mid-1920s found himself among the economic avant-garde, alongside industrialists and doctrinaires ranging from Léon Jouhaux to Louis Rénault, and from André François-Poncet to Ernest Mercier. The economic doctrine of the Faisceau was essentially that of its leader. Although

---

165    Canat, 'Le Conseil nationale économique et l'état social', *Volontaire 36*, 25 Feb. 1938.

166    Canat, 'Le Conseil national économique', *Volontaire 36*, 18 Feb. 1938.

broadened at times by Pierre Dumas, most group authors at best embellished Valois's thought, paraphrasing his work and citing his authority in economic matters. Like so many of his generation, his time in the trenches profoundly affected Valois. Entering the Great War as a convinced Maurrassian and advocate of social Catholicism, he quickly converted to technocracy. Despite the tinge of idealism present in his description of the fraternity and discipline during wartime, Valois believed that the trenches provided the blueprint for the society of the future, a crucial component of the *État combattant*. Thus the new economic order paralleled his perception of the organizational principles of the French army. Class collaboration replaced the rapport between officers and soldiers, but the structure and principles of the trenches, such as hierarchy and discipline, a highly organized and rational society, and the emphasis upon specialization remained unchanged. This schema provided the basis for Valois's entire postwar economic program, from the earliest rough outline of a syndico-corporatist society to the Faisceau des corporations, and he continually referred to the trenches as his inspiration. Where Jacques Arthuys and Philippe Barrès wrote of the *État combatant* as a continuation of the war in civil society, a strong France forged anew by the battle-hardened combatant, Valois spoke of a new economic war.[167] Eschewing the terminology of virility adopted by his confreres, he instead argued that the war generation demanded not armed struggle, but modern industrial techniques and an unceasing effort to ensure French economic predominance. The artisanal virtues of the small shop, championed in the *Cahiers du Cercle Proudhon*, were meaningless in a conflict waged according to the rules of mass production. It is therefore no coincidence that the postwar Valois championed the 'age of electricity', in which modern, concentrated industrial production ruled the day.

But there was an equally important secondary influence upon Valois's postwar thought, without which his wartime experiences could not have found their economic expression. In looking to the American industrial model, epitomized by Taylor's scientific management and Ford's rational organization, productivism became Valois's economic doctrine. This theme provided the constant thread throughout his career, developing from the primitive doctrine of the law of maximum effort in *L'Homme qui vient*, through the vague syndico-corporatism outlined in the postwar *L'Économie nouvelle*, and culminating in the organizational efforts of the Faisceau des corporations and plans for a new economic order. While he shared a concern for social justice with La Tour du Pin and De Mun, Valois was thoroughly impressed with modern capitalist production techniques, which he deemed both the economic realization of the trenches and the salvation of backwards French industry. His vision of the worker and owner mirrored those proposed by Jouhaux, Renault, and Mercier in France, and by Henry Ford in the United States: Maximum effort in minimum time for maximum benefit. High salaries and low prices encouraged consumption, gained the loyalty of the worker, and drove the *patron* continually to improve the means of production. Far from being fascist in nature, this system formed the basis of American economic success, and was enthusiastically adopted in France after the Second World War. As a member of the interwar minority advocating economic

---

167   On Barrès and Arthuys, see Chapter One.

modernization, Valois joined representatives of heavy industry, future deputies and financiers, and members of the CGT in the commercial avant-garde.

The key difference was that Valois, in keeping with his concept of the authoritarian state and the organic nation, expected production and effort to be in service of the collective rather than the individual. He opposed liberalism, because it encouraged laziness in the *patronat* and immiserated the worker, allowing communism and its ideology of class warfare to flourish, and served the law of profit rather than the nation. Yet even though his ends were anti-republican, completely opposed to the practices of laissez-faire capitalism, the means he proposed were quite common: The corporativist system of economic organization, adopted to ensure that the selfish *patronat* attended to the needs of the nation rather than the bottom line. Valois rejected the medieval corporations long championed by the French extreme-right, deeming them insufficient to meet the needs of a modern economy, instead favouring the new corporatism adopted by various industrialists in emergent modern sectors in postwar France, Italy, and Germany. His industrial organization, like those proposed by Germany's Hugo Stinnes, Italy's Edmondo Rossoni, and a variety of French technocrats, involved industrial concentration, the rational organization of production, and the specialization of labour.

It is thus difficult to accept Valois's dictum that his economy represented fascism. Various Faisceau members constantly referred to the economic 'revolution' taking place in Italy, the herald of a new European organization suitable for the age of electricity. Too late did they realize their error, that the Duce was no combination of Sorel, St-Simon, and Henry Ford, but an economic reactionary who gave free rein to Confindustria while squelching revolutionary sentiment in favour of the status quo. In his search for contemporaries, Valois might have instead looked to the boardrooms of the automotive, steel, and electricity industries, where men like Mercier and Renault agreed wholeheartedly with his Taylorist prescription for the stricken French economy.

Similarly to Valois, both the traditionalist and modernist factions of the CDF/PSF represented contemporary strains of economic thought. But unlike the Faisceau, the group divided concerning the character of the economy within the *État social français*. While the economic doctrine of the Faisceau reflected the tenets of their leader, La Rocque's ideas were frequently contested. Much like business and commerce in the interwar Republic, the CDF/PSF was clearly not of one mind regarding the form and content of the new economic order. The group found itself in this position because, as Kevin Passmore observes, they were populist in nature, attempting to bind together diverse social and economic elements within French society under its own banner, in order to attain power.[168] For the CDF/PSF ultimately desired the transformation of French state and society into the *État social français*, without which they had little reason for existence. Their situation thus differed from the one facing Valois and the Faisceau, who never attracted a membership large enough to produce competing interest groups.

Both Passmore and Klaus-Jürgen Müller claim that the CDF/PSF represented the interests of the emerging modern economic sectors, such as engineering and industry.[169]

---

168  Passmore, p. 210.
169  Müller, p. 89.

Yet La Rocque's discourse betrays a very different slant. For the traditionalists, the artisanal class and family firm were to be protected at all costs from large industrial concentration. La Rocque viciously attacked modern solutions such as Taylorism and the assembly-line model, while counter-proposing social Catholic corporatism, a system designed to protect workers' rights, owners' property, and the French farmer from the harmful effects of technical progress. In essence, the traditionalists wanted to turn back the clock to the era of the family farm, the village, and the supremacy of small business. Their solution to the failure of liberalism was to halt economic progress, and in many instances to dismantle its excessive features. Furthermore, traditionalist plans for an alternative syndicalism following the electoral victory of the Popular Front betray an interest in the potential support of the working class, and the belief that the CDF/PSF provided the only effective alternative to a socialist state. Where Valois, with the experience of the trenches fresh in his mind, was motivated by the Great War in constructing his ideal economy, the Marxist threat preoccupied La Rocque and the traditionalists a decade later. A mass-based political party by 1936, the CDF/PSF threw off the *combattant* mantle and embraced economic pragmatism. In order to implement the *État social français*, the group needed the support of French labour, the largest sector of the population in mid-1930s France.

Although artisans, farmers, and workers represented a significant portion of the CDF/PSF membership throughout the latter half of the decade, they by no means monopolized an organization that, at its 1938 height, contained up to one-and-a-half-million members. Given the belief among many industrialists that liberalism and the Republic had failed to protect the French economy, it is not surprising to find strains of modern economic sentiment within the CDF/PSF. If lower-middle class adherents hoped that the group would reverse their deteriorating social and economic status, businessmen viewed the CDF/PSF in an opposite light: As the anti-liberal and anti-protectionist vehicle through which a technocratic and rational economic order would triumph in France. Men such as Touron and Canat thus adopted positions in direct contrast to the La Tour du Pin-inspired corporatism of La Rocque and the traditionalists. Like Valois, they used the framework provided by corporatism, of national and regional regulating bodies, to create plans for a complete transformation of the French economy in which American methods would be used to bolster economic competitiveness. Much like Mercier or Renault, Touron, Canat, and the *maréchaux* represented the emerging economic modernism against which La Rocque and the traditionalists fought on behalf of the status quo.

# Chapter Three

# *La Politique du foyer*:
# The Role of Women and the Family
# in the National Community

In *Civilization without Sexes*, Mary Louise Roberts describes a 'dialectical effort to reconcile outdated domestic ideals with a changing social organization'. Although it seldom garnered front-page headlines, Roberts writes, the mobilization of women during the Great War as workers on the home front performing tasks previously exclusive to men created a postwar demand for an end to established gender roles. Previously women had been perceived as wives and mothers, cultivating the *foyer familial* in silence, but the experience of working life and the death of one-and-a-half million future husbands in battle permanently altered the face of both the French family and the workforce.[1]

To be sure, the 'woman' problem was hardly novel in postwar France. A plethora of fin-de-siècle commentators derided feminists and other 'unruly' females, whose very public demands challenged traditional gender roles. For most of the nineteenth century, the social archetype of the bourgeois wife and mother predominated. Men directed the public sphere, engaging in politics, business, and diplomacy, managing the nation's affairs and engendering prosperity. Only in the private sphere, principally the family home, did women gain a certain measure of control. However, the late century arrival of the *femme nouvelle*, whose demands for rights and modern behaviour challenged the gendered norm, and the subsequent female adoption of male roles during the Great War – primarily in the workforce – shattered the myth of 'separate spheres' so cherished by the nineteenth century middle class. By the 1920s, a growing number of women adopted 'masculine' modes of dress, seemingly abandoned strict moral codes in favour of overt sexuality, and remained a distinct presence in the factory or business concern.[2]

As a result, conservative elements anxious to return the 'weaker sex' to their maternal duties clashed with more progressive voices which argued for the expansion of career opportunities and political freedom for women. To the French right, and indeed their European counterparts, the omnipresence of working women, sexual freedom, and above all burgeoning feminist movements symbolized national decline in moral and

---

1    Mary Louis Roberts, *Civilization Without Sexes: Reconstructing Gender in Postwar France, 1917–1927* (Chicago, 1994), p. 11.

2    Ibid, pp. 7–9; Mary Louise Roberts, *Disruptive Acts: The New Woman in Fin-de-Siècle France* (Chicago, 2002), p. 6. For European gender expectations, see Victoria de Grazia, *How Fascism Ruled Women* (Berkeley, 1992), p. 6.

demographic terms. In sharp contrast to the virtuous housewife, the *femme moderne* threatened to reduce the male sex to a mere societal footnote, while undermining the sacred institutions of marriage and the family. In an era of declining birthrates, pronatalists further predicted catastrophic consequences, often likening the new woman to a traitor, intent upon subjecting France to German domination. By the nineteen-thirties, as Hitler's militarism cast a shadow over Western Europe, the government increasingly took the lead in reinforcing traditional gender roles and strengthening the family, although women continued to receive education and skills in increasing numbers.

In the midst of this maelstrom the Faisceau and the Croix de Feu/Parti social français forged their respective doctrines concerning gender and the family. Analogous to their debates about the new political order, various Faisceau views on the subject of women clashed. Certain members displayed a remarkably modern acceptance of their new-found roles as workers, while others adhered to the older stereotype of housewife and mother. Although group leader Georges Valois formulated a more cohesive position concerning the family, which the rank and file largely accepted, dissenting opinions remained. A basic contradiction resulted, in which progressive discourse flourished despite the presence of more conservative voices within the group.[3] Further clouding the issue was the fact that Valois, the leading figure in debates concerning all other aspects of the État Combattant, remained virtually silent on the question of gender.

Paradoxically, the Faisceau vision of the family owed much to traditional extreme right-wing thought. Valois's concept of the organic nation, in which each family was a living cell, echoed the discourse of prominent integral nationalists Maurice Barrès and Charles Maurras. Thus the same group which argued for increased opportunities for women adopted the opposite stance regarding the family: That it was the duty of all French adults to have children, so that the national body remained healthy. Adding even more confusion to the mix, many of the justifications adopted by the rank and file to bolster this view were geneticist in nature, corresponding to prevailing scientific theories of the day rather than specifically extreme-rightist solutions.

Despite their own authoritarian bent, the CDF/PSF were also remarkably mainstream concerning both gender and the family. Their rhetoric regarding women would not have been out of place in the conservative Republican Federation or a local peasant's league. Furthermore, their conception of the family and detailed plans for its revitalization were distinguished almost exclusively by pronatalist sentiments, a ubiquitous position in interwar France, where the Radical party and even the socialist Section française de l'Internationale ouvrière (SFIO) rallied to the defense of the family and French repopulation, and the communist party replaced its older ideal of the working woman with the *mater familias*.

---

3    This phrase is used in context only. Obviously the views expressed would not today be regarded as forward-looking. Yet in a country where women possessed no political or civil rights to speak of, and only gained the vote in 1945, the position of certain Faisceau members was quite progressive. They were not feminists, however, because they still adhered to the notion that many women preferred the life of a housewife and mother to the working-world, and encouraged them to remain in the home if possible. Yet in arguing for a full extension of freedoms to women, including the right to a career, they became aligned with the modern side in the growing debate over the role of women in society.

Thus neither the Faisceau nor the CDF/PSF ever adopted the methodology of systematic indoctrination practiced by Nazism or Italian fascism. To be sure, they deemed both women and the family crucial components of the reconstructed French nation, yet the chosen vehicle for their revitalization was not state-sponsored coercion. Neither group ever proposed a state policy for the severe repression of women or government intervention in family life as did both Mussolini and Hitler.[4] They never elaborated policies along the lines of the Italian fascist National Agency for Maternity and Infancy. In this regard, the CDF/PSF could have been the Radical party, for their proposals were variously implemented by the *Chambre Bleu-Horizon*, Pierre Laval, André Tardieu, and Édouard Daladier in his *Code de la famille*. Even the authoritarian Vichy regime, born in the aftermath of the French defeat of June 1940, broke no new ground regarding women and the family. For as Francine Muel-Dreyfus has observed, 'the vision of femininity and the sexual order mobilized by the National Revolution largely preexisted it', and Marshall Pétain's Secretariat of State for the Family and Health mainly utilized older models to recreate French gender relations.[5] Hence Faisceau and CDF/PSF plans for women and the family place the historian in an awkward position: Their ideas were commonly expressed in interwar France, while both groups were bastions of the extreme right.

# I

The role of women in the new nation and state was frequently discussed within the pages of *Nouveau Siècle* and the writings of various Faisceau members, but once again no clear consensus emerged. The newspaper's position seemed at times to be outright modern, yet certain members remained wedded to traditional and conservative thinking, arguing that a women's place was in the home, and that the family (as the cell of the nation) was above individual wants and needs. In their view, women were housewives and nothing more, fulfilling their national duty by having as many children as possible. Progressive elements within the group countered with the argument that their presence in the workplace represented an irreversible fact of modern life, and that the family must be re-defined to suit this new reality.

The Faisceau debate concerning the position of women in France unfolded at a time when increasing numbers of them called traditional gender roles into question, while

---

4     This is not to imply that the orders of the dictators were unconditionally obeyed. Their initiatives actually failed more often than they succeeded, and reality (that women needed to work in many instances) often forced both regimes to make concessions. But their intentions, to enforce women's natural maternal role, was clear. On fascist Italy and women, see Victoria De Grazia, chapters three and four, and Perry Wilson, 'Italy', in Kevin Passmore (ed.), *Women, Gender, and Fascism in Europe, 1919–1945* (New Brunswick, 2003). The Nazi case is detailed in Claudia Koonz, *Mothers in the Fatherland: Women, the Family, and Nazi Politics* (New York, 1987) and Kirsten Heinsohn, 'Germany', in Passmore, *Women, Gender, and Fascism in Europe*.

5     Francine Muel-Dreyfus, *Vichy and the Eternal Feminine: A Contribution to the Political Sociology of Gender* (Durham, 2001), p. 319. Miranda Pollard makes similar claims in *Reign of Virtue: Mobilizing Gender in Vichy France* (Chicago, 1998), pp. 123–124.

both the patriarchal elite and the man on the street demanded their re-enforcement. French legal and social practice traditionally followed the 1804 Napoleonic Code, which decreed females naturally inferior to men. Article 213 of the document admonished that 'the husband owes protection to his wife, the wife obedience to her husband', which in practice permitted male adultery, granted spousal control over a wife's finances, wages, and property, and prohibited women from bearing witness or exercising the right to vote. Lacking the intellectual or physical abilities necessary to participate in the public sphere (according to nineteenth century French men), they were consigned to a uniform existence as wives and mothers, dutifully remaining the bastions of moral rectitude. Although never as restrictive in practice, the code nonetheless provided a powerful restraint upon female empowerment. Only in 1879 with the proclamation of the Ferry education laws did women receive the tutelage necessary to engage in professional life, although they studied a uniquely feminine syllabus, weighted heavily towards the 'domestic arts' rather than classical languages or modern science.[6]

French public figures reacted with derision as each plank of the Napoleonic Code was progressively removed, beginning with the loosening of divorce laws in 1884. Unnerved by the recent defeat in the Franco-Prussian war, and the subsequent rout of the bourgeoisie during the Paris Commune, republicans voiced concerns over the simultaneous collapse of the gender order and French military might.[7] More conservative voices attributed the problem to liberal government, too weak to put women in their rightful place: the home. Authors like Maurice Barrès contrasted the impure feminist with the 'real woman', subservient and conscious of her limitations.[8] But despite the wishes of French males, women did not re-enter the domestic sphere. The coming of the Great War in 1914 emptied fields and factories across Europe, forcing the French government to legislate increased female employment in July 1916, and exclusively male professions became feminized as a result.[9] Calls to remove them from the workforce at war's end, from both government and business leaders, went unheeded and 36.6 per cent of French women continued to work in 1931; clearly, female employment was not a mere temporary expedient.[10]

Women's continued presence in the work force owed much to the postwar demographic imbalance produced by French casualties during the Great War. Following the armistice, parents feared that their daughters would be left impoverished due to the death of one-and-a-half million young men on the battlefields, worries which resulted in increased educational opportunities for girls, embodied in Minister of Education

---

6    Edward Berenson, *The Trial of Madame Caillaux* (Berkeley, 1992), pp. 105–113.

7    Ibid, pp. 114–115.

8    Roberts, *Disruptive Acts*, pp. 116–117. For Barrès's image of the perfect woman, virtuous and maternal, see *Colette Baudoche* (Paris, 1908).

9    James F. McMillan, *Housewife or Harlot: The Place of Women in French Society, 1870–1940* (New York, 1981), p. 12.

10    Karen Offen, 'Body Politics: Women, Work, and the Politics of Motherhood in France', in Gisela Bock and Pat Thane (eds), *Maternity and Gender Policies: Women and the Rise of the European Welfare States, 1880s–1950s* (London, 1991), p. 142.

Leon Bérard's 1924 standardization of schooling for both sexes.[11] Yet most French commentators, especially men, viewed women's 'usurption' of male social roles as improper. The hostility stretched across class boundaries, a phenomenon extending from the factory floor to the labour unions and management.[12] They faced equally harsh political restrictions. Not only were women unable to vote in France until 1945, but they were socialized to accept these realities from an early age. In addition, many of the vaunted educational reforms were incomplete at best. Thus in 1923, director of primary education Paul Lapie renewed Jules Ferry's dictum that girls were to spend twice as much time doing manual instruction as boys, which meant sewing, knitting, and crocheting, so that 'girls could learn to darn "as their mothers did"'. It is unsurprising that breast-feeding techniques appeared on school-leaving exams, along with cooking, cleaning and child care, a format unchanged until after the Second World War. Although it was acknowledged that women had to work in certain cases out of financial necessity, the only proposed careers open to those possessing a post-primary education were seamstress, shopkeeper, or teacher.[13] The message was clear: Even if a woman worked, she would still be expected to tend house.

Into this new conflict came the Faisceau with its sparring progressive and conservative factions. The more tolerant must have included *Nouveau Siècle* editor Jacques Roujon, for the front page of the party newspaper frequently trumpeted women's accomplishments around the world. Tennis champion Suzanne Lenglen received a front page splash in June 1926, shown *en pleine action* diving for the ball while excited fans leaned over the stadium railing in anticipation. A photograph of 'Mme. Brian-Garfield' at work in a hospital operating room adorned the front page on October 23, 1926, proudly proclaimed to be the first female surgeon ever to practice. Another front page photo, this time under the heading 'feminism', portrayed English member of parliament Margaret Bondfield presiding over the inaugural congress of female trade unions at Portsmouth. These pictures were neither offered as negative examples nor was there any derogatory remark or tone displayed. Women were simply cast as modern professionals at the top of their chosen fields.[14]

Progressive rhetoric was also present in Claude Aragonnès's weekly columns for and about women. Aragonnès, a female cousin of French philosopher Pierre Teilhard de Chardin, voiced approval of the new postwar woman, frankly stating that 'things have changed a bit since the days when a young girl had to wait in her chair to be invited to polka'.[15] That women worked was a fait accompli. Due to the gender disparity resulting from the human destruction of the Great War many girls could not even hope

11    Mary Louise Roberts, 'Rationalization, Vocational Guidance and the Reconstruction of Female Identity in Postwar France', *Proceedings of the Annual Meeting of the Western Society for French History*, 20 (1993), pp. 367–369.

12    Siân Reynolds, *France Between the Wars: Gender and Politics* (New York, 1996), pp. 106–107.

13    Linda L. Clark, *Schooling the Daughters of Marianne* (Albany, 1984), pp. 82–123.

14    'Mlle. Suzanne Lenglen, impériatrice du Tennis', *NS*, 14 June 1926; 'La Première femme chirurgien', *NS*, 23 Oct. 1926; 'Féminisme', *NS*, 14 Aug. 1926.

15    Aragonnès, 'La Choix d'une carrière (1)', *NS*, 6 July 1926. This quote displays a remarkable similarity to certain feminist observations. For example, in the feminist newspaper *Le Fronde*, which applauded that 'the time is gone when a young lady of a good

for marriage, and increasingly had to make do for themselves. In a discussion of the *Grand revue* inquiry into 'les Jeunes filles d'aujourd'hui', Aragonnès claimed that preventing women from exercising a profession was tantamount to an act of cruelty in a postwar France deprived of eligible bachelors due to the one-and-a-half million war dead. Such rhetoric in no way differed from the views expressed by parents of the day, fearing for the future of their daughters if they should be unable to marry.[16]

Her reasoning went beyond demography, however. For those women fortunate enough to find a husband, she argued, a few years of living on one's own provided a virtual apprenticeship in cooking, cleaning, and general household management. Thus the career woman actually made a better mother and wife. Furthermore, rather than condemning them to menial positions, Aragonnès argued that women should be trained in a wide array of fields, many previously exclusive to men. Echoing the sentiments of the vocational counselors, she insisted that rather than accepting secretarial or teaching positions, the best and brightest would be librarians, archivists, museum curators, work in public administration at the Ministry of Labour or Hygiene, and even in the League of Nations if they possessed a law degree or a Doctorate. Although she did not envision women managing male workers, she felt that the commercial professions should be opened to them. The new businesswomen became industrial designers or corporate secretaries, the latter contingent upon the knowledge of several languages and corporate law. Finally, although she was no feminist, arguing that women still preferred the married life of home and children, Aragonnès adopted the progressive (for 1926 France) position that married women should exercise their profession if their husband lost his job, providing much-needed financial security for the French family.[17]

Aragonnès's position is somewhat surprising, given the hostile reaction to female labour from across the contemporary political spectrum. For as James Macmillan notes, 'with the return of peace many employers began to preach the virtues of domesticity and sought to get rid of their women workers'. Postwar governments consistently tendered legislation designed to force women back into the *foyer*. Although a variety of commercial training programs catered to female labour, from the management-oriented École de haute enseignement commerciale to trade schools, few candidates ever entered prominent professions. Most remained in low-paying service-sector employment, as office workers or shopgirls, and if possible left these positions shortly after marriage.[18] That a member of the Faisceau supported a woman's right to a career is doubly surprising considering the limitations placed upon female labour in fascist Italy. Lionized by group members and leadership, Mussolini's regime tendered the 1927 Labour Charter, which reduced women's

---

family had only to know how to embroider, sing, dance, and play music'. Quoted in Roberts, 'Rationalization', p. 369.

16    Aragonnès, 'Les Jeunes filles d'aujourd'hui', *NS*, 11 May 1926. Nursing, pharmacy, and chemistry were also proposed as potential careers.

17    Ibid.

18    Macmillan, pp. 117–123, 158–162; Renate Bridenthal, Claudia Koonz, and Susan Stuard (eds), *Becoming Visible: Women in European History* (Boston, 1987), pp. 484–485.

wages to 50 per cent of the total earned by their male counterparts and denied female access to management or the free professions.[19]

Yet Aragonnès tendered an equally audacious proposal for female education, the necessary precursor to women's entrance into management and professional life. She rejected the stereotype of the female student as the *scandale de la bourgeoisie*, a black sheep of the family who lived the bohemian life. Better education neither created flappers nor encouraged feminism, she argued, but prepared a young woman for the necessary career choice. One quarter of university students were women, but most still enrolled in the faculties of letters and education, or gynecology and children's medicine, and thus chose jobs better suited to the female temperament and tastes.[20] Although reasoning that feminine studies differed from the masculine curriculum, emphasizing 'the feminine arts necessary for domestic life', Aragonnès insisted that women were to be intellectually prepared upon graduating.[21] No longer a mere appendage of their husband in the postwar world, they required a political and civic education. Furthermore, they were to be granted equal rights and protection under the law befitting their more independent status, and the option of entering politics in the *État Combattant*.[22]

Aragonnès reserved her highest praise for farm women, not only as wives and mothers but as business partners. Here she seemingly mirrored the rhetorical affectations of both Mussolini and Marshall Philippe Pétain, staunch supporters of rural females as an antidote to the decadent urban bourgeoisie, their sturdy frames capable of bearing children and tending the rugged farmhouse.[23] Yet her vision of the agrarian matriarch rejected the docility and obedience envisioned by Italian fascism and Vichy. Although farm wives were preoccupied with domestic duties and light work, and solely responsible for cooking and serving at mealtimes while the men worked in the fields, this was purely a consequence of the male position as the physically stronger sex. More than just a housewife, the agrarian woman comprised an integral part of the working farm. The farm needed specialized female labour, Aragonnès argued, easily trained through the École nationale féminine d'agriculture in Rennes and the Union pour l'enseignement agricole et horticole feminin.[24] Above and beyond cooking and raising children, women helped balance the books and ordered necessary goods, as sales, profits, and hiring presented too great a burden for the male head of the household to manage alone. As in many working class families,

19    Bridenthal et al, p. 509; De Grazia, pp. 166–174.

20    Aragonnès, 'Les Etudiantes', *NS*, 20 April 1926. For an account of the restrictions placed upon women's education, and the perception of female students as feminists, see Muel-Dreyfus, pp. 98–100, 165–170.

21    Aragonnès, 'Bachelières', *NS*, 5 Aug. 1926.

22    Aragonnès, 'Les Jeunes filles d'aujourd'hui', *NS*, 11 May 1926.

23    Various Italian leaders gave their staunch support to the Messaie Rurali (Rural Housewives) organization, and lauded rural women as perfect examples of feminine fascism. See Lesley Caldwell, '*Madri d'Italia*: Film and the Fascist Concern with Motherhood', in Zygmunt G. Baránski and Shirley W. Vinall (eds), *Women and Italy: Essays on Gender, Culture, and History* (New York, 1991), pp. 50–51. On Vichy's veneration of peasant life and farm women, see Pollard, pp. 15, 138–139.

24    Aragonnès, 'La Choix d'une carrière (2)', *NS*, 20 July 1926.

she claimed, the country wife organized the home, but also made crucial decisions concerning commercial operations.[25]

Although modern in tone, Aragonnès's writings nevertheless concluded that whatever else they could accomplish, women were always first and foremost mothers and housewives:

> If in the final analysis today's woman expands her knowledge and abilities, it must be done in the spirit of a more complete partnership with men. If her tasks increase, she must do her bit, but never forget the main thing: Her primary duty. Nature and common sense, and the unanimous opinion of husbands, demand that the housewife thinks of the family home first and foremost.[26]

The best career for a woman remained the *foyer familial*, as mother to her children. Yet Aragonnès's career girls were a far cry from Paul Lapie's students, who learned the art of keeping house and little else. Given the opposition in both government and society towards women's newfound roles, her views were benevolent in comparison despite her advocacy of family and motherhood.

Nor was she the only member of the Faisceau to adopt such a stance. Group labour expert Pierre Dumas recognized female industrial work as a permanent feature in the factory. With a negligible birthrate and the shroud of the million-and-a-half war dead hanging in the air, he argued, France was on the verge of becoming swamped by foreigners who increasingly buttressed the labour force. Acceptance of female workers effectively solved the shortage, while preserving the national character. Dumas recognized the changing role of women in modern France, writing that the corporatist Faisceau state would extend the rights and duties of working men to female labourers, adding that the male salary scale and level of respect would also be applied to them. Far from portraying them exclusively as guardians of the family home, he claimed that they had worked since time immemorial in France: had not the women now labouring in mechanized clothing factories once performed the same task by hand? Shopkeepers had always been aided by their wives, and secretaries had always been female, like most teachers after the turn of the century. Thus to Dumas it was only natural that women played a role within the nation equal to their stature at work. He invoked the example of delegations at the Faisceau's June 1926 Reims conference, which included female corporative representatives alongside their male counterparts, as indicative of this trend.[27]

Columnist Antoine Fouroux went even further, arguing that women had been forced into a form of corporate prostitution by capitalism, earning lower wages than foreign labourers. In answer to those who viewed a female presence in the workforce as immoral, Fouroux pointed to the hundreds of thousands of fathers and workers who had died on the battlefield, leaving paid labour as the sole viable option. State pensions for widows were deemed insufficient, and remarriage regarded as

---

25    Aragonnès, 'Paysans de chez nous', *NS*, 14 Sept, 1926.

26    Aragonnès, 'L'Activité féminine', *NS*, 23 March 1926.

27    Pierre Dumas, 'La Femme qui travaille doit prendre place dans nos organisations', *NS*, 11 July 1926.

impossible due to France's lop-sided demography. Soon, Fouroux warned, women would have to turn to old-fashioned prostitution in order to make ends meet.[28]

Despite the progressive bent displayed on the front page of the group newspaper and in many of its articles about women, certain elements within the Faisceau maintained a more conservative social position concerning gender. Although the group inaugurated a women's section in January 1926, the Faisceau Féminin, membership costs were prohibitively high, reducing its potential appeal. Hence women received a token role, primarily aiding male-dominated propaganda and fundraising initiatives. Jacques Arthuys admitted as much in January 1926, telling a Bordeaux crowd that their recruitment drives on behalf of the group constituted a fundamental duty, similar to the role played by female workers during the Great War. Valois and his colleagues rarely consulted members of the Faisceau Féminin, which had no active voice in the group's decision-making process. Their sole outlet was the irregular *Page de la famille* in the group's daily newspaper, which discussed cooking recipes and children's games rather than political or social issues.[29]

The rationale for this decision consistently appeared in the writing of the group's more traditional commentators, far removed from the qualified progressive statements issued by Aragonnès, Dumas, and Fouroux. The former denigrated women's new-found freedoms, attacking the ills of feminism and the moral indecency into which it propelled potential wives and mothers. They wished to turn back the clock to a time when being a woman was synonymous with remaining in the home and bearing children, the only natural and moral roles for the 'weaker sex'. While fleetingly lauding the fact that women had discovered careerism, *Nouveau Siècle* religious affairs columnist Gaetan Bernöville warned that feminism was a destructive social element. As it posed the question of women only in an individual sense, the belief placed personal pleasure and freedom above the needs of the nation, which were couched in collective and familial terms. 'If feminism is developed in the sense of individualism', he warned, 'it will lead to nothing less than the destruction of society'. A woman's sole vocation was that of mother, compatible with both Catholicism and the future of the French race.[30] Some writers justified these claims by questioning women's intelligence and abilities. Thus columnist Jeanne Loviton claimed that a female belonged in the home because tending house was her only natural talent.[31]

The loudest exponent within the group of traditional women's roles was Hubert Bourgin, the Faisceau expert on education and pedagogy. The conservative and traditionalist Bourgin rejected the notion of a modern schooling for women, positing that they should be trained as mothers alone. They had no use for masculine pedagogy, as it attempted to train national leaders and heads of families, and most

---

28    Antoine Fouroux, 'Salaire féminin vital ou prostitution?', *NS*, 27 Aug. 1925.

29    F/7/13209, note of 21 January 1926 from the Commissaire Spéciale de Bordeaux to the Directeur de la Sûreté Générale. On Faisceau Féminin membership dues, see Daniella Sarnoff, 'In the Cervix of the Nation: Women in French Fascism, 1919–1939', Ph.D. Diss., Boston College, 2001, pp. 30–32.

30    Gaetan Bernöville, 'Féminisme', *NS*, 31 July 1927.

31    Jeanne Loviton, 'L'Esprit féminin et l'esprit fasciste', *NS*, 21 Dec. 1925. For a similar argument, see Louis Masset, 'Vieilles filles', *NS*, 10 Jan. 1926.

women resumed domestic life upon graduation. Therefore the goal of the state's education program should be the training of an elite of mothers, and Bourgin called upon the state curriculum committee to regain 'the right path' in the education of young girls.[32] It is unsurprising that in later years he enthusiastically joined Vichy's education lobby, lauding the 1941 reforms instituted by Education Minister Jérome Carcopino, which mandated home economics as the primary field of study for women in an effort to force them back into the *foyer familial*.[33] Completely opposed to progressive voices within the Faisceau, Bourgin insisted upon a reassertion of male predominance in the classroom.

In sharp contrast to Aragonnès's more modern woman, Bourgin's vision of the second sex was quite sinister. As a Catholic ultra-moralist, he viewed women as innately corrupt, a feature only heightened through education. His typical woman resembled the biblical Eve, a figure directly contrasted with the virtuous mother:

> You are not the glamour girl who spends all my hard-earned cash. You are not the fashionable female who, armed with the most ludicrous intentions, has neither imagination beyond her mechanical reflexes nor any dream other than spending money on new, fake frivolous purchases. You are not the depraved, uncouth, scumbag party-girl ... You are not the idler seeking to alleviate boredom caused by the emptiness of your soul through vice or indiscretion. You are not the licentious hussy who entertains, disgusts, or frightens.[34]

Here he reacted to the postwar *garçonnes* immortalized in Victor Margueritte's million-selling 1922 novel. Like Bourgin's 'glamour girl', Margueritte's heroine adopts masculine habits and dress, displays a voracious sexual appetite, and wears bobbed hair, aspiring to nothing more than the latest fashions and the expenditure of vast amounts of money.[35] His antidote both recalls the conservative critique of the fin-de-siècle *femme nouvelle* and augurs the judgment leveled under the Vichy regime, of 'the childless coquette' who rejects her natural role as parent and spouse in favour of feminist individuality and silk stockings.[36] The truly virtuous woman remained at home, wholesome and healthy, while performing her supreme duty – maternity. Bourgin praised 'our grandmothers' as icons of womanhood, 'those modest women without ambitions or pretensions' who could run a household, clean and cook, and

---

32    Hubert Bourgin, 'Les Femmes savants, et les autres ...', *NS*, 10 Sept. 1926.
33    On Vichy's education laws, see Muel-Dreyfus, pp. 233–243 and Pollard, pp. 80–85. In 1942, Bourgin published *L'Éducation nationale*, a pamphlet designed to promote, among other things, a strictly gendered education.
34    Hubert Bourgin, *Les Pierres de la maison* (Paris, 1926), pp. 61–62.
35    Roberts, *Civilization Without Sexes*, chapter two.
36    Pollard, pp. 33–38; Muel-Dreyfus, p. 25. Vichy propaganda frequently contrasted the two images in an effort to convince women of their natural maternal role. Joshua Cole further notes the omnipresence of comparable arguments in the prewar era, quoting conservative commentator Georges Duherme, who uses language comparable to Bourgin's: 'The woman who wears a hat costing 30 Louis and who surrounds her neck with jewelry costing 1000 francs' is characterized as a 'monster' who abandons her children. In '"There Are Only Good Mothers": The Ideological Work of Women's Fertility in France Before World War I', *French Historical Studies* 19 (1996), pp. 668–669.

raise decent children. They performed this labour solely for the Motherland, like Joan of Arc or Saint-Geneviève.[37]

Bourgin reserved his greatest ire for feminists, those who appeared before parliamentary committees or marched in the streets demanding rights and work for women. He believed them to be funded by 'Jewish elements' and Soviet-Bolshevik in inspiration, and demanded their immediate dispersal. A woman was simply not capable of becoming an engineer, a doctor, or a lawyer, and should instead be forced to do her duty, defending the race against degeneration. The mother alone protected French blood and ancestral virtue in Bourgin's world-view, transmitting the national character and values to each successive generation. Thus the responsibility for the development of tomorrow's leaders depended upon female subservience.[38]

The ultimate expression of such gender differentiation appeared in the children's serial comic *Fanfan et Marinette*, which ran in late 1925 and early 1926 in *Nouveau Siècle*'s weekly *Page de la famille*. The title characters were both war orphans, whose fathers died heroically at the front, and the storyline contained numerous conservative moral messages. Although both Fanfan and Marinette were supposed to be children, the illustrator fashioned them as slightly smaller adults. Both dreamed of marrying and starting a family, a theme which emphasized proscribed gender roles. Fanfan writes to Marinette that 'when I am grown up, I will live in a house that I will build; there will be beautiful furniture inside and a gorgeous garden. And you will be my wife'. In addition to this traditional example of home and hearth, Marinette is portrayed as a virtuous housewife, folding Fanfan's clothes and leading them in prayer. The author fused such traditional discourse with the doctrine of the *combattant* – an exclusively male preserve. While Marinette tends the home, Fanfan continually alludes to his future as a soldier and communes with his father, 'who died a hero so that his little boy could live in a free country'. He is always accompanied by his faithful dog *poilu*, the term used to denote a soldier in the trenches. The lesson for children was clear: men fight to preserve France, while women act as housewives and mothers.[39]

It is somewhat ironic that a group which patterned itself so closely upon the doctrine and formation of Mussolini's Italy experienced such inner contention regarding the issue of women. While the Italian fascist revolution, in the words of Victoria de Grazia, 'fell back on the traditional authority of family and religion to enforce biologically determined roles as mother and caretakers', the majority of Faisceau writers accepted and actively promoted women's rights and freedoms despite the presence of traditionalist discourse within the group.[40] Even the staunchly conservative Bourgin adopted a gendered doctrine which echoed the papal encyclical *Casti Connubi* and a variety of Vichy propaganda initiatives far more than Mussolini's conception of the

---

37    Bourgin, *Les Pierres de la maison*, p. 65. That neither Joan of Arc nor Saint-Geneviève ever cooked or cleaned was never considered by Bourgin.

38    Ibid, pp. 68–71. On feminist conceptions of maternity and pronatalism, see Anna Cova, 'French Feminism and Maternity: Theories and Policies, 1890–1918', p. 128 and Karen Offen, 'Body Politics: Women, Work and the Politics of Motherhood in France, 1920–1950', in Bock and Thane, *Maternity and Gender Policies*.

39    See the installments from 20 December 1925–7 February 1926.

40    De Grazia, p. xi.

mother, who produced as many children as possible to buttress the Italian army in preparation for war.[41] This irony is furthered by the fact that the CDF/PSF, a group divided on almost every other major facet of their proposed nation and state, united in their conservative stance regarding women. To be sure, the occasional article praising 'modern' women appeared in their party press, but most of their writings on the subject agreed wholeheartedly with Bourgin: Women were predestined to be housewives and mothers, duties which they performed for the good of the nation.[42]

## II

In a recent overview of women and the French extreme right, Cheryl Koos and Daniella Sarnoff observe that 'the parliamentary left and right and extreme and fascist right anti-democratic leagues all agreed that more gendered order and family relations would guarantee the nation's well-being'.[43] Both republicans and their enemies alike extemporized about the ideal woman, a housewife who provided the nation with an abundance of children and tended to the orderly *foyer familial*. If a certain number had to enter the workforce out of financial necessity, primarily because they lacked a husband, such cases were to be exceptions rather than the rule. Yet there remained a crucial difference between republican and extreme right-wing or fascist gender discourse: Groups like the CDF/PSF placed the blame for the *femme moderne* squarely upon the Third Republic, perceived to be too weak to put the rowdy feminist or immoral *garçonne* in her place. Although women engaged in a variety of important activities for the extreme-rightist leagues, ranging from social service to propaganda, they were confined to 'feminine' duties, and rarely possessed any influence or leadership position. The CDF/PSF acted no differently, designating the family home as a woman's domain, where they performed their duty as housewives and mothers.[44]

Irrespective of where they cast the blame, male republicans and the extreme right alike shared identical concerns in the 1930s, because female emancipation proceeded apace despite the coming of the depression to France and its fiscal consequences. If fewer women found employment in the industrial sector, many benefited from increased educational opportunities, constituting 50 per cent of post-primary students and over 30 per cent of those enrolled at *Lycées* and *Collèges* in 1936. Most importantly, female candidates could sit for competitive exams after 1930, acquiring the necessary passport into French professional life. Women did not storm the barricades of business, law or medicine – only 510 female doctors

---

41    On the Church view, see Offen, 'Body Politics', pp. 143–144. Although Mussolini's public pronouncements, that 'women must obey' for example, resemble Bourgin's rhetoric, his ultimate ambitions differed dramatically in theory if not in practice. See De Grazia, pp. 1–2.

42    Only one clear example exists of a *Nouveau Siècle*-style laudatory piece. The 21 May 1939 edition of the *Petit journal* contained a page two article about pioneering women, including Amelia Earhardt, tennis champions, and government ministers.

43    Cheryl Koos and Daniella Sarnoff, 'France', in Kevin Passmore (ed.), *Women, Gender and Fascism in Europe, 1919–1945*, p. 168.

44    Sarnoff, 'In the Cervix of the Nation', pp. 8–9.

practiced in 1929, for example.[45] Yet they were no longer confined to the domestic sphere. Although they continued to receive lower wages than their male counterparts and be treated with derision by male-dominated trade unions, well over 30 per cent of French women found employment throughout the 1930s.[46]

Although male commentators of all political stripes reacted negatively to the dramatic increase in female visibility, it is tempting to single out the extreme right as a particularly virulent case. After all, Mussolini and the Italian fascists mobilized misogyny and anti-feminism in the service of the nation, criticizing any attempt by women to better their lot in life, while the Nazis spoke in similar terms, linking the health of the race to the preservation of the domestic sphere.[47] Although neither regime proved to be as harsh in practice, primarily due to the labour needs of their militarized economies, French leagues held comparably negative views concerning women.

But such a narrow view omits the degree to which analogous notions penetrated mainstream Gallic politics and society. Taking their cue from papal encyclicals *Casti Connubi* and *Quadragesimo Anno*, French conservatives demanded the return of women to the domestic sphere, doing their duty as wives and mothers to the exclusion of all professional aspirations. Hence the right wing École des parents, designed to combat the progressive republican education system, believed it necessary to 'rehabilitate the domestic arts, culinary science, child care, too often disdained by our young female intellectuals hungry for diplomas'. In a similar vein, a 1936 pastoral letter from French cardinals demanded a restoration of 'the unity of the conjugal bond', and the removal of women from the workplace.[48] The left reacted no differently. At the 1933 SFIO national congress, socialist women tendered a request for government financial assistance to 'conciliate and facilitate for women their functions as mother, salaried women, and housekeepers'. If they were paid to stay home and bear children, the argument ran, they would happily leave factory life behind.[49]

In such a context, CDF/PSF proposals were far from outlandish. Furthermore, as Kevin Passmore notes, the group embodied a seeming contradiction. Although Colonel de la Rocque and other leaders viewed women as passive and maternal, the desire to create a mass-based party inevitably necessitated female inclusion.[50] Hence the group actively mobilized women, which invariably removed them from the domestic sphere. On February 22, 1934 the Section féminine du Regroupement nationale autour des Croix de Feu (SFRN) first appeared, under the leadership of La Rocque's personal secretary Antoinette de Préval. This affiliate adminsitered propaganda and social assistance programs (*service social*), such as soup kitchens, children's recreation centres, and the distribution of alms to the needy. These activities corresponded to woman's 'natural domain', focusing upon feminine and

---

45    Muel-Dreyfus, pp. 98–100.

46    Bridenthal et al, pp. 481–82; Offen, p. 142.

47    On Mussolini and the Italian fascists, see Wilson, pp. 18–20. The most comprehensive treatment of Nazism and gender is Koonz, *Mothers in the Fatherland*.

48    Muel-Dreyfus, pp. 50–52, 166.

49    Offen, pp. 148–149.

50    Kevin Passmore, 'Planting the Tricolor in the Citadels of Communism: Women's Social Action in the Croix de Feu and Parti social français', *Journal of Modern History*, 71 (1999), pp. 825–828.

maternal qualities, and simultaneously afforded the group the opportunity to convert working-class women – the primary targets of SFRN activity – from communism to CDF/PSF doctrine.[51] The group considered this ancillary organization to be a priority, and consistently urged the intensified recruitment of women into the SFRN, which encompassed 525 cells by the autumn of 1935. In September of that year the *section féminine*, along with all other non-*combattant* sections of the CDF/PSF, was incorporated into the new Mouvement social français organization, which replaced the Regroupement nationale autour des Croix de Feu.[52] With the 1936 transformation of the group into the Parti social français further changes emerged: The SFRN divided into *Action civique* and *Action sociale* subdivisions.

Despite the frequent mutations, CDF/PSF women's organizations proved to be tremendously successful, attracting up to 400,000 members at their peak. However, because they had not fought in the Great War, and could not claim veteran status, female participation was strictly limited. Women were not afforded membership during the Croix de Feu years, and were noticeably absent from meetings, parades, and celebrations even after the transformation into the parliamentary PSF.[53] Such restrictions coincided with pronouncements concerning gender and the *État social français*: which soundly rejected the notion that women could adopt a profession outside of the SFRN. Despite paying lip-service to the notion of female professionals, CDF/PSF members viewed the idea as dangerous to both the economy and society.[54] Thus the party bulletin claimed that working mothers were not as healthy as those who remained in the home. Infant mortality rose significantly in families in which both parents worked, with the exposure of the pregnant mother to disease in dingy and crowded factories deemed the chief culprit. Worse still, reported the Bureau d'études sociales du PSF, working women were ignorant about household matters, and their children frequently exposed to the danger of juvenile delinquency. Their houses were filthy and their children unhealthy due to a lack of maternal care. Thus

---

51     Charles Vallin, *Aux femmes du Parti social français* (Paris, 1937), p. 5. On SFRN activities and anti-communism, see Mary Jean Green, 'Gender, Fascism, and the Croix de Feu: The 'Women's' Pages of *Le Flambeau*', *French Cultural Studies* 8 (1997), p. 234. Préval was eventually joined by two colleagues, Mlle. de Gérus (an engineer's wife) and Mlle. Féraud (like Préval, a General's daughter). See Passmore, 'Planting the Tricolor', p. 831.

52     See for example: F/7/12966, 'Réunion organisée par la Comité local du 7me Arrt. du Parti social français', 12 Feb. 1937. La Rocque made this priority clear in one of his first acts as Croix de Feu president, in CHEVS/LR 46, 'Extraits littéraux de notes prises par un de mes intimes à la suite des conférences que je lui ai faites, sur mes projets civiques, en décembre 1931'. Although precise membership numbers are unavailable, the number of sections is drawn from Jacques Nobecourt, *Le colonel de la Rocque, 1885–1946 ou les pièges du nationalisme chrétien* (Paris, 1996), pp. 287–288.

53     Green, pp. 232–236; Passmore, p. 817.

54     The exception to this rule was Marcelle Tinayre, an occasional columnist for *Le Flambeau*, and a former writer for Margeurite Durand's *La Fronde*. A staunch feminist activist, Tinayre believed it necessary for women to work if their husbands were unemployed or otherwise could not support them. See Passmore, pp. 843–844.

the group urged employed wives to abandon their jobs if at all possible, for the sake of their children.[55]

This message was brought directly to the SFRN on every occasion possible. Speaking at a meeting in March 1934, Pasteur Durleman advised women to:

> Believe in the family home. Unlike so many of your contemporaries, do not frequent those illicit places where one can never think of the beauty, the splendour of the most modest tasks of domestic life, seemingly the most banal, but in truth the most sacred thing in existence.

Durleman urged women to have as many children as possible, a burden which constituted their service and sacrifice for the French nation.[56] Pierre Kula, the head of the CDF/PSF Groupe patronale, proposed 'housework schooling' for all young girls to teach them the tricks of the trade, from washing and sewing to cooking, while others demanded training courses in natal care and household hygiene.[57]

Following Kula's suggestion, women's schooling in the new CDF/PSF state was to be largely practical. While young boys were taught leadership skills and given rigorous physical exercise, girls learned the art of composing menus. CDF/PSF male youth groups visited the factory or farm, to give them a taste of their future; girls on the other hand practiced choral singing and mastered the art of pottery.[58] Within the confines of CDF/PSF youth organizations, they were also taught fashion, cooking, household economy, and stenography, while group periodicals pictured women sewing accompanied by a caption explaining what 'la ménagère doit savoir'. Stereotypical gender roles were continuously reinforced from an early age, in an effort to reverse the societal trend towards working women, and to deter thoughts of independence or the single life. To this end, the CDF/PSF Cercle des jeunes filles youth organization deemed females the 'professors of housework', and pledged to instill the ideal of family into all of its young adherents.[59] Having received a feminine education, the final product of such training would be the perfect mother and housewife:

> The housewife acquires a calling. She prepares for her role as a mother, the most beautiful profession ... In the PSF, we give her back a penchant for humble domestic duties, and we show her the dignity of familial responsibility. We teach her the practical things which

---

55    AP/451/101, 'La Retour de la mère au foyer', *Bulletin d'information 70*; La Présence de la mère au foyer', *L'Ouvrier libre*, Sept–Oct. 1938. These same points were made practically *ver batim* in 'La Mère au foyer', *Le Haut parleur du Val et Loire*, April 1939. The latter cited examples of children forced to cook and clean for the entire household due to a lack of parental attention and care. For a similar argument, see AP/451/117, Pierre Kula, 'Essai sur un politique des allocations familiales', in *Premier congrès du Groupe patronale* (tract), p. 8.

56    'Section féminine du regroupement national autour des Croix de Feu', *Le Flambeau*, April 1934.

57    'Essai sur un politique....', Pierre Kula, in *Premier congrès du Groupe patronale*, 47; Dr. P. Rudaux, 'L'École des mères', *Petit journal*, 14 Feb. 1938.

58    AP/451/106, 'Conseils d'ordre général pour les Moniteurs et les Monitrices des groupes de 14 à 16 ans'.

59    AP/451/104, 'Cercle des filles de Croix de Feu'; Tract – *L'Oeuvre social dans le mouvement Croix de Feu* (illustrated supplement to *Le Flambeau*, May 1936); AP/451/93, 'Section féminine', Oct. 1935; AP/451/106, 'Instructions spéciales pour le Groupe d'action sociale'.

will impress the household, especially the art of cooking which our ancestors gave pride of place. The future mistress of the house similarly learns cleaning, dressmaking, sewing, puericulture, first aid, hygiene, and finally the secret of that priceless elegance which only France can offer.[60]

CDF/PSF women's organizations took advantage of every available opportunity to reinforce gender expectations, from social service providers who taught working-class women the art of tending house to newspaper columns designed to impart 'ce qu'une femme doit savoir'.[61] Such gender proscriptions, for both young girls and adults, echoed precepts espoused by the conservative wing of the Faisceau, and found their ultimate expression in the Vichy regime. The insistence upon the 'domestic arts' in the classroom, including requisite courses in housework and child care, along with the gender disparity regarding physical education and activity, were legislated by Education Minister Jérome Carcopino in August 1941 as part of a substantial reform of French pedagogy. The CDF/PSF, like Carcopino and Marshall Pétain, pledged to remove women from the factory, emphasizing that the home constituted her workplace. Further akin to Vichy education specialists and indeed the Marshall himself, La Rocque and his colleagues wedded stern moralizing to the concept of feminine education, arguing that French weakness, engendered by female decadence and illicit behaviour, could only be corrected through the suppression of selfish individualism in the domestic sphere.[62]

Just as Vichy propaganda lionized Pétain as the father of France, teaching his female children about their proper role within the *État Français*, authors portrayed La Rocque, and indeed the CDF/PSF as a whole, as the *Pater Familias* of the group's *Grande Famille*. Their prototypical icon of womanhood was Nadine de la Rocque, daughter of the *chef*, who understood her duty to serve the league and France, assenting to the patriarchal structure of the CDF/PSF and the nation as a whole.[63] Various authors consistently emphasized this theme, insisting upon feminine docility and moral rectitude. To CDF/PSF parliamentary deputy Charles Vallin, women were not only the best propagandists in both the family and the community, but created the very atmosphere of a Christian country, acting as the conscience of the nation.[64] Echoing the sentiments professed a decade earlier by Hubert Bourgin, La Rocque himself wrote of 'the gracious troop of our girls [who] will plot the function of the wife, citizen, and guardian of the home, maintaining the sacred Flame of patriotic faith'.[65] The soil of France, which represented the heart of the people, could only be properly preserved by the mother within the confines of the home. As one author chided in the *Liberté du Maine*, a family needed more than bread to survive: only a

---

60    Hélène Bailleux, 'Le PSF et la jeunesse', *Flambeau de Flandres-Artois-Picardie*, 9 April 1939.

61    Green, pp. 231–232; Passmore, p. 842.

62    Pollard, pp. 80–85; Dreyfus, pp. 233–243.

63    Passmore, p. 825.

64    Vallin, pp. 3, 5.

65    CDLR, 'Aux Fils et Filles de Croix de Feu', *Le Flambeau*, Aug. 1933. See also AP/451/93 'Note du Président-Générale', 2 Jan. 1936.

mother transmitted the *patrimoine française* to the young.[66] Maternal intervention prevented scandal, immoral behaviour, and anti-national sentiment.

The CDF/PSF also spoke out vehemently against all vestiges of feminism, portrayed as the polar opposite of the good Christian housewife. Although the group expended considerable energy combating popular women's organizations and suffrage movements, the number of interwar feminists was relatively undaunting, between 200,000 and 300,000 at most, and they were hardly a uniform bunch. To be sure, a large number espoused the political left and frequently invoked Neo-Malthusianism as the only solution to women's second-class status. However, the vast majority rejected any vestige of extremism. Older, more established organizations like the Ligue française des droits des femmes and the Union française pour la suffrage des femmes, formed during the turn-of-the-century French feminist heyday, lobbied almost exclusively for the female vote and rejected demands for immediate gender equality. Finally, a substantial number of Catholic and conservative feminist organizations appeared in the 1920s, strict devotees of Church pronouncements condemning *la femme moderne*. Thus the Union nationale pour la vote des femmes founded in 1920 by the Duchesse de la Rochefoucauld devalued female labour and supported the vote to protect wives and mothers. Despite their use of the feminist tag, the UNVF certainly rejected the antics of more radical feminists like Louise Weiss, whose *Femme Nouvelle* suffrage campaign urged women to demand their rights through street action. If anything, their program echoed the CDF/PSF demand for the return of the *femme au foyer*.[67]

Group luminaries held firm, however, and regularly cast feminists as the destroyers of tradition, family, and the motherland, and accused them of collaborating with the enemies of the nation. Vallin called feminism a 'fanatical religion', assuring his readers that the movement was inspired by communism, which pitted the female proletarian against the male capitalist.[68] Jean-Marie Gautier was equally hostile in the *Flamme des Deux-Sèvres*, insisting that:

> we are not feminists, because feminism is an idiocy ... What is this war chant, that 'woman is equal to man'? It's a ridiculous equation, which leaves the impression that one is in conflict with the other, that a woman must fight against man to win equality (!) Vanity.

The author reminded his readers that in the *Etat social français* women would be returned to their proper place. In direct contrast to the Faisceau notion that many modern woman had to work as a consequence of the postwar demographic imbalance, Gautier argued that they were victims of a horrid mistake that allowed them to adopt male roles during the Great War.[69]

Others appealed to the feminine character and delicacy of the 'weaker sex' in criticizing feminism. It was not a woman's place to descend into the street, 'de jouer les suffragettes', argued one female member. Such women forgot their familial and

---

66    'Les Femmes et le PSF', *Liberté du Maine*, May 1938 (deuxième quinzaine).
67    Reynolds, pp. 178–179, 218–219; Muel-Dreyfus, pp. 154–157.
68    Vallin, p. 1.
69    Jean-Marie Gautier, 'Vous Mesdames', *La Flamme des Deux-Sèvres*, May 1939. See also Jos Levet, 'La Famille', *L'Ouvrier libre*, March 1939.

national duties, mostly revolutionaries who sang the *Internationale* at rallies. The feminists' rough and rugged character and appearance were often contrasted with the proper French lady, who was courteous, kind, and elegant at all times. 'Is it the role of a woman, a being of daintiness and harmony, to mingle with the hateful roaring crowd, which disfigures her face and makes her look like a shrew?' asked *L'Espoir Lorrain*. Such violent behaviour belied woman's docile and nurturing nature.[70] This CDF/PSF further used this rationale to deny women access to the realm of politics. Prominent novelist and group member Colette Yvar told a crowd at the Salle Wagram in 1933 that 'women, good sir, do not like politics', urging them to remain in their normal sphere of activity – the family home.

However, despite the group's antipathy for feminism, and derisive stance towards the politicization of women, the CDF/PSF wholeheartedly supported feminine suffrage. While seemingly contradictory, given their persistent berating of women's rights campaigners, their stance was actually quite duplicitous. If some conservatives like Maurice Barrès supported the vote for women, many commentators actually envisioned the *vote familiale*, whereby the husband cast a number of ballots equivalent to the size of his family. For this reason, the right-leaning Senate rejected direct female suffrage in 1922, deferring to the wishes of the Republican Federation and other conservative parties that proffered the family vote. Even those proponents of female suffrage within the CDF/PSF and other leagues supported such initiatives solely because they believed 'the weaker sex' to be inherently conservative, defending traditional family values, and as such necessarily voting for the leagues, widening their electoral appeal. It is thus unsurprising that the concept proved exceptionally popular under the ultra-conservative Vichy regime.[71]

Given their beliefs, the group took pains to point out that suffrage neither implied genuine political participation nor contradicted femininity. Hence the *Flamme des Deux-Sèvres* claimed that a woman would inevitably cast a ballot in favour of those candidates who supported family and *foyer*; giving them the right to vote could only strengthen the nation.[72] But not all female CDF/PSF supporters were so docile concerning the vote, and some demanded that their sex be viewed as equal in all facets of national existence. To Mme. Desmons, a PSF Délégué civique fédérale, it was essential that women not only be given the right to vote, but full civil and political liberties as well: 'The poverty of social legislation for the protection of children and their mother, who often lives her life alone and shoulders a heavy burden, leads her to imperiously claim the eligibility and the right to speak her mind about social matters. That is justice!' Women were too often exploited in the working world, denied the salary, respect, and protection due to them, creating intolerably harsh conditions for the mothers of France's future generations. Desmons reasoned

---

70    Jacqueline Benoit, 'Visage des femmes', *L'Espoir Lorrain*, 24 April 1937. See also Arlette Michel, 'Femmes françaises', *L'Espoir de l'Est*, 16 Oct. 1937.

71    McMillan, pp. 178–179; Pollard, pp. 15, 35.

72    Votre devoir civique Mesdames?', *La Flamme des Deux-Sèvres*, April 1939. See also 'À la Salle Wagram', *Le Flambeau*, Dec. 1933.

that women had to be recognized as equals under the law in order to protect the well-being of the family and ancestral morality.[73]

Nor was she alone in voicing this conclusion. In November 1938, the *Volonté Bretonne* published eight letters written by young girls supporting the female vote, including one who asserted that the ballot-box was only the tip of the iceberg. Fully capable of performing all of the tasks currently assigned to men, females displayed more honesty and diligence. Women, the writer asserted, did not steal millions of francs for corrupt purposes while national defense and the French air force became dilapidated in the nation's hour of need![74] The CDF/PSF leadership itself acknowledged such views, noting that 'the labour of the French woman is indispensable to our administration, public services, factories, hospitals, and our countryside'. Such supportive words rarely appeared, however; more typically an author in the *Flambeau Morbihannais* proclaimed that it would be a catastrophe if women ran either businesses or the country. This, the author imparted, was CDF/PSF 'feminism'.[75]

## III

Although both the Faisceau and the CDF/PSF differed in their views of women's national economic and social roles, they agreed wholeheartedly on the primacy of family. Yet they mobilized antithetical arguments in support of their analogous judgments. While the Faisceau referred to the family in organic/biological terms, as the cell of the nation, the CDF/PSF adopted a staunchly pronatalist position. On the surface, the Faisceau's vocabulary was that of the traditional extreme right, which viewed France as a living organism, and consistently referred to the nation in crypto-biological terms. However, various authors combined this rhetoric with the popular interwar discipline of eugenics, a common discourse in 1920s France, and indeed Europe as a whole. The CDF/PSF position, which regarded the decline of the birthrate as the key factor, also appears somewhat extreme, but was actually quite common in 1930s parlance. The group's belief in the necessity of large families to revitalize the nation by strengthening the French population and its collective potential appeared across the political spectrum, variously adopted by the socialist and communist left, the centrist Radical Party, conservatives in the Republican Federation, and various lobbying groups.

Leading Faisceau member Maurice de Barral offered the clearest group definition of the family: the constitution of a social group whose existence and development are subordinate to a specific national *modus operandi*, emphasizing service, justice, and solidarity. Each member received a proscribed role. The head of the family (he included the mother here, not simply responsible for raising the children, but regarded as a key decision-maker) led while the children followed. Barral envisioned an identical model at the regional and national levels, where the leader took the place of the parents, while citizens were the designated offspring. Building upon his colleague's assertions, Valois further assigned specific gender roles. In a June 1926

---

73    S. Desmans, 'La Femme et la politique', *Flambeau de Lorraine*, 1 April 1939.

74    Annaick, 'Le Coin des jeunes filles', *Volonté Bretonne*, 5 Nov. 1938.

75    CHEVS/LR 9 G, Tract – 'Appel aux femmes françaises pour l'honneur et la paix'; 'Féminisme', *Flambeau Morbihannais*, 5 July 1933.

*Nouveau Siècle* article, he wrote that the mother bound the father to the soil of his ancestors, convincing him to assume a national function as the great motor of human activity, labouring for the household's survival. The nation thus became a collective of families, and those who did not marry and have children (excluding war widows, priests and the like), were considered non-entities.[76]

Barral, Valois, and other Faisceau leaders based their conception of the family on the Barrèssian notion of the soil and the dead as the lifeblood of France. According to Maurice Barrès, one of the chief spokesmen for the fin-de-siècle French extreme right, each family of solid racial stock represented a link in the national chain, preserving the history and spirit of France.[77] In binding its inhabitants together into a living whole, in which each household represented one cell, Faisceau doctrine seemingly parroted late nineteenth-century integral nationalist thought. Hence to Hubert Bourgin, the household provided and nurtured the familial cells. All institutions, from the constitution and the law to the government had arisen from *la terre*, produced by its children the French people. As it represented the pillar of the *Cité/Maison* called France, the defense of the family symbolized the protection of the living nation.[78] Valois assigned this task primarily to the mother, who kept both the father and his children on the right path, instilling the values of sacrifice and patriotism. Only the patriarchal moral code, in combination with the mother's diligent eye, prevented man's reversion to his primordial state, engaged in an unproductive life comprised solely of sleep and consumption.[79]

The father too was a central component of the familial system, providing both leadership and an example for his children. Valois's *pater familias* functioned as an educator, whose passion turned towards family, society, and the nation.[80] Using an almost Freudian analysis, Valois declared that the nineteenth century had been symbolized by a revolt against the father, with families destroyed in the name of anarchy. Declaring this rebellion absurd, he countered that every village, town, or province was in a sense familial. Because the nation was an organic whole, neither man nor his institutional creations could exist without family, yet the entire corpus of nineteenth century legislation and its executive apparatus worked against this principle. No honour or rights had been extended to society's most crucial component, resulting in the subsequent degeneration of the nation.[81] The new Faisceau state would produce a revolutionary revision of the constitution and laws in order to save the family. Individualism, the metaphysic of the Third Republic, could not co-exist

---

76    Maurice de Barral, *Dialogues sur le Faisceau* (Paris, 1926), pp. 11–12; Georges Valois, 'Aux chefs de famille', *NS*, 19 June 1926.

77    For a discussion of Barrès and integral nationalism, see chapters one and two. On Barrès's formulations of integral nationalism and *la terre et les morts*, see Michel Winock, *Nationalisme, antisémitisme, et fascisme en France* (Paris, 1990), chapter one and Zeev Sternhell, *Maurice Barrès et le nationalisme français* (Paris, 1985), chapters five and six.

78    Bourgin, *Les Pierres de la maison*, pp. 56–59, 85.

79    *Première assemblée nationale des combattants, des producteurs et des chefs de famille* (Paris, 1926), pp. 11–12. This tract contains the text of the Reims meeting.

80    Georges Valois, *La Père* (Paris, 1924), p. 9. This quote is taken from the 1924 preface and not the book itself, which was written before the war.

81    Ibid., pp. 10–12.

with the necessary social collective, and as such would be eliminated. The revolution of 1789, with its rights of man and citizen, would be replaced by an opposing one, dedicated to placing individual passions into the national framework, within which they would be subjected to rigorous discipline.

Valois believed that this accomplishment had been partially achieved during the Great War, when men had acted as a collective unit in the trenches, experiencing a unity based solely on unconscious fraternity rather than class or profession.[82] This bond represented the living nation (what Action française leader Charles Maurras had termed the *pays réél*), as distinct from the strictly legalist state enshrined within the Third Republic (the *pays légal*). All Frenchmen thus formed a second family – that of the nation as a whole – to which all who willingly sacrificed and worked for the common good belonged. The establishment of the familial unit provided both a coherent expression of this fact and assured the continuation of the French nation.

It was a short step from the notion of the nation as a collective family to the biological view of France as a living organism. Speaking to an Armistice Day rally in November 1925, Valois termed the family a cell of the national body, just as the father's profession was an extension of the *atelier familial*. Hence the proposed Faisceau state organized strictly by family and corporation.[83] Schooling encouraged moral and material prosperity, a process replicated by the church in the larger community, and by families within the new Estates-General.[84] To ensure that the voice of families and not individuals dominated the nation, the *vote familial* replaced the republican system, allowing the father a number of votes corresponding to the size of his household.[85]

Valois's rhetoric seemingly negated the group's technocratic scheme for the French economy, which focused exclusively upon industry, demanding scientific management and Fordism. Similarly, the group's veneration of the countryside conflicted with the leader's fascination with Le Corbusier and modern urbanism, the antithesis of the integral nationalist cult of *la campagne*. But the Faisceau had no intention of recreating the pre-revolutionary dream so beloved of Maurras and the Action française, or of succumbing to Barrès's veneration of *la terre et les morts*. They desired only a healthy national body, effectuated through an ultra-modern vehicle: The burgeoning science of eugenics, prevalent in postwar Europe and the predominant strand of modern medicine.

Eugenicists of all political stripes echoed the Faisceau's familial doctrine. In 1919, radical-socialist leader Édouard Herriot, no friend of the extreme right, expounded

---

82    Ibid., pp. 13–15.

83    F/7/13211–Tract 9, Georges Valois, 'Le Faisceau des combattants, des chefs de famille, et des producteurs', p. 5. On the composition and functioning of the new state, see Chapter One.

84    'Discours prononcée le 11 Novembre', *NS*, 12 Nov. 1925.

85    Georges Valois, 'La Famille', *NS*, 8 Feb. 1926. The family vote traced back to the conservatives of the 1870's, and was adopted by pronatalists in the interwar period. See Andrés Horacio Reggiani. 'The Politics of Demography, 1919–1945', *French Historical Studies*, 19 (1996), p. 733. Valois, however, did not use the term in this sense. Where the Alliance nationale argued that the family vote was owed to large families because of their greater financial contribution to the nation, he instead focused on the health of the national 'body'.

upon the nation's future in Valoissian terms: 'A nation is not a collection of individuals placed beside one another; it is a group of interlocking families. The organic cell is not the individual but the family.'[86] Although such statements are commonly associated with Nazi Germany, or fascist sympathizers in other nations, they were common throughout interwar Europe. State intervention on a hitherto unimagined scale occurred variously in liberal-democratic Great Britain (to combat tuberculosis and alcoholism), socialist-dominated 'Red Vienna' (to supervise young parents in the raising of their children), and France, where the Conseil supérieur d'hygiène sociale constructed new housing units for working-class families and engaged in large-scale 'social management'. In each country, millions of citizens participated in exhibitions, congresses, and programs designed to defend public welfare and strengthen the national body.[87] Thus it was not the Nazis, but the French republican government which declared that 'the health of the parents, conception, pregnancy, and infant were identified as privileged sites of intervention for improving the species'. Well before the advent of the Vichy regime, doctors received the right to intervene if the health of the nation appeared threatened; for example, in 1920 leading obstetrician Adolphe Pinard successfully lobbied the Chamber of Deputies into banning contraception and abortion.[88]

Yet as William Schneider notes, two strands of eugenics existed in the interwar era: Positive eugenics, exclusively concerned with social hygiene, disease prevention, and improved natal care, and negative eugenics whose goal was the perfection of the race.[89] Until the late 1930s, Mussolini's Italy supported the former program, waging war against birth control, and ensuring a steady stream of healthy babies for the economy and military through the National Agency for Maternity and Infancy. From the mandatory proscription of puericulture to a punitive bachelor's tax, fascist ministers tendered a series of laws and directives designed to raise the birthrate.[90] Groups like the Alliance nationale made similar demands in France, albeit from a conservative ideological bent, more concerned with matching German population growth than military conquest.

A certain amount of pronatalist sentiment appeared within the ranks of the Faisceau, but the group mainly argued in favour of negative eugenics, attempting to improve the quality of the national population. Valois's crypto-biological view of the French family implied a need to ensure the health of each cell in the national body. Rather than demanding more children, the group focused upon improving the current stock. However, it is important to note that neither Valois nor his colleagues ever considered the methods later adopted by the Nazis in Germany. No member of

86    Quoted in Mark Mazower, *Dark Continent: Europe's Twentieth Century* (New York, 1998), pp. 79–80.

87    Ibid, pp. 83, 87–91.

88    Muel-Dreyfus, p. 67.

89    William H. Schneider, *Quality and Quantity: The Quest for Biological Regeneration in Twentieth-Century France* (Cambridge, 1990), p. 284. It was the former that gained widespread acceptance in France after the Great War, and many of the ideas presented under its auspices are today commonly accepted practice in pediatric medicine.

90    De Grazia, pp. 53–71. On the efforts of the ONMI, see Chiara Saraceno, 'Redefining Maternity and Paternity: Gender, Pronatalism, and Social Policies in Fascist Italy', in Bock and Thane.

the Faisceau supported mass sterilization, the murderous elimination of 'biologically inferior material' or euthanasia.[91] The *État Combattant* simply intervened to ensure the health of all children by utilizing modern medical techniques. Nonetheless, the group did support what Mary Louise Roberts terms 'human engineering': the enforced scientific management of public health.[92]

Authors posited genetico-biological solutions to the problem, expounding ideas similar to then-current medical thinking.[93] To Claude Aragonnès, the density and health of a country's population were their two greatest resources, both of which had diminished during the war. The low birthrate, an infant mortality rate higher than those of England and Germany, alcoholism, and disease (tuberculosis and syphilis being the most prominent) constituted a medical disaster, a near fatal blow made harsher by the male population loss suffered during the war. Aragonnès therefore warned that the France of the future would become a colony of foreigners providing necessary industrial labour unless the population rose significantly.[94]

Although these arguments corresponded to similar views expounded by orthodox pronatalists, his solutions were genetic rather than legislative, and went far beyond the purview of positive eugenics. Aragonnès proposed a national system of social hygiene, to be given priority status alongside the ministries for economics and national defense. A full examination of the living conditions of the working class would be conducted under the auspices of the new ministry, with a further emphasis placed upon heredity and contagion. It aimed to prevent illness, bringing proper hygiene techniques into the homes of all workers and farmers, aided by propaganda campaigns in schools and the workplace. Mothers would be taught how to feed their children properly and uncover symptoms of illness by specialized female social workers and nurses during the course of home visitations, and in nutritional clinics or factory and school infirmaries.[95]

Some Faisceau members took this plan to extremes; one of them called for an Infirmière hygiène sociale to uncover and progressively eliminate 'physical and mental incapacities' in children.[96] This included below average performances at school and troublemakers at home. Such children were perceived as lethal to their families and the nation, and the author proposed their immediate removal. The theme of the incurable delinquent child as a threat to the social order often appeared in Faisceau writings. One

---

91     On Nazi eugenics, see Gisela Bock, 'Antinatalism, Maternity and Paternity in National Socialist Racism', in Bock and Thane.

92     Roberts, *Civilization Without Sexes*, pp. 207–211. The Faisceau fell short even of Vichy in this regard. Alexis Carrel and Paul Morand, the National Revolution's leading eugenicists, demanded selective breeding and the forced sterilization of persons deemed to be racially inferior. On Carrel, see Schneider, pp. 272–280. For a discussion of Morand's views, see Andrea Loselle, 'The Historical Nullification of Paul Morand's Gendered Eugenics', in Melanie Hawthorne and Richard J. Golson (eds), *Gender and Fascism in Modern France* (Hanover, 1997), pp. 101–118.

93     For examples of such initiatives, see Schneider, pp. 120–126, 135, 139–142, 284.

94     Aragonnès, 'Une Bataille à gagner: sauver la race', *NS*, 28 Nov. 1926.

95     Ibid. Here again, despite the emphasis on maternity, Aragonnès writes that these new occupations would be perfectly suited to women in search of a career.

96     S.G., 'A propos des services sociaux', *NS*, 4 Sept. 1927.

cartoon in *Nouveau Siècle* showed a young boy in tattered clothing, his face sullen and downcast, being observed by two bourgeois men in a food market. The menacing caption, 'I wonder when it will become serious; again this morning he tried to murder his grandfather and set the house on fire', transmitted a clear message: If parents could not take proper care of their children, then the state would be forced to do it for them. Such language resembled the terminology used by more extreme French and European geneticists, who argued for restrictions on marriage and childbirth for those of inferior physical or mental stock.[97] Dr. Lestrocquoy, the vice-president of the group's Corporation des médecins, agreed with the harsh language used by his colleagues, writing that military and colonial problems (and an invasion of foreign workers into factories and fields) inevitably followed by the degeneration of French racial stock.[98]

The adoption of negative eugenicist solutions merely bolstered Valois's crypto-biological view of the organic nation. In any case, when one considers the acceptance by certain sections within the group of the changing position of women in society, it becomes all the more difficult to place the Faisceau in the pronatalist camp. To be sure, Valois and his colleagues regarded the family as the pre-eminent social unit, and wanted women to bear as many children as possible, but they were by and large too realistic to expect that all would (and could) marry. Furthermore, those who adopted a scientific rather than ideological argument, such as Aragonnès or Lestrocquoy, were concerned with the quality and health of French children, and as such bolstered Valois's organic view of the nation. That the Faisceau view was completely atypical of popular pronatalist sentiment becomes even clearer when considering the example of the CDF/PSF, whose doctrine of the family mirrored that of various groups across the political spectrum, from the Radical party to the conservative Alliance nationale. If Valois and company looked to integral nationalism and eugenics for inspiration, CDF/PSF members needed only to read any available newspaper.

## IV

The CDF/PSF displayed remarkable conservatism, falling within the category of what historians call the *mouvement nataliste*, overwhelmingly concerned with the low birthrate during the interwar period and its consequences for France. In arguing for a renewal of the traditional women's roles as mother and housewife, and for the need to give the family (as a moral entity rather than cell of the nation) a pre-eminent position within the nation and the state, the CDF/PSF in fact espoused the stance taken by French society as a whole throughout the interwar period. The battle cry of the highly influential Alliance nationale that 'il faut faire naître' could have been the CDF/PSF social policy slogan.[99]

---

97    'La Jeunesse criminelle', *NS*, 1 Feb. 1926. On extreme solutions to the problem of juvenile delinquency, see Schneider, chapter six; Mazower, p. 78.

98    Dr. Lestrocquoy, 'La Problème de la natalité', *NS*, 19 July 1926.

99    Françoise Thébaud. 'Le Mouvement nataliste dans la France de L'entre-deux-guerres: L'Alliance nationale pour l'accroissement de la population française', *Revue d'histoire moderne et contemporaine*, Avril–Juin 1985, p. 276.

The group devoted significant human and material resources towards combating the low birthrate. Dozens of newspaper articles about the phenomenon appeared in the CDF/PSF press, and regional and national congresses continually devoted space to the topic. In each case, authors and speakers exhorted women to give up working outside the home, in order to care for the *foyer familial* and to have as many children as possible. The duty of the state included the support of large families with supplemental incomes and family allowances, while adopting the family and not the individual as the bulwark of the nation. France would either have more children, or be left old, infirm, and childless amongst the new familial dynamism of Germany, Italy, and the United States.

It is crucial to stress that although this program sounds severe, it was actually quite commonly accepted at the time. This is not to say that all pronatalist groups were alike. To be sure, the leaders of the Alliance nationale, a parliamentary lobbying group founded in 1896 by demographer Jacques Bertillon, incorporated concepts of extreme nationalism and anti-individualism into their platform, opinions unacceptable to more mainstream political parties. Its congresses regularly yielded a wealth of initiatives that aimed to reverse the sagging birthrate, from a bachelor's tax to state rewards and recognition for large families. Alliance propaganda demanded immediate state action to ensure French economic and military strength, particularly following the narrow margin of victory against a resurgent Germany in the Great War. The group's rhetoric echoed the pronatalist doctrine espoused by the French extreme right, which viewed national depopulation with alarm, as the birthrate fell from 21.5 per thousand inhabitants in 1920 to 14.8 in 1939. Hence the Jeunesses patriotes, Solidarité française, and above all the CDF/PSF tendered analogous demands, mirroring the Alliance program.[100]

Yet the Alliance contained many members unsympathetic to the fascist cause, including the Archbishop of Paris Cardinal Verdier, Protestant leader Pastor Marc Boegner, and the Grand Rabbi of France Isaïah Schwartz.[101] The group also attracted the support of Radical and Socialist governments, and the Ministry of Public Health paid its propaganda costs throughout the 1930s.[102] Nor was this support particularly new. Five of its members were ministers in the postwar Bloc national government, many others were among the best French physicians, and its journal *Alliance* and propaganda initiatives reached millions of ordinary French men and women.[103]

In fact, few raised objections to pronatalism on either the left or the right in interwar France. Figures as seemingly irreconcilable as Aristide Briand, Édouard Daladier, and Georges Clemenceau all expressed strongly pronatalist sentiments during the 1920s and 1930s. Furthermore, the government's Conseil supérieur de la natalité, founded in 1920 to fight French Malthusianism, included among its ranks members of the Académie française, doctors, and former parliamentarians, many of whom were of centrist or centre-leftist inclination. Deputies of all political colours also belonged to

---

100   Pollard, pp. 19, 100–103; Cole, pp. 658–666. On the Jeunesses Patriotes and Solidarité française and pronatalism, see Sarnoff, pp. 62–72.

101   Reggiani, p. 745.

102   Susan Pederson, *Family, Dependence, and the Origins of the Welfare State: Britain and France, 1914–1945* (Cambridge, 1995), p. 369.

103   Marie-Monique Huss, 'Pronatalism in the Inter-War Period in France', *Journal of Contemporary History*, 25 (1990), p. 43.

the Groupe parlementaire pour la protection de la natalité et de la famille, and used their influence to enact legislation in 1920 and 1923 which banned abortion and contraception. Both laws received the support of an overwhelming majority in the Chambre Bleu-Horizon. Exclusively motivated by pronatalist doctrine, these decisions set precedents followed throughout the interwar years. By 1932 Adolphe Landry, Minister of Labour in the Laval government and one of France's leading pronatalist activists, made family allowances mandatory in legislation that criminalized employer non-participation in national *caisses de compensation*.

Even the *pièce de resistance* of pronatalist legislation, the 1938–1939 Code de la Famille, was drafted not by the right but the Radicals in 1938, including Premier Édouard Daladier and Minister of Finance Paul Reynaud. Most importantly, at a time when even the communist daily *L'Humanité* featured a regular family page devoted to woman's role as a mother rather than a worker, the Alliance nationale (the largest interwar pronatalist group, with 35,000 members by 1930) was not alone in promoting items which found their way onto the CDF/PSF agenda, including the family vote, improved housing, and family allowances. Feminist groups, such as Cécile Brunschvicg's Union française pour la suffrage des femmes, argued for increased family allowances precisely because such action would accelerate the lagging birthrate. It is obvious then that the extreme-right did not possess a monopoly on pronatalist sentiment.[104]

The CDF/PSF press belaboured the question of the birthrate to such a degree that its family policy was almost exclusively pronatalist. Unlike Aragonnès in the Faisceau, who adopted geneticist rhetoric and viewed governmental intervention as desirable for qualitative reasons, the CDF/PSF simply wanted more French babies. La Rocque mobilized the defense of the family as his (and the group's) top priority, stating that the population crisis had robbed the nation and the soil of its people. The CDF/PSF would take the necessary steps to reverse this downward trend:

> The real problem cannot be resolved, except in the spiritual, moral, caring, and protective atmosphere of our homes. It is around them, for them, and from them that the PSF today, and the social state tomorrow, will do its duty for the family, giving children, servants, and soldiers to the motherland.[105]

In support of such arguments, Louis Dupuy warned *Petit journal* readers in March 1939 that France lost four people each day while Italy grew by 50, Germany gained 60, and 100 Japanese babies were born. Echoing Clemenceau's famous statement that the Treaty of Versailles meant nothing to France without concomitant births, Dupuy concluded that the low birthrate lead the nation to its grave.[106] One of the group's monthly bulletins in Paris agreed, claiming that the French population quickly disappeared: 'la France est en train de devenir un pays de vieillards.' Fewer producers, consumers and taxpayers meant that private enterprise and public finances

---

104   Huss, pp. 41–42; Reggiani, pp. 732, 734; Pederson, p. 368.

105   CDLR, 'La Grande misère de la famille française', *Petit journal*, 27 Dec. 1938.

106   Louis Dupuy, 'Famille et natalité', *Petit journal*, 4 March 1939.

existed in dire jeopardy, while national defense withered away at the precise moment when a hostile Germany waited to invade from across the Rhine.[107]

Such responses were hardly novel in 1930s France. In 1937 Paul Reynaud famously quipped that '41 million Frenchmen face 67 million Germans and 43 million Italians; as far as numbers are concerned, we are beaten'.[108] As Mary Louise Roberts notes, 'the crisis of depopulation became the master narrative of postwar economic, political, and gender anxiety', a nervous tic omnipresent in the late Third Republic.[109] Yet the CDF/PSF response to such threats combined Catholic and conservative appeals with the military and economic arguments favoured by figures like Reynaud. Although they consistently reminded members to do their patriotic natalist duty, the group simultaneously utilized the language found in papal encyclicals like *Casti Connubi*, of childbirth as a moral imperative. One author in the *Flambeau de Charentes et du Périgord* insisted: 'It is a moral question, because starting a family and having numerous children is a necessary civic and patriotic duty that the French people have too often forgotten.' The good father was a true patriot, but also a good citizen, the obscure hero living a decent life and helping French society to flourish.[110] Thus family became an ideal to be followed as part of the *mystique* of the CDF/PSF.

However, the group unhesitatingly rejected Faisceau-style argumentation, dismissing eugenics and biomedical solutions to the population problem. To Henri Andriot of the CDF/PSF executive committee, the nation was a moral unit rather than a biological one. In his report on the family at the first annual PSF Social Congress in May 1939, he told the audience that the familial outlook of the group was solely a product of the traditions bequeathed to France by Christian civilization. Where Valois spoke of the restoration of the national body, Andriot complained that morality had eroded in France to the extent that marriage was not taken seriously as an institution and divorce had become a mere legal formality. Moral discipline, rather than Valois's national-biological evolution, taught children the true spiritual values that governed life. At the same congress, the PSF Bureau d'études sociales echoed these sentiments, positioning the family as the necessary basis of society, but added that the national community and not the state was responsible for its moral implementation. In matters such as the divorce, the government intervened, forbidding it in all but the most extreme cases, but parents alone raised their children and transmitted the appropriate values. Thus the state would enact stronger preventative laws against abortion, referred to as the worst of all crimes by the *Flambeau de Lorraine*, and lead the fight against pornography and alcoholism. But the language used was strictly moralistic; at no point was degeneration mentioned. Good Catholics simply did not engage in such practices.[111]

---

107   CHEVS/LR 11 VI A1, A.W., 'Un Peu de démographie', *Bulletin mensuel du mouvement Croix de Feu (51e et 100e sections)*, 1 May 1936.

108   Reynaud quoted in Pollard, p. 9.

109   Roberts, *Civilization Without Sexes*, p. 107.

110   A.C., 'La Dénatalité française', *Flambeau de Charentes et du Périgord*, 6 Feb. 1938. For a similar argument, see AP/451/134, 'Extraits du rapport sur l'enfant', presented by the Bureau des études sociales, *Premier congrès social du PSF*, 16–17 May 1939.

111   AP/451/134, 'Discours sur la "défense de la famille"', presented by Henri Andriot, *Premier congrès sociale du PSF*, 16–17 May 1939; CHEVS/LR 22, 'Extraits du rapport sur "les

*The Extreme Right in Interwar France*

In this way, the CDF/PSF envisioned a less interventionist state than the Third Republic, content with moral persuasion rather than national policy implementation. Their model resembled the framework adopted by Vichy after 1940, rhetorically comparable to prewar pronatalism, but less prone to government action. Various leaders of the National Revolution decried decadence and democratic individualism, claiming that the family constituted the fundamental unit of French society. Only days after the June 1940 defeat at the hands of the Germans, whose population far outweighed their Gallic neighbours, Pétain declared: 'Too few babies, too few weapons, too few allies, those are the causes of our defeat.'[112] But for all the talk about men as producers and women as reproducers, the Commissariat général de la famille did little to actively raise the birthrate. Its role was confined to propaganda and the provision of facilities for independent efforts by the Alliance nationale and like-minded organizations.[113]

The CDF/PSF behaved in much the same way, only forming a Comité d'action familiale in 1939 to fight the low birth rate through meetings, youth groups, films and other activities. Group leaders merely put forth solutions to the decline of the family throughout the decade.[114] Although the CDF/PSF never viewed moral regeneration as an affair of state in the direct sense, group members believed that the resurrection of the French family could be aided by means of legislation. Hence the call from the Bureau d'etudes sociales for strict divorce laws and higher taxes on bachelors.[115] Through such legislation and the use of propaganda, claimed the *Ouvrier libre*, the 'religion of the family' took root in the population, instilling the desire to perpetuate the race. As a result, in the new CDF/PSF state, the family would become the focus of limited state planning, but nonetheless regain the rights that it had lost to the individual under the republican system.[116]

Thus the group fundamentally agreed with 1930s conservatives and Vichy policy-makers, who viewed the Republic as the culprit for French weakness, due to its perceived insistence that individualism and materialism trumped the common good. According to the *Flamme Tourangelle*, republican governmental authorities preferred bachelorhood or families with only one child, in order to maintain *les moeurs laïco-matérialistes* for their own profit, even at the expense of the national well-being.[117] The *Flambeau du Sud-Est* contrasted this ideology with the role of the family in preserving the French race and tradition, arguing that the low birthrate and depopulation of the countryside, abetted by the lure of materialism, produced a deterioration of paternal authority and subsequent deracination among the population. Instant gratification replaced morality, leaving France with 'a country full of individuals engulfed by the anonymous masses'. As all French genius and virtue sprang from the family and the sacrifice and discipline that it engendered – the

questions familiales"', presented by the Bureau d'études sociales, *Premier congrès sociale du PSF*, 16–17 May 1939; 'En écoutent la radio', *Flambeau de Lorraine*, 27 May 1939.

112  Quoted in Muel-Dreyfus, p. 63.
113  Ibid, p. 74.
114  CHEVS/LR 11 A, 'Plan générale d'action familiale et nataliste du PSF', 16 Feb. 1939.
115  CHEVS/LR 11 VI A 1, A. Wolff, 'Un peu de démographie (suite)', *Bulletin mensuel du mouvement Croix de Feu (51e et 100e Sections)*, 1 June 1936.
116  M. de la Palisse, 'Déficit de naissances', *L'Ouvrier libre*, Feb. 1939.
117  Volmar, 'Le Coupable', *Flamme Tourangelle*, 8 July 1939.

cornerstones of a proper Christian society – the new CDF/PSF nation would actively work for their restoration. Once again, however, the focus was solely a moral one, with the reconstitution of familial authority largely confined to the private sphere, where the father and not the state governed.[118]

Others within the CDF/PSF ranks blamed a lack of economic ethics. For *Le Flambeau* newspaper columnist Pierre Sutter, liberal individualism and materialist doctrine engendered class war and unemployment, both of which effectively corroded the working class family. While the bourgeoisie looked upon children as an impediment to the accumulation of wealth, the worker simply could not afford them. Sutter proposed as potential remedies the family vote, with a number of ballots cast proportional to the size of the family, and the *salaire familiale*. La Rocque extended this argument, attacking the republican 'cult of ease', which replaced discipline and sacrifice in a state that no longer defended the family.[119] Given such statements, it is unsurprising that the pre-Vichy Pétain lauded the group in an April 1936 interview in *Le Journal*, stating that 'The Croix de Feu represent one of the healthiest elements in this country. They want to defend the family. I approve of that. Everything stems from it'.[120]

But the CDF/PSF arguments extended far beyond simple moral platitudes, themselves certainly not confined to Pétain and the extreme right. For their plans for the resuscitation of the French family were almost exclusively financial in scope, and included propositions which emanated from every political party and natalist group during the interwar era. Pierre Kula argued that material well-being proved just as crucial to the health and development of the French family as its moral fibre, needing bread as much as virtue.[121] The group leadership agreed, placing the material defense of the household into its 1936 program, in which it called for the *salaire familial* and an increased family allowance. Only with such guarantees could the wife/mother stay at home and raise children, which lessened unemployment as women left the workplace for the *foyer*. Furthermore, all 'Malthusian legislation' which favoured only 'anonymous capitalism' would be struck down by the *État social français*, through an amendment to minimize inheritance taxes and institute a legal codex of mother's rights. Large-scale industrial expansion would be carefully monitored to insure the fair treatment of employees/fathers, no longer condemned to wander from site to site in search of work due to frequent layoffs. Finally, the state envisioned the implementation of the *vote familial* and women's suffrage to restore the family's rightful leadership

---

118  'Les Croix de Feu et la famille', *Flambeau du Sud-Est*, June 1936. This argument was not exclusive to the CDF/PSF. A variety of Social Catholic groups, influenced by Albert de Mun and the papal encyclical *Rerum Novarum*, used the same arguments, condemning both liberal individualism and capitalist materialism for the destruction of the family and morality. See Pederson, p. 394.

119  Pierre Sutter, 'Intégrons la famille dans la vie sociale', *Le Flambeau*, 12 June 1937; CDLR, 'Discours de clôture', in *Premier congrès agricole* (Saint-Brieuc, 1939), p. 14; CDLR, 'La Grande misère de la famille française', *Petit journal*, 27 Dec. 1938.

120  Muel-Dreyfus, p. 222.

121  AP/451/117, Pierre Kula, 'Essai sur un politique des allocations familiales', *Premier congrès du Groupe patronale (19 et 20 Mai 1939)*, 35.

position within the nation. The language used made clear the seriousness with which the group took the issue: 'The family has a soul which must be defended.'[122]

The CDF/PSF also frequently assailed business owners for failing to meet group standards. La Rocque abused the Popular Front's Matignon accords for non-acceptance of familial rights, asking why laws on apprenticeship and the *salaire familial* had not been included in Léon Blum's new deal for labour. Although the CDF/PSF leader applauded the gains made for working women, using the example of on-site day care centres, the leader nonetheless observed that such actions were morally weak, as children and their mothers were supposed to remain at home.[123] Dr. Philippe Encausse echoed La Rocque's critique, complaining that the accords had been written exclusively for bachelors, a fact uncontested by either the government or France's largest labour union, the Confédération Générale du Travail. He deemed any assistance for the working father a pittance, immediately erased by the rising prices of staple goods, which meant that a family of four needed the money formerly required to feed six in order to survive. Although he lauded the recent raise in family allowances by the Caisse de compensation de la Region Parisienne to 200 francs per month per child, Encausse warned against such inadequate solutions. Births numbered half of those in Germany per annum, France lost 40,000 inhabitants per year, and the race stood in danger of becoming extinct without further compensation.[124]

Owners were thus encouraged by the CDF/PSF to move far beyond the Matignon agreements. At a meeting in Lyon in 1936, La Rocque called for a true minimum wage, much higher than proposed by the CGT and sufficient to raise a large family, rather than the mere bachelor's wage currently paid out by French industry. Factory and business proprietors were encouraged to hire fathers rather than bachelors, with the former being allotted a fixed superior number of positions within each concern. In La Rocque's view, the national interest alone dictated business practices in the *État social français*. Authorities must strictly enforce the increased wage and secure employment to keep women at home: 'We demand that the married woman, the mother of the family, finally quit the factory, workshop, office, and store where she is not in her domain, in order to return to her home.'[125] Pierre Kula agreed, calling the notion that a bachelor and a father of four should earn the same wage absurd:

> In a normally constituted and demographically prosperous society, the sizable family – of at least three children – must be the rule, bachelorhood a temporary expedient (outside of special cases of voluntary celibacy, notably in religious orders), and the family with no children eliminated entirely.

---

122   AP/451/102, tract – *Parti social français: une mystique, un programme* (Paris, 1936), pp. 31–35; 'Pour une politique française', *Le Flambeau*, 19 Nov. 1936.

123   AP/451/102, tract – *Union-Esprit-Famille* (Paris, 1938), p. 13. The text is an in extenso annotation of La Rocque's January 1938 speech at the Vélodrome d'Hiver.

124   Dr. Philippe Encausse, 'Il faut sauver la famille française', *Le Flambeau*, 24 Oct. 1936. Encausse's figure of 200 francs per month given by the CCRP is well above the actual amount, which was 30 francs per month for the first child at the time he was writing, rising to 200 for each additional child after the second one. See Pederson, p. 270.

125   CHEVS/LR 20 H, 'Réunion du 15 Septembre 1936', Salle Blanchon. Lyon. La Rocque offered no figures for the new minimum wage.

Wage equalization that made the father an inferior, and family allowances lower than the actual cost per child, were to be immediately rectified by the new CDF/PSF regime.[126]

The crowning achievement of CDF/PSF policy was a complete revision of the *salaire familial*. Members proposed various schemes, all of which raised the then-standard subsidies considerably, while extending the plan to agriculture. For agricultural workers, whose average wage was 60 per cent of that of industrial workers, commentators replaced the existing equation with a scale of 1,000 francs per annum for the first child, rising substantially for each subsequent birth:

Table 3.1    Salaire Familial I

| Number of Children | Suggested Amount |
| --- | --- |
| 1 | 1000 Francs/yr. |
| 2 | 1500 Fr./yr. |
| 3 | 3000 Fr./yr. |
| 4 | 4500 Fr./yr. |
| 5 | 5500 Fr./yr. |
| 6 | 6500 Fr./yr. |
| 7 | 7000 Fr./yr. |

By contrast, a percentage of the total annual wage bill determined the supplement for the industrial worker, driving up the allocation considerably:[127]

Table 3.2    Salaire Familial II

| Number of Children | Suggested Amount |
| --- | --- |
| 1 | 10 per cent of Wage Bill |
| 2 | 25 per cent |
| 3 | 50 per cent |
| 4 | 75 per cent |
| 5 | 100 per cent |

---

126    AP/451/117, Kula, 'Essai.', pp. 36–37. This same argument was used in an article entitled 'Travail FAMILLE Patrie' by an anonymous author in the *Flambeau des Vosges*, July 1939.

127    All general wage information based on figures in Alfred Sauvy, *Histoire économique de la France entre les deux guerres, Tome 2* (Paris, 1967), pp. 510–522. Table 1 information taken from Ch. des Dorides, 'Les Allocations familiales en agriculture', *La Flamme des Deux-Sèvres*, April 1939. Table 2 information taken from Beyland, 'Questions sociales et familiales', *Ralliment du Nord*, 24 June 1937.

Writing in the *Flamme des Deux-Sèvres* in April 1939, one author proclaimed these scales sufficient to offset the cost of the birth itself, and the subsequent clothing and feeding of each child. The total cost of the plan was estimated at one and a half billion francs per annum, to be paid for by a 4 per cent tax on foreign goods, and a small tithe on French agricultural produce, with the remainder taken from the existing *caisses*.[128] This plan aimed specifically at offsetting the lagging birthrate and reconstituting the French family. Putting these words into action, the group took their principles into the Chamber, where in 1938 PSF deputies tabled a motion to make domestics and cleaning women the first recipients of the new 'woman's wage'.[129]

## V

Despite the seeming extremity of their discourse, the vast majority of CDF/PSF members never displayed sympathy for Nazi or fascist plans regarding the family. Neither La Rocque nor the rank and file mentioned Mussolini or Hitler in this context, relying solely upon moral and economic solutions, many of which were implemented during the later stages of the Third Republic. The Tardieu government legally adopted the *salaire familial* in 1932, with the CDF/PSF simply demanding increased allotments. Furthermore, Edouard Daladier's Radical government finally raised the allowances in November 1939, as part of his *Code de la Famille*, and not the right or the Vichy regime. Nor was pronatalist morality exclusive to the CDF/PSF or the extreme-right; the law of July 1920 voted by the Chambre Bleu Horizon rendered abortion and contraception illegal, measures reinforced by Daladier's initiative. Even Léon Blum's socialist-led Popular Front government established a ministry for the protection of childhood under Suzanne Lacore, whose scope included social hygiene.[130] The CDF/PSF were no aberration, and certainly not extreme or fascist in this regard. If anything, they were simply a sign of the times.

These similarities also distinguished the CDF/PSF from the Faisceau. Proponents of the extreme-right commonly adopted Valois's vision of an organic French nation: The Barrèsian notion of *la terre et les morts*, combined with Maurras's integral

---

128  Ch. des Dorides, 'Les Allocations familiales en agriculture', *La Flamme des Deux-Sèvres*, April 1939.

129  CHEVS/LR 29, Chambre des Députés/n.2501, 'Proposition de résolution tendant à inviter le gouvernement à déposer un projet de loi en vue d'instituer des allocations familiales en faveur des gens de maison et des concierges'. For similar treatments, see also Kula, 'Essai sur un politique', p. 49 and Jacques Nadaillac, 'Les Allocations familiales', in *Premier congrès agricole* (Saint-Brieuc, 1939), pp. 36–54. Although the Nazis utilized a similar idea in Germany after 1933, Nadaillac never envisioned the state control of a woman's body. The Nazis argued that a woman's life belonged to the *volk* and that state benefits existed solely to ensure proper breeding. Nadaillac's plan more closely resembled provisions instituted by the *Code de la Famille* and subsequently adopted by Vichy, aimed at stemming the rural exodus to urban centres through financial incentives to remain in the countryside and bear numerous children. On Nazi marriage loans, see Koonz, pp. 149–150, 185–191. For a discussion of Daladier's model and Vichy's adoption of it, see Pollard, pp. 24, 98.

130  Huss, pp. 42–43, 55–56. On Blum's pronatalist leanings during the Popular Front ministry, see Pederson, p. 371.

nationalism. Although certain Faisceau members mobilized negative eugenics to uphold the validity of Valois's analysis and constructed programs for potential state initiatives, they never deviated from the extreme-rightist analysis put forth by their leader. La Rocque and the CDF/PSF, by contrast, were conservative and Catholic in their moralistic stance, envisioning families as ethical units, the backbone of *Christian* civilization rather than the *fascist* nation-state. There would be no national-biological evolution within the *État social français*, but rather a state-sponsored and community-directed effort to morally cleanse society. Unlike Valois's proposed state, which enforced the regeneration of the family by dictatorial means, pronatalist initiatives in the CDF/PSF state were limited to divorce and abortion. The main thrust of activity took place in the home, the school, and the church, a troika which imposed the necessary moral education upon the young. These solutions would not have been out of place in the traditional conservative camp, and if the church is replaced by the party meeting, even the Parti communiste français – whose newspaper encouraged women to stay at home and raise large families throughout the 1930s – would have been forced to agree.

One might argue that this was simply a case in which an extremist position moved to occupy the centre. Such a notion can be easily countered with two points. Firstly, neither the French extreme right nor the fascists/Nazis forged family and gender policies based exclusively upon pronatalism and an unspoken fear of female empowerment. Rather, they wanted to strengthen the race, a corollary to their glorification of war and continental dominance. The CDF/PSF leadership had no such plans in mind, the Republic even less so.[131] Second, the extremity of the fascist and Nazi plans was in no way duplicated within the confines of the Third Republic. Where Mussolini's regime progressively barred female employment and the Third Reich embarked upon state-sponsored negative eugenics, the Republic made abortion illegal and divorce difficult (in no way different from the situation in other democratic countries at the time), but mainly offered incentives to French fathers and mothers. Thus despite demonstrating a 'right-wing' slant regarding women and the family during the interwar period, the parties of the French centre and left in no way sympathized with the fascist program, but rather expressed the wishes of a patriarchal state and society which, despite experiencing its first feminist challenges, wished to preserve the male power structure within a democratic political system. As Joan Scott writes: 'High politics is a gendered concept, for it establishes its crucial importance and public power, the reasons for and the fact of its highest authority, precisely in its exclusion of women from its work.'[132] The crucial difference for the CDF/PSF, and indeed the subsequent Vichy regime, was a critique of democratic individualism, a sense that the Third Republic itself shouldered the blame for feminine empowerment and the sagging birthrate.

The Faisceau, however, were a curious case. By a strange paradox, the same group which worshipped Italian fascism, arguing for ministries of social hygiene and state-

---

131   Certain elements within the group adopted such a platform, with some advocating the use of eugenics in social planning while others proposed a racial cleansing of the nation, but these ideas were in no way sanctioned by the group leadership.
132   Joan Wallach Scott, *Gender and the Politics of History* (New York, 1999), p. 48.

legislated family law, contained a number of more progressive voices concerning women within its ranks. So prominently heard concerning the new economic order, Valois remained virtually silent regarding women and feminism, which he viewed as less important than the installation of state-sponsored corporatism. In his absence neither the more progressive Aragonnès nor the ultra-conservative Hubert Bourgin elaborated a Mussolini-style discourse on the subject of women. The major planks of Italian fascist social policy, and particularly pronatalism, were entirely absent from Faisceau discourse. Various group writers instead recreated postwar divisions concerning gender roles.

Nor did arguing that women should be confined to the home make one a fascist. After all, the views espoused by the CDF/PSF on the question were, like their pronatalism, quite common. The archetype of woman-as-housewife/mother became the norm in a country where women were not allowed to vote and had few civil or political rights until the dying days of the Second World War. Thus a group that was extreme-rightist on a number of other counts (authoritarianism or the politics of exclusion, for example) and also quite divided in their approaches to the same issues, was united regarding women and the family precisely by holding views which appeared across the entire French political spectrum during the interwar period.

Chapter Four

# *Health, Virility, and Patriotism*:
# The Physical and Moral
# Transformation of Youth

The interwar era in France was in many ways the epoch in which youth came to prominence for the first time. Dozens of groups formed across the political spectrum which catered exclusively to a younger clientele. Youth began to assume political and social stances of their own, often encouraged by adult leaders of established political parties and groups. Most importantly, they were extremely visible during the interwar period, both in physical and ideological terms. Despite the relatively low proportion of young men and women in the various new groups (less than 15 per cent of those aged 14–20 belonged to a particular association), the proliferation of new organizations succeeded in attracting the young at an age when the struggle for an identity or a career, or the attraction of an ideology or adventurous lifestyle, loomed large. Combined with the turmoil of the Third Republic, primarily its perceived inherent instability and political gridlock, such struggles led many to turn their back on the old ways, seeking their own solutions to particular problems. Many interwar French youths rejected the past as sterile, viewing themselves as a new force, and possessing the will and ability to deliver a moribund France from its impasse. Inspired by the German *Wandervogel* and the Portuguese youth movement, they returned to nature, seeing themselves as a new knighthood, an elite alone capable of regenerating the nation.[1] As a newly radicalized bloc disenchanted with the status quo, youth were also a primary target for recruitment by various groups across the political spectrum.

The idea that youth could actively regenerate the nation especially appealed to the French right, which had derided the Republic in no uncertain terms since the days of the Boulanger and Dreyfus affairs in the late nineteenth century. A veteran of both campaigns and the acknowledged voice of the right before the Great War, Maurice Barrès set the tone in the 1890s, proclaiming French youth *déracinés*. In need of 'good soil for replanting', they were ill served by a government solely interested in forging loyal adult voters: 'From their natural order, modest but social, they progressed to anarchy, to a lethal disorder.'[2] Striking a more positive note,

---

1    Aline Coutrot, 'Le Mouvement du jeunesse, un phénomène au singulier?', in Gérard Cholvy (ed.), *Mouvements de jeunesse Chrétiens et Juifs: Sociabilité juvénile dans le cadre Européen, 1799–1968* (Paris, 1985), pp. 114–117, 120; John Hellman, *The Knight-Monks of Vichy France* (Montreal, 1993), pp. 5–7.
2    Maurice Barrès, *Les Déracinés* (Paris, 1928), p. 464.

certain authors strove to join the Barrèssian critique with a more hopeful future outlook. In their 1912 survey of the doctrine and attitudes of prewar youth, Henri Massis and Alfred de Tarde claimed that youth, despite their treatment at the hands of the Republic, were prepared to cast aside weak bourgeois morals in the service of heroism and virtue. Using the rhetoric of generational conflict, they insisted that 'in all matters, it is his distinguishing characteristic to create order and hierarchy, just as his elders created disorder and ruin'.[3]

Yet for all of their bluster, Catholics and conservatives expended little effort to enlist youth in the prewar era. Only the royalist Action française, which successfully recruited students into the Camelots du Roi and the Institut d'Action Française, enjoyed any real success in this regard. Founded in 1908, these Maurrassian youth initiatives were not replicated before 1914, despite their success in attracting the younger generation to the royalist right.[4] In the interwar era, however, the right-wing agenda appeared much more prominently in France. Newspapers, journals, and reviews containing Catholic content mushroomed, creating what John Hellman has termed a religious revival: 'A wave of enthusiasm seems to have touched some school teachers, army officers, priests, and a certain segment of the bourgeoisie nurtured by the religious revival that had been flourishing in France since the late nineteenth century.'[5] Rejecting the anticlericalism of the founders of the Republic, right-wing partisans lauded Barrès, literary icon Charles Péguy, and war hero Marshall Lyautey. Equally repulsed by parliamentary democracy, they demanded the restoration of church, morality, and discipline in place of individualism and liberal capitalism.

Both the Association catholique de la jeunesse française (ACJF) and the Scouts represented this trend. They emphasized moral revivalism and the need for youth to take control of their own lives in order to better society. The ACJF, an umbrella organization comprising the Jeunesses Chrétiennes groups (ouvrières, agricoles, étudiants, maritime) for both boys and girls, the Union Chrétienne des jeunes garcons/ filles, and the French YMCA, appealed directly to youth in a staunchly anti-Marxist tone, emphasizing spiritual regeneration. The Jeunesse ouvrière chrétienne (JOC) in particular proved an immediate success, gaining 65,000 adherents by the mid-1930s, while their newspaper *Jeunesse ouvrière* enjoyed a circulation of 270,000 copies per issue.[6] Although not explicitly political, the Scouts, with their emphasis on hierarchy, uniforms, and physical accomplishment, were equally adamant that youth should be inculcated with virtue, healthy in both body and spirit. Most importantly, they

---

3        Robert Wohl, *The Generation of 1914* (Cambridge, 1979), p. 9.

4        Eugen Weber, *Action française: Royalism and Reaction in Twentieth-Century France* (Stanford, 1962), pp. 53–55.

5        Hellman, pp. 7–9.

6        Yves-Marie Hillaire, 'L'Association Catholique de la jeunesse française, les étapes d'une histoire (1886–1956), *Revue du Nord*, no. 261/262, avril–septembre 1984, p. 913; Oscar Cole-Arnal, 'Towards a Lay Apostelate of the Workers: Three Decades of Conflict for the French Jeunesse ouvrière Chrétienne (1927–1956)', *Catholic Historical Review*, Vol. LXXIII (2), April 1987: 211–227. Membership numbers and circulation figures taken from Oscar Cole-Arnal, 'Shaping Young Proletarians into Militant Christians: The Pioneer Phase of the JOC in France and Québec', *Journal of Contemporary History*, 32 (1997), pp. 510–513.

successfully recruited 125,000 members by 1939.[7] Both the ACJF and the Scouts proved far more attractive than left-wing youth groups during the interwar era. The Jeunesses communistes garnered only 12,000 adherents by 1925, and PCF attempts to forge a scout movement in the 1930s (the Pionniers Rouges) failed miserably. Similarly, the Jeunesses socialistes were only moderately successful, gathering 55,000 youths by 1935.[8]

Neither the ACJF nor the Scouts were politically motivated per se. Although both organizations attempted to train future leaders, they operated on a social level, omitting strictly political discourse. Yet they were not the only groups interested in youthful potential. The extreme-right too sought to draw youth into their fold during the interwar era. Unlike the ACJF or the scouts, however, these organizations rejected the Republic, instead training a young vanguard to defeat democracy and usher in an authoritarian state. By the 1920s and 1930s, each extreme right organization contained a youth wing, complete with various centres, meetings, and uniforms incorporating primary, secondary, and university students. The Parisian middle class and urban universities proved especially fertile, the former assigned to the shock troops while the latter agitated within the confines of the school. All were instilled with extreme nationalism (which often devolved into xenophobic sentiments) and urged to adopt the militaristic values of sacrifice for the nation, discipline, and violence against 'the enemy'.[9]

The Faisceau and the CDF/PSF displayed a similar interest in youth. However, unlike the Action française – whose Camelots du Roi were dedicated to hooliganism – neither viewed youth as mere street troops, to be utilized against the state in the interests of a counter-revolution. Nor did they share the vision of youth as an anti-communist vanguard associated with fellow organizations like the Jeunesses patriotes and their student wing the Phalange universitaire which provided shock troops to disrupt leftist meetings. Leadership and rank-and-file alike also rejected the socially conscious working-class ACJF youth or the physically fit and virtuous scout. Rather both the Faisceau and CDF/PSF took the spirit of the age – the concept of youth as a new elite vanguard, and their dissatisfaction with a decadent and sterile Republic – and combined it with their own socio-political aspirations. As the future French elite, they learned nationalist and military values not merely for agitational purposes, but as the ideological basis for the new nation and state in which they were to play a leading role. Only by harnessing the best and the brightest, they argued, could France regain the world predominance lost as a consequence of the Great War.

7    Gérard Cholvy, 'Les Organisations de jeunesse d'inspiration Chrétienne ou Juive, XIXe–XXe siècle', in Cholvy, pp. 44–46; Philippe Laneyrie, *Les Scouts de France* (Paris, 1985), pp. 51, 80, 86; Rémi Fabre, 'Les Mouvements de jeunesse dans la France de l'entre-deux-geurres', *Mouvement social*, no. 168, juillet–septembre 1994, p. 11.

8    On communist youth initiatives, see Susan Brewer Whitney, 'The Politics of Youth: Communists and Catholics in Interwar France', Ph.D. Dissertation, Rutgers University, 1994, p. 17. For socialist efforts, see Christian Delaporte, 'Les Jeunesses socialistes dans l'entre-deux-geurres', *Mouvement social*, no. 157. octobre–décembre 1991, p. 33; Pascal Ory, *La Belle illusion: Culture et politique sous le signe du Front Populaire* (Paris, 1994), pp. 769–772.

9    See Bertram M. Gordon, 'Radical Right Youth Between the Wars', *Proceedings of the Fifth Annual Meeting of the Western Society for French History*, 1978.

However, their respective approaches to the question of youth markedly differed. The Faisceau vision of youth was two-fold. For war veterans within the group, like Valois and Jacques Arthuys, youth symbolized the soldiers who had served France at the front during the Great War, sacrificing themselves as a fraternal generation for the nation. The task of the young *combattant* was now to win the peace as they had emerged victorious from war, by toppling the decadent Republic and then forging a new, vibrant fascist state.

Such a vision owed much to the doctrine of early Italian fascism, the Faisceau's chief inspiration, echoing the sentiments of Giuseppe Bottai and Giovanni Gentile among others. But neither Valois nor Arthuys actually designed a program for youth. Content to issue slogans, they left the blueprint in the hands of Hubert Bourgin, the ex-Lycée professor and staunchly conservative admirer of Charles Maurras and Maurice Barrès. As a non-combatant, Bourgin ignored Valois's call to 'win the peace'. He instead proposed the cult of the soil and social Catholic ideals for young recruits, concepts steeped in moralism and tradition, rather than Italian fascism. Where other members of the group focused upon the militarization of youth, using will, heroism, and sacrifice to topple the decadent Third Republic, Bourgin demanded moral and physical education, to instill students with non-republican values. Although never openly expressed, the tension between the two positions is clear: Valois and Arthuys favoured the values of the *anciens combattants*, while Bourgin wished to create good Christians and Frenchmen.

Conflicting plans for youth also existed within the ranks of the CDF/PSF, yet to a much lesser degree. Their approach differed from that of Valois's group, for La Rocque and his confreres prioritized the recruitment of youth. As a larger entity, with greater available human and material resources, the CDF/PSF employed a variety of activities and initiatives to inculcate French youth with their mystique. Before 1936, this implied the cult of tradition and the motherland, along with leadership, discipline, will, and the values of the trenches, reinforced in student centres, *colonies de vacances*, and youth propaganda. These traits corresponded to Valois's soldier-producer, and the CDF/PSF likewise wished to mold youth in the image of their *combattant* fathers. Once the group transformed into the Parti social français in June 1936, however, they became populist in nature, and membership increased exponentially.[10] Thus a more traditional program for youth emerged, involving detailed proposals for a national education system and a complete reform of the teaching profession, to create a physical, moral, and intellectual elite of workers, fathers, and soldiers.

Although disagreements occurred within the group regarding the content of the system, the diametrically opposed factions within the Faisceau were absent in the CDF/PSF. The doctrinal framework established by La Rocque, Jean Daujat, and Jean Mierry was never seriously challenged. Despite minor disputes, all sides agreed to the restoration of religious values, healthy and disciplined youth, and morality in both school and the *foyer familial*. Dissent regarding youth came only from those in favour of a more extreme notion: The concept of human engineering through physical education and sport. Some within the group argued that this was necessary to reverse degeneration, that youth were raw material, to be sculpted into a new type

---

10    For a discussion of the group's populism after 1936, see Chapters One and Two.

of French man and woman. Where La Rocque wanted strength and morality, those who favoured more harsh physical training demanded the perfection of the race.

# I

Just as the Faisceau were divided regarding politics and the state, and the roles of women and the family in the nation, two distinct voices again emerged on the subject of youth, represented by war heroes Georges Valois and Jacques Arthuys on one hand, and conservative academic Hubert Bourgin on the other. Valois and Arthuys represented the mentality of what Robert Wohl has called the Generation of 1914, those who came of age during the Great War. Both men took part in the nationalist revival in France in the years before the conflict, a precursor to the explosion of youth movements in the twenties and thirties. Like many young intellectuals at the time, they saw the events of 1914 as a harbinger of national regeneration, in which a higher spiritual order replaced the decadent France of the prewar period. To these men, the trench experience demonstrated the innate superiority of action over reason, a natural human preference for national unity rather than class conflict, and sacrifice and fraternity.[11] Most importantly to Valois and Arthuys the youthful war veterans, instilled with the virtues of the trenches, desired to bring their warlike mentality into the civic arena, to win the peace as they had won the war. This was not the rhetoric of the scouts or the ACJF. To Valois, 'for all of us, the war was a prodigious school ... a bath in the deep waters of our people', training a youthful vanguard for the fight against republican decadence and the fascist future.[12]

Following the logic of notable youth movements of all political stripes during the interwar period, both Valois and Arthuys addressed the younger generation from a doctrinal perspective, primarily by invoking the theme of generational conflict. Represented in the Faisceau press by parliamentarians of all stripes from Poincaré to Caillaux, the *vieux équipe* was blamed for all vestiges of French weakness, while the young were cast in the dual role of the principal victims of 'old men' in government and their democratic modus operandi, and the saviours of France in her hour of need. But as a *mouvement des anciens combattants*, the Faisceau also viewed youth as the heroes of 1914–1918, representing the values of the trenches.[13] Hence the characteristics attributed to them were militaristic, such as physical ability, virility, and the mentality of the warrior. They became the soldiers and producers of the future, whose baptism by fire took place in the heat of battle, which had constituted for the younger generation of Frenchmen their first true life experience of any kind. These youthful *combattants* symbolized renewed French greatness, the sole creators of the National Revolution, a duty for which they had prepared in the trenches.[14]

---

11    Wohl, pp. 215, 231.

12    Georges Valois, *D'Un siècle à l'autre: Chronique d'une génération* (Paris, 1924), p. 267.

13    Arthuys bluntly told a reporter that 'the real Faisceau was formed on 2 August 1914'. See F/7/13209, 'Ya-t-il vraiment un 'fascio' à Paris?', *Le Journal*, 7 Dec. 1925. For similar statements, see Jacques Arthuys, 'Les Combattants, le patriotisme, et l'ordre', *NS*, 4 Jan. 1926 and F/7/13211, Tract 5, Georges Valois, 'La Conquête de l'avenir', 1926.

14    F/7/13208, Faisceau meeting at the Sociétés Savantes, 29 Jan. 1926.

This vision provided an integral component of the Faisceau doctrine from the beginning. Speaking at the first group meeting in Paris, in November 1925, Arthuys called youth a 'new harvest' and 'the voluntary avant-garde of an immense renaissance movement', embodying the spirit of the victory. They had sacrificed their bodies and souls for France, placing the nation above themselves in direct contrast to the democratic individualism of the Republic. Arthuys further argued that youth became an indissoluble fraternity during the war. While fighting in unison the young soldiers experienced a love of the nation that springs from the 'depths of the race'. To Arthuys, this served to demonstrate that French survival depended upon a reconstitution of the national collective of which the younger generation, steeped in the values of fraternity, will, hierarchy, and sacrifice discovered in the trenches, were now living representatives. Wartime experiences made them impatient, ready to resume the battle of the Marne against the weak and decadent Republic. The war would not be over, Arthuys thundered, until the younger generation removed the 'leeches' in government from French soil as the Germans had been before them and forged *l'État Combattant.*[15]

The latter point was the crucial one for the Faisceau, who viewed youth as both eager to exercise power and inherently anti-parliamentary and anti-republican. Youth, Valois professed, were interested solely in action. Thus the experience of the front operated as a line of generational demarcation. Speeches and debates were anathema to the young men of 1914, and the deputies who prattled on in the Chamber symbolized the old way of thinking. They represented the generation of the defeat of 1871, in direct opposition to the youthful 'generation of the victory', having come of age during the disastrous Franco-Prussian war and its aftermath during the 1870s. Valois believed that the old guard were conditioned to accept French weakness as a fait accompli, and that this attitude had governed their conduct during the Great War, a conflict which they had experienced solely through debates in the Chamber of Deputies and newspaper articles. They had neither fought for the nation at the front, nor experienced the concerted effort of hundreds of thousands to win on the battlefield, incapable of appreciating the positive revaluation produced by will, heroism, and national discipline. Despite their lack of effort and sacrifice, the older generation retained the levers of power after the war as custodians of a debilitated nation.[16] Youth, by contrast, perceived only a people rejuvenated by victory, climbing towards greatness through a collective effort. Valois believed that the generation of 1914 wanted to cast aside the older caste of war profiteers, mercantilists, and *embusqués*, ready to both lead and be led, waiting to rise up and take power upon receiving the signal: 'They have understood, they understand better each day, that they were victims of defeated old men, and that we will only see the true face of France once the generation of the victory seizes power.'[17]

---

15    'Discours prononcée le 11 Novembre', *NS*, 12 Nov. 1925. On Arthuys's notion of the État Combattant, see Chapter One.

16    F/7/13211, Tract 5, Georges Valois, 'La Conquête de l'avenir', 1926; Georges Valois, 'L'Arrivée des nouvelles équipes et la jeunesse', *NS*, 5 Oct. 1926.

17    George Valois, *La Politique de la victoire* (Paris, 1925), p. 93.

The Faisceau thus specifically linked themselves to the hopes and ambitions of the war generation. As only a new mass movement could vanquish the *vieux équipe* of the Republic, youth were by inclination and necessity fascist:

> Swift, to the point, disliking idle chatter, full of a taste for action, they wait in seeming indifference to be called upon for a great undertaking. They await the national leader and his team. They want orders. They wait for us to give the signal to attack a putrefied world where cowards, war profiteers, swindlers, dealers, blackmailers, assassins, homosexuals, and pimps pretend to be leaders or form the funeral procession for elected officials.[18]

Should they remain passive, the nation would be relegated to second-class status. For the generation of 1871 represented failure, their legacy visible throughout Europe in the communist menace, the plummeting franc, the rule of foreign plutocracy, and the political and financial predominance of New York, Frankfurt and London over the Latin nations. Worse still, trumpeted Philippe Barrès, those in power, too weary to contemplate the use of force in order to staunch the threat, ignored the menace across the Rhine.[19] Son of the revered Maurice Barrès, he wrote that the nation's youth must act for the salvation of France before it was too late. As Arthuys sternly warned, there was no third way; one either favoured the *Révolution nationale* of the *combattants* and *jeunes producteurs* or represented fatigue, disorder, and decadence.[20]

The Italian fascists provided the model of creative energy and youth for the Faisceau, a movement whose dynamism Valois and others frequently compared to their flabby republican neighbours. To Valois, fascism represented 'the cry of the new Italy, young and ardent, who grow with a stunning quickness, and who want to live'. Its youth were living expressions of the Italian creative genius, harnessed by Mussolini who gave them a soul, a doctrine, and the will to elevate the nation to a superior level. In the East such a society also existed, in the form of communism, a phenomenon equally at odds with the venerable 'legitimate' democracies. Yet communism was flawed, a system where the masses starved and the bureaucracy ruled, a virus that spread slowly across the globe while inexorably destroying those nations it infected. If France was not to fall victim to the barbaric hordes from Russia, Valois opined, the younger generations must adopt fascism, since democracy was crumbling and no longer afforded sufficient protection to the nation.[21]

In championing fascism as both a movement of youth and the only effective barrier against the threat of communism and the decadence of weak republican institutions, Valois and Arthuys mobilized arguments identical to those expressed by prominent Italian fascists. Mussolini himself maintained that Italy represented a revolution of youth against old Europe; their efforts produced a higher civilization.[22] He took it for granted that youth alone regenerated the nation, striking down the venerable liberal bourgeoisie in the name of a new man. Echoing Valois and Arthuys, Giuseppe Bottai,

---

18    Ibid.

19    Philippe Barrès, 'Le Mal': Veulerie. La Remède: Jeunesse.', *NS*, 2 Feb. 1926.

20    Jacques Arthuys, 'L'Urgence de la révolte', *NS*, 14 Feb. 1926.

21    Georges Valois, 'L'Ancienne et la nouvelle Europe', *NS*, 18 Sept. 1926.

22    Michael A. Ledeen, 'Italian Fascism and Youth', *Journal of Contemporary History*, 4 (1969), pp. 137–138.

the editor of leading Italian fascist journal *Critica Fascista*, called for leadership by natural selection, whereby the youthful veterans of the Great War assumed leadership positions.[23] Although somewhat duplicitous in its rhetoric, for youth were expected to express simple obedience to the regime and worship of Mussolini, in the mid-1920s the Italian government conscripted them into various organizations designed to train a new elite. Formed in April 1926, the *Opera Nazionale Balilla* conscripted boys and girls under the age of 18 from various cities and provinces. Boys were subjected to rigorous exercise routines and physical examinations to increase their virility, and brought to museums and monuments to foster a love of the fatherland. Although trained first and foremost as future mothers and housewives, girls were similarly expected to demonstrate the appropriate 'fascist spirit', contributing to the perfection of Italy.[24]

Such ideas subsequently became the ideological and practical impetus for Pierre Drieu la Rochelle, Robert Brasillach, and the French fascist intellectuals a decade later. Describing the riotous events of 6 February 1934 in his novel *Gilles*, Drieu adopted the terminology of Valois or Mussolini:

> [Young] hands roughly grasped him. Eyes questioned him with passionate insistence. 'Come with us.' In an instant he was transformed. Looking to his left and right, he became surrounded by ... the fear and courage which had directed the war. Their blazing whips cracked. He threw himself against the current of the crowd surging backwards. Like that night in Champagne, when the front line had collapsed; like that morning at Verdun when he had arrived with the 20th Corps, after which all were consumed by the sacrifice of the cover divisions.[25]

Similarly, in 1934 Thierry Maulnier wrote of youth rejecting decadence, willing to act in the service of the nation rather than parliamentary democracy.[26] Such talk again appeared during the Vichy years, particularly in the Chantiers de la Jeunesse and the Ministry of Sport under the watchful eyes of Marshall Philippe Pétain and General de la Porte du Theuil, and in the education ministry during the tenure of Abel Bonnard from April 1942 onwards. Each championed the notion of a new man, formed by a disciplined and virile young elite. The organization of these energies, particularly in physical activity, would eradicate old individual and liberal habits, creating what Brasillach called a 'new human type'.[27]

Given their similar interests, one might presume that the Faisceau attempted to emulate the Italian example, producing youthful cadres in the service of the National

---

23     Paolo Nello, 'Mussolini e Bottai: due modi diversi di concepire l'educazione fascista della gioventù', *Storia Contemporanea*, 8 (1977), pp. 335–339.

24     Tracy H. Koon, *Believe, Obey, Fight: Political Socialization in Fascist Italy, 1922–1943* (Chapel Hill, 1985), pp. 91–94, Michel Ostenc, *L'Education en Italie pendant le fascisme* (Paris, 1980), pp. 240–255.

25     Pierre Drieu La Rochelle, *Gilles* (Paris, 1939), p. 433. For a detailed examination of fascist themes in this novel, see Michel Winock, 'Une parabole fasciste: *Gilles* de Drieu la Rochelle', in *Nationalisme, antisémitisme, et fascisme en France* (Paris, 1990), pp. 346–374.

26     Zeev Sternhell, *Neither Right Nor Left* (Princeton, 1996), p. 260.

27     On Vichy and the organization of youth, see W.D. Halls, *The Youth of Vichy France* (Oxford, 1981), pp. 34–36, 190–199. Brasillach quoted in David Carroll, *French Literary Fascism: Nationalism, Anti-Semitism, and the Ideology of Culture* (Princeton, 1995), p. 105.

Revolution. But the group's leadership never made any direct appeal for the formation of a new and virile order. This is not to say that Valois and Arthuys rejected the notion that young males possessed the qualities of heroism, sacrifice, and virility that Mussolini and the later French fascists ascribed to them. They simply did not engage in any systematic attempt to create such an order. Unlike later groups such as the CDF/PSF or Jacques Doriot's Parti populaire français, which drew up precise plans for the reconstitution of a young elite, Faisceau leaders issued only vague and unambitious slogans.

Thus despite the verbal prioritization of youth by the group leadership, Faisceau organizations specifically dedicated to the younger generation paid little attention to mass recruitment: The Jeunesses fascistes [JF] and the Faisceau universitaire [FU], founded in December 1925 and January 1926 respectively. Unlike the other leading extreme-rightist groups of the day, the Action française and the Jeunesses patriotes, the Faisceau did not direct propaganda specifically at youth.[28] The JF encompassed all members aged 20 and younger, but its membership never rose above a few hundred Parisian students, a far cry from the 1,000 Camelots du Roi who roamed the streets of Paris at the time. Local police in the provinces recorded the presence of additional sections in St.-Quinton, Reims, Chateau Thierry, and Verdun. However, the number of adherents remained relatively low in each case. In Toulouse, local officers estimated 150 members, mostly 'young intellectuals' of approximately 30 years of age. The latter observation reveals a rather fluid Faisceau definition of youth, a notion shared with the Camelots du Roi among others.[29] Nonetheless, like the Camelots and Phalange universitaire, the role of the JF was confined to recruitment, the dissemination of group propaganda, fund-raising activities, and the distribution of *Nouveau Siècle*. The JF lacked the violence of the Camelots and the military style of the Phalange, however, and the non-existence of police records regarding their activities strongly suggests that they rarely saw street action.[30]

The FU, headed by the young lawyer Philippe Lamour, received more attention from the Faisceau. Lamour lauded youth as a modernizing force, a theme which he continued to promote in the post-Faisceau years as the editor of *Plans*, a journal fusing anti-parliamentarism and syndicalism with avant-garde art and architecture.[31] Given their leader's determination, the FU at least merited a semi-regular column

28 F/7/13208, 'Chez les fascistes', police report, 26 May 1926.

29 F/7/13208, untitled Sureté Générale memorandum, 6 Jan. 1926. This document further mentions that only a portion of the paltry 110 legionnaires in Chateau Thierry were youths. For the Toulouse membership, see F/7/13210, memo of 5 July 1926. The Camelots were notorious for accepting members well into their 60s. See Weber, p. 64.

30 CHEVS/V 45, Faisceau 'Manuel de délégué', Aug. 1926; Allen Douglas, *From Fascism to Libertarian Communism: Georges Valois Against the Third Republic* (Berkeley, 1992), p. 115. As Douglas elsewhere attests, the Faisceau were victims more often than perpetrators. See 'Violence and Fascism: The Case of the Faisceau', *Journal of Contemporary History* 19 (1984): 689–712.

31 On Lamour and *Plans*, see John Hellman, *Emmanuel Mounier and the French Catholic Left* (Toronto, 1981), pp. 57–58; Jean-Louis Loubet del Bayle, *Les Non-conformistes des années 30: Une tentative de renouvellement de la pensée politique française* (Paris, 1969), part one, chapter two; Sternhell, pp. 202–203.

in the group's newspaper. But the Faisceau devoted few resources towards its growth, and as a result the student initiative attracted only 500 members in Paris and slightly over 100 in Toulouse.[32] Valois and his colleagues remained preoccupied with economic and political matters, neglecting recruitment despite the group's failure to attract young newcomers.

## II

Despite their lack of initiative towards youth and the resulting low level of interest displayed by Parisian students – the principal target of irregular FU recruitment campaigns – the Faisceau managed to concoct elaborate plans for the rejuvenation of French schools and universities in which students were to play a pivotal role. That these proposals for educational reform were conservative rather than fascist in nature, and in certain cases representative of fairly common concerns, reflects Valois and Arthuys's lack of involvement in their formulation. In their place stood Hubert Bourgin, an arch-Catholic traditionalist, whose vision of youth had little in common with the *anciens combattants* in the group. Bourgin was a graduate of the prestigious École normale supérieure at the Rue d'Ulm, an agrégé and Doctor of Letters. Upon leaving the ENS he found employment at the Lycée Louis-le-Grand in Paris, and authored several specialized works on the topic of education. He had been a member of the Proudhonian wing of the SFIO before the war, and served under Albert Thomas during the conflict, only to resign due to his mounting patriotism and his disapproval of the defeatism and political wrangling of the socialists during wartime.[33]

Bourgin was not an *ancien combattant*. A stanch Catholic moralist and educator, his concerns regarding youth parroted ideas long present in right-wing discourse. Since Jules Ferry's fateful declaration that his ministry would 'organize humanity without God', the right – and particularly the extreme-right – warred openly with the Republic concerning the school curriculum. From 1882 onwards, the state's free and primary laic education replaced Catholic dogma with 'moral and civic instruction' designed to convert youth to the republican cause. Needless to say, the right would have none of it. By the postwar era, prominent Catholics demanded the Répartition proportionnelle scolaire, through which the government funded both confessional and public schools on a per capita basis. Although the campaign failed, along with attempts to reinstitute mandatory Latin courses in 1923, the election of the left-centrist Cartel des Gauches government the following year produced yet another round of heated rhetoric. Education, claimed rightist A.G. Michels, had fallen victim to the Masonic conspiracy running France. Socialist educators working tirelessly for Moscow, he charged, transformed French youth into fodder for the Republic, ignoring the *patrie*.[34]

In keeping with such attitudes, Faisceau plans for educational reform owed more to Maurice Barrès than to Mussolini, and much of the platform that the group

---

32    F/7/13208, untitled Sureté Générale memorandum, 19 March 1926; F/7/13210, Commissaire spéciale de Toulouse to director of the Sureté Générale, 5 July 1926.

33    Douglas, *From Fascism to Libertarian Communism*, p. 75.

34    John E. Talbott, *The Politics of Educational Reform in France, 1918–1940* (Princeton 1969), pp. 24–29, 52–53, 100–104.

favoured was traditional in nature. To be sure, Bourgin paid lip service to the concept of the future fascist elite, in direct contrast to the theoreticians produced by republican schools. He half-heartedly adopted the Valoissian notion that an education should train the future renovators and innovators of the fascist nation and state; all instructors would necessarily be men of action rather than empty talk: The professor as educational engineer. In the new fascist state, all study served to propel national activity forward, even in such passive disciplines as history or literature.[35]

Such talk should have betrayed a blatantly fascist mindset, echoing appeals from Italian leaders like Achille Starace to forge a healthy body and combative spirit for youth.[36] However, Bourgin was no ideological carbon-copy of Valois or Mussolini. The legitimacy of his elite rested upon ancestral morality, region, and soil, instead of their position as a new leadership endowed with virility, will, and productivism:

> The students are faithful disciples of their masters, and their philosophical successors. They are the inheritors of ancestral virtues and the descendants of families, sanctified by the immense sacrifices of the past. They are the representatives and leaders of their communities, called upon to resurrect them using the pulsing energy at the centre of the national intellect, and also to bring to it the sometimes forgotten insight emanating from the eternal rivers of the provinces.[37]

Where Valois and Arthuys focused upon the construction of a new fascist nation and state based upon the doctrine of renovation and innovation, the old *Normalien* looked instead to the intellectual purification of pedagogy. In adopting such a curricular bent, Bourgin hoped to dispel the intellectual decadence permeating twentieth-century higher education. The abandonment of positive duties in favour of empiricism, careerism, and political party doctrine had in his view resulted in the jettisoning of reason and morality, and the de-emphasizing of creative ability in French schools. Criticism of this state of affairs came regularly from the left and the right in the nineteen-twenties, but to no avail, as political groupings preached reform solely to garner votes. Thus to the more traditional Bourgin, far from producing fascist youth, the Faisceau would instead elude the traps of partisan politics and bickering, creating a new education system in which action in thought replaced 'modernized bohemianism'. In Bourgin's mind, the first tangible step towards this goal was the restoration of the university as a corporative body. The clientism and sectarianism that divided the republican *Facultés* would be eradicated, a move accompanied by an elevation of the material and moral situation of both professors and the administration.[38]

None of these points were particularly original, as any contemporary reader of Maurras, Barrès, or even Ernest Renan and Frédéric Le Play would attest. Such observations frequently appeared during the Third Republic years, when low state subsidies prevented the expansion and modernization of already inadequate library and laboratory facilities, and the consequently low enrollment (some *facultés* in the

---

35    Hubert Bourgin, 'Le Rôle des Faisceau universitaire dans la nation', *NS*, 6 March 1927.

36    Nello, pp. 355–358

37    Hubert Bourgin, 'L'État et la corporation', *NS*, 10 Feb. 1926.

38    Hubert Bourgin, 'L'État et la corporation', *NS*, 13 Feb. 1926.

provinces contained only a handful of students even after the Great War) provided the government with the rationale to further restrict funding. For as Theodore Zeldin notes, by the Second World War 'the universities were still shackled by the outdated ambitions of Napoleon and still enslaved to the secondary schools'.[39]

Hence Bourgin's preoccupation with morality and old-fashioned corporative discipline. Yet he further alleged the existence of a conspiracy to weaken the French education system that betrayed the influence of the Maurrassian extreme-right. Bourgin contrasted his proposed system with the republican one, deriding the sacrifice of schooling to the political ends of diverse electoral, doctrinal, and sectarian interests. Modern universities, he cried, were mere fiefdoms for parliamentary patrons and the Masons, to form loyalists rather than educate. To this end, all instructors from the primary school teacher to the elite professoriate of the *Grandes Écoles* were socialist and *cegetiste*. Echoing the traditional rightist sentiment of the *République des professeurs*, he pointed to Théodore Steeg (former head of the École normale supérieure), and Paul Painlevé (former Mathematics instructor) as examples of those who had committed treason by using the French academe for republican careerism alone.[40] Echoing Marshall Pétain's call throughout the Vichy years for a curriculum emphasizing *travail, famille, patrie*, designed to combat *l'anti-France* with Christian and moral teachings, Bourgin demanded a corporative education ministry. There ministers would purge all suspect (i.e. republican and communist) teachers, while assuming responsibility for the adjudication of the school curriculum on all levels.[41]

Bourgin reserved his greatest ire for the primary school system, however. Here he echoed Barrès's notion from *Les Déracinés* that children were indoctrinated with false scientism and immoral republican orthodoxy rather than receiving a Catholic and national education befitting French youth. Bourgin further assailed the lack of morality in the primary classroom, charging that children were taught the Kantian categorical imperative rather than the common shared realities of material and spiritual life. The call for neutrality in the education statute was merely an excuse for republican and socialist school-teachers to eradicate religion, nation, and soil from the school in favour of positivism and science.[42]

Yet Bourgin was no Charles Maurras, dreaming of a return to pre-revolutionary France. He recognized the changing nature of technology and society, and the

---

39    Theodore Zeldin, *France, 1848–1945* (2 Vols, Oxford, 1977), vol. 2, p. 326.

40    Hubert Bourgin, 'L'Université et la politique', *NS*, 30 July 1926.

41    Hubert Bourgin, 'Le Faisceau et l'enseignement national', *NS*, 25 June 1926. On this point, the Faisceau as a whole were agreed. See Maurice de Barral, *Dialogues sur le Faisceau: ses origines, sa doctrine* (Paris, 1926), p. 13. On Pétain's vision, see W.D. Halls, pp. 7–9. The concept of a national corporation for education was a much-discussed initiative on the extreme-right in the 1930s, proposed by Weygand, Pétain, and the Cercle Fustel des Coulanges among others.

42    These sentiments permeate Bourgin's writings. The best summery of them pre-dates the formation of the Faisceau by three months. See 'Le mercantilisme dans l'enseignement national', *Cahiers des États-Généraux*, Aug. 1924, pp. 231–241. Bourgin faithfully copies Barrès, almost to the letter. See Maurice Barrès, *Les Déracinés* (Paris, 1924), pp. 33, 36–37. For a Faisceau-era replication of these arguments, see Hubert Bourgin, 'Le Faisceau et l'enseignement national', *NS*, 25 June 1926.

role which they necessarily played in the new state. Although he never espoused Valois's Henry Ford/Le Corbusier-inspired economic and political model, Bourgin acknowledged that the future needed 'producers, technicians, and leaders, capable of understanding, of wishing, and of realizing the transformations of which the present is composed'. In this regard, the primary school was pivotal, preparing the producer for his future profession. The curriculum necessarily provided a physical and moral, rather than a strictly intellectual education. The pedagogy of strength and skill, what Bourgin called the acquiring of a 'cerebral and muscular culture' through 'moral and physical gymnastics' replaced dogma and politics. Having completed this process, students would be evaluated based on ability, and directed either into secondary schools which formed a national elite for private enterprise and the public administration, or to technical and trade schools.[43]

However, despite paying lip service to the need for science and technology in the classroom, Bourgin reserved his greatest concern for the laicization of the primary school. Here he sounded almost like the *vieux grand-père* castigating the young rascal caught misbehaving, as he chided the reader that only through the adoption of a moral curriculum could proper discipline be imposed and respect for instructors and parents restored. In an age when families protested even the vestige of discipline in the classroom, he cried, it was not surprising that Soviet teachers abounded in French schools.[44] Here Bourgin again directly presaged ideas which took root under the Vichy regime, where Pétain and General de la Porte du Theuil argued that sport and physical activity increased the moral and physical health of the nation, through an emphasis on discipline and collective activity. The idea of competition as a moral regenerative tool, akin to George Hébert's prewar natural method, appealed to Bourgin as a character-building technique.[45]

True to such traditional concerns, Bourgin took as his model school the École des Roches in Verneuil. Founded in 1899 as an institution faithful to Le Play's principles of social science, the school dedicated itself to French humanism, characterized by the imposition of discipline and virtue, and the formation of a French physical and moral elite.[46] Bourgin most admired its dedication to physical activity, regaling *Nouveau Siècle* readers with descriptions of the gymnastics, fitness, and hydrotherapy sessions taken by every student in the afternoon. Classes were held in the mornings, leaving the rest of the day for physical activity, which culminated in the extra-curricular practice of team sports. Bourgin further lauded the moralism at work within the school. Instructors and their families ate together with the students, and professor's children participated in afternoon fitness activities, lending the institution an atmosphere of fraternity and the inculcation of family as a social ideal. Furthermore, all students received strict moral preparation and religious instruction to ensure their correct formation as Christian children. The transmission of these ideals, claimed Bourgin, prepared the student for his future duty as a worker, producer, father, and

---

43  Hubert Bourgin, 'L'Université et le devoir présent', *NS*, 18 Sept. 1927.
44  Hubert Bourgin, 'La Discipline', *NS*, 20 Aug. 1925.
45  Halls, pp. 190–199.
46  Laneyrie, p. 47.

soldier.[47] Perhaps inspired by his visit to the École des Roches, less than three months after returning he announced the formation of a scout section within the Faisceau sportif, in a *Nouveau Siècle* article entitled 'L'education physique et morale de notre jeunesse'. Scoutism, he wrote, prepared youth physically and morally for the *cité moderne* and trained future soldiers. In this way the 'propagators of the race' would be taught their primordial duties: will and work.[48]

The Faisceau was an ideological house divided concerning youth, just as they were factionalized when discussing the roles of women and the family after the *Revolution nationale*. Valois and Arthuys painted a portrait of youth as the new avant-garde, bringing the energy and values of the trenches into the nation and state. These constructors of the future contrasted with old republican personnel and values, and the decadence that they represented. To Valois, youth naturally accepted fascism, and he looked to Mussolini's Italy as a role model for the younger generation in France. Yet the conservative Bourgin developed all of the group's concrete plans. In contrast to Valois and Arthuys, he advocated a return to traditional morality, the restoration of discipline, and conservative nationalism, proffering ideas that betrayed the influence of Maurras, Barrès, and Le Play far more than Mussolini.

## III

Far less divided than the Faisceau, The Croix de Feu/Parti social français differed substantially in their approach to the question of youth in the renovated nation and state. Although the group leadership and rank and file agreed upon the primacy of youth, believing the younger generation to be the architects of a renewed France, they devoted significantly greater human and material resources to the issue. For example, the CDF/PSF funded several highly successful youth organizations to indoctrinate students and children with the *mystique Croix de Feu*. Yet the question of what ideas were to be transmitted and how they were to be disseminated within the *État social français* led to a certain level of disagreement. Furthermore, the precise role which youth were to play within the new France, although never openly debated, was the subject of various plans with differing conclusions, ranging from conservative to eugenicist in nature. From these contrasting perspectives, the group attempted to indoctrinate youth via meetings, articles, and tracts, while simultaneously proposing a plethora of educational and fitness initiatives to mold a new anti-republican leadership elite.

Certain segments of the CDF/PSF leadership and rank and file evinced pessimism about the capabilities and world view of nineteen-thirties youth. Valois and his confreres agitated during a time when the heroism of the Great War remained relatively fresh in popular memory. French woes like the fall of the franc could be solved, various Faisceau luminaries argued, if only youth wrested control of the state away from the republican menace. Certain CDF/PSF writers, in contrast, did not see the younger generation in such a promising light. Speaking at a meeting of the Fils et

---

47     Hubert Bourgin, 'Comment L'École des Roches conçoit et donne l'education morale', *NS*, 13 Aug. 1926.

48     Hubert Bourgin, 'L'Education physique et morale de notre jeunesse', *NS*, 5 Nov. 1926.

filles des Croix de Feu (FFCF) in 1933 at the Salle Wagram in Paris, Charles Goutry complained that youth lacked the aptitude for heroism. They in no way resembled their fathers and older brothers who willingly sacrificed everything to defend the nation. Modern youth instead prioritized the attainment of personal pleasure above the common good. The younger generation, he bemoaned, displayed neither spirituality nor idealism, eschewing democracy, Catholicism, and communism in equal measure.[49] The group laid the blame for this sorry state of affairs squarely on the republican government. Like Valois and Arthuys, the CDF/PSF bemoaned the apathy displayed by the older generation towards youth. Thus while La Rocque derided the new generation's rampant pessimism, he specifically blamed the Republic for shackling its young. In attempting to start a career they encountered nepotism and cronyism at every turn, and hence looked to foreign models (communism, nazism, fascism) for salvation, rather than French tradition.[50]

Such observations were not the exclusive purview of the CDF/PSF. Other voices on the right, and particular those belonging to the 'generation of 1930', a group of youthful and disaffected intellectuals, tendered equally vociferous criticism of republican officials, projecting similar worries about the success of Nazism or communism in France. Coalescing around periodicals like *Esprit* and *Plans* in the 1930s, they assailed republican weakness as an invitation to Sovietization or fascistization west of the Rhine. Writing in the journal of the group Ordre Nouveau in the mid-1930s, Denis de Rougement bluntly stated: 'Faced with jackbooted youth, bareheaded, open-shirted, with which our press likes to rally the troops, what do we have to offer? A potpourri of imitation stiff collars, rosettes, fat stomachs, and bowler hats'. Given Italian, German, and even Soviet success, he proclaimed, the sterile parliamentary liberalism of the Third Republic alienated French youth.[51] By 1936, analogous writings appeared in the *Flambeau*. That June, the paper published an article by Pierre Drieu la Rochelle, soon to become a convert to fascism himself, which declared that youth were on the march against parliamentarism and capitalism in every European country except France. The 'irresponsible bourgeoisie' would be overthrown by either communism or the Croix de Feu, he trumpeted, and French vitality depended solely upon the latter option. Like Arthuys and Valois a decade earlier Drieu envisioned no third way:

> [E]verywhere in Europe, from North to South and East to West (except in England), under regimes that become more and more numerous and decisive, authority and discipline – fascism or communism – undertake the most admirable and formidable effort to awaken the human race, to eliminate the 'cancan' from cities, to demolish all that is narrow and ugly and dirty, re-establishing contact with nature.[52]

---

49     *Le Flambeau*, July 1933.

50     CDLR, 'Manifeste Croix de Feu', *Le Flambeau*, 4 April, 1936.

51     Quoted in Jean-Louis Loubet del Bayle, 'Une tentative de renouvellement de la pensée politique française', *Nouvelle Revue des Deux-Mondes* 5 (1975), pp. 330–331. Such sentiments were regularly expressed by youthful members of the right and extreme-right in the 1930s, particularly Ordre Nouveau, *Plans*, *Esprit*, and the Jeune Droite, along with intellectuals like Thierry Maulnier and Robert Brasillach. See Del Bayle, *Les Non-Conformistes des années trente*, *passim* and Sternhell, chapter seven.

52     Drieu la Rochelle, 'Pour sauver le peau des français', *Le Flambeau*, 27 June 1936.

The CDF/PSF voiced many of the same concerns, but rejected fascist and communist solutions in equal measure. Despite pessimistic assertions about the political orientation of French youth, both leadership and rank and file alike believed that such choices were purely a manifestation of anti-republican sentiment. Given the CDF/PSF as an alternative to communism or foreign fascist dictatorships, young French men and women would switch sides, their concerns adequately addressed. To La Rocque, the goals of French youth were identical to those of his group, 'torn by their loathing of disorganized improvisation, revolutionary methods, and their distaste for the invalidated systems of useless theories. They wish at once to protect the national soil and to revive it'. Like youth, the CDF/PSF actively opposed the 'old guard', he claimed. Furthermore, wrote one author in the *Flambeau du Sud-Ouest*, contemporary youth differed dramatically from the first postwar generation in their realism. The young men and women of the 1920s had been driven purely by materialism, whereas family, security and a strong work ethic replaced this fantasy in the subsequent decade: 'On their own, they turn towards greater spiritual principles. They have seen the damaging effects of materialism ... If the youth of a race is the image of its future, then we can have faith in the destiny of our people'.[53]

Thus the CDF/PSF conception of youth differed substantially from that of the Faisceau. They shared neither Bourgin's moral pessimism, nor Valois's and Arthuys's notion of the young veteran continuing the effort of the trenches by constructing a fascist state. Instead, La Rocque and his confrères viewed French youth as a physical and moral elite which would transform republican France into a nation and state run according to the principles of social Catholicism and reactionary authoritarianism. The group would remake youth into national leaders, thoroughly transforming their physical, intellectual, and moral character from an early age. In order to effectuate this program, they focused upon four recruitment schemes: Youth organizations, the elaboration of their doctrine to the young both within these organizations and in group newspapers and activities, educational reform, and physical fitness.

Initially, the group concentrated principally upon constructing an organizational framework. Because they attracted a far greater number of supporters than the Faisceau, La Rocque and the CDF/PSF possessed significantly larger human and material resources to devote towards youth. They also prioritized the recruitment of the young and their ideological and physical incorporation into the group. Thus while the Faisceau universitaire and Jeunesses fascistes contained barely 1,000 members between them, and Faisceau leaders courted support from banking and industry for the Faisceau des corporations, the CDF/PSF consistently attracted thousands (and later tens of thousands) of young members into a myriad of organizations.[54]

---

53    CDLR, 'La Génération qui monte', *Petit journal*, 15 Dec. 1938; Maxence van der Meersch, 'La Jeunesse', *Flambeau du Sud-Ouest*, 7 Jan. 1939.

54    CDF/PSF student meetings, camping expeditions, and youth gatherings regularly attracted hundreds to thousands both in Paris and the provinces. Although Paul Chopine's estimate of 32,000 Fils et Filles des Croix de Feu by 1932 is excessive, there was clearly much interest in the group's youth wing. Charles Vallin's estimate that there were 30,000 CDF/PSF students in various group organizations in December 1938 seems much more plausible. See AP/451/117, 'Extraits du rapport sur l'activité du parti presenté par M. Charles Vallin, Deputé de Paris, Directeur de la Propagande du PSF', 3e Congrès Nationale du PSF, 3 Dec. 1938.

First and foremost came the CDF/PSF youth wing – the FFCF, founded in June 1930 by the group's first President, Maurice d'Hartoy and run by founding member Duke Pozzo di Borgo. One of the most successful initiatives during the Croix de Feu years, the FFCF attracted 10,000 members by August 1933.[55] By 1935, membership rose dramatically, necessitating a reorganization of the group into three sections – 'A', 'B', and 'C' – corresponding to age and gender. Group 'A' contained all children under the age of 13, while groups 'B' and 'C' represented boys aged 13–16 and girls aged 13–21 respectively. Young men went on to join the Volontaires nationaux, which contained all male members between the ages of 16–21, while women could join the Section feminine if wishing an active role in the group, or the Mouvement social français (the CDF/PSF charity and social work umbrella organization) for a more nominal expression of sympathy.[56]

The latter stipulation underscores the differing gender roles projected for youth. According to the Action sociale branch which supervised CDF/PSF youth programs, girls received training for their future roles as mothers and housewives, learning the love of the *foyer familial*, in order to defeat their vain, coquettish, and nervous tendencies. Light exercise and housework drills (menu planning, for example) were ideal in this regard. In need of a more rigorous program, the Foyer des jeunes filles serviced teenagers. There they received a 'familial, social, intellectual, and artistic education', including household management and hygiene, stenography, and singing or embroidery. Throughout these activities, instructors emphasized discipline, directing young women to study historical figures like Joan of Arc and Saint Génévieve who epitomized CDF/PSF principles.[57]

Naturally, boys received quite different treatment. As the future French elite, leader-instructors ran their sections, usually members of the Volontaires nationaux or the CDF/PSF proper. Each Thursday and Sunday boys were offered a variety of 'masculine' pursuits, including sports, outdoor activities, and the songs of 'old France', along with a plethora of physical education exercises and lessons. While the ideal girl exhibited 'feminine' qualities like altruism and sensitivity, young men were taught to be confident, willful, and skilled in the arts of manual labour. According to group directives, egoism, timidity, and destructive behaviour were to be eradicated, replaced by heroism and courage, and a healthy admiration for men like General Lyautey, Vercingétorix, and aviator and group icon Jean Mermoz: Figures

---

55    This figure is the group estimate, and thus probably somewhat inflated. In *Le Flambeau*, Feb. 1933.

56    CHEVS/LR 36 – 'Reglement générale de l'association 'Les Fils et Filles de Croix de Feu'', 17 Feb. 1935; Jacques Nobecourt, *Le Colonel de la Rocque 1885–1946, ou les pièges du nationalisme chrétien* (Paris, 1996), pp. 194–195. Many students were introduced to the movement through the VN, such as the young François Mitterand, whose story typifies the recruitment process. See Pierre Péan, *Une jeunesse française: François Mitterand, 1934–1947* (Paris, 1994), chapters 1–3.

57    CHEVS/LR 36 – 'Instructions spéciales pour le groupe d'action sociale'; AP/451/104 – 'Creation des groupes C et des Foyers des jeunes filles', Oct. 1935.

who personified the CDF/PSF ideal. Finally, the group offered career preparation, including visits to factories and farms, and clinics on professional skills.[58]

Regardless of gender, both boys and girls participated in the *colonies de vacances*, an initiative of Pozzo di Borgo which took hundreds of children to the seaside, countryside and mountains each summer, from the Savoie to Brittany.[59] Various camps existed, corresponding to age group and gender: For boys and girls under 13, boys age 13–16, and then girls 13–16 and 16–21 respectively. The group wished to involve as many children as possible, and thus priced the *colonies* modestly, asking seven to ten francs per day for each child registered. Those unable to pay due to lack of funds could negotiate a lesser fee, or have their child subsidized by donations regularly solicited in various group newspapers.[60]

On the surface, the *colonies de vacances* resembled like-minded initiatives in 1930s France offered by a plethora of organizations. The Popular Front government took an active hand in propagating summer camps for boys and girls, particularly those whose parents were unemployed or lacked the means to send their children to the privately run Union française des colonies de vacances et oeuvres en plein air (for Catholics) or Ligue d'union française des oeuvres des vacances laïques. Socialist and communist youth groups also offered *caisses de vacances*, along with *foyers des jeunes* in the winter season. For those parents unconvinced of the benefits afforded by the *colonies*, the Scouts and Éclaireurs presented comparable opportunities.[61]

However, the CDF/PSF *colonies de vacances* were not the woodland outings of the Union française or the boy scouts. If anything, they resembled the Chantiers de la jeunesse, the Vichy-era initiative designed to regiment unemployed and listless youths after the fall of France. Although lacking the military component of the Chantiers, the group's program contained a similarly Catholic and nationalist message, emphasizing collective discipline, leadership, and patriotism. Both also propagated a belief in the necessity of physical fitness.[62] Children of all ages in the CDF/PSF camps received regular visits from La Rocque and other leaders, reminding them of their duty and the need to maintain discipline at all times.[63] The group newsletter *Service social* elaborated upon their moral component: 'The *colonies de vacances* are coming. They will bring an ardent and joyous youth to all the provinces in France, who will loudly proclaim the PSF ideal and its doctrine of reconciliation

---

58     AP/451/104 – 'Groupe B (Garçons)', Oct. 1935; CHEVS/LR 36 – 'Instructions spéciales pour le groupe d'action sociale'.

59     APP/Ba 1857-Report of the Commission into the Events of 6 February 1934, p. 1635; CHEVS/LR 41 – 'Colonies de vacance: Été 1937'; *L'Heure française*, 10 July 1937.

60     'Nos Camps', *Le Flambeau*, 1 June 1935; 'Pour les colonies de vacances de nos enfants', *L'Heure française*, 10 July 1937. For an example of the calls for donations, see 'Colonies de Vacances', *Flambeau du Sud-Ouest*, 3 July 1939.

61     Pascal Ory, *La Belle illusion: Culture et politique sous le signe du Front Populaire* (Paris, 1994), pp. 764–771.

62     On the Chantiers de la Jeunesse, see Halls, pp. 288–296; Pierre Giolitto, *Histoire de la jeunesse sous Vichy* (Paris, 1991), pp. 551, 578–580.

63     Sean Kennedy, *Reconciling France Against Democracy* (Kingston and Montréal, 2007), pp. 104–106.

and appeasement, expressed in singing and peals of laughter.'[64] Similarly, although the daily activities seemed innocuous, from gymnastics and exercise to cleaning up the campsite, the physical regimen could be harsh, and youths were frequently mobilized in rather un-childlike pursuits. Much like the Chantiers, 80 boys at one camp at Yolet in 1938 assisted local peasants with their manual labour, making hay and baling it. Girls at Doux and a boy's camp at Chaudesaigues performed similar feats.[65] Children returned physically fit, 'tanned' and 'radiantly healthy', *Le Flambeau* claimed in July 1935.[66]

Alongside the *colonies de vacances*, the CDF/PSF sponsored other, more specialized youth organizations, most of which served to prepare them for the *renovation nationale*, during which the group would acquire control of the state and rebuild France in its own image. Thus the group founded Foyers agricoles Croix de Feu in October 1935, with the goal of making instructional and recreational activities available for young rural members. Participants were expected to demonstrate 'l'esprit national' and an appropriate friendly disposition. In return, rural youth gained access to sports fields, a library, and numerous CDF/PSF-sponsored activities, including lectures and films praising agrarian life.[67] More ambitious, the Travail et Loisirs program debuted in 1936, created by La Rocque's friend and CDF/PSF youth icon Jean Mermoz, and run by the Colonel's trusted confidante Antoinette de Preval, director of the CDF/PSF Service sociale. These subsidiaries offered protection from the dangers of the street to working-class children with two employed parents. The program provided day-care, nurseries and a wide variety of activities for children such as excursions to the opera and the symphony, yet also served to further the potential indoctrination of its charges.[68]

Linked with Travail et Loisirs, a physical education initiative appeared in 1934, entitled La Société de préparation et d'éducation sportive (SPES). Formed by Gaëtan Maire and run by Jean Mierry, a rising young leader in the Volontaires nationaux, the SPES offered a preparatory program for training the future CDF/PSF national elite. Under its auspices, Maire established 12 Centres d'éducation physique in Paris and the provinces aimed specifically at youth, including libraries, weekly talks on subjects such as hygiene, morality, and the colonies, and the screening of films and documentaries about physical fitness. At the third national party congress in December 1938, PSF deputy Charles Vallin estimated that 2,000 lessons per month were given at the centres under SPES guidance. Finally, there was the Aero-Club

---

64    CHEVS/LR 41, *Service social*, April 1938. The Colonies also reinforced the CDF/PSF view regarding gender roles. Here one mother's comment tells the whole story: 'Ma fille est revenue engraissée, joyeuse, disciplinée, ayant appris plus en chant, gymnastique, ménage que pendant tout une année de l'école'. In 'Colonies de vacance', *L'Auvergne nouvelle*, 9 Oct. 1936.

65    'Colonies de Vacances', *L'Auvergne nouvelle*, 9 Oct. 1938.

66    '3000 enfants dans nos camps de vacances', *Le Flambeau*, 20 July 1935.

67    AP/451/104, Section feminine, 'Reglement des Foyers agricoles Croix de Feu', Oct. 1935.

68    Philippe Rudaux, *Les Croix de Feu et le PSF*. (Paris, 1967), 209; Nobecourt, p. 658; Weng-Ting Lung, 'L'Historique et la doctrine des Croix de Feu et du Parti social français', Unpublished Thèse du Droit, Université de Nice, 1971, pp. 91–94.

Jean Mermoz, which trained future French aviators, taught airplane mechanics, and developed a love for the excitement of flying among youth.[69]

Jean Mierry also provided the guiding hand behind the Groupe universitaire PSF and 18 Centres sociales universitaires in Paris, constituting the most ambitious group effort at youth indoctrination. Each centre included a reading room complete with party tracts and newspapers, and a billiards room with ping-pong tables and a piano. Such an 'atmosphère de saine cameraderie' was thought healthier than the smoky and dingy cafés where trouble and immorality awaited the student. A subsidized restaurant enabled the financially strapped youth to purchase a warm and healthy meal, and a library provided a number of academic volumes for afternoon or evening study. Needy students were also encouraged to apply for special group bursaries and prizes, and given lodging if lacking a proper room of their own. Weekly conferences augmented these amenities, talks given by PSF members (young lawyers or doctors, for example) and student commissions on the *Profession organisée* designed to aid the aspiring professional in choosing a career. During these meetings students working together in professional groups (lawyers, business students, etc.) discussed corporative problems. Finally, the CDF/PSF student program demanded charitable works, in the form of group-sponsored factory visits and volunteer initiatives in working-class neighborhoods.[70]

## IV

Each of these organizations served to indoctrinate the child or student with the CDF/PSF *mystique*. They were aided in this purpose by newspaper articles, propaganda, and mass rallies aimed specifically at the younger generation.[71] But what precisely did this entail? What were youth being taught by their saviours in the CDF/PSF? During the Croix de Feu years, the lessons were frequently nationalist, militarist, and conservative, combining appeals in favour of discipline and character-building with anti-socialism and anti-republicanism. As a *mouvement des anciens combattants*, Croix de Feu youth leaders frequently alluded to the trench experience, attempting to inculcate the young with the values of the soldier. By 1936, however, as their membership and influence grew at a prodigious rate, the group began to focus on the

---

69    AP/451/104, Section feminine, 'Centres d'éducation physique avec foyer-bibliothèque', Oct. 1935; AP/451/117, 'Extraits du rapport sur l'activité du parti, presenté par M. Charles Vallin, Député de Paris, Directeur de la propagande du PSF', 3 Dec. 1938; F/7/12966, 'Réunion organisée par la section de Saint-Georges du 9ème Arrdt. du Parti social français', 24 Feb. 1937.

70    AP/451/104, 'Centre sociale universitaire', Oct. 1935; Rudaux, pp. 204–205; André Blanchet, 'Visite au Centre universitaire à Paris', *La Flamme*, 22 April 1938; CHEVS/LR 41, Jean Bernard, 'Le Centre universitaire', *L'Étudiant social*, April 1938.

71    CHEVS LR 22, 'Extraits du rapport sur l'enfant' presenté par le Bureau d'études sociales, 1er Congrès Sociale du Parti social français, 16–17 May 1939. The report urged adult members of the group to attend meetings regularly with their children, and encourage them to read extensively about the group's beliefs because youth merely awaited an authentically French *apostelat concret* whom they would follow.

role of youth within the *État social français*. Thus after their transformation into the Parti social français, both leadership and rank-and-file undertook extensive plans for a renewed education system. Yet certain members went far beyond *lycée* or university curricula, arguing for the creation of a new man through eugenicist methodology. Again auguring the discourse prevalent within the Vichy regime, this faction favoured the physical transformation of French youth within the renovated nation and state.

First and foremost during the Croix de Feu years came the concept of discipline, taught continuously before 1936 in various physical fitness programs (such as the SPES or the *colonies de vacances*) and more directly in printed form. To this end, articles frequently appeared on the special children's back page of the group newspaper. For example, a November 11, 1932 piece urged children to utilize the disciplinary style with which their fathers won the Great War:

> Sons of the veterans of 1914, when you ascend to the unknown with your fathers, know that at that moment the admiring looks of the joyful crowd are multiplied. Because the true sacrifice will never be forgotten ... It is what formed our unity, it is what creates yours. Your discipline will be intimate: it will be like the spirit and the flame, inherited, indivisible, and total.[72]

Discipline alone was insufficient, however. Youth were to serve and sacrifice everything for the greatness of the *patrie*, continually placed above the individual by group authors, an ideal transcending both material gain and personal desires. Speaking to a crowd of members and their children at the Salle Wagram in August 1932, youth leader Laignel called for a recreation of the fraternity and unity of the trenches, in which the love of the nation replaced class loyalty. One teenage member echoed his sentiments: 'Having lost everything, your comrades in arms, your blood, your money, you have reconstituted the best credit in the world: France.'[73]

La Rocque himself elaborated upon these themes on the youth page, where he preached the absolute obedience of order, will, and faith in the collective, as 'only their worship can dispense vitality to the race, greatness to the fatherland'. Discipline meant the acceptance of responsibility and initiative, and an end to the current passivity in youth. Children would be taught to exercise their will, to regenerate the 'robust Gaul of our ancestors'. To save the race, each youth learned his personal role, upon which the nation as a whole depended, and from which he must not deviate.[74] Speaking to a group of university students at Magic-City in May 1935, La Rocque made this point abundantly clear: 'You are intellectuals, or are becoming intellectuals; from this fact, you have and will have a great duty to fulfill towards society. If you work only for yourselves, you do not interest me.' Contrasting the bourgeoisie who did not understand their social role with the current ardent youth,

---

72    Trézien, 'Disciplines', *Le Flambeau*, 11 Nov. 1932; Trézien, 'La Commandement et la bienveillance', *Le Flambeau*, 1 Feb. 1933.

73    Un 'Fils', 'Servir', *Le Flambeau*, 11 Nov. 1932; *Le Flambeau*, Aug. 1932; Un 'Fils', 'Avec le sourire', *Le Flambeau*, Nov. 1932.

74    CDLR, 'Méditation', *Le Flambeau*, Sept. 1932.

he called upon the new generation to do their duty to the nation, to win the peace as their fathers won the war.[75]

The CDF/PSF ascribed a two-fold role to this youthful elite. First, youth ushered in the new France as the vanguard of the movement towards the *État social français*. Writing in the pages of the *Flambeau*, one youth leader called them the reserve corps of the Croix de Feu – the new *combattants*. They wielded the principles of their fathers in the trenches – will and heroism – to beget a new society based upon hierarchy, discipline, and strong leadership. As a logical extension of this role, Croix de Feu youth were expected to recognize and defeat the enemy (most importantly the socialist and communist left) in all its vestiges, from the PCF or ARAC to the Secours rouge internationale and the Jeunesses socialistes. To this end, they received a comprehensive list of leftist parties and organizations, complete with logos and symbols.[76] Having memorized them, young members acted accordingly, and the group rewarded children of all ages for acting in the best interest of the organization and the nation. It awarded a bronze medal to one youth who, 'attacked by ten communists, resisted victoriously and carried out his mission in spite of the fury of his adversaries'. Various children earned the gold medal for breaking up anti-patriotic meetings, being a 'véritable apôtre de la mission Croix de Feu', and showing an exceptional understanding of the concepts of order and authority.[77] Such activities made it abundantly clear that the Croix de Feu youth were not to be confused with the JOC or the French boy scouts.

However, following the group's transformation into the PSF in June 1936, the conception of youth was significantly altered. As a mass party with a membership above 500,000, the PSF could no longer afford to be seen purely as a *mouvement des anciens combattants*, expounding the discipline of the trenches and militant anti-communism. Hence with the possibility of electoral victory came a second conception of youth, above and beyond the vanguard of the *renovation nationale*. More traditional in scope, party leaders now spoke of youth as the future leaders of France within the *État social français*, replacing the old and tired generations currently in charge. In a manner which would have raised no objections from the conservative Fédération républicaine, this new caste were described as 'that which is the best, and also the most worthy of selection among the whole'.[78] Professor Sargent, a group representative from the Academy of Medicine, told a student gathering in Paris that this select few, elevated by talent or by birth to a position of superiority, ruled the nation as administrators rather than soldiers.[79] Now the young would be the Lyauteys and Napoleons of their chosen fields, the generals directing economy,

75    F/7/13963, 'Réunion privée organisée par la Groupe universitaire du Mouvement social français des Croix de Feu', Magic-City, 21 May 1935.

76    Trézien, 'Réalités', *Le Flambeau*, Jan. 1933; AP/451/93, 'Des insignes qu'il faut connaître'.

77    'Citations', *Le Flambeau*, 1 Aug. 1933. For a similar example directed at university students, see: *Étudiants: il depend de vous* (Paris, n.d. (PSF)), pp. 1–2, 6, 8–11, 15–16, 20–23.

78    'Centre universitaire: Le Rôle des élites', *Flambeau du Sud-Ouest*, 25 Dec. 1937.

79    'Une confirmation, un point de départ: La Réunion de rentrée des étudiants de Paris', *L'Étudiant social*, Jan. 1939.

government, and society.[80] Yet to create such an elite required more than *colonies de vacance* and propaganda. They required training and development to eradicate the moral and physical flabbiness resulting from republican apathy.

As Bourgin had done a decade earlier, La Rocque and the CDF/PSF leadership looked to educational reform as the solution, the vehicle with which to train their new national cadres. Articles and speeches highly critical of the republican education system actually predated the formation of the PSF, appearing semi-regularly in *Le Flambeau*. From 1934 onwards leaders lamented the lost cult of tradition in French pedagogy, lamenting that France produced no capable elite. Its teachers, emissaries of Moscow sent to sow the seeds of revolution within the syndicalist Confédération générale du travail rather than educate according to national needs, were the worst culprits. 'We do not want the public education system where our children go to consist of schools of systematic demoralization', the writers of a group tract proclaimed in agreement, 'where revolutionary masters teach them hatred and contempt for France and its glorious past'.[81]

Yet by 1936, group efforts went beyond mere criticism of teachers and the curriculum, demanding the return of spirituality to the primary and secondary classroom as the first step towards a renewed national (rather than international and republican) education system. Here the group stance resembled that of Maurice Barrès and Paul Bourget, more akin to Bourgin's Catholic and conservative young man than the rhetorical exhortations to discipline and will that characterized Croix de Feu youth propaganda.[82] To the PSF, any renovation of the French education system necessarily began with the destruction of atheism and anti-religious sentiment embedded in the state school curriculum. In essence, the group argued a position long dear to the French right, that from the Ferry reforms onwards, the Republic had waged war against Catholic and moral education. Thus the CDF/PSF engaged in what Antoine Prost terms the battle of *anciens* against *modernes*, the proponents of classical education (particularly Latin, Greek, and religious instruction) against laic advocates of pedagogical modernity (emphasizing a more technical and scientific curriculum).[83]

In 1936, this argument intensified with the ascension to power of the socialist-led Popular Front government, whose young and exuberant education minister Jean Zay was a reformist supporter of laic pedagogy. A journalist and lawyer by profession, he possessed little experience in the field, but immediately distinguished himself through ambitious curricular reorganization, raising the school leaving

---

80    André Maurois, 'Réflexions sur le commandement', *L'Étudiant social*, Jan. 1939; AP/451/82-Tract, 'Étudiants françaises'.

81    Lt.-Colonel Francois de la Rocque, *Service public* (Paris, 1934), pp. 117–118, 227; CDLR, 'Instituteurs', *Le Flambeau*, 30 March 1935; Anon, *Pourquoi nous sommes devenues Croix de Feu* (1934), pp. 4–5.

82    For a discussion of Bourget's *Le Disciple* and Barrès's *Les Déracinés* as archetypes of extreme-rightist views on Catholicism and education, see the chapter on education and the right by Françoise Mayeur in Jean-François Sirinelli (ed.), *Histoire des droites en France: Tome 3-Sensibilités* (Paris, 1992), pp. 701–702.

83    Antoine Prost, *Histoire de l'enseignement en France (1800–1967)* (Paris, 1968), pp. 250–251.

age to 14, and dividing the lycée curriculum into technical and classical streams.[84] Although he evinced little genuine anti-Catholic sentiment, Zay's right wing critics vociferously attacked his every move, buoyed by fears that Léon Blum's ministry would 'Sovietize' France. Referring to the premier's religion, conservative academic Marcel Jouhandeau derided plans for an *école unique* as 'Jewish reform'. Along similar lines, *La Croix's* Jean Giraud termed Zay's proposal to impose state regulation on education up to 14 years of age 'the installation in our country of an atheist and socialist totalitarian state'.[85]

Given such anti-reformist hostility on the right, it is only natural that the CDF/PSF joined the fight against government intervention. The defense of religious instruction was absolutely necessary, various writers claimed, and thus both instructors and schooling for the young would be the choice of the father rather than the state, to protect the Catholic education system.[86] Writing in the *Flamme des Deux-Sèvres*, the President of the Thouars section warned that a monopoly of education excluded any educator whose curriculum included God and family. The 'French Marxist state' should not be permitted to ruin the younger generation, he wrote, by 'injecting unhealthy ideas into young heads'.[87] The issue concerned the formation of decent Frenchmen, Academician Edmond Jaloux wrote in the PSF daily newspaper, for a child's parents alone ensured that he or she received a moral education, in order to assure his/her future development into good citizens and patriots.[88] In practice this meant the installation of a rigid CDF/PSF curriculum, in which all 'non-patriotic' education would be jettisoned in favour of an emphasis upon family, Catholic values, and the nation in the classroom.[89]

This necessitated a total reform of the teaching profession. Interwar French teachers had led the laic charge first under the Cartel des Gauches and again with renewed vigour after the election of Blum's ministry. Among the most militant were members of the Syndicat national des instituteurs, affiliated with the CGT. The teachers union regularly hurled insults at the Church, and rejected any role for Catholics in education. They also participated en masse in the counter-demonstrations of 12 February 1934, launched in good measure against the Croix de Feu. With 112,000 members by 1939, the SNI represented a substantial foe; thus the CDF/PSF spared no effort in attacking

---

84    Ibid, pp. 417–419. Lycées were the secondary schools of a more academic bent, designed to produce teachers and the future French elite.

85    Ory, pp. 706–707; Talbott, p. 214. Thus Talbott's claim that critics 'imputed to Zay designs that he did not have'.

86    For example, 'Parlons encore de l'enseignement', Georges Alexandre, *La Flamme des Deux-Sèvres*, July 1939.

87    'L'Enseignement libre menacée', J. Maume, *La Flamme des Deux-Sèvres*, May 1939.

88    On the defense of Catholic education, see 'Pour le peuple, par le peuple', supplement to *Le Flambeau*, 11 April 1936; AP/451/106 – Tract, 'Pour nos chers vieux', n.d. [1936?]; CHEVS/LR 20 H, 'Réunion du 15 Septembre 1936', Salle Blanchon-Lyon; 'Les Epidémies morales', Edmond Jaloux, *Petit journal*, 7 Nov. 1938.

89    Léon Diagoras, 'Le PSF et l'école', *Flambeau de Flandres-Artois-Picardie*, 11 Sept. 1938.

republican educators.[90] Rejecting the religious neutrality of the Ferry laws as a tool to further the Masonic enslavement of Christian France, Georges Alexandre, CDF/PSF municipal councilor for Deux-Sèvres, called for the immediate dismissal of all 125,000 (*sic*) laic teachers of whom 96,000 were socialists and communists taking orders from Moscow.[91] Training in the republican Collèges des instituteurs did not adequately prepare teachers, he complained, but merely indoctrinated them, rooting out religious and national sentiment. In this way sociology (Durkheim's 'deformed thought') replaced morality.[92] As part of the reconstruction of France, La Rocque foresaw the removal of the CGT from education, allowing non-socialist educators, currently bullied by 'subversive forces' into teaching an anti-patriotic curriculum, to regain its footing.[93] Only by restoring order in the classroom could the future leaders of France be properly formed, which necessitated a purge of all republican and leftist elements and their replacement with instructors who understood the primacy of national and Christian values.

The new state's moral watchfulness extended to the curriculum itself, which was to become more traditional in scope, in stark contrast to Blum and Zay's moves away from Greco-Latin studies in primary and secondary education, consigning them to a classical stream which competed with the modern and technical variants.[94] Like Bourgin a decade earlier, PSF deputy Charles Vallin clearly enunciated a conservative pedagogical position, telling an audience in Lyon that: 'The only right and duty of the state is to impose a respect for the laws of the land upon educators, whether laic or Catholic ... and above all a respect for the great principles upon which rest the existence of the family and the fatherland'.[95] In the words of Auguste Bailly, youth were to be filled with French ideas and traditions, 'imprégné d'un tel idéal'. The state acted to preserve Latin and Greek, and literary classics such as La Fontaine and Racine, bringing to life genuinely French qualities and talents. Such classics were to be studied not for their intellectual value, but because all supported a natural order of society and the universe, rejecting base individualism and encouraging 'the purest qualities of the race'.[96] Denuded of their latent anti-intellectual bent, such traditionalist sentiments would not have seemed out of place

---

90    Ory, p. 85; Prost, pp. 390–395.

91    Georges Alexandre, 'De l'enseignement', *Flamme des Deux-Sèvres*, July 1939.

92    Pierre Brissac, 'Libérer les instituteurs, c'est libérer l'intelligence française', *Le Flambeau*, 19 Sept. 1936. For an equally rabid attack on 'socialist' teachers in the same issue, see P. Menand, 'Traîtres à la France et semeurs de haine'.

93    CDLR, 'La Problème de l'éducation', *Le Flambeau*, 23 May 1936. Although a current of pacifism pervaded the teaching profession and interwar pedagogy, the school curriculum never rejected patriotism. See Mona Siegel, *The Moral Disarmament of France: Education, Pacifism, and Patriotism, 1914–1940* (Cambridge, 2004).

94    According to Talbott, Zay proposed that 'each child's teachers would deliberate on whether he should be advised to follow the classical, modern, or technical option, differentiated by the emphasis given to Latin, a modern language, or technical education'. Thus ancient languages were to be jettisoned in all but the classical stream. Talbott, p. 228.

95    AP/451/108, 'Réunion de 15 Septembre 1936'. On Blum and Zay's attempts to modernize the curriculum, and the resulting upheaval, see Ory, pp. 693–694.

96    Auguste Bailly, 'Aux sources', *Le Flambeau*, 11 May 1935.

in one of Bourgin's articles for *Nouveau Siècle*. Nor would the Travail et loisirs recommended reading list for school-children have caused a stir: Dumas, Balzac, and Hugo nestled alongside more 'modern' works by Alphonse Daudet and Anatole France.[97] Alongside the strong pedagogical emphasis on tradition and responsibility went moral formation. Echoing Bourgin's complaints about the decline of standards, Gillette Ziegler decried the fact that students did not read Barrès or Péguy in the classroom, leaving the young with no appreciation for the importance of France in the world and no experience with distinctly French forms of thought.[98]

Other members voiced more practical concerns. Echoing the pedagogical doctrine that emerged during the Vichy regime under Education Ministers Jacques Chevalier and Jérome Carcopino, one author criticized the lack of a moral component in the republican curriculum, which trained artists and philosophers rather than the artisans and farmers who represented the bulk of the French population. In a country where 45 per cent of the labouring class worked in agriculture, schooling should prepare the student for his true career, through technical education that concentrated on technical development rather than rhetoric.[99] PSF Ardennes activist Marcel Aucouturier further included the scientific skills necessary in the modern factory and farm. Where Jean Zay proposed professional courses for students aged fourteen to seventeen destined for industry or commerce, complete with factory-schools for the worker, Aucouturier included agriculture. All schooling concerned first and foremost scientific and technical progress, directed by a 'Commission nationale de l'enseignement'.[100]

Both the defense of tradition and technology-based learning found their way into CDF/PSF plans for a new Grand Ministère de l'Education nationale. Just as the Ministry of Defense ensured the security of the nation and the Finance Ministry defended French business, so too the new Education Ministry defended the 'French soul', linking the arts, scientific research, the protection of children, technical and physical education, and health and hygiene. For all intents and purposes the new ministry adopted a dual role, training the future elite and workers while simultaneously

---

97    AP/451/171, 'Les Éditions des loisirs'.

98    Gillette Ziegler, 'L'École et la Patrie', *Petit journal*, 14 Feb. 1939. Such ideas were equally apparent in fascist Italy during the 1930s. Under education minister Cesare de Vecchi, the Italian classics were almost exclusively assigned from 1936 onwards, from Dante and Boccaccio to D'Annunzio, to provide a 'Roman' education. The creation of a properly Italian curriculum received the blessing of Mussolini, who stated to the Council of Ministers in November 1928 that textbooks must introduce students to 'what Italy has been in history, in literature, the sciences, and the arts'. See Ostenc, pp. 190, 338–363. Unlike the CDF/PSF, however, de Vecchi simultaneously prioritized the writings of Mussolini and militarized the classroom setting. Although they wished to 'gallicize' students, the Parti social français had no wish to establish a cult of La Rocque or create young soldiers ready for battle.

99    J. Cathelineau, 'L'Apprentissage contre le chômage des jeunes', *Le Flambeau*, 1 May 1937. Compare with a Vichy manual for morality in the school curriculum: 'It is a matter of implanting a hard-working and courageous youth in the earth, which provides France with its daily bread and assures it of a virile and strong soul'. In Giolitto, pp. 229–231.

100   Marcel Aucouturier, *Au service des Croix de Feu* (Charleville, 1936), p. 162; Marcel Aucouturier, *Programmes socialistes et programmes sociaux* (1938–1939), p. 4. No further details about the CNE were appended.

seeking to indoctrinate youth.[101] The scholastic form, composed of the *primaire, post-primaire*, and *secondaire* levels, would remain unchanged in the new state. It was the content that would be significantly altered, to 're-educate' the masses.

The architect of the final CDF/PSF plan for educational reform, philosopher and CDF/PSF sympathizer Jean Daujat presented his completed proposal in a 1939 *Étudiant social* article entitled 'L'Université dans l'*État social français*'. Daujat began by stating that French traditions and values, and the motherland herself, were currently nothing more than a 'rotting corpse'. Only by creating a new man could the situation be rectified, a phenomenon best initiated through the re-education of the nation's youth 'because it is [youth] who are the most permeable, the most capable of being molded, and because it is they who will be the France of tomorrow for which we labour'. Such action would break the republican/Masonic stranglehold on education and restore the 'French soul'. Despite the seeming hypocrisy of such a statement, Daujat proclaimed that the new education system would nevertheless be free of any totalitarian impulses, respecting personal, confessional, and professional liberty, while the state simply controlled the process through regulatory measures to ensure that the common good was maintained.[102]

In practical terms this meant a national curricular monopoly in which the state propagandized through the classroom. Like Bourgin, however, Daujat here thought more in terms of upholding traditional morality than the construction of La Rocque's new nation based on principles of discipline, will, and leadership. He circumscribed for the new Ministry of Education the defense of morality (especially against pornography and Malthusianism) and the fight against 'immoral' propaganda as the primary directives in this regard, for both educators and students alike. Protection and encouragement were given to all subjects that contributed to French civilization, whether scientific or artistic in nature. Like La Rocque, however, Daujat also believed the development of physical health in youth to be a top priority for the new education system, necessary for the intellectual and moral health of the nation as well as its physical well-being. Furthermore, and quite unlike the republican Ministry of Education, this new body controlled and shaped all media which affected the 'French heart and soul', including books, the press, theatre, cinema, and radio, to remove corrupt political influences. Somewhat ironically, such a plan had been considered by none other than Jean Zay, who in 1936 proposed a fusion of the Secrétaire d'État à l'Éducation nationale with that for l'Expression nationale, linking pedagogy and media in a new Ministère de la Vie culturelle. However, Zay had quite different ends in mind, wishing to streamline government and facilitate cross-ministerial policy-making. Conversely, Daujat wanted to replace pernicious republican influences with the virtues of the *patrie* and the Christian morality of the family.[103]

Daujat assigned a dual role to the new system, combining the wishes for an elite education of La Rocque and the group leadership with the demands for a more

---

101   AP/451/117, 'Extraits du rapport sur l'enseignement par Stanislas Devaud, Deputé de Constantine, et François de Polignac, Deputé de Maine et Loire, 3 Dec. 1938.

102   Jean Daujat, 'L'Université dans L'*État social français*', *L'Étudiant social*, Feb. 1939.

103   Ibid. For a sketch of the Zay plan, see Ory, p. 178.

technical education asserted by Aucouturier and others. In the hands of either the parish priest or a local corporative body, the new *enseignement primaire* instilled in the child all necessary knowledge of life in France, from history and geography to language instruction and morality. To the *secondaire* fell the task of forming the elite, its primary function being to teach judgment, reason, and understanding. True to his conservative vision of secondary education, Daujat criticized the number of baccalaureate degrees awarded in contemporary France, arguing that only those possessing truly gifted intelligence qualified under the new system. Strict entrance examinations were to be taken by all potential candidates, with successful applicants of meagre means receiving state subsidies. Like Aucouturier, Daujat proposed to leave post-primary education unchanged, its object being to train workers, artisans, and agricultural labourers, imparting the skills required in their respective professions. Yet unlike the republican arrangement, Catholic schools were to be given one half of all funding by the new state, to encourage religious instruction, and both diplomas would be considered equal by both the state and corporations. In line with the traditionalist faction of Bailly and Ziegler, Daujat also proposed that the curriculum contain heavy doses of Greek and Latin, as France was the product of Greco-Roman civilization, and intensive language and literature studies together with philosophy and history. Despite recalling the archaic Napoleonic system in its tone, and rejecting interwar movement away from a purely classical curriculum, Daujat's program nevertheless conceded the importance of mathematics, biology, and the physical sciences, to be offered at both the secondary and university levels.[104]

Daujat's scheme was remarkably similar to the conservative and traditional plan put forward by Bourgin in the Faisceau press, although the CDF/PSF gave considerably less thought to post-secondary education than the *vieux Normalien*, who at times seemed the embodiment of Rénan's famous dictum 'c'est l'université qui fait l'école'. To a certain degree, the lack of attention paid to higher education reflected demographic reality in the nineteen-thirties. While 4 million French children attended primary schools by 1939, only slightly more than 5 per cent participated in the secondary stream, and only 76,405 attended university or one of the *Écoles normales*.[105] Those who formulated the group's education policy were not graduates of the *Grandes écoles*, and the CDF/PSF focused their attention on the lower intellectual strata, which were in any case better suited to transmit the group's doctrine and form worker-citizens for the new *État social français*, but still capable of teaching will, discipline, and sacrifice for the motherland, the essential traits of the new leadership elite. La Rocque and the party leadership were less interested in creating intellectual leaders, preferring the development of physical fitness, virility, Christian morality, and nationalism to physics or philosophy. The true leader was a man of action, for whom words and ideas should not exist *pour-soi*.

Hence the greatest group concern regarding universities was their perceived raison d'être as propaganda centres for leftist and republican values. For as Antoine Prost notes, André Thibaudet's portrait of the *République des professeurs* did not stray far from the truth in interwar France. Many belonged to laic organizations or

104   Ibid.
105   Zeldin, p. 292, Ory, p. 46.

the Ligue des droits de l'homme, the enemies of the CDF/PSF. Although few actually adhered to the far left, like their schoolteacher brethren, the extreme-right made no inroads either. Of the latter, those who did successfully enter the university faculties, like Maurice Bardèche or Georges Bidault, found themselves marginalized.[106] Given this state of affairs, the CDF/PSF rejected the 'decadent' curriculum being taught by professors, which omitted French and Italian humanism – studies appropriate to a Latin institution of learning – in favour of foreign (i.e. German) methods. The only proposed solution was again Daujat's: the agglomeration of all post-secondary institutions into a *Université nationale*, a corporate body which assumed responsibility for monitoring both the curriculum and the professoriate, establishing common rules of organization and sponsoring a wide array of national student conferences and contests in all fields.[107] Such vague assertions were a far cry from Bourgin's vision of the universities as the focal point of a renewed France from which ardent and youthful leadership cadres emerged. Worse still, Daujat failed to address perceived structural weaknesses in a system which desperately needed fixing. Universities were simply of little consequence in a new nation where the intellect served the state but did not lead it.

# V

Hard work, will, and proper moral fibre could not be maintained from behind a desk. Thus the CDF/PSF made physical education and sport for youth an absolute priority, holding to the dictum that a sound mind was predicated upon a sound body. They were certainly not the exclusive purveyors of this doctrine in 1930s France. Sports and fitness organizations mushroomed throughout the decade, with hundreds of thousands of ordinary French men and women forming or joining football, gymnastics, or cycling clubs. Much of this activity came as a result of initiatives undertaken by the socialist-led Popular Front government, the CDF/PSF's political nemesis, from 1936 onwards.

Like the CDF/PSF, Blum's team favoured the institution of more rigorous physical education programs in French schools, to buttress fitness and hygiene, and inculcate proper character. The Popular Front government was not wholly original in this regard, continuing a trend which dated from the founding of the Third Republic. Analogous governmental initiatives appeared between 1871 and 1914, when concerns about a resurgent Germany produced demands for patriotism and discipline among French youth, without which the 'betterment of the race' could not be achieved. Blum's government was deeply imbued with pacifism and anti-militarism, however, and bellicose lessons for contemporary youth were deemed inappropriate by socialist ministers. Only the radicals, and particularly the coterie surrounding Under-Secretary of State Pierre Dézarnaulds, found such ideas fashionable. A doctor by vocation, Dézarnaulds tendered a legislative plan to institute mandatory physical education

---

106   Prost, pp. 367–369.

107   Statements and motions of the inaugural PSF national conference/18–20 Dec. 1936, in *Le Flambeau*, 26 Dec. 1936; *Le Parti social français devant les problèmes de l'heure*, 1936; Jean Daujat, 'L'Université dans l'*État social français*', *L'Étudiant social*, Feb. 1939.

for schoolchildren aged 6–16, including extracurricular regimens and the creation of physical education teacher-training programs within the *Écoles normales*. Concomitant to this initiative, Minister of Public Health Henri Sellier demanded 'the physical and hygienic surveillance of children and young people'. Students would be visited biannually by physicians to establish *fiches de contrôles* for each individual.[108]

The Dézarnaulds/Sellier plan bore a striking resemblance to many of the initiatives proposed by the Parti social français. Blum and Zay naturally rejected such extreme measures, instead decreeing a mere five hours per week of physical education in primary and secondary schools. Nonetheless, the Popular Front government did expend significant human and material resources in the service of the physical regeneration of France. Blum's ministry created the nation's first Conseil supérieure des sports in July 1936, to transform the weakened urban-industrial masses into healthy French citizens. Through the auspices of an October 1936 government commission for the 'construction, acquisition, and fixing-up of stadia, swimming pools, and sports fields', Minister of Sport and Leisure Léo Lagrange spent considerable sums to upgrade physical education facilities, arguing that sport provided moral unity, along with joy and dignity to young people. He simultaneously instituted the Brevet sportif populaire, a certificate of merit designed to 'initiate in the youthful masses a movement towards physical education and an introduction to sport'. Not merely confined to champions, the Brevet was awarded to those who could run, swim, or compete at elementary or advanced levels. Unsurprisingly given its mass appeal, 420,000 French youths obtained it in 1937, and by the late nineteen-thirties many camped, cycled across the country, and joined the scouts and *éclaireurs* in ever-increasing numbers, encouraged by both governmental directives and grass-roots concern for the physical fitness of the young.[109]

Lagrange's success did not go unnoticed, and many competing political organizations proffered the gospel of physical education, from the Jeunesses communistes, whose youth newspaper *Avant-Garde* declared 'we don't want the race to degenerate', to the Jeunesses ouvrières chrétiennes, who attempted to forge a Catholic and virile working-class elite.[110] Various CDF/PSF members participated in comparable initiatives. PSF deputy Jean Ybarnégaray was appointed to the Comité nationale des sports, for example, sponsored by Lagrange to provide playing fields and sports equipment across France.[111] Members of the group also praised the Brevet sportif populaire, arguing that it effectively fought the degeneration caused by the modern factory, which had replaced human muscular effort with the machine.[112] But the CDF/PSF were not interested in simply making French youth fit enough to be deemed healthy by the state. Their paragon of the virile male was CDF/PSF youth

---

108    Ory, pp. 650–661.

109    Julian Jackson, *The Popular Front in France: Defending Democracy 1934–1938* (Cambridge, 1990), pp. 132–133; Ory, pp. 650–665, 725–734, 769–772.

110    Susan Whitney, 'The Politics of Youth: Communists and Catholics in Interwar France', Ph.D. Diss., Rutgers University, 1994, pp. 158, 307–310.

111    Ory, pp. 731–732. Ybarnégaray continued to actively promote physical education, culminating in his appointment as Vichy's first Minister of Youth in July 1940.

112    Pierre Apesteguy, 'Le Sport doit être obligatoire pour l'enfance', *Pétit Journal*, 31 Aug. 1937.

icon Jean Mermoz, the war hero who won the Chevalier de la Legion d'Honneur at 21, commanded an air squadron at 30, and successfully negotiated the Atlantic in high style flying his own aircraft. The epitome of the leader and the soldier, he was far more relevant than a neighborhood footballer. To La Rocque, Mermoz embodied the virtues of the ultimate Frenchman: military discipline, physical prowess, and moral piety.[113] Youth were thus expected to be in perfect shape, and group leaders believed that the new state should facilitate the transformation.

They made this point abundantly clear on numerous occasions. To the Travail et loisirs national committee, sport encompassed purely utilitarian, rather than strictly entertainment, values. Even after Lagrange's reforms, the committee bemoaned in 1939, only the strong – those least needy – engaged in physical activity. The weak majority did not develop at all, especially the youth of the industrial *banlieues*, who became victims of alcoholism and disease at an early age. Only through the institution of a rigorous scholastic policy of physical education could this trend be reversed: 'Conceived in a real, measured, and useful form, with a guiding moral idea, this constitutes an element of vitality and virility par excellence and as such must be part of education.'[114] As with the Brevet sportif populaire, the idea was to create strong men rather than champions. Far from being a mere tool for expansion of the physique, the committee claimed, such educative preparation proved indispensable for instilling the new national doctrine in young men:

> This education of the body is equally useful for inculcating children with the virtues at the root of the community, such as discipline, order, the altruistic spirit, and teamwork. In the context of sport, it requires courage, virility, devotion, and a sense of responsibility.[115]

Thus the intellectual, moral, and physical formation of the new leadership corps was assured, and each child considered as an individual national cell, to be nurtured and developed to its fullest potential.

Both Travail et Loisirs and the SPES, along with several CDF/PSF members, formulated plans designed to strengthen youth through physical education. Children in the *État social français* were to develop 'l'esprit national' from an early age, and in turn France would obtain 'muscular and fully grown children, healthy in body and spirit'.[116] This necessitated first and foremost an intensification of mandatory sports and fitness activities in schools.[117] But physical education alone was deemed insufficient, unless accompanied by a moral and authoritarian tone. Thus at the second annual PSF national congress in November 1936, SPES consultant Dr. Philippe Encausse demanded the mandatory attainment of the Brevet sportif populaire for admission into any career or government post. To effectuate this program, all 38,355 communes in France would receive proper playing fields and sports facilities, while morally suspect physical

---

113 Raoul Follereau, 'L'Archange', *Volonté Bretonne*, 5 Feb. 1939; 'Les Puissances d'exemple', *Le Flambeau*, 4 April 1936.

114 AP/451/171, 'Travail et loisirs: Assemblée générale du 2 Janvier 1939'.

115 Ibid.

116 'Les Croix de Feu', *La Flamme Catalane*, 1 March 1936.

117 CHEVS/LR 11 VI A 1, A. Laventureux, 'Jeunesses (suite)', *Bulletin mensuel du mouvement Croix de Feu (51e et 100e sections)*, 1 May 1936.

education instructors were to be removed from their posts immediately.[118] Quite unlike Popular Front legislation, such initiatives envisioned the creation of a generation with the strength and stamina of champions; an aquatic diploma, for example, granted only to those capable of swimming 33 metres in 50 seconds.[119]

Such rigorous demands recalled the 'natural method' of physical education designed in 1906 by French naval officer Georges Hébert far more than the requirements for the Brevet sportif populaire. First applied to troops during the Great War, *Hébertisme* proscribed a thoroughly rigorous exercise regimen, designed to root out physical impurities while imbuing a sense of 'moral regeneration' in recruits. Hébert insisted upon peak performance in a wide variety of activities, including swimming, running, jumping, climbing, and self-defense. Practiced for hours each day, fitness projected the perfection of the body and purification of the mind, addressing the need for a 'virile culture by means of violent and dangerous exercises'.[120] This method proved tremendously appealing to the French right, espoused by various groups and individuals, including the CDF/PSF. After 1940, *Hébertisme* also became the official doctrine of physical education under the Vichy regime. Commissioner for Education and Sport Jean Borotra, a former tennis champion and PSF supporter, believed that it could transform youth into a healthy and vital corps, regenerating the race. Combined with marching and 'order drills', school children participated in this program, as did the Compagnons de France and Chantiers de la Jeunesse.[121]

True to the *Hébertiste* code, the SPES was expected to act as an extra-curricular adjunct to scholastic programs, instilling in youth a strong sense of conscience, discipline, service, and obedience.[122] Thus the bad habits encouraged in republican schools and factories would be removed root and branch. To SPES director Gaëtan Maire sport contained both physical and moral activity, encouraging the collective and negating individualism while turning the weak into robust youth. In emphasizing teamwork and camaraderie, physical education counteracted the republican vices of materialism and individual gain, creating strong workers, managers, fathers, and soldiers.[123] Maire planned to accomplish this work in three phases. First the SPES stressed the development of the body, including exercise for muscles and respiration. Thus the physically inadequate youth slowly enlarged his previously unused capacity. Step two encompassed a strict educational regimen, teaching the human potential for strength, speed, resistance, and defense. Here the goal was 'the perfection of natural gestures ... towards the establishment of improved performance'. Finally, the application stage was reached, during which a collective mobilization of physical

---

118    Dr. Encausse, 'Rapport sur l'éducation physique et sportif', *Petit journal*, 26 Nov. 1937.

119    *L'Oeuvre sociale dans le mouvement Croix de Feu*, May 1936. This tract was an illustrated supplement to the group newspaper.

120    Halls, p. 199. Hébert quoted in Hellman, *The Knight-Monks of Vichy France*, p. 74.

121    Ibid; Giolitto, pp. 196–199. It should be noted that the success of *Hébertisme* with schoolchildren was minimal at best, mainly due to severe food shortages during wartime.

122    AP/451/151, 'Cours pour monitrices des jeunes'.

123    Gaëtan Maire, 'Education physique et sport', *L'Ouvrier libre*, April 1939; AP/451/152 – untitled SPES information pamphlet.

ability was initiated. Maire's description of the final product rejected any individual and intellectual thought or act, a synthesis of the entire vision held by La Rocque and the CDF/PSF leadership of the young future leader within the new nation and state: 'It appeals to a freely-given discipline, a desire for collective achievement, a continuous implementation denuded of any partisan or exclusive idea, in the spirit of genuine camaraderie and complete confidence.'[124]

Although infused with an authoritarian moralism, such ideas did not much differ from many Popular Front initiatives, including the Dézarnaulds/Sellier plan. The latter likewise argued for increased physical education, to encourage discipline, hygiene, and the strengthening of the French nation. Like the CDF/PSF, Dézarnaulds openly admired *Hébertisme*, whose writings influenced his vision of the transformation of youth, while Sellier made allusions to the defense of the 'race'. Even Léo Lagrange made similar pronouncements.[125] But there was a more sinister side at work in certain factions of the CDF/PSF, especially within the SPES, far removed from the initiatives of Lagrange and the Popular Front. It is true that Maire frequently proclaimed the SPES to be an organization solely interested in the propagation of physical exercise, seeking only to better the health and hygiene of French youth. Nor were his anti-individualism and use of the SPES to spread the group doctrine uncommon tactics in interwar France. The French communist party used the latter in various clubs with a similar goal in mind: the transformation of youth into comrades working to build a new nation and state, while the former was standard fare among the European right.[126]

Yet Maire and many CDF/PSF authors went much farther than their colleagues on the French left or right. They proposed the creation of a new man, through the utter transformation of youth on all levels: intellectual, moral, and especially physical. To be sure, Maire and like-minded members never approached the proto-racialist theorizing of French eugenicists. Although xenophobic sentiments existed elsewhere in the group, concepts such as René Martial's inter-racial grafting theory, in which foreign traits allegedly weakened the population by infiltrating its stronger blood type, found little sympathy in even the most extreme group proposals regarding youth.[127] Neither did these authors advocate the racial manipulation keenly endorsed by the Nazis. Under the auspices of the *Schutz Staffeln*, German eugenicists aimed to eliminate the weak and unfit, not to improve the individual. Thus Maire never proposed legislation akin to the 1933 Law to Prevent Hereditary Sick Offspring, which empowered race tribunals to eradicate the mentally ill and physically weak. Nor did they adhere to the racial typing promoted by the Hitler Youth for schoolchildren, culminating in the establishment of *Erziehungsanstallen* academies to train an aryan elite for the SS and military.[128]

---

124   AP/451/151, G.A. Maire, note of 10 July 1938.

125   Ory, pp. 659–661; Jackson, p. 134.

126   For Maire's claims see AP/451/151, G.A. Maire, note of 10 July 1938 and AP/451/152, 'Note sur le but et le programme des SPES', 15 June 1938. For the comparable case of the French communists, see Ory, pp. 78–79; Whitney, pp. 112–117.

127   Schneider, pp. 242–248. For an analysis of those within the CDF/PSF who adopted xenophobic discourse, see chapter five.

128   Arnd Krüger, 'Breeding, Rearing and Preparing the Aryan Body: Creating Supermen the Nazi Way', in J.A. Mangan (ed.), *Shaping the Superman: Fascist Body as Political Icon*

But Maire and his coevals went much farther than La Rocque and the bulk of the CDF/PSF, whose concept of youth formation consisted of educational reform, training, and fitness. Their proposed elite combined Lyautey and the Front Generation, Christian principles, and old-fashioned conservatism. Conversely, eugenicists in the group adopted the opposite position: That the nation and state would be best served through the creation of a physically and intellectually flawless youth. Maire and the SPES wished to remove all traces of physical and mental weakness from France, strengthening the nation by manipulating the population through selective physical training. Nor was this process to be introduced gradually, but rather implemented by the new state, involving mandatory training of the human body and mind in order to achieve the maximum human potential from each citizen.

In fact, SPES propaganda claimed that: 'Above all, our basic goal is not to create champions, but much more reasonably and usefully to *fabricate men* (my italics).'[129] These directives were delivered to the instructors responsible for administering SPES programs in Paris and the provinces. Various CDF/PSF writers consistently used such principles to describe the birth of the new nation and state, with special references continuously made to youth. Writing in the *Flambeau* in May 1937, Francis Georges claimed that it was the mission of the CDF/PSF to create a new breed of Frenchman, leading the nation into a glorious future through faith and will: 'This is our task in an age when brusque changes will crush the old leadership, thrusting us towards a future open to creators, where there is no place for those with neither the perceptiveness nor the will to anticipate and control events that pass them by.' How these specimens were to be conceived and propagated within society was left to the reader's imagination.[130]

Others were far less vague. In sounding the alarm about the French need for an organization comparable to the Hitler Youth, one author justified his position with the claim that 'we must consider the future of the race!'.[131] A writer in the *Flambeau de Bourgogne* took this argument to its logical extreme, stating that all education in the *État social français* would be physical training, because 'an education by and large is one of the senses, the cerebral centres, and the motor organs'. This process paralleled biological evolution, leading to the complete development and transformation of the human body, and ultimately the perfection of man, his physical and moral qualities exploited to the highest level possible. Youth were to be the focus of this program, in which the causes of enfeeblement to the human capital would be eliminated.[132]

Despite certain rhetorical similarities to Nazism or fascism, the CDF/PSF clearly rejected experimentation and racial theorizing, however. Their new youth would not be supermen, but ordinary French children. Nonetheless, the group clearly envisioned a state-mandated effort, in which the *État social français* molded the young. Such action proved necessary, lamented Pierre Apesteguy in the *Petit*

---

129   AP/451/151, 'Réunion de travail pour les moniteurs sportifs SPES'.
130   Francis Georges, 'La Drame de la jeunesse', *Le Flambeau*, 1 May 1937.
131   Artiste, 'Education nationale', *Le Flambeau*, 14 March 1936.
132   'Éducation sportive', *Flambeau de Bourgogne*, 14 March 1937.

*journal*, because the modern life of the factory, excessive leisure, and the automobile created 'a net degeneration of the human being'.[133] Once again, the SPES possessed the tool for the implementation of state policies. According to Dr. Encausse, such work had already begun in various CDF/PSF organizations. Speaking at the second national group congress in 1937, he stated that the SPES had embarked upon a plan to establish medico-psychological files for youth, granting a measure of control to the collaborative effort of group doctors and physical education specialists.[134] Maire made clear the purpose of such work in a memorandum that explicitly rejected the methodology of eugenicists in favour of physical education and a propagandistic school curriculum, but nevertheless enthusiastically adopted their goal:

> Physical degeneration is the defect of civilized peoples who neglect physical culture. In order to fight it, Europeans everywhere are organizing against intensive intellectual culture, an excess of which imbalances organic strength. This new faith excites doctors, teachers, philosophers, sportsmen, and politicians. Like men, societies suffer the consequences of their bad hygiene. Like families where the moral and intellectual education was depraved, entire states have been badly raised, cowardly and feeble. Nevertheless, experience demonstrates that these mental and psychological anomalies are nothing more than educational defects, which can be corrected by physical education and the practice of rugged sports ... The child must necessarily be considered the seedling of the country and the spirit of the nation, not merely as a future voter ... to the men responsible for this reorganization ... who are imbued with the most flawed ideas regarding inescapable, hereditary physical degeneration, and who are unaware of the extent to which living matter is plastic, and fervently regenerative.

Europe as a whole had risen up against the primacy of intellectual culture, an excess of which 'throws organic forces off balance'. Thus it was imperative that the SPES seek out and correct mental and physical anomalies.[135]

## VI

Faisceau and CDF/PSF plans for youth were not without precedent. The Third Republic itself acted in the same way, using schooling, conscription and the army, and even sport to take youth under its wing. With so much time spent under the influence of its loyal servants, various ministers theorized, young men and women would inevitably support the status quo. It was this concept that drove Jules Ferry in 1882 to weaken the stranglehold of the Catholic Church on education, an organization which he viewed as a bastion of anti-republican reaction. Ferry knew that the fidelity of the masses could be ensured through the indoctrination of their children, and acted accordingly. After their time in the schoolhouse the young were stripped of their

---

133   Pierre Apesteguy, 'Le Sport obligatoire pour l'enfance', *Petit journal*, 31 Aug. 1937. See also AP/451/103-Tract, *Que veut le Parti social français*, Dec. 1936.

134   Dr. Encausse, 'Rapport sur l'éducation physique', *Petit journal*, 26 Nov. 1937. Here again, there exists a marked resemblance to the Dézarnaulds/Sellier plan. The medical observation/ control of youth was also a key component of Vichy's policies, in Giolitto, pp. 203–204.

135   AP/451/151, G.A. Maire, note of 10 July 1938.

familial ties, and shipped off to the military or higher education for finishing touches, a captive audience already softened up by primary and secondary school teachers.[136]

But this carefully implemented scheme went awry during the interwar period. Prevented from obtaining political power or even the vote in most cases, youth proved to be exceptionally receptive to extreme-rightist attacks against republican decadence and French weakness. Faisceau and CDF/PSF plans for youth represented distinctive attempts to harness this energy, redirecting it towards the construction of a new nation and state to be built according to group principles. Thus a host of extreme-rightist groups in the nineteen-twenties and thirties took up Valois and Arthuys's optimistic belief that youth would abandon democracy in favour of the politics of the trenches, influenced by their experiences during the Great War. These leagues, from the young intellectuals of Ordre Nouveau, *Esprit*, and *Plans* to the CDF/PSF and Parti populaire français, echoed the Faisceau proposition that a National Revolution, which symbolized the union, fraternity, and spirit of the *combattants* had merely to present itself as a viable option in order to succeed. Communism, the only other available choice, was antithetical to the young because they had fought for the nation, and not a specific class. Whether fascist or conservative many right-wing organizations and leagues thus urged young members to adopt the military discipline and voluntarism of the trenches, in the service of a 'renovated' France devoid of democratic sentiment.

But for all its subsequent popularity, the doctrine expounded by Valois and Arthuys was bound to remain unrealized, not least because the exact role of youth in their proposed fascist nation and state remained obscure. Both men answered in language full of vague assertions, slogans, and avoidance. Primarily concerned with the establishment of a new economic order, they tackled the question only in the most general terms. Furthermore, the vision of the *combattant* espoused by Valois and Arthuys was itself a fiction. As Robert Wohl writes:

> Intellectuals from these [middle] classes dreamed of a spiritual revolution that would eliminate the exploiters and the exploited and fuse all sectors of a society into a unified and conflict-free community ... The 'generation of 1914' was therefore first of all a self-image produced by a clearly defined group within the educated classes at a particular moment in the evolution of European society. It was both an attempt at self-description by intellectuals and a project of hegemony over other social classes that derived its credibility and its force from circumstances that were unique to European men born during the last two decades of the nineteenth century.[137]

Although the postwar generation shared Faisceau concerns about national decadence, they were not ready to win the peace as they had triumphed in war. The architecture of Valois and Arthuys's entire project rested upon the utopian notion that youth were inherently fascist because fascism best represented the values of the trenches. In other words, it rested upon assumptions not shared by the young soldiers on whose behalf the two men spoke.

---

136  Yolande Cohen, *Les Jeunes, le Socialisme et la guerre: Histoire des mouvements de jeunesse en France* (Paris, 1989), pp. 19–20.

137  Wohl, p. 209.

Only Hubert Bourgin, a non-combatant whose interests were conservative rather than fascist in nature, attempted to address these issues. The so-called 'fascist professor' exclusively tackled the restoration of discipline and hierarchy in society, and the reintroduction of Catholic virtues and hard work in youth. Where Valois worshipped the machine gun, Bourgin idolized the strap. Like Barrès and Maurras before him, the old *Normalien* wished to return to the days before the Ferry laws and republican youth policy. Rather than the trenches, his ideals embodied the family farm and the village church, symbolic of an idyllic life that Frenchmen had lost to the decadent, immoral, and individualistic Republic. In an effort to combat this malignant development he proscribed a strict moral and physical regimen for contemporary youth, to train them for their future responsibilities as workers, fathers, Catholics, and patriots.

Such traditional attitudes were a far cry from Valois and Arthuys's modernizing fascism. But Bourgin, too, prefigured a doctrinal emphasis prevalent within later extreme-rightist initiatives. In particular, his Catholic and moral bent, and his insistence upon the primacy of discipline and physical effort, presaged currents which emerged within the Vichy regime from 1940 onwards.[138] *Pétainiste* education ministers Jacques Chevalier and Abel Bonnard, himself an ex-member of the Faisceau, emphasized a combination of moral instruction and discipline in the new school curriculum. Like Bourgin, they derided the Masonic and communist influence which had dominated pedagogy under the Third Republic, introducing legislation to remove any teacher seen as 'an element of disorder, an inveterate politicizer, or incompetent'.[139]

Nowhere were Bourgin's ideas more evident than Uriage, the leadership school established in 1940 by Pierre Dunoyer de Segonzac with Vichy's approval. Run by Segonzac and Hubert Beuve-Méry, another Faisceau sympathizer, the school provided a curriculum seemingly drawn directly from Bourgin's columns in *Nouveau Siècle*. The Uriage charter of 1941 rejected individualism and democracy, materialism and decadence in equal measure. In their place, the school proposed authority, hierarchy, and sacrifice, forging an elite in the service of the nation. To Segonzac, physical and moral learning clearly outweighed intellectual exercises, while the Uriage newspaper *Jeunesse ... France!* mimicked Bourgin's appeal to the soil, as necessary nourishment for the French race. Surely Bourgin, rather than Chombert de Lauwe, could have written that 'we have to place the maintaining of unity among the most urgent tasks ... the defence of our spiritual patrimony based on Christian civilization'.[140]

Like Bourgin, the CDF/PSF vision of future generations for the most part remained conservative in scope. But they were much more ambitious. With hundreds of thousands of members after 1934, and over 1 million by 1938, group leaders believed that *État social français* within reach, and viewed the initiation of youth as a crucial component of its success. They thus created an entire array of agencies for their indoctrination. Where Valois and Arthuys issued vague proclamations, La Rocque and his team left no stone unturned: A completely revised education system,

---

138   In this regard, it is interesting to note that Vichy borrowed the Faisceau concept of the National Revolution, first used by Bourgin, Valois, and Arthuys two decades earlier.

139   Halls, pp. 18–36, 71–72, 113–115. Perhaps emboldened by the success of his platform, Bourgin reintroduced many of his interwar ideas in a 1942 work entitled *L'École nationale*.

140   Hellman, *The Knight Monks of Vichy France*, pp. 59–63, 120.

the celebration of family life, a new and mandatory national physical education program, and youth activities and clubs figured among the initiatives which the group either funded during its existence or proposed for the future. The CDF/PSF as a whole aimed, despite disagreements regarding specific details, to transform republican youth into loyal members of the *État social français*. Young men and women were to become fervent nationalists, believing Catholics, ardent devotees of physical education, and the building-blocks of the future nation and state.

Thus the CDF/PSF also augured the doctrine and practice of Vichy-era youth policies. For as Jean-Louis Gay-Lescot writes, wartime youth ministry leaders tied the fate of French state and society to a morally and physically robust youth, implemented through the 'establishment of a new conception of the...role of physical education and sport within pedagogy and society'.[141] Many former group members were in fact directly responsible for the formulation of Vichy youth policy, including Jean Ybarnégaray at the Ministry for Family and Youth in 1940, Jean Borotra as Minister of Sport in 1940–1941, and Félix Olivier-Martin as Secretary of State for Youth in 1943–1944. All three men participated in CDF/PSF planning and organization for youth during the previous decade, including proposals for a reorganized education system and the use of propaganda to constantly remind the younger generation of their duty. In this way, the group was more modern than the Faisceau. Although quite conservative in many instances, the CDF/PSF understood the resources at the disposal of the state to inculcate its population. As the most susceptible members of society, youth were to be the primary targets. It is not surprising then that Gaëtan Maire and others made the leap from indoctrination to perfection via the elimination of human weakness through physical, moral, and intellectual education. In the view of La Rocque, Daujat, or Mierry, the new state morally and ideologically formed children; Maire's proposals simply extended the group's plans into the physical sphere.[142]

It is important to stress, however, that neither the Faisceau nor the CDF/PSF, nor even the extreme-right as a whole during the interwar era, alone insisted that the state should ensure the proper formation of youth. Many French youth groups utilized staunchly Catholic and conservative rhetoric, their appeals to a sense of community and 'healthy attitudes' prefiguring the turn against republican orthodoxy. Just as Valois, Arthuys, and Bourgin or La Rocque, Mierry, and Maire rejected parliamentarism and decadence, so too did scout leaders, the JOC, and many others preach the gospel of physical prowess and moral regeneration. Likewise, many of their members eventually joined extreme-rightist leagues or involved themselves with Vichy initiatives like the Chantiers de la jeunesse. In the words of Philippe Laneyrie, such a drift seemed to reflect the tenor of the age:

141   Jean-Louis Gay-Lescot, 'La Politique sportive de Vichy', *Cahiers de L'Institut d'histoire du temps present* 8 (1988), p. 55.

142   Here too the Vichy analogy can be detected. Not only did Colonel de Sonzy from the Sécrétariat-général de la jeunesse remark upon the 'plastic' character of youth much like Maire and others in the CDF/PSF, but the regime bombarded youth with *Pétainiste* propaganda emphasizing the benefits of the National Revolution, and the necessary role of youth in the reconstruction of France. See, for example, Giolitto, p. 459.

It is a *reactionary* movement, in the etymological sense of the word. That is to say, it is defined against the secularism and anti-clerical politics of the Third Republic, against materialism (both Marxist and capitalist), against the latitudinarian morals of liberal society, against the various ingredients of triumphant urban civilization, against the phenomenon of massification, and against democracy as a political system.[143]

This statement could have applied equally to both the Faisceau and CDF/PSF. In an era in which youthful anti-republicanism abounded, the extremity of their solution – a complete transformation of youth by both nation and state and vice versa – differentiated both groups.

---

143   Halls, p. 133, Laneyrie, p. 109.

# Chapter Five

# The Politics of Exclusion: Jews and Foreigners in the New Nation and State

Previous chapters have discussed Faisceau and CDF/PSF plans for a renovated French nation and state, which in many respects resembled similar initiatives under the authoritarian Vichy regime, born in the aftermath of the decisive German victory in June 1940. Wasting little time following the Nazi triumph, right-wing luminary and First World War hero Marshal Philippe Pétain formed a non-parliamentary government, and signed an armistice with the victors who divided the nation into a German-occupied north and a sovereign French southern zone. Under Vichy's watchful eye, various ministries and organizations began a transformation of French politics, economy, and society according to the dicta of the extreme right-wing National Revolution, a catch-phrase used to differentiate Pétain's new order from the decadent, parliamentary Third Republic.

Nowhere is this more evident than in the politics of exclusion mandated by the new government. To be sure, exclusionary policy was hardly novel in France. From the Boulanger and Dreyfus affairs in the late nineteenth century onwards, conservative and extremist groups regularly harnessed anti-Semitism and xenophobia, tendering demands which ranged from forced conversion to the outright elimination of Jews and foreigners. As the culmination of these struggles against the Third Republic, Vichy was unsurprisingly preoccupied with the politics of exclusion. Thus from the first months in power onwards, various ministers promulgated legislation designed to remove Jews and foreigners from public life, and eventually from French soil altogether.

This process began in August 1940, less than two months after Vichy's inauguration, when Minister of Justice Raphaël Alibert revoked the naturalized status of tens of thousands of foreigners living in the Vichy zone. In subsequent years the Commisariat général aux Questions juives (CGQJ), under the leadership of arch-conservative anti-Semite Xavier Vallat until March 1942, and thereafter Nazi sympathizer Louis Darquier de Pellepoix, used anti-Semitic legislation to withdraw the citizenship and civil rights of foreign and Algerian Jews. They concomitantly removed French Jews from public service, the officer corps, the arts, journalism, and professions such as law and medicine. In addition, the Service de contrôle des Administrateurs provisoires seized Jewish businesses and property. These actions were so thorough that they surpassed even Nazi planning in the occupied zone.[1] CGQJ efforts culminated in round-ups and

---

1    Susan Zuccotti, *The Holocaust, The French, and the Jews* (New York, 1993), chapter three. As Gérard Noiriel notes, such *Vichyiste* actions against Jews often echoed

deportations in summer 1942, carried out not only by the Nazis in northern France, but enthusiastically in the southern zone as well. Almost 75,000 Jews were sent to Polish death camps by the end of 1944 in this manner.[2]

Historians agree that Vichy's repressive policies and deportations, made possible by active French participation and not the direct product of Nazi pressure, must be viewed as the culmination of a long-standing anti-Semitic and xenophobic tradition in France. As Pierre Birnbaum writes:

> From the perspective of the actual fate of the Jews, Vichy began well before Vichy, because the most virulent anti-Semitism was given free reign throughout the interwar era, inspiring in both Paris and the most remote provinces everything from physical violence to an incalculable number of books, satires, pamphlets, and severe threats.[3]

At first glance, the Faisceau and CDF/PSF seem unlikely candidates for such harsh tactics. Unlike the Nazis in Germany, for example, neither group mobilized an ideology based principally on race. For Hitler and his followers, all facets of the proposed nation and state, from social legislation to foreign policy, were directly linked to the 'Jewish Question'. Various Faisceau and CDF/PSF members frequently adopted the opposite public stance: That anti-Semitism and xenophobia had no place in the newly renovated nation and state.

However, such benevolent pronouncements served to obscure the omnipresence of xenophobia within the Faisceau and CDF/PSF. Laurent Joly describes the existence of an anti-Semitic *famille de pensée* in the decades before Vichy, often twinned with anti-communism, the defense of Catholicism and tradition, and frequently enunciated in rational or legal terms rather than Nazi-style emotive appeals to the mystique of the French race.[4] Although by no means the only forefathers of Vichy, both the Faisceau and the CDF/PSF inundated their sizable memberships with the very ideas realized by the National Revolution after June 1940.[5] If their ideological foundations were not exclusively based upon racialist assumptions, the leadership and rank and file of both groups nonetheless viewed the exclusion of Jews and foreigners as one of paramount importance to the renovation of the nation and state. This notion was consistently presented in various articles, tracts, and speeches. Despite the presence of only 200,000 Jews in interwar France, they were portrayed as the masters of international finance, infiltrating the highest corridors of power, and members of a foreign race which had successfully invaded France unbeknownst to the general public. The newly powerful foreigner, who had colonized France and stolen French

---

policies initiated by the Third Republic. See *Les Origines républicaines de Vichy* (Paris, 1999), chapters three and four.

2    Michael R. Marrus and Robert O. Paxton, *Vichy France and the Jews* (Stanford, 1982), p. 343.

3    Pierre Birnbaum, *Une mythe politique: la république juive* (Paris, 1995), p. 34.

4    Laurent Joly, *Vichy dans la 'solution finale': Histoire du Commissariat général aux Questions juives* (Paris, 2006), pp. 33–34.

5    For example, the regime's terminology was often borrowed from the Faisceau and CDF/PSF. The phrase 'National Revolution' was frequently used by Valois, while Vichy's slogan 'travail, famille, patrie' had been on the front page of *Le Flambeau* throughout the 1930s.

jobs and privileges away from her native sons, joined the Jew in the Faisceau and CDF/PSF pantheon of enemies. To create conditions of prosperity and security, they would be forcibly excluded from the nation.[6]

It is equally important to note that neither group simply parroted the Catholic and conservative rhetoric of Dreyfus-era anti-Semites like Charles Maurras, Maurice Barrès, and Edouard Drumont, who argued for a tangled xenophobic conspiracy in which Jews and foreigners played leading roles. Instead, the sheer violence and scope of the Faisceau and CDF/PSF attacks render them unique, particularly within their historical context. For the Faisceau mounted their campaigns from 1924–1927, during a time of relative acceptance of Jews and foreigners when most right-wing figures had abandoned them. Similarly, the CDF/PSF began their attacks in 1932, two years before renewed xenophobia recaptured public attention in France. Finally, both the tone and proposed solutions of the Faisceau and CDF/PSF set them apart from all but the most extreme racial ideologues associated with *Gringoire* or *Je suis partout*. Hence well before the Vichy years, both groups inculcated their members with the politics of exclusion, providing a conduit which laid the groundwork for popular passive acceptance and active participation in xenophobic policies after the French defeat in June 1940.

# I

To more clearly understand the importance of this conceptual continuity, it is necessary first to introduce the broader context of French extreme right-wing anti-Semitism and xenophobia. Neither original nor marginalized, Faisceau and CDF/PSF attitudes in fact represent a crucial link to similar widely-held precepts predominant at the turn of the century. This proved especially true for the Faisceau, whose leadership and rank and file agitated during the relative calm and tolerance of the nineteen-twenties, far removed from the turbulent prewar era.

French Jews were first emancipated in 1791 during the revolutionary era, when the National Assembly granted them citizenship and constitutional rights. However, legal equalization more fully emerged under Napoleon, who bestowed consistorial status on French Jewry, aligning their religion and community with Protestantism and the Catholic faith. Consequently rabbis joined their Christian colleagues as employees of the state from the 1830s onwards. Concomitantly, official Jewish organizations like the Consistoire israèlite and the Alliance israèlite universelle adopted an assimilationist bent, dedicated to transforming a previously marginalized people into a solid caste of loyal French citizens.[7] Furthermore, after 1871 Jews

---

6     Both Lazare Landau and Pierre Birnbaum estimate the Jewish population in 1930s France, including recent immigrants, to have been no more than two hundred thousand. In Lazare Landau, *De l'aversion à l'estime: Juifs et Catholiques en France de 1919 à 1939* (Paris, 1980), pp. 41–44; Birnbaum, *Un mythe politique*, p. 157. Michael Marrus and Robert Paxton further estimate the presence of 2.5–3 million foreigners, in *Vichy France and the Jews*, pp. 34–35.

7     Paula Hyman, *From Dreyfus to Vichy: The Remaking of French Jewry, 1906–39* (New York, 1979), pp. 6–9. Hyman notes that even the AIU, founded in 1860 as an

proved overwhelmingly loyal to the Third Republic, primarily due to their liberal political orientation and an appreciation for laic policies which obviated the return of state-sanctioned anti-Semitism.

Yet despite the rapid assimilation of Jews in France, and their fervent patriotism, popular anti-Semitism reappeared in the 1840s. Xenophobic screed was initially embraced by the left, beginning with Fourrier disciple Toussenel's *Les Juifs, rois de l'époque*, which appeared in 1845. Along with Proudhon, and later socialist leader Jules Guesde, Toussenel characterized Jews as foreign peddlers and corrupt parasites, out to take money from honest Frenchmen. In each case, the authors targeted bourgeois Jews, and particularly bankers like the Rothschilds and Pereires. Motivated by class concerns, they eschewed racial anti-Semitism in favour of the perceived financial predominance of French Jewry.[8]

By the 1880s, however, conservative and clerical groups began to utilize anti-Semitic rhetoric of a different variety, linked to racial stereotypes and political protest rather than financial complaints. Catholic newspapers like *La Croix* criticized Jews for their ardent republicanism, and frequently perpetuated myths and stereotypes concerning Jewish religious practices.[9] In addition, throughout the early history of the Third Republic various extreme right-wing authors, journalists, and political figures routinely denounced Jews and foreigners, claiming that their presence within the nation poisoned France. Led by the notorious anti-Semitic writer Édouard Drumont, whose treatise *La France juive* and newspaper *Libre Parole* (which sold 200,000 copies daily at its peak) were phenomenally successful, xenophobes ran for parliament and took to the streets.[10] By the late nineteenth century, the extreme right increasingly blamed French economic and political failings squarely on Jews and foreigners. This trend was epitomized by the Dreyfus Affair, when the ensuing furor split the country in two, pitting those who believed that Dreyfus had been framed against those who proclaimed him guilty, not least because he was 'un-French' – despite the fact that his family were Alsatian patriots of long-standing French citizenship, and little proof existed of the Jewish officer's guilt.[11]

Dreyfus eventually received a presidential pardon in 1899, with the trial verdict set aside in 1906, but the divisiveness created by the affair did not disappear. For many Catholics, extreme-rightists, anti-Semitic intellectuals, and xenophobes, the case offered proof that the Jew conspired against France, a traitor and hoarder of

---

international organization based in France, dedicated itself to the promotion of the French political model abroad.

8     Ralph Schor, *L'Antisémitisme en France pendant les années trente* (Paris, 1992), pp. 9–11; Marrus and Paxton, pp. 29–32.

9     Zuccotti, p. 12.

10    Marrus and Paxton, pp. 27–34. The authors recount the political success of Francis Laur, who ran for office in 1889 with the aid of the Ligue nationale antisémitique. Laur maintained strong ties with Édouard Drumont and the Boulangists. See Stephen Wilson, *Ideology and Experience: Antisemitism in France at the Time of the Dreyfus Affair* (East Rutherford, 1982), pp. 171–172, 213–214.

11    For an examination of the extreme-right's views on Dreyfus, see James F. McMillan, *Dreyfus to De Gaulle: Politics and Society in France, 1898–1969* (New York, 1985), pp. 3–12.

money, with tentacles spread throughout Europe and the world, bent on domination.[12] In his highly influential *Vers un ordre sociale chrétien*, social Catholic philosopher René de la Tour du Pin called Jews money-hungry usurers who believed in their own innate racial superiority. In league with foreigners, Freemasons, and Protestants, they aimed to control France. As such, both Jews and immigrants were to be treated as dangerous foreigners, and preferably expelled from the nation.[13] In a similar vein, nationalist deputy and author Maurice Barrès, whose best-selling novels introduced a generation of young French intellectuals to the notion of 'the soil and the dead', wrote that no Jew could be truly French because 'for us, the motherland is the soil and our ancestors, it is the earth and our dead. For them, it is the place where they find the greatest personal interest'. Neither could the foreigner claim truly Gallic roots, because his ancestors were not nourished by the wheat and tradition of France.[14]

Such sentiments continually appeared in the late nineteenth and early twentieth century. Groups like the royalist Action française and the Ligue des patriotes regularly participated in demonstrations against Jews and foreigners, while anti-Semitic authors such as the racial geneticist Vacher de Lapouge and Drumont found substantial readerships.[15] After 1906, however, such figures were increasingly marginalized, and French Jews enjoyed a 'golden age', as the *ralliement* brought Catholics and conservatives back into the republican fold. By the 1920s, the anti-Semitic and xenophobic fervour diminished. The *fin de siècle* divisions over the Panama and Dreyfus scandals, along with the purveyors of exclusionary rhetoric, receded from public view. For the French public looked favourably upon Jewish participation in the war effort, and especially at the front. Thus the Union sacrée, initiated to end political divisiveness for the duration of the conflict, proved equally effective in reconciling Christians and Jews. In the postwar era, such sentiments resulted in the rejection of previously popular anti-Semitic figures. Drumont died in 1917, and *Libre Parole* ceased publication seven years later, its readership having declined steadily during the preceding decade. Long a staunch anti-Dreyfusard, Maurice Barrès expressed more favourable sentiments at war's end, arguing that Jews formed an integral component of the 'diverse spiritual families of France'.[16] Given the lack of postwar support for anti-Semitism, it is not surprising that even prominent leagues like the Jeunesses patriotes minimized such sentiments in their programs.[17]

---

12    See Wilson, *Ideology and Experience*, parts two and three; Venita Datta, *Birth of a National Icon: The Literary Avant-Garde and the Origins of the Intellectual in Modern France* (Albany, 1999), chapter four.

13    René de la Tour du Pin, *Vers un ordre social chrétien* (Paris, 1987), pp. 257–273.

14    Maurice Barrès, *Scenes et doctrines du nationalisme* (Paris, 1987), p. 50. See also pp. 67–69.

15    On the success of Vacher de Lapouge, see William H. Schneider, *Quality and Quantity: The Quest for Biological Regeneration in Twentieth-Century France* (Cambridge, 1990), pp. 59–63, 236–239. For an account of Drumont's position as doyen of the prewar extreme-right, see Frederick Busi, *The Pope of Antisemitism: The Career and Legacy of Édouard-Alphonse Drumont* (Lanham, 1986).

16    Millman, *La Question juive*, pp. 38–40; Hyman, pp. 34–35.

17    Neither the Jeunesses patriotes nor the Légion, two of the largest extreme-rightist groups, maintained an anti-Semitic stance during the 1920s. Furthermore, the Action française,

**II**

While others lost interest in anti-Semitism at war's end, one league remained faithful to anti-Semitic rhetoric: The Action française. Formed in 1899 in the wake of the Dreyfus Affair, the group pledged to restore the French monarchy and fight against the *Quatre États Confédérés*. According to leader Charles Maurras, Jews led the *Quatre États*, the weak offspring of tailors and peddlers who streamed into France from Eastern Europe. Many were of German origin, thundered Maurras, dedicated to turning France into a 'German-Yiddish' state.[18] A public menace to French state and society, the Jew represented a foreign invader whose legal expulsion alone could restore a properly Gallic body politic.[19] This group attracted the young Georges Valois, who became a member in 1906 and subsequently the resident expert on economic affairs. Although not exclusively attracted by his xenophobia, he nonetheless adopted Maurras's anti-Semitism along with his royalism. Valois's articles in the group newspaper and his various publications during his time in the royalist camp consistently derided the 'Jewish bourgeois plutocracy', which sought to defraud Frenchmen of their gold.[20]

Maurras's organization achieved its greatest success in the decade before the Great War, carrying the anti-Dreyfusard torch during the period of Republican resurgence. Its rise to prominence interrupted by the outbreak of hostilities in 1914, the royalist faction never regained its former position of strength on the French right. After brief postwar success in 1919, the group entered into a period of slow decline in terms of membership and influence, while interest in their brand of anti-Semitic politics weakened considerably.[21] Valois thus moved away from the Maurrassian fold upon forming the Faisceau in 1925, and seemingly jettisoned anti-Semitic rhetoric in the process.

On the subject of the so-called Jewish question, the Faisceau appeared to publicly reject anti-Semitic sentiment. Fascism united men of all confessions through love of God, country and one's fellow man, and Valois proclaimed the 'national school' of

---

long among the staunchest opponents of Jews and immigrants, somewhat downplayed such themes in response to public apathy. See Soucy, *French Fascism*, chapters two and three, and Millman, *La Question juive*, p. 40.

18    See Ernst Nolte, *Three Faces of Fascism* (New York, 1969), pp. 164–166. Such sentiments permeated Maurras's writings, for example *Enquête sur la monarchie* (Paris, 1924), pp. 257–258. This work was originally published in 1900.

19    Joly, *Vichy dans la 'solution finale'*, pp. 49–50.

20    For examples of Valois's early adoption of Maurrassian anti-Semitic and xenophobic rhetoric, see variously: CHEVS/VA 21, 'Nationalisme et syndicalisme, rapport présenté au IVe congrès de l'Action française, le 7 Décembre 1911, par M. Georges Valois'; 'La Bourgeoisie capitaliste', Georges Valois, *Cahiers du Cercle Proudhon*, Dec. 1912, pp. 229–245; Georges Valois, *La Monarchie et la classe ouvrière* (Paris, 1924); 'L'Affaire Ferrer en France', in *Histoire et philosophie sociales* (Paris, 1924). The latter originally appeared in *Action française* in 1909.

21    For an analysis of the group's steady decline see Eugen Weber, *Action française* (Stanford, 1963), parts two and four. The waning popularity of the Action française is best illustrated by the circulation of their daily newspaper, which dropped from 60,000 copies in December 1925 to just over half that amount by the end of the decade.

fascism open to all the spiritual families of France.[22] With no proscribed faith, wrote Maurice de Barral, the fascist state would not tolerate any form of philosophical or religious persecution.[23] The era of Drumont and the Dreyfus Affair had officially ended, with only a few minor incidents in Paris and the provinces as the remains of their legacy. The group listed prominent Jewish authors of the day, including Edmond Fleg, André Spine, and Israël Zangueil, while lauding new Jewish clubs such as the Union universelle de la jeunesse.[24] Valois further publicly condemned group manifestations of anti-Semitism. When faced with a member who loudly accused 'the Jews' of being the culprits during a presentation against parliament and the banks, he decried such sentiments in no uncertain terms, stating: 'You speak of the Jews, dear comrade! In their defence, it must be said that these so-called Jews are often people who are not Jewish'. He finished by voicing opposition to any violent action directed at Jews in France.[25]

But such public rejections of anti-Semitism and xenophobia hid a vastly different agenda. Given the lull in racist theorizing that followed the Great War, and the seeming unpopularity of such sentiments in the 1920s, it is hardly surprising that Faisceau members publicly avoided anti-Semitic rhetoric. In an age of state-sponsored immigration, enacted to counter the dearth of working-age French males, few voices proclaimed the xenophobic creed. Even Action française luminary and staunch anti-Semite Léon Daudet lost his seat in the Chamber of Deputies during the 1923 election.[26] By 1924, as the Bloc national collapsed, authors like Barrès, Drumont, and Paul Bourget, once the beneficiaries of large readerships, no longer wielded tremendous influence. Thus Valois sought to distance himself from the older, less dynamic right, proclaiming that his group represented the values of the 'age of electricity'.[27] When given any opportunity to reach a wider audience, at large open-air meetings for example, he declined to publicly espouse anti-Semitic views.[28]

Despite the group's public stance, there were few Jews in the Faisceau. Jean Mayer and the Parisian lawyer Jacques Marx were both marginal members and occasional contributors to *Nouveau Siècle*, but neither held any position of importance.[29] True,

22    F/7/13211, Georges Valois, Tract 9: 'Le Faisceau des combattants, des chefs de famille, et des producteurs', p. 7.
23    Maurice de Barral, *Dialogues sur le Faisceau: Ses origines, sa doctrine* (Paris, 1926), pp. 9–10.
24    Gaeton Bernöville, 'La Question Juive', *NS*, 18 Sept. 1927.
25    CHEVS/VA 21, Grande réunion privée sous le présidence de M. Georges Valois, 2 Nov. 1926.
26    Weber, *Action française*, pp. 151–152. The group as a whole garnered a mere 328,000 votes, slightly more than a third of the communist tally.
27    See, for example, 'Nationalisme et socialisme', *NS*, 25–26 January 1926 and 'Le Fascisme: conclusion du mouvement de 1789', *NS*, 14 July 1926.
28    At large gatherings in 1926 at Verdun and Reims, the question of Jews in France was not raised by speakers. See, for example, *Première assemblée nationale des combattants, des producteurs et des chefs de famille* (Paris, 1926) and Allen Douglas, *From Fascism to Libertarian Communism* (Berkeley, 1992), pp. 105–111.
29    Clarence D. Tingley, 'Georges Valois and the Faisceau: Post-Apocalyptic Politics in Twentieth-Century France', *Proceedings of the Annual Conference of the Western Society for French History*, 3 (1976), p. 387; Millman, *La Question juive*, p. 90.

Victor Mayer, a Jewish shoe manufacturer from Paris, provided financial backing, as did an engineer named Salomon, but they were uninvolved in the group's affairs.[30] The only other mention of Jewish members came in the form of a letter in the appendix to Valois's book *La Politique de la victoire*, in which a 'young Israelite Frenchman who loves God and his country' named Soloman Nathan agrees that youth are reactionary.[31]

One Jewish figure who did play a more significant role in the Faisceau, albeit briefly, was René Groos, a charter member of the Action française and a rabid anti-Semite. During his tenure as the literary critic for *Nouveau Siècle* in late 1924, Groos professed hatred for his people in a book entitled *Le Problème juif* (published by Valois at the Nouvelle Librairie Nationale). Indeed, the Faisceau membership lists contained a number of established anti-Semites. Mathilde Dubert, the only woman to write for the group's newspaper, formerly contributed to Édouard Drumont's virulently anti-Semitic *Libre parole*. Moreover, Jean Delettre, a member of the Faisceau staff, formerly participated in the Camelots du Roi, and became heavily involved in a campaign of harassment against Jewish merchants.[32]

Most significantly, anti-Semitism continually found a place within the doctrine of the Faisceau. Pierre Dumas, the Faisceau expert on syndicalism and labour, and a member of the group's management committee, stated at a public meeting in March 1926 that the Soviet Union and international bankers such as the 'Hungarian Jew' Horace Finaly, the Director of the Banque de Paris et des Pays-Bas, funded Cartel des Gauches electoral propaganda.[33] Various group authors reiterated the prewar notion, prevalent on the extreme right, that twelve Jewish bankers and socialists formed a tactical alliance in order to control France, their seeming ideological incompatibility a ruse designed to mask a joint political agenda. Commenting upon socialist party leader Léon Blum and the SFIO national congress in November 1925 Antoine Fouroux derided the supposed predominance of Jewish interests within the party. Providing the driving force behind the entire movement, 12 Jewish bankers enabled Jean Jaurès to found the left-wing newspaper *L'Humanité* and overcome the Guesdist faction while steering the party into parliamentary opportunism. Thus to Fouroux, Gallic socialism represented Judeo-German mysticism, upholding the Marxist concept of class rather than the natural French belief in *la Patrie*.[34]

---

30    Robert Soucy, *French Fascism*, pp. 97–98. Soucy uses the presence of Mayer and Salomon to demonstrate the lack of anti-Semitism in the Faisceau, stating that it was avoided for fear of a loss of funding. Yet such a view exaggerates their roles. Neither held positions of any importance within the Faisceau, published in the group newspaper, or addressed public meetings.

31    Georges Valois, *La Politique de la victoire* (Paris, 1925), p. 126.

32    Soucy, *French Fascism*, p. 108. The Camelots du Roi was the youth wing of the Action française.

33    F/7/13209, Metz Police Commissioner to Director of the Sureté Générale, 'Au sujet d'une réunion privée de propagande de la section de Metz du 'Faisceau' à Metz', 27 March 1926. This was a further elaboration upon his long-held notion that the Cartel was being led by Jewish, Masonic, and foreign interests. See Pierre Dumas, 'L'organisation ouvrière', *Cahiers des États Généraux*, Dec. 1924.

34    Antoine Fouroux, 'Pourquoi Blum a été battu au conseil national', *NS*, 12 Nov. 1925; Antoine Fouroux, 'D'un mythe révolutionnaire du 1er Mai à l'organisation de la justice

The anti-Semitism of Dumas and Fouroux paled before that of Franz van den Broeck d'Obrenan, an ex-member of the Action française and one of the main financial backers of the Faisceau. D'Obrenan outlined his racist doctrine in a 1926 book entitled *Introduction à la vie nationale*, which was not only published by the Valois-controlled Nouvelle Librairie Nationale, but dedicated to him as well.[35] There can be no doubt as to the seriousness with which Valois took the work and its author, as *Nouveau Siècle* carried prominently placed advertisements for the book.[36] This occurred despite the fact that d'Obrenan presented an anti-Semitic caricature worthy of Drumont (an author who Valois himself previously quoted with approval), taking the form of a dialogue between an ordinary Frenchman (M. Dupont) and a stereotypical Jew (M. Pollack).[37]

D'Obrenan began by citing philosopher Ernest Renan to the effect that Jews formed a secret society in the same vein as the masons. France and Europe literally fell under the spell of the Jewish international, which aspired to rule them both.[38] This was a consequence of the position of Jewry in the world, as descendants of the biblical Cain, the archetype of the wanderer, in staunch opposition to the French character Abel, representative of the sedentary farmer. The latter owned the earth, adopting the Latin way of life, which involved ownership of, and communion with the soil: 'The need for a stability, order, and perpetuity of everyday life that stand in violent contrast to the vagrancy, the taste for risk, the messianism, and the appetite for destruction of the Jews.'

This dissimilarity extended to their preferred system of government, with the Jew demanding an autocracy, as in the Bible. To d'Obrenan, this explained their leading role in the creation and propagation of the Soviet system, termed the Asiatic conception of slavery opposed to the traditional Latin way of life.[39]

Nor were the French greedy speculators, a quality which d'Obrenan believed to be specifically Jewish. The Frenchman had simple needs, such as a home and a quiet and secure old age, and nothing more. The language and description used by d'Obrenan evoke the Barrèssian notion of 'the soil and the dead', and its portrayal of the wandering Jew who rejected the rootedness of the French *paysan*. Thus M. Dupont expatiates upon:

---

dans la nation', *NS*, 30 April 1925. On the portrayal of the Jew as simultaneously revolutionary and financially predominant, see Schor, *L'Antisémitisme*, pp. 121–123.

35    The dedication reads as follows: 'À Georges Valois: Qui a su, malgré l'orage, tirer de la fondrière la cloche de Varennes, embouché jusqu'a l'essieu. Le Soleil est revenu; qu'importent les piques des mouches?', Van den Broeck D'Obrenan, *Introduction à la vie nationale* (Paris, 1926).

36    See, for example, page two of the 11 May 1926 edition.

37    For Valois's praise of Drumont, see *La Politique de la victoire*, p. 111.

38    D'Obrenan, *Introduction*, pp. 12–15.

39    Ibid., pp. 26, 32. On the incompatibility of Jews and the soil, see Birnbaum, *Une mythe politique*, pp. 172–173. This notion was frequently expounded by extreme-rightist authors like Barrès and Drumont. In Birnbaum, *Un mythe politique*, pp. 134–146; Michel Winock, *Nationalisme, anti-sémitisme, et fascisme en France* (Paris, 1982), p. 171.

the civil servant who indefatigably awaits his retirement, the artisan who dreams of a house in the village of his birth, which he abandons only when his ashes are joined with those of his parents in the cemetery, the farmer, the small shopkeeper.

M. Pollack answers ominously that the Jew is a natural nomad, in contrast to the Barrèssian notion of the perfect Frenchman. The Jews moved out of the desert and into civilization, becoming bankers and merchants, all part of a greater plan in which 'a banker born in Frankfurt ... sends one son to London, another to Paris, still another to Vienna: International finance is thus created'.[40] The end result is to be the plunder of all nations, and their eventual destruction at the hands of international Jewry. Government and finance have become the realm of Jewish power, and the Jews bankrupt the state, buying it piece by piece, with the eventual goal of complete ownership and control. To prove this point, d'Obrenan invoked the *Protocols of the Elders of Zion*, the nineteenth-century 'document' forged by the Tsarist secret police in Russia, who presented it as a guidebook to Jewish world domination tendered at an 1897 Zionist congress.[41] The Jews' secret plan, M. Dupont relates, is detailed in this work, a document which has 'deeply penetrated the ambitions and secret plans of your brethren, and nothing has yet predicted the future with such precision and exactitude'.[42]

Marxism provided one of the most powerful Jewish tools, claimed d'Obrenan, a rabbinical philosophy, messianic and materialist. In response to the Eastern European ghetto experience, Jews created communism to gain the revenge promised by God against the unbelievers. Their apocalyptic zeal turned a lower middle-class community of shopkeepers and salesmen into ardent socialists, who eventually seized control of the Russian revolutionary movement. The revolution therefore manifested God's promise that one day all of humanity would be Jewish.[43] d'Obrenan ends his portrait by echoing sentiments that the Nazis began to voice in Germany at the time: 'the only reasonable attitude today is total action, brutal action, massive action, and intelligent action, action that polarizes energy, awakens goodwill, and disperses our enemies.' Only those Semites who fought in the Great War would be spared; 'more French than Jewish', they proved with their blood and lives that they followed France rather than the decrees of international Jewry.[44]

## III

In publishing such a work and advertising it prominently in the group newspaper, Valois made clear his sympathy for d'Obrenan's virulent beliefs. Although his own writing from the Faisceau period was not as harsh, he made many of the same points nonetheless. Writing in *Action française* in March 1925, six months after he founded

---

40    Ibid., pp. 37, 42–43. The notion of an international and cosmopolitan Jewish financial conspiracy was frequently mentioned by leading figures on the extreme-right from Drumont to Action française luminary Léon Daudet. See Birnbaum, *Un mythe politique*, pp. 268–277.

41    Schor, *L'Antisémitisme*, p. 126.

42    D'Obrenan, *Introduction*, pp. 39–41, 47–48.

43    Ibid., pp. 60–64, 71–74, 127.

44    Ibid., pp. 141, 55.

the veteran's organization that would become the Faisceau, Valois invoked the biblical story of the golden calf to describe the history of the Jewish people.[45] The Jews constructed a new version in the contemporary world – a modern, plutocratic, and international economy. Its followers included both Jews and 'Judaic Christians', who sought gold for gold's sake. Like Moses in the Bible, Karl Marx was the Jewish prophet fighting the golden calf, preaching that only through suffering could the Jews once again become the chosen people, while attracting thousands of ghettoized Eastern Europeans along with sections of the Western bourgeoisie as adherents. Due to their nomadic status, they did not understand the law of nature and the necessity of attachment to the soil, easily driven to excess unlike the prudent French farmer. Industrial production, their chosen economic vehicle, led to a frenzy for gold, brought on by limitless opportunities. Valois wedded the Barrèssian notion of the Jew as nomad, unable to appreciate the virtues of the soil because of his excessive greed, with the conversionary rhetoric frequently presented by Catholic anti-Semites in newspapers like *La Croix*. Hence unlike d'Obrenan, during his years in the Action française Valois foresaw a more peaceful remedy to the Jewish character, through the implementation of a Christian economy which emphasized moderation as a first step toward a hopeful mass conversion of Jews, 'for which each Christian must pray'.[46]

Not only Jews, but Christians led astray by Jewish economic values would be made to see the errors of their ways. Writing in *Nouveau Siècle*, Valois called for an injection of religious spirit into the economy, in which Jews would work for justice, alongside Catholics and Protestants, to neutralize the plutocracy, the modern form of the golden calf. Instead of Marxist utopias, the Jews should follow the human and universal Christian justice, which guaranteed fair prices, wages, and salaries through moral obligation.[47] A state mobilization of the 'revolutionary spirit of Israel' allowed them to simply switch allegiances.[48]

Unfortunately, those Jews who joined the international financial plutocracy were beyond redemption. Valois spent his career waging a verbal war against this supposed conspiracy, the leadership of which he continually attributed to Jews. During his Action française years he called them *la bourgeoisie juive*, an economic international that wormed its way into financial predominance throughout Europe.

---

45    Valois maintained a regular column in the royalist paper until November 1925, when the Faisceau was formalized. The group's existence predated this by one year, however, having been formed on Armistice Day of the previous November, centred upon the *Nouveau Siècle* newspaper.

46    Georges Valois, 'Le Puits de Jacob', *Action Française*, 29 March 1925. This theme was also taken up in the pages of *Nouveau Siècle*, in an article that was practically a verbatim restatement. See 'Communistes', 19 March 1925. In the latter, Valois called Karl Marx 'the last prophet of Israel', and stated that truly French Jews rejected his doctrine because they were not nomads, as were their Russian brothers. He clearly stated that communism was a Judeo-Slavic creation, however.

47    Georges Valois, 'La Révolution nationale II: La Révolution économique', *NS*, 27 Aug. 1925. See also *La Politique de la victoire*, pp. 38–39, and F/7/13211, Tract 5-Georges Valois, *La Conquête de l'avenir,* 1926.

48    Georges Valois, 'L'État national, la révolution économique, et Israël', *NS*, 25 Feb. 1926.

The socialist movement provided an excuse to build a private army to protect Jewish interests. Furthermore they had trained a whole new caste – the *bourgeoisie judaïsante* – corrupting their good Catholic morals and substituting the American capitalist values of the primacy of profit and individualism. Both bourgeois types, having perverted and exploited the impoverished French worker, ruined the nation through their lack of morality. These Jewish people were 'foreign leeches' out to steal French money, using control of the state, the press, the army, and the education system to do it. The financial powers headed the conspiracy to control France, led by 'men with Jewish names'.[49]

The equation of the Jewish bourgeoisie with financial hegemony and greed was hardly novel. Nineteenth-century socialists invoked similar imagery in their slanderous critiques of French Jewry, usually accompanied by a list of prominent bankers: Rothschild, Worms, Lazard Frères, the Pereire brothers, and Thalmann often received mention, alongside a detailed explanation of their 'German' or foreign origins. However, such attacks seldom devolved into calls for anti-Semitic violence. Instead, they replaced the medieval stereotype of the Jew as usurer with calls for the political suppression of powerful Jewish financial interests, linked to republicanism and bourgeois power under the Second Empire and the Third Republic.[50] However, Valois's vision was suffused with violence in a manner more consistent with Drumont, envisioning the downfall of the 'eternal Jew', the Semitic 'banker-king'.[51]

Thus in the postwar era, Valois wrote that German-Jewish financiers mobilized revolutionary sentiment and Wilsonian internationalism for the purposes of economic colonialism, which could only be defeated 'under the law of the warriors who rise up from the soil, and it is in those times that Israel trembles and prays in the ghettos'.[52] All of the financiers Valois named throughout the twenties were Jewish, with Horace Finaly, Dumas's 'Hungarian Jew', as the ringleader. Despite the fact that Finaly was a naturalized citizen and an officer of the Légion d'Honneur, Valois referred to him as a foreigner, continually making reference to his Jewishness.[53]

Valois indeed viewed Finaly as the main backer of the Cartel des Gauches, and the man in control of a large part of French industry through his ownership of the Banque de Paris et Pays-Bas, aided by a legion of revolutionaries, engineers, politicians, journalists, generals, and ambassadors. Finaly and his mysterious foreign partners had variously aided the development of Prussian power, the Great War, internal strife in France and the Russian Revolution. All of the named accomplices were Jewish: 'The world remembers the interventions of New York bankers, Otto Kuhn, Jacob Schiff,

49    Georges Valois, 'La Bourgeoisie capitaliste', *Cahiers du Cercle Proudhon*, Dec. 1912, pp. 229–245; Georges Valois, *La Monarchie*, pp. 295, 297–305; F/7/13195, 'Conférence royaliste de M.M. Arnal et G. Valois', *Le Nouvelliste*, 7 Feb. 1910.
50    Schor, *L'Antisémitisme*, pp. 135–137; Birnbaum, *Un mythe politique*, pp. 43–46.
51    On Drumont's vision, see Winock, *Nationalisme*, pp. 219–220.
52    Georges Valois, 'Sur deux questions morales et politiques', *Action Française*, 15 March 1920.
53    Georges Valois, 'La Religion laïque contre les combattants et les producteurs', *Action Française*, 22 March 1925. This argument appeared again numerous times in the Faisceau press, although Valois substituted the concept of mysterious and unknown names for Jews in his thesis. All of the names that he did list, however, were those of Jews.

and others, in favour of Lenin and of Trotsky, and in favour of a united Germany.'[54] Sassoon did the same, working from his base of power in Great Britain.[55] These men placed agents everywhere, including politicians who adopted measures contrary to the national interest, Masonic industrialists, and of course the press and intellectuals.

Once again, clear criteria for the Jew as enemy emerged through the critique of Finaly. That he was a Hungarian Jew, wrote Valois, was of secondary importance. If he had served the French state no one would have questioned him, yet Finaly's lust for money and power led to a betrayal of the nation.[56] His Jewishness became an issue because he did not serve the national interest (i.e. the national interest according to Valois), and the Jew only proved acceptable if he thought and acted in a correct manner. Thus in 1926 the group's newspaper applauded Octave Homberg's opposition to the Bérenger-Mellon accords on the repayment of French war debts, and supported him for the presidency of the Valois-organized Semaine de la Monnaie the following year, while Finaly had to be expunged from the nation.[57]

One is tempted to argue that Valois only practiced selective anti-Semitism, that the issue concerned adherence to Faisceau doctrine, and not religion or race. Yet he singled out Jews for criticism, rarely extending his argument to include Christians. However benevolent the tone, the stereotype remained clearly in evidence. To be sure, Valois distinguished between patriotic and malevolent Jews in certain instances. But the former necessarily adopted the extreme right-wing platform of the Faisceau, rejecting both parliamentarianism and socialism, while working for the nation rather than individual profiteering.

Moreover, the appeal of such a platform to Jews was severely limited, as most enthusiastically supported the Third Republic. For as Pierre Birnbaum notes, from the Dreyfus Affair onwards French Jews adopted a staunchly pro-republican stance, believing (rightly or wrongly) that the system provided both political/economic opportunities and a bulwark against anti-Semitism. Commenting upon the sudden influx of Jews in republican governments after 1871, Birnbaum writes:

> They loved it with devotion, propagated its values, rushed into its protective arms, even going so far as to constitute its true administrative families, anxious to ensure the proper functioning of public service. They were the new heroes, whose slightest acts and gestures were honored in Jewish circles, whose promotions within the state were endlessly commented upon [within the Jewish community].[58]

54    'Chronique de la semaine', *NS*, 2 April 1926. That the notion of supporting Lenin and the Kaiser at the same time was quite antithetical seems never to have been considered by the author.

55    'La Réunion du 2 Novembre au Cirque du Paris', *NS*, 7 Nov. 1926.

56    Georges Valois, 'Horace Finaly', *NS*, 5 Sept. 1926.

57    Millman, *La Question juive*, p. 87. CGQJ head Xavier Vallat used similar logic in his 1940 attempt to exclude war veterans from the regime's anti-Semitic legislation. See Joly, *Vichy dans la 'solution finale'*, pp. 91–92.

58    Pierre Birnbaum, *The Jews of the Republic: A Political History of State Jews in France from Gambetta to Vichy* (Stanford 1996), p. 2.

In any case, throughout his oeuvre Valois provided a negative analysis of the Jewish character, claiming that most Jews posed a dire threat to the French nation and state. He also quite willingly tolerated more severe opinions, as evidenced in his publication of d'Obrenan's work and Fouroux's articles. Far from attracting Jews, such attitudes could only have the opposite effect.

Clearly Valois did not have a Road to Damascus experience regarding anti-Semitism upon forming the Faisceau. Far from leaving such sentiments behind upon quitting the Action française, he continued to espouse xenophobia, as did various key members of the group. Nor did their anti-Semitic rhetoric exist in a vacuum. By keeping such discourse active at a time when the vast majority of the French populace had abandoned it, the Faisceau became a link between prewar anti-Semites and the return of their doctrine in the 1930s. While the Action française languished in decline, and the reputations of Drumont, La Tour du Pin, and other prewar xenophobes diminished in the postwar era, Valois and his confreres actively promoted a similar agenda.

## IV

In discussing Vichy's treatment of Jews, Michael Marrus and Robert Paxton write that 'there was no sharp break in 1940; there was, rather, a long habituation through the decade of the 1930s to the idea of the foreigner – and especially the Jew – as the enemy of the state'.[59] That this notion prevailed beyond the corridors of power, enthusiastically endorsed by much of the French population, explains the willing acceptance of many repressive measures mandated by the CGQJ, at least before deportations to the east began in summer 1942.

At first glance, this thesis seems surprising, for the 'golden age' of French Jewry continued into the 1920s, a decade largely devoid of popular xenophobic sentiment. As immigrants laboured to reconstruct France and Jewish war veterans proudly marched with their Christian confrères, the influence of virulent anti-Semites like Drumont receded. The most telling proof came from the Catholic Church, long devoted to mass conversion, and among the chief exponents of the stereotypical Jew: A nomadic, greedy, and power-hungry creature who had killed Christ, and now attempted to enslave an agrarian and pious nation. Under the leadership of the progressive Pope Pius XI, Rome rejected anti-Semitism in the 1920s, placing the Action française on the papal index of banned organizations. In their stead came the left-wing social Catholicism of the Jeunesse ouvrière chrétienne, and newspapers like *Sept*, *Temps Present*, and *l'Aube* dedicated to a similar agenda. Following suit, Catholic intellectuals like Jacques Maritain and Emmanuel Mounier openly decried racial theorizing, and even *La Croix* printed philo-Semitic articles for the first time in its history under the influence of new editor Abbé Merklen. There were exceptions of course, most notoriously ex-liguer and Drumont disciple Georges Bernanos, who continued to publish xenophobic pamphlets and books throughout the interwar era. Yet official policy remained

---

59    Marrus and Paxton, p. 54.

unchanged throughout the 1930s, culminating in the 1938 anti-Nazi papal encyclical Mit Brennender Sorge, which strongly condemned Hitlerian racism.[60]

However, by the 1930s French popular opinion once again turned towards anti-Semitism, principally due to the effects of the depression, which struck France only in 1932, and waves of immigration after 1933 as Jews fled Nazi persecution. Suffering from the effects of the slump and resulting chronic unemployment, workers tended to blame Jews (and particularly Jewish immigrants) for stealing jobs from French workers. The arrival after January 1933 of 25,000 German refugees fleeing Hitler's regime reinforced this popular anti-Semitism. Although initially welcomed by the state, the newcomers faced the possibility of exclusion throughout the decade as successive ministries introduced ever-harsher immigration policies aimed primarily at preventing Jews from settling in France. In addition, members of the syndicalist Confédération générale du travail, the Confédération générale du Patronat français, local Chambers of Commerce, and various French professional organizations took to the streets to participate in anti-Semitic and xenophobic protests. By 1938, newspapers variously accused the newcomers of spying for Hitler, attempting to push France towards war with Germany, and colonizing professions like medicine and jurisprudence.[61] Opposition frequently devolved into medico-biological justification for exclusion. As the refugee wave picked up steam, one police agent mused in November 1933: '[Jews] will soon constitute groups of discontented and violent exiles: Veritable ghettos from the moral point of view, as well as the point of view of hygiene!'[62]

Yet it was the election of the Popular Front government in May 1936 that brought renewed anti-Semitism into the mainstream of French society. Socialist party leader Léon Blum became the first Jewish premier in French history and the object of derision for leaders from across the political spectrum. The *Dépêche de Toulouse*, one of the chief press organs of Blum's allies in the Radical party, rejected Popular Front leniency towards Jewish immigrants, claiming that they were undesirable because they refused to assimilate. Within his own organization Paul Faure, executive editor of the socialist daily *Le Populaire*, complained that Jews demanded war with Hitler simply to protect their German brethren.[63] More disturbing than renewed anti-Semitism on the centre and left, however, was the growth and evident strength of the xenophobic extreme-right, especially during the Popular Front years. Often derisively labeled 'our masters', Blum and various Jews within the Popular Front ministry, including Jean Zay, Georges Boris, Jules Moch, and Pierre Mendes-France were characterized as a 'Jewish team' of foreign Talmudists in the pay of the Soviet Union.[64]

Given free rein in the Chamber of Deputies and municipal councils across France, anti-Semites like Xavier Vallat and Louis Darquier de Pellepoix, the future leaders of

60    Asher Cohen, *Persécutions et sauvetages: juifs et français sous l'occupation et sous Vichy* (Paris, 1993), pp. 40–41.

61    The best history of Jews and immigrants in 1930s France is Vicki Caron, *Uneasy Asylum: France and the Jewish Refugee Crisis, 1933–1942* (Stanford, 1999).

62    Ibid., p. 20.

63    Ibid., pp. 286–290.

64    Birnbaum, *Un mythe politique*, pp. 319–323. Interestingly, Birnbaum notes that only 20 of 237 personnel in Blum's ministries were Jews.

Vichy's CGQJ, lambasted Blum with few objections from their fellow representatives.[65] Similarly, anti-Semitic newspapers enjoyed tremendously success, particularly after Blum's ascension to the Matignon. Although pro-Nazi dailies such as *Je suis partout* rarely sold more than 80,000 copies, openly anti-Semitic newspapers like *Gringoire* (650,000 copies sold per issue), *Candide* (465,000 copies), and *L'Ami du Peuple* (460,000 copies) reached hundreds of thousands daily, many of them newcomers to the extreme-right. In addition, publishers printed 1.8 million xenophobic tracts and 95,000 books and brochures, many produced by services like Henry-Robert Petit's Centre de documentation et de la propagande, specialists in the burgeoning industry of racial publishing.[66] Greater in number than even their Dreyfus-era counterparts, they also evinced a much more violent tone, frequently calling for popular assaults against Jews, while employing increasingly damning rhetoric. Thus Céline's 1937 *Bagatelles pour un massacre* demanded a pogrom, to rid France of putrefied Judaism. Furthermore, his fellow extreme-rightist intellectuals Pierre Drieu la Rochelle, Robert Brasillach, and Lucien Rebatet lauded Hitler and the Nazis who, they claimed, had discovered a satisfactory solution to the Jewish question.[67]

One group is frequently minimized in such discussions: The CDF/PSF and its leader Colonel François de la Rocque.[68] As the largest extreme right-wing movement in 1930s France, with over one million members by 1938, the group is frequently presented as proof that the leagues, and possibly the French population, were not overtly anti-Semitic. If such a massive organization resisted the xenophobic temptation, the argument runs, then surely the actual penetration of anti-Semitism into French society was limited. La Rocque's contemporaries on the right were certainly concerned with the group's perceived philo-Semitism, accusing the CDF/PSF of befriending the Jews, and reserving scathing criticism for the group's perceived inaction in the face of Blum and the Popular Front. Céline bluntly referred to him as 'La Rocque-ghetto', while *Je suis partout* stalwart Lucien Rebatet lumped the CDF/PSF in with 'Blum's team' in his wartime book *Les Décombrés*.[69] In a similar vein, a tract produced by the Centre de documentation et de la Propagande reacted furiously when La Rocque seemingly rejected anti-Semitism at a 1937 Algerian rally, claiming

65   Hyman, p. 201.
66   Schor, *L'Antisémitisme*, pp. 30–35.
67   Hyman, pp. 200–201.
68   Most authors claim that the CDF/PSF did not engage in the practice of anti-Semitism in a systematic fashion. See, for example, Jacques Nobecourt, *Le Colonel de La Rocque, 1885–1946 ou les pièges du nationalisme chrétien* (Paris, 1996); Philippe Machefer, 'La Rocque et le problème antisémite', in *La France et la question juive, 1940–44* (Paris 1981). Others are less charitable, but still argue for a limited anti-Semitism within the group. In his work on French fascism, Robert Soucy correctly notes that La Rocque practiced political, rather than racial anti-Semitism, accepting right-wing Jews but professing disdain for leftists and immigrants. However, he claims that all-encompassing xenophobia appeared only in the Alsatian and Algerian sections. In *French Fascism: The Second Wave, 1933–1939* (New Haven, 1995), pp. 152–158. This view is seconded by Richard Millman in *La Question juive*, pp. 219–228, 256–267.
69   Céline quoted in Schor, *L'Antisémitisme,* p. 79; Rebatet quoted in Birnbaum, *Un mythe politique*, p. 166.

that this *bobard de la réconciliation* enabled the Jewish peril. The anonymous author accused the CDF/PSF of playing a 'double game' with Jews, afraid to reject them for fear of the political consequences.[70]

For his part, from the group's beginnings La Rocque publicly disavowed anti-Semitism on numerous occasions, speaking of an ideal fraternity of men, including Jews, all of whom held different philosophical and religious beliefs, but nonetheless adopted 'the cult of patriotism and love for French ways'.[71] However, Jewish organizations and press organs did not agree. Both the immigrant newspaper *Parizer Haynt* and the mainstream *Samedi* published articles condemning CDF/PSF anti-Semitism in France and Algeria, forcing *Le Flambeau* to claim in March 1934 that such rumours were the work of the group's adversaries. La Rocque empathetically added in an adjoining letter that 'the Croix de Feu have never been anti-Semitic'.[72] But the questions did not disappear. Mere weeks later, the left-wing Ligue internationale contre l'antisémitisme [LICA], founded by Eastern European immigrant's son Bernard Lecache, forcefully restated the earlier claims, demanding a denunciation of xenophobia from the CDF/PSF leadership. This time La Rocque authorized the publication of a letter in the LICA newspaper *Droit de Vivre*, which dismissed any division by race, confession, or class within the ranks of the Croix de Feu. He further listed instances when *Le Flambeau* published philo-Semitic articles.[73]

The letter temporarily placated Lecache and LICA, but the following year members of the CDF/PSF itself began to publicly question the group's stance concerning Jews. In October 1935, the director of propaganda received a letter from a member demanding to know their precise attitude regarding anti-Semitism. By December, Grand Rabbin Maurice Liber wrote personally to La Rocque to ascertain the leader's position. In each case, the group defended itself with quotations from various publications – La Rocque's claim in his 1934 work *Service public* that France represented a 'magnificent synthesis of all races', for example – and a solemn declaration to root out any anti-Semitism in the group. As an organization open to men of all confessions, officials stated, the CDF/PSF did not tolerate the slander or persecution of any minority.[74]

Following the 1936 Popular Front ban of the extreme right-wing leagues, the group transformed into the more sedate Parti social français, but continued to receive staunch criticism regarding anti-Semitic behaviour and ideas from a variety of Jewish organizations, from LICA to the Consistoire Israèlite. By 1938, La Rocque enlisted the aid of Henri de Kerellis, a good friend and leading figure in the conservative Republican Federation, who publicly stated that the CDF/PSF were more benevolent

70   *La Rocque et les Juifs: Un nouveau scandale!* (Paris, 1937).
71   *Le Flambeau*, Oct. 1931. For a more public proclamation, see APP Ba 1857, excerpts from the 'Rapport fait au nom de la commission d'enquête chargée de rechercher les causes et les origines des événements du 6 février', 1620.
72   'Nos Documents', *Le Flambeau*, 1 March 1934; Hyman, pp. 227–28.
73   'Une lettre du Colonel de la Rocque', *Droit de Vivre*, 25 March 1934.
74   AP/451/93, 'Mouvement Croix de Feu/Service de la Propagande', 25 Oct. 1935; CHEVS/LR 48, La Rocque to Grand Rabbin Maurice Liber, 4 Dec. 1935. See also a letter published by La Rocque in *Le Journal* in CHEVS/LR 11 VI A 2.

towards Jews than Italians under Mussolini. Meanwhile the April 1938 party bulletin urged speakers to refrain from any and all anti-Semitic rhetoric in speeches.[75]

But such pronouncements were limited to the Paris-based leadership, and seldom received the endorsement of the rank and file. Furthermore, few Jews were actually members or sympathizers of the CDF/PSF, and almost all of them from Paris/Île de France. Before La Rocque's ascension to the group presidency, *Le Flambeau* mentioned honours given to a M. Lévy, the president of the 10th section. Additionally, in 1932 a M. Marx presided over the 16th section and served on the Comité Directeur. La Rocque's secretary Edouard Carvalho and personal physician Raymond Benda were also Jewish, but few members were Jews and none retained any significant position within the group.[76]

One prominent Jew who did support the CDF/PSF was Rabbi Kaplan of the synagogue at Rue de la Victoire in Paris. A sympathizer until 1936, he frequently led memorial services for right-wing veterans and spoke at various group functions. However, Kaplan hardly represented mainstream French Jewry. His well known distaste for Jewish immigrants and his sympathy for the far right set him apart from most contemporaries. Thus Kaplan consistently ran into trouble with Jewish organizations and was forced to stop holding CDF/PSF ceremonies in 1937, due to criticism from LICA that he aided the cause of French fascism. As the pressure mounted, he eventually backtracked, stating that the group had been invited solely on orders from the Consistoire Israèlite.[77]

---

75    'L'Époque', Henri de Kerellis, *L'Époque*, 28 April 1938; 'Au sujet des campagnes antisémites', *Bulletin d'informations* 75, 30 April 1938. The group also attempted to portray La Rocque as an ardent philo-Semite. See Jacques de Lacretelle, *Qui est La Rocque* (Paris 1936), p. 24.

76    In only one instance did a rank and file member pronounce his displeasure with anti-Semitism: A.M. Pinçon from the 8th section called for the collaboration of Catholics, Protestants, Jews, and Muslims for the good of the fatherland. In F/7/12966, 'Réunion organisée par le comité local du 8me Arrt. du Parti social français', 16 Feb. 1937. On Jewish group leaders, see *Le Flambeau*, Dec. 1929, Feb. 1930, and 1 June 1932. According to Paul Chopine, Marx resigned in 1935. In *Six ans chez les Croix de Feu* (Paris, 1935), p. 125. See also CHEVS/LR 48, letter from Carvalho to Gilles de la Rocque, 3 Dec. 1971. He lists Blumenthal and Seligmann, La Rocque's pilots, as other Jews involved in the group. On Benda, see Claude Popelin, *Arènes politiques* (Paris, 1974), p. 37. Until 1935 Popelin was a member of the CDF/PSF youth wing, the Volontaires Nationaux. Richard Millman also lists a Léon Koscziusko as Vice-President of a Paris section, but does not name it. He further claims that Grand Rabbin Maurice Eisenbeth was member number 13,725, and that he left the group in 1932. See his 'Les Croix de Feu et l'antisémitisme', *Vingtième Siècle*, no. 38 (1993), p. 50. Pierre Machefer lists Jean Bonnard (Secretary of the Centre Universitaire and President of the Fédération de Paris-Sud) and André Bloch (Carvalho's cousin and member of the 6th section). See 'La Rocque et le problème antisémite', in *La France et la question juive, 1940–44*, pp. 96–98. Finally, a memo from the German occupation government lists the President of the Alpes-Maritimes section, an employee of the Rothschild bank, a Paris Municipal Councilor, and a PSF-sponsored candidate in Nice. In CDJC XL VI-32 and XL VI-37.

77    For a complete stenograph of a meeting at the synagogue, see APP/Ba 1853, memo of 14 June 1936. La Rocque sat with a member of the Rothschild family and right-wing Jewish lawyer Edmond Bloch, while Kaplan lauded the group in his speech for being 'sans distinction d'opinion'. On Kaplan's activities at Croix de Feu meetings, see 'Section féminine

Such activity served to mask a harsher reality: That the leadership and rank and file of the CDF/PSF were overtly anti-Semitic to varying degrees. The group's earliest active entrance into the public sphere occurred in March 1931, during the riots in Paris protesting the play *L'Affaire Dreyfus* by Jewish author Jacques Richepin. The piece provided a detailed description of the officer's suffering during and after his trial, and consequently the CDF/PSF derided it as an example of German treachery, which aimed to recreate the divisions present in *fin-de-siècle* France. They not only demanded that the play be banned, but joined the notoriously anti-Semitic Action française in the streets to voice their objections.[78]

That the play was labeled German is hardly surprising, considering La Rocque's vocal refusal to accept foreign Jews into the French nation. He made this clear in an interview given to *Le Journal* in 1936, qualifying his rejection of anti-Semitism by juxtaposing 'good Jews', who had fought in France during the Great War and were seen as consistently patriotic, 'with the two or three visiting Israelites, in direct contact with certain powerful international financiers who will ... unleash a wave of reproach which will victimize their fellow Jews'.[79] La Rocque here reiterated two of the principal interwar stereotypes concerning French Jewry. The notion that foreign Jews failed to 'do their bit' at the front frequently appeared in interwar extreme-rightist publications, expounded by groups like the Jeunesses patriotes and Action française.[80] Similarly, the differentiation between French and foreign Jews was quite commonly made in 1930s France. Assimilated and often bourgeois, French Jews were frequently distinguished from Yiddish-speaking, deeply religious, and left-wing new arrivals in the press and on the street.[81] However, La Rocque's intent was explicitly political in nature, directed at Léon Blum's 'Jewish team'. Patriotic and anti-Marxist Jews were welcome in France, according to the group leader, and the CDF/PSF happily opened its ranks to all such citizens irrespective of religious faith.[82]

La Rocque's purported philo-Semitism was thus disingenuous, masking an underlying xenophobia. During a 1936 rally in Alsace, for example, he chastised a member who yelled 'down with the Jews' in the same manner as Valois a decade earlier, stating: 'I don't want to hear it. I said what I said, and those who don't

---

du Regroupement national autour des Croix de Feu', *Le Flambeau*, April 1934. He was a featured speaker at the meeting. For criticism of Kaplan, see 'Soyez républicaine, on vous poindra! Soyez fascistes, on vous oindra!', *Droit de Vivre*, 25 March 1934; 'Les Croix de Feu à la synagogue', *Droit de Vivre*, June 1935. See also, Hyman, pp. 227–28.

78     'L'Affaire Dreyfus', *Le Flambeau*, April 1931; *La Relève*, March 1931; Maurice Genay, 'Notre action, nos buts', *Le Flambeau*, May 1931.

79     'Déclarations de La Rocque', *Le Journal*, 17 March 1936. La Rocque continued to make the distinction between patriotic French Jews and their foreign counterparts throughout the history of the CDF/PSF, even during the Vichy era. See *Disciplines d'action* (Clermont-Ferrand, 1941), pp. 97–99.

80     Birnbaum, pp. 152–158. Paula Hyman writes that the allegations were untrue: In fact, a higher percentage of Jews (including immigrants) than Christians died during the Great War. Hyman, pp. 55–57.

81     Hyman, p. 30. It is worth noting that this distinction appeared under Vichy as well, particularly in the case of Admiral Darlan. See Marrus and Paxton, *Vichy France*, pp. 85–87.

82     CDLR, 'Repérés', *Le Flambeau*, 15 Aug. 1936.

approve of the Christian doctrine which guides the PSF can get lost! ... Despite M. Blum, I welcome the Jews.' Yet he qualified this statement, claiming that Jews first had to pledge allegiance to Franco-Christian tradition. Those who refused to do so, like Blum and the socialists, termed 'parasites from all civilizations', not only betrayed France but the Jewish people as well. Only the acceptance of the PSF doctrine conferred citizenship.[83]

This position was hardly confined to La Rocque's speeches. In 1937, the PSF monthly bulletin loudly rejected anti-Semitism. The group believed in Christian civilization, the author proclaimed, respecting all minorities if they were willing to live according to Gallic customs and beliefs. Yet once again, immigrant Jews were portrayed as despicable, and the author adopted an uncompromising tone:

> Having said that, it must be added that there exist in certain regions, notably Alsace and Algeria, unassimilated recent immigrants among the Jewish population, voluntarily estranged from the national community that they nonetheless want to join. Jewish patriots know this, and are the first to deplore it, embarrassed by it. Alongside them, we condemn this latent, uncontrolled invasion ... We consider as foreigners all those who through their comportment, beliefs, and conduct distance themselves from the nation, even if they can buy French citizenship.[84]

French Jews were thus encouraged to reject their foreign brethren if deemed unacceptable to the PSF.[85]

La Rocque and others in the Paris-based leadership practiced selective anti-Semitism, reaching out to French Jews who might adhere to CDF/PSF doctrine, while rejecting immigrants and leftist sympathizers. This stance was not uncommon in 1930s France, where hostility towards immigrants became increasingly prevalent as the decade progressed. More often than not, Jewish refugees bore the brunt of popular anger, and their French brethren worried about the presence of newcomers from Central and Eastern Europe, hoping that each new influx would not undermine their own secure existence.[86] However, with the exception of rabid racial anti-Semites like the staff at *Je suis partout* or *Gringoire*, natives remained unscathed. Given this state of affairs La Rocque, who made a clear distinction between French and foreign Jews and professed acceptance for those who adhered to CDF/PSF doctrine in no way distinguished himself.

Outside of Paris, and particularly among the rank and file, the situation differed dramatically. There a much more violent anti-Semitism persisted, exclusively based upon race rather than politics. Such beliefs reflected the view that all Jews belonged

---

83    AP/451/103, tract – 'Qu'est-ce que le P.S.F.?', Dec. 1936, 13.

84    AP/451/101, 'La P.S.F. et la question juive', *Bulletin d'information* #18, 9 Feb. 1937.

85    *Le Parti social français devant les problèmes de l'heure*, PSF Premier Congrès National, 18–20 Dec. 1936, pp. 219–224. La Rocque agreed with the latter point, stating at the same rally that Jews voted democratically as a bloc for the left, and thus worked against the group's national revolution. In *La Flamme*, 28 Oct. 1938. For a response to their rhetoric, see 'Le Colonel repondera t-il?', *Droit de Vivre*, Jan. 1935.

86    See Caron, *Uneasy Asylum*.

to a common racial type, and consequently threatened the nation. As such, doctrinal compatibility proved insufficient: they had to be eliminated from the French nation to ensure its survival. In this regard, various members wrote of a massive conspiracy in which Jews attempted to undermine France for their own personal ends.

Loyal to the laic Third Republic, which granted them citizenship and opportunity even at the highest levels of government, French Jews had long been accused of political machinations to foment urbanism and capitalism at the expense of traditional values and industries. Action française leader Charles Maurras infamously referred to Jews as 'the state within the state', and blamed the French revolution for allowing them to control France from behind the scenes.[87] CDF/PSF members likewise called Jews 'our masters', rigging elections and directing a cartel that secretly dominated the nation in tandem with the Freemasons, the press, corporations, and banks. To the *Volonté Bretonne*, this alliance directed European affairs, from the Russian Revolution to the emergence of the decadent Weimar Republic in Germany. Jews called themselves the chosen people, the author bemoaned, but were really 'yids', using Marxist revolutionary rhetoric to seize French property piece by piece. Most importantly, these *barbe-à-réfugies* contradicted the good Bréton peasant, a hard-working patriot far removed from disloyal foreigners who had not fought in the Great War and served as Hitlerian agents-provocateurs out to make Frenchmen speak Yiddish.[88]

Various CDF/PSF members wed the notion of the Jew as political master to the nineteenth-century stereotype of the innately greedy Semite, never tiring of robbing Frenchmen blind. Lyon partisan Pierre Melon menacingly described him as the source of all French scandal and larceny:

> Oh, they always buy at a quarter or a fifth of the price! The Israelite *bande noir,* forever on the lookout for a French peasant's land, money in hand, ready to pay bankruptcy prices or agree to ruinous mortgages. All the Staviskys, the friends of ministers creating agencies, banks, and credit unions where, easy as pie, everyone can get into debt and be foreclosed in no time at all.[89]

In the CDF/PSF rank and file's anti-Semitic vision, Jews did this dirty work with the willing collaboration of the 200 families. This century-old extreme-rightist myth concerning the largest shareholders in the Bank of France was updated accordingly for

---

87    Birnbaum, *Un mythe politique*, pp. 35–39, 312–319.

88    Le Goin PSF, 'Memez tra?', *Volonté Bretonne*, 20 April 1938. For a similar argument, see an article protesting Jewish businesses in the *Volonté du Centre*, 28 May 1938. Such statements can be readily compared with Vichy-era pronouncements. CGQJ leader Xavier Vallat used the same argument on various occasions, for example in *Les Nouveaux Temps* on 4 April 1941: 'Le problème juif qui a pris, des avant cette guerre, une acuité redoutable, se pose de manière générale. Ainsi, une minorité ethnique, mal assimilée et qui, très souvent d'ailleurs, ne veut pas s'assimiler, s'est installer dans la nation, a voulu prendre les leviers de commande, diriger le pays selon des tendances, des reflexes de l'esprit, qui appartiennent a cette race et ne correspondent pas a notre nature'. Quoted in Joly, *Vichy dans la 'solution finale'*, p. 147.

89    Pierre Melon, 'Avis à la France', *Volontaire 36*, 15 April 1938.

the Popular Front era, with the financial oligarchy buying Léon Blum's Premiership, led by Lazard-Frères, Rothschild, and their fellow *rupins*.[90]

Like Valois and the Faisceau before them, the CDF/PSF also more often than not accused such Jews of leftist sympathies, a charge leveled against both French and foreign-born alike.[91] The personification of the Jew as a natural socialist was of course Léon Blum. The French right and extreme-right continually took the Popular Front to task, proclaiming its responsibility for all of the ills that befell France during its 1936–1937 and 1938 ministries. Numerous critics remarked upon Blum's Judaism, positioning his government as representative of the bitter reality that Jews slowly but surely gained complete control of France. Despite the presence of only four Jews in the June 1936 ministry, his 'Jewish team' was accused of collusion with Nazi Germany, Bolshevizing the nation, and ruining the economy through social welfare programs. Moreover, the right viciously objected to Blum as a 'foreigner' in a position reserved for true Frenchmen. On June 6, 1936, future CGQJ head Xavier Vallat warned the Chamber of Deputies: 'I tell you that to govern the peasant nation that is France, we would be better off with somewhat whose origins, however modest they are, are rooted in the entrails of our soil, rather than a sly Talmudist.' That few protests were heard after Vallat finished is telling, for even radicals proved susceptible to slanderous attacks against the new Premier. No less an authority than Senator Joseph Caillaux denounced Blum as a leader 'without enough French soil on the soles of his shoes'.[92]

However, the CDF/PSF were not content to merely criticize Blum, but instead argued that his success proved the need to exclude Jews from the nation. Certain authors have argued that the group's campaign against Blum was strictly a political one, directed at the socialist rather than the Jew.[93] However, it encompassed Jewry as a whole, and ceased only with the outbreak of the Second World War, well after the Popular Front disappeared. Blum was not the symbol of a Jewish Marxist, but a target because he was perceived to be a Marxist *Jew*, a foreigner despite the fact that he was a French citizen by birth, came from an old Franco-Jewish family, and attended the prestigious École Normale Supérieure.

At a September 1936 party meeting, Charles Vallin exemplified this trend, openly joking about Blum's Judaism. To the delight of a laughing audience, Vallin quipped:

90    See variously Adrien Lesur, 'Physionomie éléctorale', *Bulletin Mensuel du Mouvement Croix de Feu du XVIIe Arrondissement*; 'Parti social français', *Temps Nouveaux*, 5 Dec. 1936; Jean Murols, 'Incohérences financieres', *Le Flambeau*, 6 March 1937; Marcel Aucouturier, *Au service des Croix de Feu* (Charleville, 1936), pp. 234–237; Marcel Aucouturier, *Programmes socialistes et programmes sociaux* (1938–39), p. 9.

91    'Socialisme et Marxisme', *Flamme Tourangelle*, 26 Nov. 1938; P. Budan, 'L'Universel échec du Marxisme', *Flambeau de Charentes et du Périgord*, 12 Dec. 1937. See also B.P., 'La Réforme de l'État', *La Flamme Vendéenne*, 1 Sept. 1938.

92    Vallat quoted in Birnbaum, *Un mythe politique*, pp. 327–333. Caillaux quoted in Caron, *Uneasy Asylum*, p. 270. The four Jews in Blum's ministry were Education Minister Jean Zay, Secretary-General Jules Moch, Under-Secretary of State – Education Cécile Brunschvicg, and Minister of the Interior Marx Dormoy.

93    The best example of this argument is Millman, *La Question juive*, pp. 219–228, 256–267.

I have the impression that the day will come when Mr. Léon Blum, outflanked on all sides, will be forced into exile. What rock will have him? Maybe Sainte Hélène ... maybe Mount Sinai, who knows? (laughs).

But Vallin pushed beyond mere jest, continuing in a much more hostile tone:

It's about time that Mr. Blum, Mr. Rosenfeld, and the others get the hell out, along with their great ancestors. They should leave us, the French, to run our own affairs while they mind their own business (applause).[94]

To Vallin, the Jew clearly had no place in France, and belonged elsewhere. The theme of Blum as a foreigner-in-disguise frequently appeared in group discourse, often including the mispronunciation of names and words in a 'Yiddish' style which marked Vichy-era publications. One such example occurred during a February 1937 meeting at Bécon-les-Bruyères, when a M. D'Alloue denounced the Popular Front leader: 'Mr. Blum, you come from Luisgerg in Eastern Prussia, your country of origin, and your name is Karrefoucaschtang!'[95] Such pronouncements also appeared in CDF/PSF newspapers, often in the form of cartoons, a favoured tactic of the extreme-rightist press from the 1890s onwards. Prominently displayed on the front page, the drawings characterized Blum in a rabbinical coat and hat, with long hair and a beard, and the peyot worn by Chassidic Jews, adorned with such captions as 'Blum, alias Karfunkelstein'.[96]

This nickname appeared frequently in anti-Semitic publications like *Gringoire*, along with many other stereotypical characteristics adopted by CDF/PSF authors and artists. Newspapers from *Action française* to *Je suis partout* wrote in similarly derisive terms, calling Blum *le juif errant*. His essay 'On marriage', which advocated sexual freedom, left the socialist leader open to all manner of accusations, from pederasty to femininity. Even figures like the respected left-wing novelist André Gide privately noted Blum's 'foreign' and 'Jewish' character traits.[97] But the tone used by CDF/PSF critics most resembled the discourse found on the fringes of the extreme-right. Much like Robert Brasillach and company, the group referred to the Popular Front using a crypto-biological lexicon which mirrored the Nazi demonization of Jews so prominent in 1930s Germany. At a 1937 rally in Constantine, Algeria, La Rocque compared Blum's government to a degenerative illness, calling it a 'microbe of pus' which had attached

---

94    CHEVS/LR 20 H, Parti social français, 'Réunion du 15 septembre 1936', Salle Blanchon-Lyon.

95    F/7/12966, 'Réunion organisée par la section de Bécon-les Bruyères du Parti social français', Salle Mermoz, 18 Feb. 1937.

96    On the mispronunciation caricature, see Schor, *L'Antisémitisme*, pp. 54–61. On the anti-Semitic cartoons, see Hyman, *From Dreyfus to Vichy*, 14. Citation from *Liberté du Maine*, Aug. 1939. See also the *Volontaire 36* of 16 Dec. 1938 and *La Flamme* of 20 May 1938, in which Blum is pictured at his desk embezzling government funds, with a Star of David painted on the wall above a safe, besides which is a painting labeled 'papa', of a crudely drawn Jew with a bulbous nose, scraggly beard, and yarmulke. The cartoons appeared in a variety of regional group publications.

97    Tony Judt, *The Burden of Responsibility: Blum, Camus, and Aron and the French Twentieth Century* (Chicago, 1998), pp. 74–77.

itself to the previously healthy flesh of France. The CDF/PSF Provençal newspaper was even more explicit, referring to the group as the sole antidote against the Popular Front 'disease': 'Decomposing and putrid, they resist all disinfection, and can only be destroyed by using all of the preventative measures taken to protect us against filth and excrement.' Yet the author remained optimistic, cheerfully announcing that 'the surgeon is ready to perform the needed operation, and the necessary amputations will be swiftly carried out to save the healthy parts of the country'.[98]

In their work on Vichy France and the Jews, Michael Marrus and Robert Paxton quote various Vichy-era government ministers and authors using precisely the same phraseology. Xavier Vallat, for example, spoke of the CGQJ as surgeons performing an operation to save France from the Jewish parasite that sickened her. Such rhetoric culminated in the 1941 exhibition entitled 'Les Juifs et la France', sponsored by L'Institut d'études des questions juives, whose centrepiece display portrayed the 'gangrenous' Popular Front. Receiving the blessing of the occupation government in Paris, the showing attracted more than 300,000 visitors, and functioned as a platform for the French Union for the Defense of the Race among other organizations.[99] Yet there existed one crucial difference between the anti-Semitism of the Vichy era and that of the Third Republic: The Jewish community, and indeed Léon Blum himself, could defend themselves against the charges launched by the extreme-right. The Premier assailed his critics in a 1936 *Le Populaire* article entitled 'I am French', rebutting various anti-Semitic accusations with characteristic aplomb, foreshadowing his stellar defense at the 1941 Riom trial. Invariably, however, CDF/PSF members dismissed counter-attacks as smoke and mirrors, designed to obscure the nefarious menace of his 'Jewish team'.[100]

Despite his pronouncements that the CDF/PSF rejected anti-Semitism, La Rocque rarely commented upon regular xenophobic outbursts within the group. The only public disagreement between the leader and the rank and file concerned Nazi Germany. On this subject La Rocque never wavered. To be sure, he declared, two or three Jews were involved with international finance, and perhaps pushed France towards war with Germany for personal gain rather than patriotic impulse. But to

---

98    'L'Emouvante et noble discours de La Rocque', *La Flamme*, 16 July 1937; 'Aurore', *L'Heure Française*, 10 July 1937.

99    Marrus and Paxton, *Vichy France*, pp. 87–95, 298–300; Birnbaum, *Un mythe politique*, p. 118.

100    On Blum's defense, see Judt, *The Burden of Responsibility*, p. 77. For the CDF/PSF response, see Ph. Thibaud, 'Réflexions sur la propagande Hitlérienne', *Liberté du Maine*, May 1938 (2me Quinzaine). For just such a purpose, the *Volonté du Centre* published a list of all Jews in Popular Front Ministries, designed to serve as both a warning and a hint for possible future action. See 'La France aux français', 2 Jan. 1937. The article reprinted material originally published in *Gringoire*. Also Devaud quoted in *Le PSF devant les problèmes*, pp. 219–224. For other CDF/PSF pronouncements on the Jewish 'responsibility' for anti-Semitism see AP/451/101, *Bulletin de Documentation (PSF)* 44, 1–8 June 1937. La Rocque himself argued similarly to the crowd at a 1937 Metz rally, claiming that Jews engaged in un-French activities and hence deserved blame. In 'Mehrere tausend Personen jubeln La Rocque in Nice und in Metz', *Flambeau de l'Est*, 30 April 1938. He further stated that any strikers, as well as unwanted Jewish refugees, would be expunged from the nation.

punish all Jews for the actions of a minority was out of the question. The revocation of citizenship solved the problem, he stated, and the CDF/PSF scoffed at the notion of universal exclusion, particularly considering the many Jews who fought for France during the Great War. He also responded firmly to Kristallnacht in November 1938, when the SS and ordinary Germans assaulted Jews and burned synagogues: 'Could you imagine France with intellectual, cultural, and racial totalitarianism?' Hitler and the Nazi racism were no answer to French problems, he maintained.[101] Writing on the same topic in the group's information bulletin three days later La Rocque remained equally adamant:

> For us, it is not a question of 'anti-Semite' and 'philo-Semite', but a strictly French one. We consider as foreigners all those, Jews or non-Jews, who by their attitude, beliefs, and behaviour remove themselves from the nation, even if they have acquired French citizenship ... But racism is the worship of the physical species. It excludes assimilation, persecutes families, and destroys places of worship. It is thus the opposite of Christian civilization and tradition, of Frenchness.[102]

Once again, various group members disagreed, taking the opposite position and sympathizing with Hitler and the Nazis, and demanding measures that later emerged under Vichy. True, wrote one author, Nazi brutality was barbaric, but one could not welcome Jews with open arms, giving them leave to occupy the country and all of its top posts. If the CDF/PSF rejected outright violence, then at least France should have complete control over immigration, a new national police force empowered to act without compromise, and a regulation of professions by nationality.[103] Surely Xavier Vallat and the CGQJ would have agreed. Marcel Aucouturier voiced even greater approval of Nazi policy, remarking that the Germans cleaned up the country, their youth once again healthy, now that the Jews and communists had been relegated to their proper position: Below that of true Germans.[104]

Among the most pronounced exponents of the notion that Jews were inassimilable, and its violent corollary, were the Alsatian sections. The extreme right enjoyed tremendous support throughout Alsace-Lorraine in the 1930s, including both French leagues and Nazi sympathizers in favour of German expansion into the area. The CDF/PSF alone numbered 20–30,000, and like their *liguer* brethren group activists were careful to address local interests.[105] Historically popular across the region, xenophobia received much attention in CDF/PSF meetings and newspaper articles. The *Flambeau de l'Est*, the group's Alsatian newspaper, regularly contained anti-Semitic diatribes, criticizing Jewish immigrants and characterizing Jews as inferior 'economic vultures'.[106] The ringleaders were foreigners 'of fresh date', and only

---

101   Text of CDLR speech in *Flambeau Normand*, 19 Nov. 1938.

102   AP/451/101, 'L'Agitation antisémite', *Bulletin d'Informations* 90, 22 Nov. 1938.

103   F. Dehl, 'Question juive toujours', *Flambeau de Flandres-Artois-Picardie*, 27 Nov. 1938.

104   Marcel Aucouturier, *Au service*, pp. 109, 125–127.

105   Samuel Huston Goodfellow, *Between the Swastika and the Cross of Lorraine* (Dekalb, 1999), pp. 3–9.

106   Ibid, pp. 145–146.

immediate and severe action could eliminate the 'wheelings and dealings of the Jewish race'. Answering critics who labeled their platform anti-Semitic, the paper blamed Jews themselves, who caused xenophobia by behaving improperly: The PSF was not anti-Semitic, simply 'anti-Dreck-Juden'.[107]

In keeping with this premise, during the 1936 electoral campaign for the provincial legislature, Alsatian Croix de Feu members distributed tracts describing the Jewish 'poisoning of the race', including details of theft and murder against Frenchmen. Group writings also frequently alluded to *nettoyage*, a term which applied to both the political and racial reconstruction of the nation.[108] Hence the local PSF section chiefs jointly demanded the mass expulsion of Alsatian Jews during their 1937 annual meeting in Strasbourg. Finally, a November 1938 resolution adopted by the PSF Bureau Politique d'Alsace in Mulhouse condemned 'Jewish nationalism' as a serious threat to France, and opposed citizenship for newcomers fleeing Nazi Germany. As usual, the group blamed Blum and the Popular Front for such problems. La Rocque personally named the socialist leader at an April 1938 meeting in Metz, calling for the expulsion of all unwanted strikers and refugees, and an end to official government aid for their cause.[109]

Yet for all the bluster of the Alsatian sections, by far the greatest opposition to La Rocque's conditional anti-Semitism came from Algeria. The colony's 35,000 Jews were granted French citizenship and the right to vote by the 1870 Crémieux Decree, but this did little to quell a long anti-Semitic tradition there and the impoverished local community remained second-class citizens for all intents and purposes.[110] First exported to North Africa by leading French anti-Semites Edouard Drumont and Jules Guérin during the Dreyfus Affair in the 1890s, xenophobia became entrenched in Algerian political life. Led by the mayor of Algiers Max Régis, the Ligue Anti-Juive d'Alger sent four deputies to the Chamber in 1897, while anti-Semites gained control of every municipal council in the colony. Violence against Jews regularly occurred after 1871, and stereotypes permeated the local press in Algiers, Constantine, and Oran, comparing the newest citizens to ghettoized parasites whose crimes included usury and barbarism.[111] Although the French government gradually cracked down on dissenters after a vicious pogrom in 1898, which destroyed Jewish neighbourhoods, anti-Semitic groups again received electoral support during the interwar era. Variously led by xenophobic activists like Dr. Jules Molle and Henry

107 'Antisemitismus und Rassenhetze', *Flambeau de l'Est*, 30 April 1938.
108 AP/451/103, Tract – 'Qu'est-ce que le PSF?', n.d. (1936).
109 'Mehrere tausend Personen jubeln La Rocque in Nice und in Metz!', *Flambeau de l'Est*, 30 April 1938; Claude Mislin, 'Les Croix de Feu et le Parti social français en Alsace (1930–39)', Diplôme d'IED, Institut d'Études Politiques de Strasbourg, 1981–82, pp. 33–35.
110 Emanuel Sivan, 'Stéréotypes antijuifs dans la mentalité Pied-noir. Les Relations entre Juifs et Musulmans en Afrique du nord, XIXe–XXe siècles: actes du Colloque international de l'institut d'histoire des pays d'outre-mer' (Paris, 1980), p. 166; Jonathan K. Gosnell, *The Politics of Frenchness in Colonial Algeria, 1930–1954* (Rochester, 2002), p. 149.
111 Sivan, 'Stéréotypes antijuifs', pp. 161–165; Gosnell, *The Politics of Frenchness*, pp. 149–151; Genevieve Dermenjian, *La Crise anti-juive oranaise, 1895–1905* (Paris, 1986), pp. 140–144; Elizabeth Friedman, *Colonialism and After: An Algerian Jewish Community* (South Hadley, 1988), pp. 19–24.

Coston, alongside members of the metropolitan leagues and their indigenous counterparts, the movement dominated local and regional politics, once again electing mayors, city councilors, and representatives to the *Délégations financières* in each department.[112]

Unsurprisingly, the CDF/PSF enjoyed tremendous success in Algeria in the 1930s, gathering almost 10,000 members in the departments of Alger and Oran alone by August 1935, and operating *La Flamme*, a daily newspaper.[113] The group forged links with a variety of anti-Semitic leagues, including the Action française, Parti populaire français, and the Rassemblement nationale d'action sociale, run by the mayor of Oran and notorious xenophobe Gabriel Lambert.[114] Naturally, few Jews ever joined the group, despite the substantial number of veterans present in each department. One unnamed member appears on the rolls in Ain-Beida, a small community southeast of Constantine, and Lucien Bensimon regularly attended meetings in the capital despite protestations over his origins, which eventually caused his departure from the CDF/PSF in October 1934.[115] Thereafter, Jews only appeared at group meetings on behalf of the parties of the left, usually as protesters.

Much like their metropolitan compatriots, local members vociferously condemned racism, claiming that the CDF/PSF accepted all races and religions, and that French patriotism and anti-communism were the only requirements for membership. Speakers at group meetings assailed Algerian anti-Semitism, characterizing such sentiments as un-Christian and divisive. Thus an Algiers lawyer named Bricault vigorously criticized Nazi racial legislation in front of a 3,000-strong audience at the Cinema Majestic in November 1935, while the President of the Oran Volontaires nationaux warned his charges to avoid violence against Jews, many of whom came from 'authentically French' families dedicated to the *mystique Croix de Feu*.[116] Paul

---

112   On Dr. Molle, see Millman, *La Question juive*, pp. 192–195. For a discussion of Coston's Algerian years, see Pierre Assouline, 'Henry Coston: itinéraire d'un anti-Sémite', *L'Histoire* 148 (1991): 56–60. Little research has been done concerning the leagues in Algeria. For brief treatments, see Francis Koerner, 'L'Extrême-droite en Oranie (1936–1940)', *Revue d'histoire moderne et contemporaine* 20 (1973): 568–594 and Jacques Cantier, *L'Algérie sous le régime de Vichy* (Paris, 2002), pp. 22–31. Cantier notes that the anti-Semitism of the leagues reached its zenith under the Vichy regime, which received an enthusiastic welcome in Algeria. For an examination of the Algerian anti-Semitic rhetoric of one league in particular – the Parti Populaire Français of Jacques Doriot – see Laurent Kestel, 'The Emergence of Amti-Semitism Within the Parti Populaire Français: Party Intellectuals, Peripheral Leaders and National Figures', *French History* 19 (2005), pp. 375–381.

113   Archives d'Outre-Mer (AOM) GGA/3CAB/47, 'Renseignements receuillis en juin 1935 sur Croix de Feu, Volontaires Nationaux et Briscards', and note of 11 July 1935, Prefect of Algiers to Governor-General.

114   On the group's relations with Gabriel Lambert and the various leagues, see AOM Oran/3121, 'Rapport du Capitaine Roubaud', 24 August 1935, and untitled police report, 16 September 1937; AOM Oran/466, 'Réunion Croix de Feu et Volontaires Nationaux', 9 April 1936.

115   AOM Constantine B/3/323, Cabinet du Commissaire de Police, 'De l'activité des Croix de Feu', 16 July 1935; AOM Constantine B/3/707, 'Réunion des Croix de Feu et Volontaires Nationaux', 5 July 1934, and 'Rapport', 1 November 1934.

116   AOM Alger 1K/26, 'Réunion Croix de Feu', 25 November 1935; AOM Oran/466, Chef de la Sûreté Départementale to Prefect of Oran, 27 November 1935.

Levas, the President of the CDF/PSF in Constantine, went even further, issuing a 1936 communiqué that instructed all members that the league 'gathers together war veterans without distinction of race, religion, or doctrine'. Both Levas and La Rocque reminded the Algerian sections that soldiers at the front made no distinction among their fellow *poilus*, instead labouring and fighting in unison, a pattern and experience which solely determined citizenship.[117]

However, much like comparable pronouncements from the metropolitan CDF/PSF, the rhetoric of the Algerian sections failed to obscure severe anti-Semitism, which exceeded the worst verbiage of their French counterparts. The terminology and themes employed echo those mobilized during the pogroms of the 1890s in both their violence and intensity. To begin with, the CDF/PSF leadership and rank and file demanded the immediate exclusion of Jews from European life in the colony, by force if necessary. From the Crémieux Decree onwards, anti-Semites boycotted Jewish businesses and assaulted inhabitants of urban ghettos, alleging that Jews dominated the economy and local politics, preventing the success of Europeans. Although the notion of Jewish dominance belied the reality of poverty and immiseration within each local community, where most inhabitants eked out a living as petty merchants, a torrent of vandalism, assault, and abuse flourished in Algeria.[118] Bestselling novels like *Cagayous anti-juif*, popular newspapers from the *Depeche de Constantine* to the *Echo d'Oran*, and a flurry of tracts and stickers in every town worked to educate the population about the nefarious Jew, whose tentacles reached into every pot and threatened the European and his livelihood.[119]

The Algerian CDF/PSF likewise detailed 'Jewish crimes', and demanded the exclusion of members of the community who did not embrace the *mystique Croix de Feu*. Jews were variously accused of masterminding the Bolshevik revolution in Russia, manipulating American politics in order to control the national agenda, and envisioning global domination through the auspices of international finance, led by 'M.M. Baruch, Kuhn, Loebe et cie. de New York, et leurs coreligionnaires de Londres et d'Amsterdam', who followed the orders of their partners in the Komintern.[120] They were also deemed to be war profiteers. One group member in Bougie unfavourably contrasted the loyal effort of the *indigènes* during the Great War with local 'parasites', who struck it rich while French and Arab soldiers perished.[121] The group's Algerian newspaper *La Flamme* frequently appended anti-Semitic cartoons to these discussions. Each depicts the stereotypical Jew, an overweight figure with bulbous, hooked nose, outsized lips, and greasy, curly hair and beard, in

117   AOM Constantine B/3/522, 'Communication du Président du Comite départementale [1936]'; AOM Alger 1K/75, 'Parti social français: réunion privée présidée par le Colonel de la Rocque', 2 July 1937.

118   Friedman, *Colonialism and After*, pp. 18–19; Richard Ayoun and Bernard Cohen, *Les Juifs d'Algérie: 2000 ans d'histoire* (Paris, 1982), pp. 133–139.

119   Sivan, 'Stéréotypes antijuifs', pp. 160–165; Dermenjian, *La Crise*, pp. 140–144.

120   Pierre-Louis Ganne, 'Tout contre le rapprochement Franco-Hitlérien!', *La Flamme*, 23 December 1938; Pierre-Louis Ganne, 'Le Gang et le contre-gang', *La Flamme*, 25 November 1938.

121   AOM Constantine B/3/327, Commissaire de Police de Bougie to Prefect, 15 December 1936.

addition to pointed teeth. The character always wears an ill-fitting banker's suit with a Star of David on the front breast pocket, while accompanying captions contend that the Jew represents an alien presence on French and Algerian soil, which cannot be nationalized. One such example portrays an Eastern European Jew, wearing a shabby fur coat with cigar in hand, speaking to a butler in a cabinet minister's drawing room. While well-dressed onlookers patiently wait their turn, the interloper announces that 'the President is expecting me: Ephraim Krankfünchsteinblatt. I have come from Czernovitch to replace Stavisky in the good graces of French justice … that is, if there is a ministerial portfolio available!'.[122] Such depictions in no way differed from those present in stridently anti-Semitic publications like *Libre Parole*, which found fertile ground in 1930s Algeria for campaigns against Jews and their supposed political machinations.

Much like their metropolitan counterparts, the Algerian CDF/PSF designated Léon Blum as the worst example of the Jewish threat to France and North Africa. Local members blamed the Popular Front leader for the low French birthrate due to his supposed advocacy of divorce and unbridled sexuality, and depicting him as the quintessential queer dandy – weak, thin, and nervous.[123] Naturally, the effeminate Jew distributed the most important ministerial portfolios to other members of the 'synagogue', including Jean Zay and Georges Mandel. Blum's 'Jewish team' engaged in ruinous financial practices, following the orders of their Muscovite masters, and concomitantly attempted to transform Algeria into a huge ghetto, run by Jews and subservient Arabs.[124]

Most odiously, they attempted to nationalize the *evolués*, the Arabic elite, through the 1936 Blum-Viollette bill. Tendered by former Governor-General Maurice Viollette in response to the Charter of Demands issued by the Algerian Muslim Congress in June 1936, the legislation proffered citizenship to 25 000 educated *indigènes*. Lauded by local assimilationist figures like Dr. Bendjelloul and Ferhat Abbas as a solution to increasing Arab frustration, it was soundly rejected by the *Pied-noirs* as the first step towards political and economic equality between Arabs and Europeans.[125] La Rocque and the PSF Commission des Affaires indigènes countered with the status quo: That any Muslim could receive citizenship if they agreed to renounce traditional customs and authorities, including Koranic law, and exclusively honour the French legal code. Given their attachment to Islam, few Arabs agreed to abandon their civil status, a refusal consistently voiced after the

---

122 'Le futur tabou', *La Flamme*, 13 January 1939. The stereotypical Jew frequently appeared in group discourse, contrasted with the virtuous and law-abiding Frenchmen. Addressing a meeting in Constantine, Mme. Vicrey of the local PSF women's auxiliary brought the argument to its logical conclusion, declaring: 'Monsieur, a Constantine, on est Français ou Juif!' In AOM Constantine B/3/327, 'Parti social français', 8 November 1936.

123 AOM Constantine, B/3/635, 'Parti Social Français', 24 October 1938; 'L'Homosexuel', *La Flamme*, 14 October 1938. The latter cartoon characterizes Blum as an effete, coiffed lover, sidling up to a butch Roman legionnaire.

124 See variously AOM Alger 1 K/75, 'Rapport/Commissaire Centrale de Police', 1 February 1937 and 'Parti Social Français', 9 April 1938; Constantine B/3/635, 'Parti Social Français', 8 April 1938.

125 On the Blum-Viollette bill and its subsequent failure, see John Ruedy, *Modern Algeria: The Origins and Development of a Nation* (Bloomington, 1992), pp. 139–144.

government first tendered the offer in the 1865 *sénatus-consulte* (a fact not lost on the CDF/PSF's Algerian membership).[126]

Although the group certainly pilloried Viollette, its members lambasted Blum and Algerian Jewry, decrying the legislation as an attempt to convert Muslims to communism while inspiring separatist sentiment among the *indigènes*.[127] They released a tract in French and Arabic designed to discourage Arabs from listening to Jews, the slavish devotees of the doctrine of Karl Marx (termed *leur nouveau prophète*) who attempted to lure unsuspecting Muslims out of their mosques with a variety of false promises. Those unfortunate souls who heeded this call became thieves and traitors, and inevitably ended up in prison.[128] Others termed Viollette's plan 'the gift of the Jews', and implied that the proposed law aimed to create a Judeo-Marxist state.[129]

In the final analysis, Algerian members judged Blum in the same fashion as the metropolitan CDF/PSF: As a foreigner at odds with French traditions and expectations, taking orders from the synagogue rather than acting in the public interest. Yet the local response to Blum and his co-religionists went much further, unmasking a violent racism beyond even the most severe xenophobia present in the French sections. Speaking to an audience at Constantine's public university in January 1937, PSF deputy Paul Creyssel called for violence against those who rejected the group's overtures: 'if we extend our hand to the Jews and they spit on it, then our fist will be raised to expel them.'[130] Mere months after Creyssel's outburst, sympathizer and Constantine Mayor Morinaud told an audience of ardent supporters, including PSF parliamentary representative Stanislas Devaud, section President Colonel Gros, and a group of Volontaires nationaux, that the Jewish minority worked in tandem with local communists to undermine his government.[131] Given the regularity of such vitriol, it is perhaps unsurprising that rabid anti-Semite René Barthélemy, Algerian publisher of the new *Libre Parole* and Secretary-General of the fascist Regroupement national, frequently addressed group meetings, discussing the perilous 'Judaic international' and demanding a violent campaign against local Jews.[132]

Group members frequently invoked Jewish 'racism' as a rationale for their campaigns against Algerian Jews. Various authors declared that the community constituted a homogeneous entity, voting with pro-Semitic prejudice for parties of disorder and treason solely on the basis of each candidate's race. Thus the 2,400-

---

126   Pierre Machefer, 'Autour du problème algérien en 1936–1938: La Doctrine algérienne de PSF: Le PSF et le projet Blum-Viollette', *Revue d'histoire moderne et contemporaine* 10 (1963): 147–156.

127   'Le Problème Algérien', *L'Heure Française*, 10 July 1937.

128   AOM Alger 1K/75, 'Appel aux musulmans', 17 March 1937.

129   'PSF et racisme', *La Flamme*, 22 July 1938; 'L'Algérie française v-t-elle faire les frais des combinaisons de M.M. Mandel et Lecache?', *La Flamme*, 26 May 1939.

130   AOM Constantine B/3/635, Rapport – Sûreté Départementale de Constantine, 3 January 1937.

131   AOM Constantine B/3/522, Rapport – Sûreté Départementale de Constantine, 13 May 1936.

132   AOM Constantine B/3/635, 'Parti social français', 14 August 1936 and Commissaire de Police de Batna to Sous-préfet, 27 April 1937.

strong Constantine bloc thwarted any non-Jewish/socialist candidate, voting as directed by the rabbinate. Bernard Lecache and LICA were deemed the worst Jewish racists, allied variously with Blum and the Popular Front, and financiers like Rothschild. Controlled by international banking interests, they accused the CDF/ PSF of anti-Semitism on orders from Moscow, and ordered Jewish voters to support left-wing candidates.[133] With this in mind, and to promote exclusionary policies, *La Flamme* printed stories of Judeo-communist activity in Algeria, designed to demonstrate Jewish power. One such tale involved a local professor badgered by Semitic Marxists who sang the 'Internationale' in his classroom, part of a 'witch-hunt' which led to the instructor's dismissal.[134] La Rocque himself perpetuated the notion at the PSF Federal Congress in October 1938, claiming that Algerian Jews exclusively supported left-wing parties in municipal and national elections. As a result, he declared an economic boycott of Jewish businesses until community leaders allowed their charges to vote with their conscience.[135]

Of course, the North African extreme right did not traditionally confine its displeasure to newspaper columns and public rallies. In 1884, an Algiers mob assaulted the Jewish quarter and burned down stores owned by Jews, pillaging those of sympathetic Christians for good measure. Urged onwards by Max Regis's violently xenophobic newspaper *L'Anti-juif*, which demanded that Europeans 'water the tree of liberty ... with Jewish blood', rioters in 1897–1898 destroyed the entire Jewish quarter. The fervour soon spread to Constantine and Oran, where youthful mobs careened through the streets, screaming 'death to the Jews!', looting and pillaging stores and synagogues, and occasionally brutalizing or murdering the inhabitants.[136]

---

133  On racial voting, see Pierre-Louis Ganne, 'Un dernier mot sur la question juive', *La Flamme*, 1 August 1937. On the LICA, see variously 'Nous souhaitons malheur à l'Angleterre', *La Flamme*, 22 April 1938; 'Les Racistes en action', *La Flamme*, 29 April 1938; Pierre-Louis Ganne, 'Sommes-nous encore en démocratie?', *La Flamme*, 3 June 1938; Pierre-Louis Ganne, 'Logique', *La Flamme*, 25 November 1938; *La Flamme*, 22 December 1938. For similar attacks against *American Hebrew* magazine and the newspaper *Alger Républicain* see 'Ce qu'il y a derrière la course à l'alliance russe', *La Flamme*, 16 June 1939; 'Heureux les imbéciles', *La Flamme*, 20 Jan. 1939. That Jews did not actually vote *en bloc* in the 1930s was never mentioned. Neither did the PSF address the real reason for left-wing success – that the extreme right often split its ballots. Thus the SFIO won seats in the 1936 Oran election, but only due to the presence of two candidates from the leagues: Marcel Gatuing for the CDF/PSF and Gabriel Lambert. In Koerner, 'L'Extrême-droite en Oranie', p. 574.

134  'Un savoureux manifeste', *La Flamme*, 22 April, 1938 (reprint of a tract distributed in Oran); 'L'Incroyable odyssée d'un professeur français poursuivi par la vindicte de communautés juives', *La Flamme*, 19 March 1938.

135  La Rocque's dictum was relayed by memo to all members in Algeria. For the full text, and the positive response of local conservatives and the Algerian extreme right, see 'Aux adhérents PSF', *Dépêche de Constantine*, 14 January 1939. It also received mention at group meetings. See, for example, AOM, Constantine B/3/635, Rapport – Police Spéciale Départementale de Constantine, 15 January 1939. Also 'La Voix du pape', *L'Avenir*, 14 November 1938. The editors might well have been reading the pages of *La Flamme*, which made the exact same points in the months leading up to the boycott. See, for example, Pierre-Louis Ganne, 'Sommes-nous encore chez nous?', 3 June 1938 and 'La Race prétendue élue', 10 July 1938.

136  Friedman, *Colonialism and After*, pp. 19–24; Dermenjian, *La Crise*, pp. 74–94.

In the 1930s, local CDF/PSF sections engaged in similar activities, frequently attacking Jews across Algeria in a comparable effort to eliminate undesirables. Although these actions never approached the scale of the 1890s riots, they went far beyond the exploits of the group's metropolitan membership, which never engaged in anti-Semitic episodes despite their tough talk. In fact, while the Paris leadership took part in ceremonies honouring Jewish war dead with Rabbin Kaplan at the Rue de la Victoire synagogue, the Algerian sections participated in street violence against local Jews. During the Constantine pogrom of August 5, 1934, which culminated in 25 deaths and 200 pillaged stores, Croix de Feu sections incited the crowd.[137] Moreover, following the electoral victory of Blum and the Popular Front in 1936, the group's elected representatives in Constantine called for anti-Semitic pogroms, while the local leadership in Oran collaborated with the Parti populaire français in street demonstrations in the Jewish quarter.[138]

Indeed, the 1936 election campaign unleashed a wave of anti-Semitic violence in Algeria, and various metropolitan extreme right-wing leagues and their colonial counterparts engaged in xenophobic actions designed to intimidate Jewish voters and left-wing candidates. The CDF/PSF actively participated in each department, joining Gabriel Lambert's Rassemblement national d'action sociale and collaborating in street demonstrations with the Parti populaire français and Unions latines.[139] However, the group needed neither partners nor encouragement to attack Algerian Jews.[140] In the aftermath of a celebratory rally on April 1936, feting Devaud's successful run for parliament, a 2,000-strong crowd spilled out into Place de la Brèche in Constantine, screaming 'a bas les juifs, il faut les prendra par le nombril!' and 'les youpins au ravin!' before storming the Jewish quarter and terrifying local residents and merchants along the Faubourg St. Jean.[141] Neither did the violence cease after the campaign ended: one of the most extreme incidents occurred at an Oran train station in August 1936. It began on the platform, where Jews and *colons* engaged in a shouting match, and continued during the commute, escalating into a full-scale brawl. Although the conductor temporarily restored order, 20 CDF/PSF supporters boarded the train at Hennaya, and attacked every Jew they could find, seriously injuring five passengers.[142]

---

137   CHEVS/LR 33, General Notes, 'Affaire du Constantine, août 1934'.

138   Michael Ansky, *Les Juifs d'Algérie du décret Crémieux à la Libération* (Paris, 1950), p. 71.

139   Michel Abitbol, *Les Juifs d'Afrique du nord sous Vichy* (Paris, 1983), pp. 20–21; Koerner, 'L'Extrême-droite en Oranie', pp. 574–577.

140   AOM Constantine B/3/522, reports of 19 March, 31 March, and 30 April 1936. These tactics were used well after the campaign ended, and fighting between CDF/PSF members and Jews was a regular occurrence in Constantine. See, for example, Constantine B/3/635, Rapport – Police spéciale du Constantine, 12 December 1938. The report details an incident between the group's local Treasurer and a group of Jews, in which the former raised his arm in the fascist salute and yelled 'je suis français, moi!', provoking a riot.

141   AOM Constantine B/3/522, 'Elections legislatives', 27 April 1936.

142   AOM Oran/3121, 'Rapport du Capitaine Thoude, commandant la section du Tlemcen, sur un incident survenu en gare d'Hennaya avec Israélites et colons', 20 August 1936.

Clearly there existed a deep chasm between the views of La Rocque and the CDF/PSF. The leader consistently advocated non-violence, and distinguished between French and foreign Jews: All French citizens were French, while all others were not welcome, regardless of race. Yet many within the group disagreed, including members of the inner circle. Worse still, the naysayers supported racial anti-Semitism and violence against Jews. The Algerian sections in particular clearly proved to be an exception to any moderation displayed by the CDF/PSF in Paris or the provinces, for their anti-Semitism in word and deed certainly matched the vitriolic spite of the French xenophobic press and the street violence of the Camelots du Roi and like-minded organizations. Colonial anti-Semitism was by no means confined to the CDF/PSF during the 1930s; in fact, the extreme-right enjoyed tremendous success among the *Pied-noirs*, dominating local politics and captivating a mass audience. Yet it is curious to note that the constant cries of 'a bas les juifs!' heard at almost every CDF/PSF meeting were never opposed by the Paris-based leadership. It is true that La Rocque again disagreed concerning tactics, rejecting fisticuffs in favour of an economic boycott, and condemning the use of drastic language in France and Algeria alike, but his distinctions were not shared by many in the group's metropolitan and colonial sections.

Moreover, in contrast to the limited exposure of newspapers like *Je suis partout*, CDF/PSF exclusionary rhetoric was directed at a membership which exceeded one million by 1938. It is worth noting that their ideas were realized by the authoritarian Vichy regime in 1940, which acted in an atmosphere of popular apathy. All of the themes adopted by Xavier Vallat, Darquier de Pellepoix, and their minions appeared in the CDF/PSF's newspapers, tracts, and speeches well before the June 1940 defeat and its authoritarian consequences. The group characterized the Jew as a scheming foreigner, allied with international finance and the left, who secretly controlled parliamentary politics from behind the scenes and lusted after French gold. A parasite that lacked Gallic blood, his very presence weakened the nation, leaving France vulnerable to Nazi aggression, Soviet-inspired revolution, and Muslim uprisings. None of these depictions would have seemed out of place in the anti-Semitic press, radio addresses, and exhibitions omnipresent under Vichy. Thus the tasks of Vallat and the CGQJ, and their dire consequences for French Jewry, were certainly facilitated by the mass indoctrination of CDF/PSF members during the preceding decade.

# V

A xenophobic creed, in which foreigners were deemed equally dangerous to the health of the nation, accompanied the anti-Semitism pervasive within the Faisceau and CDF/PSF. Fearing the growing numbers of supposedly un-French elements migrating to France each year, the leadership and rank and file of both groups wrote extensively on the issue. Immigrants were seen to be taking advantage of French hospitality, and in many cases using France as a base for their own nefarious (often communist) activities. Like their Jewish confrères, foreigners ultimately aimed to take control of the nation and at the expense of true Frenchmen. Many members thus adopted a virulent position, based upon racial stereotyping, which advocated the violent eradication of foreigners.

Despite their popular acceptance in 1920s France, the Faisceau were not among those extending their hand to the immigrant labourers expected to replace the one-and-a-half million working-age males lost during the Great War. Most of the newcomers were Eastern and Southern Europeans – Italians, Poles, Czechs, and Spaniards – to whom the government granted salaries and benefits comparable to those enjoyed by the average French worker. For the most part, the population supported such measures. There were exceptions to be sure, brief moments of unrest precipitated by unemployment or fiscal woes, during which the public called for repatriation or a special immigrant tax, but they faded quickly. Similarly, occasional demands for vigilance against communist or fascist sympathizers among the newcomers produced no sustained action or polemic against immigrants. For better or worse, foreign labour proved necessary throughout the decade, a fact emphasized by business owners and management on numerous occasions.[143]

Thus racist sentiment proved to be relatively mild in the postwar decade. Yet the harshness with which they condemned foreigners set the Faisceau apart from more casual contemporary xenophobes. Valois and his colleagues mobilized existing arguments, but added an extreme and often violent critique of their own, more Action française racism than socio-economic complaint. Various members criticized perceived governmental irresponsibility concerning immigration policy, while more conservative voices declared an invasion of foreign workers due to a low birthrate. All agreed, however, that foreigners were not welcome in France, and that the new fascist state would take immediate and severe action to eliminate their presence.[144]

Contrary to their public disavowal of anti-Semitism, no member of the Faisceau adopted a similar stance against xenophobia. Hubert Bourgin warned that France existed in disarray due to a lack of recognition from the newcomers of *l'héritage paternel et maternel*. There were foreigners everywhere in France, warned Bourgin, who were nothing but 'cannibals'. 'Sommes-nous encore chez-nous?' he groaned. In a book chapter entitled 'The Garbage', Bourgin placed *métèques* first among the rubbish: Those who could or would not assimilate, and came to France only to make money. They gave nothing back to the country, were corrupt and thieving, and never worked, exploiting French cities as places for the pursuit of decadent pleasures. Claiming that most were parasites, Bourgin allotted them no place in the French *maison*.[145]

*Nouveau Siècle* frequently attacked the state's 'overly lax' immigration policy. An unsigned July 1926 article criticized the Paris chief of police for not keeping exact data regarding the whereabouts of foreigners in the capital, including the number of immigrants residing in the city, their place of origin, and their activities. Most of them,

143   Ralph Schor, *Histoire de l'immigration en France de la fin du XIXe siècle à nos jours* (Paris, 1996), pp. 50–52, 64–75, 112–114. Like Caron, the author denotes a shift from acceptance to exclusion in the 1930s and not the preceding decade: 'More or less accepted in the 1920s [immigrants] commonly found themselves rejected in the subsequent decade'.

144   An analysis of the socio-economic critique of immigrants in 1920s France can be found in Schor, *L'Opinion français et les étrangers* (Paris, 1985), pp. 415–435.

145   Hubert Bourgin, *Les Pierres*, pp. 8, 156–157. Coined by Action française leader Charles Maurras, the term 'métèque' – or 'alien' – refers to both atheists and foreigners. Alongside Jews, Protestants, and Freemasons, this category of undesirable formed the Quatre États Confédérés.

the author surmised, arrived in France for the sole purpose of starting a civil war, and the article closed with a sarcastic warning to 'sleep, Parisians surrounded by *Métèques*, you are being well guarded!' Group member Jacques Reboul asserted that a steady stream of undesirables from other nations came to France to live well, and to encumber already overburdened French public services, a malevolent force which injured the nation. Immigrants and foreigners regularly harassed and insulted French citizens, warned Reboul, and the government had to take steps to control the 'monkeys'.[146]

In assailing the quantity of foreigners living in France, Faisceau members frequently portrayed immigrants as an invading force. France was en route to becoming a colony of foreigners, cried *Nouveau Siècle* writer Louis Masset in March 1926, for some Parisian schools reported that as many as two-thirds of their students were of foreign origin. Despite the presence of only 230,172 foreign children in France, he claimed that some French students could no longer even go to school, as their places in the classroom had been filled. Masset declared the plight of the French worker to be even more unjust. In the tourist industry where so many native Frenchmen were unemployed, eight out of ten hotel workers were foreigners. *Anciens combattants* went without homes, Masset groaned, as immigrants took all the housing and never worked hard, lazing about and drinking or smoking all day.[147]

Group sympathizer Ambroise Rendu extended this argument to the countryside, where 'two million' foreigners had bought up 'the land of our fathers'.[148] To Rendu, immigration policy should have as its mission the protection of the French race and traditions, lest defence of the *tricolore* be left to immigrants' sons. A virtual foreign invasion, he claimed, allowed Italians to take control of French agricultural production in the South-West of France. Because no governmental regulation prevented the acquisition of land by foreigners, the majority of children in certain villages in the Gers or Lot-et-Garonne were Italian. Rendu lamented the loss of racial purity, warning that 'little by little, the foreign blood mixes with our blood, altering the exterior character of our race'. Nor would Italians, remaining faithful to their country of origin, accept French customs and traditions. Rendu proposed that 'occupied ancestral territory' be given to farmers from Alsace-Lorraine. The new Faisceau state, he declared, would end immigration and immediately undertake the task of assimilating the three million or more foreigners already on French soil.[149]

Immigrant workers, whether rural or urban, were the target of a virulent hate campaign within the pages of *Nouveau Siècle*, whose writers claimed that they constituted a dire threat to the safety and vitality of the French nation. Echoing Masset and Rendu, Antoine Fouroux wrote of a veritable foreign invasion, calling

---

146 'Les Etrangers à Paris', *NS*, 30 July 1925; Jacques Reboul, 'La Question des étrangers', *NS*, 14 Aug. 1926.

147 Louis Masset, 'Une Colonie pour les étrangers', *NS*, 7 March 1926. Statistics on foreign children appear in Schor, *L'Opinion française*, p. 362.

148 A member of the Action française and close friend of Charles Maurras, Rendu severed his ties with the Faisceau in 1926, after Valois and his confreres initiated a press campaign against the royalist group. See Weber, *Action française*, pp. 94, 152; Douglas, *From Fascism*, pp. 93–99.

149 Ambroise Rendu, 'La Terre de France', *NS*, 26 Feb. 1925; Ambroise Rendu, 'L'Infiltration étrangère', *NS*, 11 June 1925.

the new arrivals inassimilable revolutionaries on the run from their native countries. He reserved the greatest ire for Polish workers: '[The] Poles, who we have been able to band together in large industrial cities, are for the most part Jews, designated by the term Pollacks.' Pierre Dumas added the notion that the foreign labourer stole jobs from the French worker, and received better protection and perks than his counterpart in the process. Dumas believed that the clothing industry exemplified the plight of the true French labourer, where an entire colony of 'Pollacks' worked for starvation wages, causing moral and material sickness among French workers.[150]

The Faisceau declared the real culprit to be the revolutionary left, the communist and socialist parties, and their allies in the syndicalist CGT and CGTU, who supported foreign workers to further their own revolutionary agenda.[151] Dumas insisted that 'Pollacks' ran the latter, adding that each time its Parisian adherents cried 'Vive l'Internationale', they did so at the insistence of foreign masters. Describing a special propaganda office of the CGTU which supplied foreign language speakers, Fouroux similarly claimed that the communist party used immigrant labour as shock troops, and especially refugees from Mussolini's Italy or Primo's Spain. Omnipresent Soviet agents posed as factory workers or agricultural labourers, pursuing Bolshevik aims and recruiting fresh troops for the coming civil war.[152]

The threat thus went beyond the immigrant workers themselves, seen as a problem for which there was an easy solution: Expulsion. Socialists and communists were a different matter, equally at odds with the nation yet less conspicuous, aiming to bring the revolution from Russia to France. As one anonymous article in *Nouveau Siècle* menacingly reported:

> The red terror shakes the bourgeoisie who quickly become Leninists in the wink of an eye. As for the incurable, the intruders who will never agree to the application of integral Marxism in a ruined motherland, Chinese centurions already trained in the Paris suburbs will quickly knock some sense into them. And when Frenchmen are shot down, their

---

150    Antoine Fouroux, 'Une soirée à l'Union des corporations françaises', *NS*, 2 April 1925; Pierre Dumas, 'Le Travailleur français, dupé par la CGT doit trouver un asile au Faisceau', *NS*, 28 Feb. 1926; Pierre Dumas, 'Les Ouvriers français ...', *NS*, 5 Feb. 1927. This theme was present throughout Dumas's career. See for example 'L'Organisation ouvrière', *Cahiers des États-Généraux*, Dec. 1924: 'And we are aiding the birth, the development, of a formidable American-style moral slavery. Moreover, ask about the composition of a medium-sized metallurgical factory, whether in Paris, Marseilles, Lille, or Nantes, and they will tell you that, as in America, workers of ten to fifteen nationalities are employed there: That the French worker is the real foreigner.' (498).

151    L. Marcellin, 'Le Rubican à rebours', *NS*, 16 July 1925. The split in the syndicalist camp dated from September 1921, when communist militants left the increasingly reformist CGT to form the CGTU, affiliated with the Third International.

152    Pierre Dumas, 'Les Ouvriers français ...', *NS*, 5 Feb. 1927; Antoine Fouroux, 'Les Ouvriers étrangers sont encadrés dans l'armée communiste en vue de la guerre civile', *NS*, 26 March 1925. Articles on Soviet agents, usually minute, appeared on a regular basis in the Faisceau press. For a larger example, see 'Les Ouvriers agricoles Russes en France', *NS*, 24 Sept. 1925.

goods pillaged, and their national treasures ransacked, when the German drags his heavy boots to take part in the cleansing, we will surely know all the sweetness of paradise.[153]

By far the worst crime committed by the communists in the eyes of the Faisceau was the exploitation of the unwitting French worker.[154] Valois reminded his audience at Verdun in February 1926 that many communist workers had once been prepared to make the ultimate sacrifice for the French nation in the trenches. Barbaric emissaries of Moscow hoodwinked these brave patriots into believing that the factory owner was to blame for their misery.[155]

## VI

Valois and the Faisceau operated during a time when immigration did not provoke widespread concern within French society. Although not alone in their anti-foreigner stance (the Action française and Jeunesses patriotes were equally rabid), such groups were the exception and not the rule. By the 1930s, however, the entire political spectrum became permeated with varying degrees of xenophobia. As a group containing over one million members by 1938, the CDF/PSF represented a large portion of this constituency, functioning as an extreme proponent of the renewed violent polemic against foreigners.

Historians Gérard Noiriel and Vicki Caron have noted the presence of a long-standing French tradition of welcoming immigrants, dating from the French revolutionary era, when the 1793 constitution provided them with legal status for the first time. Although occasional lapses in tolerance occurred, in the 1890s during the Dreyfus affair for example, the post-World War One era in no way departed from the established tradition of acceptance.[156] Hence by 1931, approximately three million foreigners lived in France, mostly Poles and Italians working in mines, factories, and farms. Only Jewish immigrants tended to settle in Paris or other urban centres, mainly in the Pletzl, the impoverished Parisian slum buttressing the third and fourth *arrondissements*.[157]

The onslaught of the depression in 1932, at which time production plunged by more than 25 per cent, led to the economic victimization of foreigners in varying degrees. While the total number actually fell by more than half a million during the next four years, primarily due to unemployment, a large segment of the population angrily accused the newcomers of stealing jobs from honest Frenchmen.

---

153 'Le Coup d'état du 3 Août', *NS*, 30 July 1925. Similar arguments appear in F/7/13210, Tract – 'Tu n'est pas communiste? Non, mon camarade, tu n'es pas communiste', and d'Obrenan, *Introduction*, 66, 91; La Politique socialiste', *NS*, 3 Jan. 1926.

154 Antoine Fouroux, 'Ouvriers français, qui faire pour éviter la misère?', *NS*, 2 July 1925.

155 'Au marché couvert', *NS*, 28 Feb. 1926. See also Philippe Barrès, 'Précisons encore', *NS*, 8 Jan. 1926; F/7/13208, note of 15 May 1926. Barrès also accused the 'men from Moscow' of collaboration with Arab nationalists, specifically Abd el Krim, in an effort to destroy the French empire.

156 Caron, p. 5.

157 Hyman, pp. 65–71; Marrus and Paxton, pp. 34–45.

Simultaneously, France began to receive an influx of refugees, primarily Jews fleeing Nazi repression in Germany: In 1933 alone up to 25,000 sought political exile. Where Polish and Italian workers earned the ire of union members and employers' associations, the refugees angered educated Frenchmen, for they were overwhelmingly skilled professionals. As a result, doctors and lawyers entered the fray, demanding the exclusion of Jews from the free professions.[158] Nonetheless, the immigrant population grew substantially by the end of the decade, and by 1939 France surpassed the United States as the country containing the most foreigners per hundred thousand inhabitants (515 against 492), and refugees became a much-debated topic in government, the press, and among the general population. Every facet of French life became embroiled in the struggle, from the number of foreign students in schools and universities to the political affiliations of the newcomers.[159]

Right wing groups, such as the Republican Federation, began to publicly espouse xenophobic sentiment by 1936–1937. The left proved to be equally affected, as evidenced by an April 1937 article in *L'Humanité* which attacked foreign spies and *agents provocateurs*, a common theme during the 1930s, and chided the Popular Front for its inability to keep foreigners out of the country. The article concluded that 'we must clean up Paris and France'. No less an authority than communist party leader Maurice Thorez agreed, shouting to a crowd at the Vélodrome d'Hiver in September 1937: 'When we cry France for the French, it means: Spies out! Murderous agitators out!'[160] Thorez went on to accuse recent immigrants of abusing French hospitality.

Centrist governments agreed with both ends of the political spectrum. Only during the Popular Front years did refugees receive favourable treatment, albeit limited to those already within French borders, for the government steadfastly refused to issue new visas. By 1938, however, paternalism disappeared amid the clamour over German expansion into Austria and Czechoslovakia, the anti-Semitic violence of Kristallnacht, and the looming reality of renewed immigration. In May of that year, Radical Minister of the Interior Albert Sarraut enacted legislation obliging non-citizens to obtain identity cards and inform the police of any change of address, restricting their right to work, and stripping all foreigners of the right to vote. Finally, the new law imposed a five year waiting period on all citizenship applications.[161]

Such sentiments leave the impression that the xenophobia of La Rocque and the CDF/PSF simply followed a general social trend. Yet however unwelcoming French society may have been towards immigrants in the 1930s, the group's leadership and rank and file stood out in the virulent scope and violence of their critique. Much like the Faisceau, the CDF/PSF remained aloof from popular sentiment due to its menacing tone, offering a policy of exclusion without exceptions, within a discursive framework which often rivaled the worst that *Gringoire* or *Je suis partout* could muster. Theirs was not a momentary xenophobia, to be resolved through prohibitive

158   Hyman, pp. 65–68; Caron, pp. 8–16.

159   Ralph Schor, *L'Opinion français*, p. 663.

160   Ibid., pp. 661–662. On the popular theme of the refugee as spy, see Caron, pp. 187–194.

161   Schor, *L'Opinion français*, p. 667; Caron, chapter six (Blum/Popular Front), p. 171–176 (events of 1938).

legislation, but rather an all-out assault on a racial and cultural influx perceived to have ruined France. Moreover, the solutions proposed by the group once again augured the exclusionary legislation of the Vichy regime.

Unlike the group's anti-Semitism, its criticism of foreigners evinced little disagreement between leadership and rank and file. La Rocque's theoretical xenophobia first emerged in his 1934 work *Service public*, and remained unchanged throughout the decade. He began by condemning racism, which 'goes against nature and common sense'. To the CDF/PSF leader, the French race represented a magnificent synthesis which denied xenophobia within its borders. Nevertheless, he considered the issue of foreigners problematic, specifically the uncontrolled perpetual immigration which resulted in mass racism:

> Paris and the big cities, especially Marseilles, are saturated with deportees, *interdits de séjour*, and the deracinated. The inordinate ease of naturalizations, without a sufficient waiting period, has introduced a growing multitude of undesirables into society.[162]

Although La Rocque did not believe that all foreigners were suspect, he worried that many used Nazi persecution to cover up a variety of crimes, including conspiracy and espionage on behalf of Germany. However, he rejected specific criticisms of Jewish refugees: the real question involved immigration *en-soi*, and there existed no difference between a Jewish or non-Jewish newcomer. All abused French hospitality, taking jobs away from French citizens, while encouraging revolution and chaos in *la Patrie*. Only stern legislation permitted the elimination of 'parasitic' foreigners, including a severe naturalization statute designed to weed out undesirables.[163]

As the decade progressed La Rocque's tone evolved from quasi-benevolence towards immigrants to outright confrontation. At the third PSF national congress in December 1938, he drew a clear distinction between assimilated Frenchmen and newcomers, protesting against 'the invasion of foreign elements' which caused renewed racism in France.[164] He further demanded a complete revision of the 'hateful and abusive' naturalizations of the previous ten years, and a special tax for immigrants conducting business and/or living in France. Two weeks later, he regaled readers of the group's *Petit Journal* daily newspaper with tales of immigrant intrigue on behalf of international finance, communism, and foreign powers, concluding with a call of 'France for the French'.[165]

La Rocque's exclusionary doctrine rested upon the socio-economic rationale that fueled mainstream xenophobia in 1930s France: Immigrants took French jobs, voted communist, and never assimilated into the *patrie*. Various CDF/PSF members

---

162    Lt.-Colonel François de la Rocque, *Service public* (Paris, 1934), pp. 157, 159.

163    Ibid., pp. 160–162. La Rocque also proposed the elimination of foreigners who took away French jobs in a November 1934 interview with the *Petit Journal*. See the reprint in extenso in *Le Flambeau*, Nov. 1934. La Rocque later took this theme to the government, writing to Senatorial candidates in October 1935 to outline the need to expunge foreign economic influence and terminate immigration. See *Le Flambeau*, 19 Oct. 1935.

164    AP/451/117, 3me Congrès National du PSF, 'Déclaration du PSF, présentée par le Président du parti', 4 Dec. 1938.

165    La Rocque, 'La France française', *Petit Journal*, 18 Dec. 1938.

similarly discounted immigration for economic reasons. In her study of Jewish refugees in France, Vicki Caron claims that middle-class concerns about unwanted competition, combined with the deleterious effects of the depression, generated much of the hostility towards newcomers. Thus even normally staid periodicals, many of them staunchly republican, joined the chorus of denunciation by portraying immigrants as inassimilable, revolutionary, and lazy. However, the CDF/PSF began assailing foreign labour well before the refugee crisis of 1934, beating the government and the middle-class (the principal backers of the economic argument, and the group's largest contingent of supporters) to the punch by two years.[166] Thus its rhetoric tended towards the extremism of the Vichy years, when corporatist policies disguised a concerted commercial campaign against Jewish capitalism and its foreign workforce, both of which would be forcefully replaced by French professional organization after the exclusion of undesirables. To this end, in November 1932 *Le Flambeau* addressed the issue of unemployment, crying foul over the existence of 300,000 jobless Frenchmen. How could this have happened, when French businesses employed two million foreigners? The author proposed a simple solution: The mandatory replacement of every departing immigrant with a Frenchman, reducing the number of foreigners to a suitable level.[167] La Rocque himself entered the fray during a nationally broadcast radio address on April 24, 1936, in which he claimed that with the implementation of the *profession organisée*, 'we will no longer see French workers in the streets and hordes of foreigners congesting poor neighbourhoods, receiving welfare, straining budgets, and contaminating the population'.[168]

Conversely, others within the group demanded exclusion based upon the superiority of the French race, and emphasized the danger in allowing foreigners to taint racial purity. Their conclusions relied upon bio-medical terminology comparable to the language of right-wing geneticists like René Martial, who infamously commented that foreigners displayed 'an oriental mentality that frequently nullifies our intentions as well as our efforts'. He further declared that immigrants were 'impelled to defraud, steal, and avoid the honest life'.[169] The writings of Martial and others proved to be extremely influential under Vichy, and many of his colleagues found themselves employed by government agencies in both zones during the war years.

Taking their cue from Martial, many CDF/PSF writers emphasized sickness and degeneration. The *Volonté du Centre* referred to each member of the French nation as a cell in a living organism poisoned by the introduction of 'foreign parasites'. Similarly, Jean Madigner, writing in the *Volontaire 36*, claimed that 'we cannot allow colonies of recent arrivals to settle among us, maintaining the brutal and unstable instincts of primitive races'. Despite the evident strength of French blood, capable of withstanding

---

166   Caron, pp. 278–283, 358.
167   'Appel pour les chomeurs', *Le Flambeau*, 11 Nov. 1932. This issue was frequently raised by CDF/PSF members. See Magny, 'Le Chomage', *Le Flambeau*, 1 Feb. 1932; AP/451/103, Tract – 'Qu'est-ce le PSF', 13; Anon., *Pourquoi nous sommes dévenues Croix de Feu*, 1934; Louis Recoules, 'Qualité', *Le Flambeau*, 11 Jan. 1936.
168   CHEVS/LR 38, 'Déclaration du Lt.-Colonel de la Rocque, radiodiffusée le 24 avril 1936'.
169   Caron, p. 78.

a certain level of assimilation, Madigner warned that France must retain its national traits, composed of families nourished upon French wheat and tradition.[170]

The group's transformation into the parliamentary PSF only made their rhetoric more hostile. Various authors wed racial and bio-medical critiques with more populist economic arguments, producing a portrait of the immigrant as foreign invader. The issue no longer concerned protection for the battered French worker, but rather immediate action against dangerous and unhealthy foreigners.[171] The most detailed such critique came from parliamentary deputy Charles Vallin, whose writing tied together all of the various themes present in the group's xenophobic discourse. While proclaiming that racism ran counter to French culture and the principles of Western civilization, Vallin nevertheless argued that it was unfair to import foreign labour while so many French workers remained unemployed. While he recognized that the low French birthrate produced the need for limited immigration, he derided the subsequent 'veritable invasion'. According to Vallin, France had woken up one morning to find colonies of immigrants camped along various stretches of her territory, creating a dire national security threat. These encampments represented a threat to the moral and mental health of the nation, and a severe hygiene problem. Although some of the three million foreigners living on French soil respected the rules, Vallin acknowledged, many others were economic parasites. Was it acceptable for a French *Tabac* to close, sending its clients to an immigrant? He bluntly responded: 'We don't think so. We demand that all foreigners based in France be hit with the majority of taxes.'[172]

Speaking on behalf of the group, Vallin demanded the strict physical and moral control of prospective immigrants, and the immediate expulsion of undesirables. A severe exam would be administered before the attainment of citizenship, and a PSF government pledged to review all naturalizations from the preceding decade in order to weed out the unwanted. Once a candidate received acceptance, Vallin's proposed immigration tax immediately took effect, with exceptions granted solely to war veterans from French campaigns.[173]

The notion that foreigners colonized France found a willing audience in the countryside, where farmers demonstrated little tolerance for refugees and immigrants. Peasant anger often resulted from perceived government apathy towards the plight of the French farm, battered by the ongoing economic slump and concomitant low prices. Reacting to the 1937 Serre plan, which envisioned the resettlement of thousands of Eastern European newcomers in slightly populated agrarian departments, the extreme right-wing newspaper *Choc* asked if 'our Burgundy was going to become a Zionist colony?'. CDF/PSF rural members wholeheartedly agreed,

---

170  Le PSF Moyen, 'Éloge de l'égoïsme de parti', *Volonté du Centre*, 22 April 1939; Jean Madigner, 'Fécondation artificielle', *Volontaire 36*, 15 Sept. 1936.

171  *Volonté du Centre*, 13 Feb., 1937; Albert Carpide, 'La France française', *La France sauvée par la PSF*, Oct. 1937. The latter was a special colour magazine devoted to the PSF platform. For a similar argument, see 'Protégons le travail français', *Volonté du Centre*, 28 May 1938.

172  Charles Vallin, 'Il faut régler la question des étrangers', *Petit Journal*, 19 Oct. 1938. For an identical argument, see 'Das Problem der Auslander', *Flambeau de l'Est*, 30 April 1938.

173  Charles Vallin, 'La Question des étrangers', *Petit Journal*, 3 Nov. 1938. Vallin's call for expulsion was not exclusive to the CDF/PSF leadership. See the article concerning immigration in the *Volontaire 36*, 8 May 1938.

lambasting successive governments for allowing un-French elements to defile the soil and its ancestral dead. Thus in December 1933, the *Flambeau* declared that France had fallen victim to an invasion from the steppes, desert, and other foreign lands. Recalling the presence of three million foreigners on French soil, the author of one article claimed that the newcomers farmed 586,000 hectares of land. Its field and culture increasingly lost in the swamp of immigration, the French race consequently suffered from acute anemia.[174]

It was a simple step from criticism to exclusion, enacted in a virulently xenophobic article written by Jacques Le Roy Ladurie, which portrayed the farmer as a victim of malignant foreigners. A group sympathizer, Ladurie's Union centrale des syndicats agricoles (the largest such network in 1930s France) worked alongside the CDF/PSF in support of Henry Dorgères's Peasant Front, an organization dedicated to the creation of an authoritarian, corporatist state which largely resembled La Rocque's *Profession organisée*. In his article, Ladurie sounded a profoundly Barrèssian note, berating the government decision to lower production targets while 300,000 foreigners, many of whom worked 'stolen' French soil, dominated agriculture and refused assimilation.[175]

The immigrant-as-colonizer motif was further embraced by CDF/PSF youth organizations. During the 1930s students of all political colours vigorously opposed immigration from a purely economic perspective, fearing a saturated job market. French doctors and medical students alike protested against the presence of foreigners in their faculties, despite the low proportion of newcomers among those enrolled in various courses. Riots occurred in Paris and the provinces throughout 1934–1935, led by Secretary-General Marchandeau of the Confédération des syndicats médicaux, a staunch xenophobe who demanded restrictions on the naturalization of immigrants, and their admission into French universities. By 1938, similar rhetoric appeared within the Chamber of Deputies. Republican Federation stalwarts Louis Marin and Fernand Laurent regaled representatives with tales of 'recently naturalized foreigners [who] constitute in commerce as well as in certain liberal professions, and especially in medicine, inadmissible competition to French citizens'.[176]

However, CDF/PSF student critiques betrayed a violent bent far removed from Marin and his conservative cohorts. They reproached foreigners for abusing French hospitality and colonizing the nation, noting the threat to the job market. Yet their answer was the expulsion of foreigners, and not a mere revision of the naturalization statute. In April 1935, *Le Flambeau* justified this stance through assertions that foreign students abused French hospitality, studying in a chosen faculty and then

174   'Invasion étrangère', *Le Flambeau*, Dec. 1933. See also party agricultural secretary Jean Duval's 'La Vie agricole', *Flamme Vendéene*, 15 Jan. 1939. On the Serre plan and the extreme-right reaction, see Caron, p. 215.

175   Jacques Le Roy Ladurie, 'Paroles paysannes', *Le Flambeau*, Sept. 1933; Robert O. Paxton, *French Peasant Fascism: Henry Dorgère's Greenshirts and the Crisis of French Agriculture, 1929–1939* (Oxford, 1997), chapters one, three, and four. La Rocque warned that the CDF/PSF could never accept foreigners tilling French soil, referring to those who settled in the countryside as Spanish anarchists and communists, fleeing Franco and the fascists. In *1er congrès agricole, 16–17 février 1939* (Saint Brieuc, 1939), p. 16. This point was also made by a M. Heintz at the 1936 regional congress in Alsace, in *Qu'est-ce que le P.S.F.*, pp. 4–5.

176   Caron, pp. 29–32, 238.

remaining in the country despite popular resistance to their continued presence. That students chose Gallic universities presented no serious problem, merely continuing a centuries-old practice resulting from the French position at the centre of Christian civilization. But for the government to permit their overwhelming presence in various professions proved unacceptable. The article concluded with praise for a recent student conference resolution to bar foreigners from practicing any profession in France or her colonies, until ten years from the receipt of citizenship.[177]

Thus the complaints of CDF/PSF youth members went far beyond socio-economic criticism. Authors instead asserted that immigrant students likened France to a conquered country. Despite the relatively low number of foreigners enrolled in university courses, in April 1938 *L'Espoir de l'Est* complained that Asians and the 'olive-faced' predominated in French universities: 'They install themselves in the vanquished country. They benefit from our weakness, occupying positions which are normally reserved for our compatriots. Their temporary emigration becomes an occupation.'[178] Furthermore, the author unhesitatingly referred to the unwillingness of foreigners to perform civic duties, including military service. Upon graduating the student earned an easy naturalization, changed his name, and subsequently robbed Frenchmen of their careers.

Hence at the second annual PSF student conference in March 1939, members floated a motion demanding restrictions on the admission of foreign students into French institutions. Only after a strict examination of the candidate's intellectual and moral qualifications, along with proof of adequate financial resources, would they be permitted to enter the country. Although PSF students opposed racism in principle, the text read, they would not hesitate to expel those who did not meet their criteria.[179] These proposals were later enlarged in the PSF student newspaper *L'Etudiant sociale*. Writing in May 1939, Pierre Suire claimed that it was a French tradition to accept foreign students in French universities, if the newcomers were 'discreet and genuine ambassadors'. But the current crop disrespected their hosts, abused native hospitality, and used the university as a forum for partisan political battles. While those immigrants who faced persecution or utter poverty in their country of origin would be allowed to remain in France, the remainder were to be removed, to ensure employment for French students upon graduation. France was a Christian country, Suire concluded, whose traditions demanded respect from all those who crossed the border, including visiting students.[180]

## VII

Zeev Sternhell has written of the French extreme-rightist attitude that:

177    André Delacour, 'Science ou profession?', *Le Flambeau*, 20 April 1935. For similar arguments, see Trézien, 'Le Sentiment de la grandeur', *Le Flambeau*, Dec. 1933; 'À la Sorbonne', *Le Flambeau*, 23 March 1935.

178    'Les Etudiants étrangers', *L'Espoir de l'est*, 2 April 1938. See also 'Le Dernier né se porte bien', *Flambeau de Sud-Ouest*, 22 May 1937. The term olive-faced refers to students of Arabian descent.

179    *La Flamme*, 10 March 1939.

180    Pierre Suire, 'Les Etudiants étrangers', *L'Etudiant Sociale*, May 1939. Suire was the President of the Group's Centre Universitaire.

No legal fiction can convert a Rumanian Jew into a Frenchman. It can convert him into a French *citizen*, but it cannot make him into a *Frenchman*. To be a French citizen and to be a Frenchman are two quite different things ... Hence, according to organic nationalism, Léon Blum, though a renowned and successful literary critic, could not possibly understand Racine. He could not plumb the depths of seventeenth-century French literature because his brain and heart were foreign to the inner essence of the text, even though he could understand the language and analyze the linguistic forms.[181]

It was this type of thinking which drove the Faisceau and CDF/PSF to make the politics of exclusion central to their projected transformation of the nation and state. Despite proclamations to the contrary, both groups openly displayed anti-Semitism and xenophobia throughout their existence. Although Jews and foreigners were not assigned the doctrinal importance present in the Nazi worldview, the Faisceau and CDF/PSF nonetheless prioritized the 'Jewish question' and derided immigration. As a result, their racist doctrine cannot be minimized or ignored.

Because it was active during the 1920s, a period in which anti-Semitism and xenophobia were largely absent from public discourse, while the traditional extreme right languished in relative obscurity, the Faisceau represents a crucial link between prewar racism and the next wave in the 1930s. While the vast majority of the French populace abandoned fin-de-siècle anti-Semitism and welcomed foreign labour as a solution to the postwar manpower shortage, the Faisceau spoke in terms that betrayed the influence of *La France juive* and the Action française. Although the group disbanded in 1928, well before the depression generated a renewal of xenophobic sentiment in France, its mobilization of racial doctrine helped bridge the gap between late nineteenth-century racism and the renewed polemic of the subsequent decade.

Similarly, although they agitated during the stormy 1930s, when anti-Semitism and xenophobia re-emerged throughout France, the CDF/PSF promulgated an uncompromising racial typology. Although popular accommodation of Jews and immigrants abruptly ceased with the onset of the depression in 1932, few voices demanded outright expulsion with the vigour of La Rocque and his confreres. Various CDF/PSF members mobilized rhetoric equaled only by the extreme xenophobes of *Je suis partout* and *Gringoire*, eschewing economic rationale in favour of racial stereotyping and calls to violence. Thus like the Faisceau, the CDF/PSF, an organization which surpassed one million members by 1938, preserved the drastic anti-Semitism and race hatred so prevalent in France before the Great War.

Consequently, the road to Vichy, in its xenophobic manifestation, passed through the Faisceau and the CDF/PSF, to be taken up with renewed vigour by a plethora of groups from across the political spectrum. The debate over the role of ordinary French men and women in the repression of Jews during the Vichy years continues today. Yet there can be no doubt that *Vichyiste* anti-Semitic legislation and concomitant state action represented an actualization of various extreme-right programs propagated throughout the existence of the Third Republic. The plans tendered by the CGQJ, Xavier Vallat – himself a founding member of the Faisceau and subsequent supporter of the CDF/PSF, and his successor Louis Darquier de Pellepoix (another ex-CDF/PSF member) were not conceived in a vacuum; they represented the culmination of

---

181   Zeev Sternhell, *Antisemitism and the Right in France* (Jerusalem, 1988), p. 13.

sixty years of anti-Semitic and xenophobic propaganda. During the 1920s and 1930s, various Faisceau and CDF/PSF members effectively propagated this world-view.[182]

Like Drumont and Vallat, both groups continually referred to Jews and foreigners as a dangerous, malevolent force bent on destroying France, even if they were naturalized citizens. To Fouroux and Dumas, or Devaud and Vallin, the Jew served either international socialism or the interests of big business, both incompatible with the national good. Employing racial stereotyping and conversionary rhetoric, Valois and La Rocque similarly placed 'dangerous' (and particularly foreign) Jews at the head of a vast conspiracy that aimed to infiltrate the corridors of power and subvert French interests in the pursuit of profit. Although they never openly supported d'Obrenan or the Algerian CDF/PSF, hoping that Jews could be converted to the group's doctrine, both men nonetheless published and actively promoted them, lending the group's name and publications to such efforts.

Neither was Faisceau and CDF/PSF xenophobia mere socio-economic complaint. Like Jews, foreigners were declared extremely dangerous by a variety of group members. In both cases, authors deemed foreigners to be racially incompatible with Frenchmen, poisoning the national bloodstream and colonizing France. Immigrants began their sojourn by taking advantage of local hospitality, all the while scheming against the national interest. Consequently, the Faisceau and CDF/PSF labeled them criminals, financial opportunists who slowly bought up French land and capital, while immigrant labourers worked as Soviet spies, preparing the country for the coming revolution.

There were exceptions to be sure; to La Rocque, a war veteran such as Rabbin Kaplan could qualify for membership in the CDF/PSF nation. Likewise, Valois's non-socialist Jew who abandoned financial and political gain, agreeing absolutely with group principles, could join the Faisceau. Yet even enthusiastic participants remained suspect, and during the Third Republic years, when Jews and immigrants shied away from supporting or voting for the extreme right, exceptions of this kind were rare indeed. Hence more often than not, the Jew or foreigner symbolized the conspiring enemy, ruling France from the shadows, the other who bore full responsibility for French weakness and whose expulsion would reinvigorate the nation. The elimination of this enemy represented the crucial preliminary step towards the establishment of the Faisceau *État Combattant* and the CDF/PSF *État social français* based upon group principles, just as it became a condition for the establishment of the new order at Vichy two decades later.

---

182 On the road to Vichy thesis, see Denis Peschanski, *Vichy, 1940–44: Contrôle et exclusion* (Paris, 1997), pp. 20–23; Marrus and Paxton, chapter 2. On the continuing debate in France concerning the Vichy years, see Henry Rousso, *The Vichy Syndrome: History and Memory in France Since 1944* (Cambridge, 1991). On Vallat and the Faisceau, see his memoirs *Le Nez de Cléopatre: Souvenirs d'un homme de droite, 1919–1944* (Paris, 1957), pp. 131–133. Vallat left the Faisceau in 1926, following Valois's rupture with the Action française, and later briefly joined the Croix de Feu before enjoying success as a deputy for the Republican Federation in the 1930s. See also Laurent Joly, *Xavier Vallat (1891–1972): Du nationalisme Chrétien à l'antisémitisme d'État* (Paris, 2001). On Darquier, see Laloum, *La France antisémite de Darquier de Pellepoix.*

# Conclusion

In his work on the 'reactionary modernism' of interwar German intellectuals, historian Jeffrey Herf writes that:

> The reactionary modernists were nationalists who turned the romantic anticapitalism of the German right away from backward-looking pastoralism, pointing instead to the outlines of a beautiful new order replacing the formless chaos due to capitalism in a united, technologically advanced nation.[1]

Ernst Jünger, Carl Schmitt, Werner Sombart, Oswald Spengler, Martin Heidegger, and Josef Goebbels knew that the state could not be strong yet simultaneously technologically backward. They thus combined the traditional conservative goal of *Gemeinschaft* with the hated *Gesellschaft*, mobilizing the trappings of modernity in the service of an authoritarian ideal. Heavily influenced by the experience of the trenches and the socio-technological changes wrought by the Great War, the reactionary modernists sought to mobilize technology in furtherance of blood and race, to realize full German potential. In so doing, writes Herf, they 'interpreted technology as the embodiment of will and beauty', an irrational means to the ends of national community and self-realization in contrast to soul-less intellectual discourse.[2]

The German intellectual phenomenon described by Herf bears certain similarities to the programs of the Faisceau and CDF/PSF across the Rhine. Enthralled by the trench experience, both wished to import the *mentalité* of the *combattant* into civilian life. They too looked beyond capitalism, which they derided as artificially divisive, to a gilded future in which an authoritarian state defended conservative principles. Rejecting both liberal capitalism and socialism in equal measure, the leadership and rank and file of the Faisceau and CDF/PSF wished to transform the nation and state, moving beyond the decadent, materialist, and frail Third Republic. Finally, both groups contained fervent believers in the primacy of technology, that mechanization could effectuate the desired political, economic, and social metamorphosis.

Beyond these superficial similarities, however, lay a diverse reality of competing designs far beyond the scope of their German counterparts. To begin with, the various positions adopted by factions within the Faisceau and CDF/PSF were uniquely French. Their proposed renovation of the nation and state did not exist in a vacuum, but as part of a well-defined national tradition. Within the Third Republic, elements of both the left and the right continually sought to seize power in order to allow the renovation of existing institutions, from the rise of General Boulanger and the founding of the revolutionary Parti ouvrier français in the late 1880s onwards. By 1924, when the Faisceau was founded, the Republic had already fought off a series

---

1    Jeffrey Herf, *Reactionary Modernism: Technology, Culture, and Politics in Weimar and the Third Reich* (Cambridge, 1984), pp. 2–3.
2    Ibid., pp. 24–25, 30.

of diverse challenges: Guesdist socialism, revolutionary syndicalism, the 1890s anarchist wave, the rise of the extreme-right in the wake of the Dreyfus affair, the subsequent prewar royalist vogue led by Charles Maurras and the Action française, and the newly formed communist party.

The conservative faction within the Faisceau drew heavily upon their extreme-rightist antecedents, invoking Maurras, Maurice Barrès, and social Catholicism in formulating its doctrine. Yearning in like manner for the 'true France' of tradition espoused by the dissatisfied right throughout the republican years, they were conscious of the continuity present in their discourse. Even Valois, whose hyper-modernism aroused the suspicion of his more traditional confreres, was not particularly novel. His influences were either French (Sorel, Le Corbusier) or shared with an emerging economic *avant garde*, for figures such as Léon Jouhaux, Ernst Mercier, and Louis Renault equally admired Henry Ford and Frederick Taylor. Thus the first fascist group in France, characterized by distinctly Gallic heritage and ambition, bore little resemblance to its Italian or German counterparts.[3] Similarly, certain factions within the CDF/PSF adopted positions found on the Republican left and right, such as economic rationalization and *planisme*, while others looked to French social Catholic doctrine and the *idéologie des combattants* for inspiration. In an era when the diminishing radical centre was vulnerable to the dynamism of the left and the right, especially following the 1934 formation of the Popular Front, previously marginalized ideas became common political currency.

Furthermore, neither the Faisceau nor the CDF/PSF was monolithic. Rather than adopting technology and modernism in the service of a reactionary agenda, both groups were divided into traditionalist and modernist factions, themselves occasionally subdivided into different positions. Further compounding this heterogeneity of doctrine were disagreements about the form and content of the new nation and state, which often corresponded to commonly-held ideas or plans.

Valois's technocratic state and economy were not *sui generis*, and elicited opposition from conservatives within the group who instead proffered a hierarchical, authoritarian, and social Darwinist vision which mirrored various nineteenth and early-twentieth century Catholic and reactionary French writers. Such positions further echoed the theoretical postures of certain contemporary industrialists, *combattant* leagues and right-wing political figures. Similar disagreements occurred regarding the position of women in the new nation, where progressive and traditionalist stances within the Faisceau corresponded to analogous republican positions concerning feminist demands for the political, legal, and economic equality, while their vision of the post-*Révolution nationale* French family incorporated integral nationalism, negative eugenics, and old-fashioned pronatalism. Their plans for youth were similarly divided. Valois's young fascist engineer, representative of the generation of 1914, confronted Hubert Bourgin's moral educator, emphasizing discipline, obedience, and social Catholicism. Both, however, drew upon the revolt of interwar youth against a Republic perceived as weak and decadent, and Bourgin's prescription in particular resembled the credo of the Scouts or Association Catholique

---

3    For an analysis of the key differences between Mussolini's fascist regime, and the Faisceau perception of it, see chapters one and two.

de la jeunesse française. Finally, although members unanimously agreed that Jews and foreigners were undesirable, the Faisceau's exclusionary solution varied greatly, ranging from restricted immigration to outright elimination.

This situation was even more acute within the ranks of the Croix de Feu/Parti social français. Like the Faisceau, the CDF/PSF was remarkably heterogeneous, and many of the convictions expounded by the various factions were commonplace. Unlike the Faisceau, however, the group was not divided cleanly along two ideological lines. As a genuine mass movement, with over one million members by 1938, the group could not possibly manufacture unanimity. Many followers perceived the CDF/PSF to be a non-traditional vehicle towards the achievement of limited reform, often restricted to one specific area of the nation or state: Touron or Canat, for example, wrote exclusively in reference to the new economic order. But neither figure provided great detail regarding government or social policy. Others, including La Rocque, conversely argued in favour of the *Etat social français*, an integral transformation of France according to group doctrine.

The political and economic plans of various CDF/PSF leaders, including La Rocque, were steeped in the social Catholicism of De Mun and La Tour du Pin. They were equally influenced by the trench experience, much like the Union nationale des combatants and other veterans associations. CDF/PSF technocrats who opposed the anti-modernism of their leaders instead proposed state planning and rationalization. Unlike their Faisceau counterparts a decade earlier, however, their demands were common currency in 1930s France, foreshadowing the post-1945 reconfiguration of the French economy under the guidance of Jean Monnet. Group views regarding women and the family were less divided, yet equally common. In adopting a staunchly anti-feminist and pronatalist platform for the new nation, CDF/PSF leadership and rank and file alike aligned themselves with a burgeoning movement which garnered support across the political spectrum. For an impressive and diverse array of prominent Republicans supported pronatalist organizations like the Alliance nationale. Similarly, the legislative path which culminated in 1939 with Edouard Daladier's Code de la Famille included the *salaire familial* and restrictions on contraception and abortion among its provisions. By the mid-1930s, Léon Blum's Popular Front government, the Radical party, and even the communist PCF spoke openly of a woman's natural role as mother and housewife, and supported the preservation of the French family.

Neither were conflicting CDF/PSF policies regarding youth and education aberrant. Calls for a more traditional and Catholic curriculum dated from the preceding decade, when conservatives in the Chamber of Deputies mounted campaigns for the restoration of state funding for Catholic schools and the re-imposition of Latin and Greek as mandatory subjects. In such a milieu demands for an end to republican laic education were hardly surprising, and the solution of social Catholic and conservative CDF/PSF members – emphasizing discipline, order, and moral and physical education – was certainly not particular to the group. The concept of education as propaganda drove Jules Ferry's reinvention of French pedagogy in the early 1880s, while Front Populaire youth minister Leo Lagrange and the Jeunesse Chrétienne movement proposed similar strategies for energizing contemporary juveniles. Those voices within the CDF/PSF which called for the formation of a young leadership elite based on talent, and still others concerned with skill development, further reflected established public opinion. Even the most extreme on the issue, those who proposed the creation of a new man through physical and moral regeneration, reflected the spirit of the age. Nor was CDF/PSF exclusionary rhetoric unprecedented: From the mid-1930s onwards, socio-economic anti-Semitism and xenophobia were increasingly apparent throughout French society.

Yet the Faisceau and the CDF/PSF did not merely parrot contemporary doctrine. In many instances, the extremity of their solutions differentiated them from their republican counterparts. Valois's hyper-modern productivist state shared affinities with the blueprints of Léon Jouhaux, Louis Renault, or André Tardieu, who attempted to implement technocratic and *planiste* reforms as Premier in 1930–1931. But the Faisceau leader had a far more revolutionary transformation in mind. Where Ernest Mercier or Jouhaux preached the gospel of rationalization and scientific management for industry, Valois invoked a state and government run according to such principles. Furthermore, he portrayed the nation in organic terms, delegating the preservation of morality, tradition, and social order to the newly empowered French family. Similarly, the demand of Hubert Bourgin, Philippe Barrès, and Jacques Arthuys for a return to tradition through the installation of an authoritarian regime was echoed during the nineteen-twenties only by the Action française, the Légion, and similar extreme-rightist organizations. Bourgin's conservative re-conceptualization of French education, for example, hinged upon the transformation of society as a whole, in which an authoritarian and hierarchical state replaced parliamentary democracy. Thus while his pedagogical program might have received the approval of French conservatives, his means and ends would not, for the Republican Federation and the Alliance Démocratique supported the Third Republic. More severely, the proto-geneticist leanings of Aragonnés and the eliminationist anti-Semitism of Van den Broek d'Obrenan went far beyond the scope of any opinions expressed by more mainstream political parties or social organizations.

CDF/PSF conclusions were equally severe. Although influenced by social Catholicism and the trench experience, La Rocque's authoritarian state, artisanal and agrarian economy, and emphasis upon moral and physical conformity, were anathematic to the Christian youth movements so popular in 1930s France. The blatant xenophobia of traditionalists within the group, along with their strident anti-republicanism and rejection of economic modernity, were likewise closer in tone to the extreme-rightist leagues than mainstream conservative right. The same was true for the technocratic and modernizing *planistes*, who like Valois went far beyond limits deemed acceptable by industry and government during the 1930s. Although economic modernizers entered government posts in 1936–1937, and economic rationalization was in vogue during the 1930s, a complete transformation of the nation and state never retained substantial public or ministerial support. Only marginalized figures such as Marcel Déat argued for a complete metamorphosis of French economy and society. Likewise, the anti-Semitism and xenophobia displayed by the CDF/PSF leadership and rank-and-file far outstripped the socio-economic complaints heard throughout French society from 1933 onwards. With the exception of La Rocque, the CDF/PSF critique of Jews and foreigners was based on race, and not the unemployment rate. Various members claimed that undesirable *étrangers* were unassimilable aliens whose mere presence ruined France. Such rhetoric rivaled the obloquy prevalent in the xenophobic pages of *Gringoire* and *Je suis partout*, more akin to the speeches of Xavier Vallat about Blum and his 'Jewish team' than mainstream discourse.

It is tempting to argue that both groups were simply representatives of a society-wide shift to the right, that the Third Republic in its closing stages itself adopted many doctrinal features long popular on the extreme-right. After all, the Faisceau and CDF/PSF were undeniably extreme-rightist in orientation, and yet advocated ideas which existed within the Republic. Yet such a parallel is superficial at best. The Faisceau were most influential during the era of the left-wing Cartel des Gauches, while the CDF/PSF rose to prominence alongside the socialist-led Popular Front. Although both the Cartel des Gauches and the Popular Front adopted limited versions of right-wing gender and youth policies, the radicals, socialists, and communists who continued to represent the electoral majority never abandoned their core political and social beliefs. Furthermore, with the exception of the PCF and the leagues, all of the political parties in the interwar period remained faithful to the parliamentary democracy of the Republic, never envisioning a complete transformation of the nation and state. Although they occasionally bent towards the extreme-right, the left and centre never switched sides.

The ideological pluralism of the Faisceau and CDF/PSF instead resembles the Vichy regime which replaced the Republic following the German victory in June 1940. Although they were by no means singularly responsible for the advent of Pétain's government, there were broad similarities between the two leagues and the Vichy experience. From 1940–1944, disagreements arose concerning all aspects of the nation and state: politics, economics, gender, family, youth and education, and the politics of exclusion. That the conflicts were overt during the Vichy era, rather than simmering under the surface, was a product of structural differences: The struggles for control within various ministries in the southern zone were matters of state, while the appearance of unity was necessary for the Faisceau and CDF/PSF during the drive to power. Yet the overall experience, of opposing factions with differing plans for the new nation and state, remains analogous.

Like the Faisceau and the CDF/PSF, the first *Vichyistes*, under the leadership of Marshall Philippe Pétain, unanimously supported a complete transformation of France. Their proposals greatly resembled the dicta put forth by conservative and social Catholic factions in both groups. It was no accident that the slogans of the Vichy era – the *Révolution nationale* and *Travail, Famille, Patrie*–were coined by the Faisceau and CDF/PSF during the preceding decades. Driven by organic nationalism, in which the individual existed only within the family, corporation, region, and nation, this doctrine portrayed the leader (Pétain) as the saviour and ultimate expression of the state. The regime aligned itself against republican decadence, personified by the Jew, foreigner and communist, and instead embraced moral regeneration. The *anti-France* of the republican enemy was replaced by a variety of exalted figures: The mother (representing tradition), the peasant (social harmony, Catholicism, the soil), and the *combattant* (youth, discipline, patriotism).[4]

---

4    Denis Peschanski, *Vichy 1940–44: Contrôle et exclusion* (Paris, 1997), pp. 20–23.

As in the Faisceau and CDF/PSF, this unanimity quickly evaporated. Figures from across the political spectrum regarded the new regime as an opportunity for change. Plans were tendered by a multitude of diverse personalities, affecting all areas of political, economic, and social life, ranging from social Catholicism and integral nationalism to pagan tribalism, corporative federalism to bureaucratic centralization, and communal economic organization to technocracy. Like the Faisceau and CDF/PSF, Vichy officials sought a third way between laissez-faire liberal capitalism and its parliamentary politics on one hand, and communism on the other. Their visions of the new France, however, reflected personal agendas and defeated any attempts at consensus.[5]

In the realm of economics, for example, traditionalists believed the family farm to be the basis for the new French economy. This massive return to the soil, supported by Pétain and Pierre Caziot, Vichy's first Minister of Agriculture in 1940–1941, was bolstered by the artisan-based corporatism of René Gillouin and Jules Verger who, much like La Rocque, supported a moral economy based upon the social Catholic *profession organisée*. These plans were resolutely opposed by technocratic modernizers, led by Finance Minister Yves Bouthillier, and Ministers of Industrial Production René Belin, Pierre Pucheu, François Lehideux, and Jean Bichelonne, as well as Caziot's replacement in the agriculture ministry, Jacques Le Roy Ladurie. Industrialists and engineers by trade (with the exception of the ex-CGT activist Belin), they strove to modernize the French economy, implementing state management of industry and agriculture, economic planning, and the rule of experts. Theirs was the technocratic modernization proposed by Valois, Dumas, and Lusignac within the Faisceau, and the *Maréchaux*, Canat, and Touron in the CDF/PSF. Believing the French defeat to have been the product of economic backwardness, they paid lip service to the traditionalist program, but ignored its initiatives in practical terms. With their triumph in the fall of 1941, the organic communitarian ideal of the farmer and artisan was relegated to the dustbin.[6] Although neither the Faisceau nor the CDF/PSF witnessed this success, the conflicts during the Vichy years seem all too familiar to the scholar of either group.

Similar disagreements occurred regarding youth, as they had in the Faisceau and CDF/PSF. Within the education ministry, the rationalization of French pedagogy championed by Jérome Carcopino was bitterly contested by the staunch clericalism of Jacques Chevalier, whose concept of reform involved the re-imposition of a traditional and Catholic moral education upon French youth. In the same vein, former tennis champion and *Commissaire Général à l'Éducation générale et aux Sports* Jean Borotra, former scout leader and director of the Chantiers de la jeunesse General de la Porte du Theuil, and the leaders of the Uriage *école des cadres* favoured an emphasis upon the creation of a new order through a harsh physical regimen.

---

5     See Robert Paxton, *Vichy France: Old Guard and New Order. 1940–1944* (New York, 1972), chapter two; Julian Jackson, *France: The Dark Years, 1940–1944* (Oxford, 2001), part two.

6     Paxton, pp. 200–221, 268–271; Richard F. Kuisel, *Capitalism and the State in Modern France: Renovation and Economic Management in the Twentieth Century* (Cambridge, 1981), chapter five.

Viewing their efforts as both dangerous and incompatible with the goals of the national revolution, especially the Uriage espousal of communitarian personalism, the Catholic and conservative Conseil national at Vichy continually thwarted their efforts. Hoping to root out teachings incompatible with the prevailing *Pétainisme*, authorities also closely monitored the Compagnons de France work groups and Chantiers de la jeunesse, called the 'avant-garde of the national revolution' for their role in indoctrinating youth with the values of hard work, order, and discipline. Again, one finds in such infighting a parallel with the Faisceau and CDF/PSF experience. All of the elements present in both groups – the Catholic and traditional, the creation of a new order and new man, the meritocratic elite, and the modernization of the education system were represented in the Vichy ministries for education, youth, and sport.[7]

Even on the subject of exclusion, there was frequent disagreement among Vichy government ministers and officials at the Commissariat générale aux Questions juives. Much like the differing opinions in the Faisceau and CDF/PSF, the matter was simply one of degree: How far was the process of exclusion to progress? Within the two groups, opinions ranged from the acceptance of genuinely 'French' Jews to the violent exclusion of all Jews and foreigners. The debate concerning exclusion took place within the same parameters at Vichy, focusing upon the extent to which the regime would act against undesirables. In debating anti-Semitic measures, for example, Admiral Darlan, the head of state throughout 1941, clearly differentiated between French Jews and foreigners, much like La Rocque had done in the CDF/PSF, or Valois in the Faisceau. Yet the views of CQJC head Xavier Vallat were akin to those held by the rank and file in both groups. A virulent anti-Semite, he demanded the suppression of all Jews, and the withholding of all rights and privileges from them. Vallat interned French Jews in concentration camps while deporting foreigners to Germany. His rhetoric and actions, however, were temperate compared those of his successor, Louis Darquier de Pellepoix, an eliminationist anti-Semite dedicated to bringing Nazi racial policies to France.[8]

The comparison, however, goes well beyond doctrine. Although Georges Valois, a convert to the left after the demise of the Faisceau, perished as a resistor in Bergen-Belsen in January 1945, other former members resurfaced under the Vichy regime, most notably Bourgin and Vallat.[9] La Rocque was given a seat on the Conseil

---

7    Paxton, pp. 153–165; W.D. Halls, *The Youth of Vichy France* (Oxford, 1981), pp. 132–134, 187; John Hellman, *The Knight-Monks of Vichy France: Uriage, 1940–1945* (Montréal and Kingston, 1993), pp. 15–16, 50, 74, 139–141, 163–181.

8    Peschanski, pp. 143–179; Michael R. Marrus and Robert O. Paxton, *Vichy France and the Jews* (Stanford, 1995), especially pp. 83–96, 283–286; Laurent Joly, *Vichy dans la solution finale: histoire de Commissariat générale aux Questions juives, 1941–1944* (Paris, 2006), part two.

9    On Vallat's experience in the Faisceau, see his memoirs, *Le Nez de Cléopatre: Souvenirs d'un homme de droite, 1919–1944* (Paris, 1957), pp. 131–133. Vallat was subsequently a member of the CDF/PSF. He left the Faisceau in 1926, after the rupture with the Action française, and the CDF/PSF, after its transformation into a parliamentary party. A member of the conservative Fédération Republicaine, Vallat chose to remain with that organization.

national and a minor post within the Vichy administrative apparatus, but quickly abandoned them for the reconstituted PSF (renamed the Progrès social français in August 1940), whose independence he stressed. Irate at the inattention of Vichy to the group program, La Rocque became a minor resistor and was arrested by the Gestapo in March 1943 for aiding British Intelligence. Yet some of his former colleagues trod a quite different path: Jean Ybarnégaray (Minister of Family and Public Health, subsequently Minister of Youth, in 1940), Paul Creyssel (Secretary-General for Propaganda in 1943), Félix Olivier-Martin (Secretary-General for Youth in 1943), and Stanislas Devaud and Charles Vallin (members of the Conseil national) all actively collaborated.[10] Many rank and file CDF/PSF members also supported different factions within the Vichy regime, including Darquier de Pellepoix.[11]

In the final analysis, factions within both groups agreed on very little. Angered by the perceived decadence and weakness of the parliamentary Republic, fearful of the potential for success on the left, and yearning for a new order, the various leaders and members banded together to forge a French future in their own image. In the process, they provided a microcosm of Vichy, and prepared the way for its programmatic success. Although the results were remarkably different – failure for the Faisceau, limited success for the CDF/PSF, and the exercise of power for the *Vichyistes*, their ultimate experience was a common one. Diverse conservative, extreme-rightist, and technocratic notions of the new nation and state defined the Faisceau and CDF/PSF, much as the plans of the traditionalists, technocrats, social Catholics, and ardent nationalists defined the Vichy regime.

---

10    Paxton, pp. 251–252; Sean Kennedy, *Reconciling France Against Democracy: The Croix de Feu and the Parti social français, 1927–1945* (Kingston and Montréal, 2007), chapter seven. Vallin eventually fled Vichy, joining De Gaulle in London in September 1942.

11    On Darquier de Pellepoix in the CDF/PSF, see Jean Laloum, *La France antisémite de Darquier de Pellepoix* (Paris, 1979), p. 16. He abruptly left the group in December 1935, believing La Rocque to be a 'perfumed dictator'.

# Bibliography

**Personal Interviews**

Gilles de la Rocque and Jacques Nobecourt, July 1997.

**Archival Sources**

*Archives Nationales (AN):*

F7 (General Police): 12863, 12950–12955, 12959–12963, 12965–12966, 13195, 13197, 13208–13212, 13241, 13245, 13247, 13249, 13320, 13983, 14817
AP 451 (Fonds de La Rocque): 10, 70, 81–84, 91, 93, 101–104, 106, 108, 117–118, 120–121, 124–125, 128, 134, 140, 151–152, 170–172

*Archives d'Outre-Mer (AOM):*

Governor-General of Algeria (GGA): 3CAB/47
Alger: 1K/26, 1K/75
Constantine: B/3/323, B/3/327, B/3/522, B/3/635, B/3/707
Oran: 466, 3121

*Archives de la Préfecture de Police/Paris (APP):*

APP/Ba: 1853, 1855–1858, 1894, 1902, 1952, 1980, Boite 'Croix de Feu'

*Bibliothèque Nationale (BN):*

LB: 57/16185

*Centre de documentation juive contemporaine (CDJC):*

XLVI: 32, 37

*Centre d'histoire de l'Europe du vingtième-siècle (CHEVS):*

Fonds La Rocque: 4, 6–7, 9, 11–15, 18–22, 29, 33–36, 38, 41, 43, 45–46, 48, 60–62, 70
Fonds Valois: 12, 21, 25, 44–45

**Periodicals**

*Action française*
*L'Auvergne nouvelle*
*Bulletin mensuel du Mouvement Croix de Feu (51e et 100e sections)*
*Bulletin des Associations Croix de Feu du Département d'Alger*
*Bulletin du Mouvement Croix de Feu en Algérie*
*Cahiers du Cercle Proudhon*
*Cahiers des Etats Généraux*
*Droit de vivre*
*L'Espoir de l'Est*
*L'Espoir Lorrain*
*L'Étudiant sociale*
*Faisceau Bellifontain*
*Le Flambeau*
*Le Flambeau de Bourgogne*
*Le Flambeau de Cannes*
*Le Flambeau de Charentes et du Périgord*
*Le Flambeau de l'Est*
*Le Flambeau de Flandres-Artois-Picardie*
*Le Flambeau de Franche-Comté et Territoire de Belfort*
*Le Flambeau de l'Indochine*
*Le Flambeau de l'Isère*
*Le Flambeau de Lorraine*
*Le Flambeau Marocain*
*Le Flambeau du Midi*
*Le Flambeau Morbihannais*
*Le Flambeau Normand*
*Le Flambeau du Sud-Est*
*Le Flambeau du Sud-Ouest*
*Le Flambeau des Vosges*
*La Flamme*
*La Flamme Catalane*
*La Flamme des Deux-Sèvres*
*La Flamme du Midi*
*La Flamme Tourangelle*
*La Flamme Vendéenne*
*Le Haut parleur du Val et Loire*
*L'Heure française*
*L'Humanité*
*L'Informateur du Syndicats professionnel français des industries chimiques et
    branches connexes*
*L'Information Angevine*
*La Liberté du Maine*
*Nouveau Siècle*
*L'Ouvrier libre*

*Petit journal*
*Le Populaire*
*Pourquoi s'en faire?*
*Les Professionnels de la STA (SPF)*
*PSF Bulletin d'informations*
*Quinze-Vingts Bercy*
*Le Ralliement du Nord*
*Réalité*
*La Relève*
*Rénovation républicaine*
*Revue critique des idées et des livres*
*Revue universelle*
*Samedi*
*Service social*
*SPF*
*SPF de l'aéronautique*
*SPF automobile*
*SPF Banque et Crédit*
*Le Temps*
*Temps nouveaux*
*Le Terrien*
*Volontaire 36*
*Le Volontaire de l'Ouest*
*La Volonté Bretonne*
*La Volonté du Centre*

## Contemporary Sources

Aries, Nel. *L'Économie politique et la doctrine catholique*. Paris: Nouvelle Librairie Nationale, 1923.
Arthuys, Jacques. *Les Combattants*. Paris: Nouvelle Librairie Nationale, 1925.
——. *Comment éviter la banqueroute*. Paris: Nouvelle Librairie Nationale, 1922.
Aucouturier, Marcel. *Programmes socialistes et programmes sociaux*. Imprimeries A. Chaduc, 1938–39.
——. *Programme du Parti social français*. Ardennes: Imprimerie P. Anciaux et co., 1938.
——. *Au Service des Croix de Feu*. Charleville: Impression des Ardennes, 1936.
Barrachin, Edmond. *Le Parti social français devant le pays*. Société d'Éditions et d'Abonnements, 1937.
Barrès, Maurice. *Scènes et doctrines du nationalisme*. Paris: Éditions du Trident, 1987.
——. *Les Déracinés*. Paris: Plon, 1924.
——. *Amori et dolori sacrum*. Paris: Plon, 1921.
——. *Colette Baudoche*. Paris: Nelson Éditeurs, 1908.
Barrès, Philippe. *La Guerre à vingt ans*. Paris: Plon, 1924.

Bourgin, Hubert. *Les Pierres de la maison*. Paris: Nouvelle Librairie Nationale, 1926.

——. *Cinquante ans d'expérience démocratique*. Paris: Nouvelle Librairie Nationale, 1925.

Brasillach, Robert. *Une génération dans l'orage*. Paris: Plon, 1968.

Brière, Jean. *La Tartuffe démasqué: Réponse à Georges Valois*. Paris: Les Étincelles, 1928.

Chopine, Paul. *Six ans chez les Croix de Feu*. Paris: Gallimard, 1935.

Comité de vigilance des intellectuels antifascistes. *Les Croix de Feu, leur chef, leur programme*. Paris, n.p., 1935.

Daladier, Edouard. *Prison Journal, 1940–1945*. Boulder: Westview Press, 1995.

De Barral, Maurice. *Dialogues sur le Faisceau: ses origines, sa doctrine*. Paris: Éditions du Faisceau, 1926.

Debay, Jean. *Remise du fanion à la sous-section Blida-Mitidja*. n.p, 1934.

D'Obrenan, Van den Broeck. *Introduction à la vie nationale*. Paris: Nouvelle Librairie Nationale, 1926.

Drieu la Rochelle, Pierre. *Chronique politique, 1934–1942*. Paris: Gallimard, 1943.

——. *Gilles*. Paris: Gallimard, 1939.

——. *Socialisme fasciste*. Paris: Gallimard, 1934.

*Étudiants: il dépend de vous*. Paris: Imprimerie Artistique Moderne, n.d. (PSF).

Forest, Pierre. *Le Parti social français et le syndicalisme*. Lyon, 1937.

Gorgolini, Pietro. *La Révolution fasciste*. Paris: Nouvelle Librairie Nationale, 1924.

Hautclocque, F. *Grandeur et décadence des Croix de Feu*. Paris: Éditions la Bourbonnais, 1937.

Lacretelle, Jacques. *Qui est La Rocque?* Paris: Flammarion, 1936.

La Rocque, François de. *Disciplines d'action*. Clermont-ferrand: Éditions du Petit journal, 1941.

——. *Paix ou guerre*. Paris: SEDA, 1939.

——. *Service public*. Paris: Grasset, 1934.

*La Rocque et les juifs: un nouveau scandale*. Paris: Centre de Documentation et de Propagande, 1938.

La Tour du Pin, René de. *Vers un ordre sociale chrétien*. Paris: Éditions du Trident, 1987.

Le Corbusier. *Urbanisme*. Paris: Éditions Vincent, Fréal & Co., 1966.

Le Play, Frédéric. *On Family, Work and Social Change*. Chicago: University of Chicago Press, 1982.

Loyer, Pierre. *Vue d'ensemble sur la politique intérieure et extérieure. Conférence fait le 23 novembre 1935 à la réunion des membres des Croix de Feu-Centraux*. n.p., 1935.

*L'Oeuvre sociale dans la mouvement Croix de Feu*. n.p., 1936.

Malherbe, Henri. *La Rocque: un chef, des actes, des idées*. Paris: Plon, 1934.

Maurras, Charles. *Kiel et Tanger*. Versailles: Bibliothèque des Oeuvres Politiques, 1928.

——. *L'Avenir de l'intelligence*. Paris: Ernest Flammarion, 1927.

——. *Enquête sur la monarchie*. Paris: Nouvelle Librairie Nationale, 1924.

Mussolini, Benito. 'The Political and Social Doctrine of Fascism', *International Reconciliation* 306 (1935): 5–17.

Nusbaumer, E. *L'Organisation scientifique des usines*. Paris: Nouvelle Librairie Nationale, 1924.

Parti social français. *1er congrès agricole, 16–17 février 1939*. Saint Brieuc: Les Presses Bretonnes, 1939.

*Le Parti sociale français devant les problèmes de l'heure*. Paris, 1936.

*Le Parti social français et la semaine des 40 heures*. Paris: Service de Propagande, 1937.

*Parti social français: une mystique, un programme*. Paris: SEDA, 1938.

Petit, Jacques. *De la Rocque est-il un chef?* Paris: Société française de Librairie et d'Éditions, 1937.

*Pourquoi nous sommes devenues Croix de Feu*. n.p., 1934.

*Première assemblée nationale des combattants, des producteurs et des chefs de famille*. Paris: Nouvelle Librairie Nationale, 1926.

Pucheu, Pierre. *Ma vie*. Paris: Amiot-Dumont, 1948.

Pujo, Maurice. *Comment La Rocque a trahi*. Paris: Fernand Sorlot, 1937.

Rebatet, Lucien. *Les Décombrés*. Paris: Les Éditions Denoël, 1942.

Renaud, Jean. *J'accuse La Rocque*. Paris: Société d'Éditions Populaires, 1937.

Semaine de la monnaie. *La Politique financière et monétaire de la France*. Paris: La Maison du Livre Français, 1922.

*Union-Esprit-Famille*. Paris, 1938.

Vallat, Xavier. *Le Nez de Cléopâtre: souvenirs d'un homme de droite, 1919–1944*. Paris: Éditions les Quatre Fils Ayman, 1957.

Vallin, Charles. *Aux femmes du Parti social français*. Paris: SEDA, 1937.

Valois, Georges. *L'Homme contre l'argent*. Paris: Librairie Valois, 1928.

——. *Basile, ou la politique de la calomnie*. Paris: Librairie Valois, 1927.

——. *Le Fascisme*. Paris: Nouvelle Librairie Nationale, 1927.

——. *L'État syndicale et la représentation corporatif*. Paris: Nouvelle Librairie Nationale, 1927.

——. *Contre la mensonge et la calomnie*. Paris: Nouvelle Librairie Nationale, 1926.

——. *La Politique économique et sociale du Faisceau*. Paris: Éditions du Faisceau, 1926.

——. *La Politique de la victoire*. Paris: Nouvelle Librairie Nationale, 1925.

——. *L'État, les finances et la monnaie*. Paris: Nouvelle Librairie Nationale, 1925.

——. *La Religion de la laïcité*. Paris: Nouvelle Librairie Nationale, 1925.

——. *D'un siècle à l'autre: chronique d'un génération*. Paris: Nouvelle Librairie Nationale, 1924.

——. *Histoire et philosophie sociales*. Paris: Nouvelle Librairie Nationale, 1924.

——. *La Monarchie et la classe ouvrière*. Paris: Nouvelle Librairie Nationale, 1924.

——. *Le Père*. Paris: Nouvelle Librairie Nationale, 1924.

——. *La Révolution nationale*. Paris: Nouvelle Librairie Nationale, 1924.

——. *La Reconstruction économique de l'Europe*. Paris: Nouvelle Librairie Nationale, 1922.

244 The Extreme Right in Interwar France

——. *L'Économie nouvelle*. Paris: Nouvelle Librairie Nationale, 1919.

——. *Le Cheval de Troie*. Paris: Nouvelle Librairie Nationale, 1918.

——. *La Réforme économique et sociale*. Paris: Nouvelle Librairie Nationale, 1918.

——. *Les Manuels scolaires*. Paris: Nouvelle Librairie Nationale, 1911.

——. *L'Homme qui vient: Philosophie de l'autorité*. Paris: Nouvelle Librairie Nationale, 1906.

Valois, Georges and Coquelle, Georges. *Intelligence et production*. Paris: Nouvelle Librairie nationale, 1920.

Veuillot, François. *La Rocque et son parti*. Paris: Librairie Plon, 1938.


**Books**

Abitbol, Michel. *Les Juifs d'Afrique du nord sous Vichy*. Paris: G.P. Maisonneuve & Larose, 1983.

Adereth, M. *The French Communist Party: A Critical History (1920–84)*. Manchester: Manchester University Press, 1984.

Affron, Matthew and Antliff, Mark, ed. *Fascist Visions*. Princeton: Princeton University Press, 1997.

Alexander, Martin S. and Graham, Helen. *The French and Spanish Popular Fronts*. Cambridge: Cambridge University Press, 1989.

Andreu, Pierre. *Le Rouge et le blanc*. Paris: La Table Ronde, 1977.

Ansky, Michael. *Les Juifs d'Algérie: du décret Crémieux à la libération*. Paris: Éditions du Centre de documentation juive contemporain, 1950.

Ayoun, Richard and Cohen, Bernard. *Les Juifs d'Algérie: 2000 ans d'histoire*. Paris: J.C. Lattès, 1982.

Baránski, Zygmunt G. and Vinall, Shirley W., eds. *Women and Italy: Essays on Gender, Culture, and History*. New York, St. Martin's Press, 1991.

Becker, Jean-Jacques and Berstein, Serge. *Histoire de l'anticommunisme*. Paris: Olivier Orban, 1987.

Bellanger, Claude. *Histoire générale de la presse française, Tome 3: De 1871 à 1940*. Paris: Presses Universitaires de France, 1972.

Berenson, Edward. *The Trial of Madame Caillaux*. Berkeley: University of California Press, 1992.

Bernard, Philippe and Dubief, Henri. *The Decline of the Third Republic*. Cambridge: Cambridge University Press, 1986.

Berstein, Serge. *Histoire du parti Radical*. 2 Vols. Paris: Presses de la Fondation Nationale des Sciences Politiques, 1982.

Birnbaum, Pierre. *The Jews of the Republic: A Political History of State Jews in France from Gambetta to Vichy*. Stanford: Stanford University Press, 1996.

——. *Une Mythe Politique: la République juive*. Paris: Fayard, 1988.

Blinkhorn, Martin. *Mussolini and Fascist Italy*. New York: Methuen, 1984.

Bock, Gisela and Thane, Pat eds. *Maternity and Gender Policies: Women and the Rise of the European Welfare States, 1880s–1950s*. London: Routledge, 1991.

Bonnefous, Édouard. *Histoire politique de la Troisième République*. Vols. 4–5. Paris: Presses Universitaires de France, 1960.

Bridenthal, Renate, Claudia Koonz, and Susan Stuard, eds. *Becoming Visible: Women in European History*. Boston: Houghton Mifflin, 1987.

Brun, Gerard. *Technocrates et technocratie en France (1914–1945)*. Paris: Éditions Albatros, 1985.

Burrin, Philippe. *La Dérive fasciste: Doriot, Déat, Bergery, 1933–1945*. Paris: Seuil, 1986.

Busi, Frederick. *The Pope of Antisemitism: The Career and Legacy of Edouard-Alphonse Drumont*. Lanham: University Press of America, 1986.

Cantier, Jacques. *L'Algérie sous le régime de Vichy*. Paris: Odile Jacob, 2002.

Capitan-Peter, Colette. *Charles Maurras et l'idéologie d'Action française*. Paris: Éditions du Seuil, 1972.

Carls, Stephen D. *Louis Loucheur and the Shaping of Modern France, 1916–1931*. Baton Rouge: Louisiana State University Press, 1993.

Caron, Jeanne. *Le Sillon et la démocratie chrétienne, 1894–1910*. Paris: Plon, 1967.

Caron, Vicki. *Uneasy Asylum: France and the Jewish Refugee Crisis, 1933–1942*. Stanford: Stanford University Press, 1999.

Carroll, David. *Nationalism, Anti-Semitism, and the Ideology of Culture*. Princeton: Princeton University Press, 1995.

Chadwick, Kay, ed. *Catholicism, Politics and Society in Twentieth-Century France*. Liverpool, University of Liverpool Press, 2000.

Chevalier, Maurice. *Histoire de la Franc-maçonnerie française*. Paris: Fayard, 1975.

Cholvy, Gérard, ed. *Mouvements de jeunesse Chrétiens et Juifs: sociabilité juvénile dans le cadre Européen, 1799–1968*. Paris: Éditions du Cerf, 1985.

Clark, Linda L. *Schooling the Daughters of Marianne*. Albany: SUNY Press, 1984.

——. *Social Darwinism in France*. University of Alabama Press, 1984.

Cohen, Asher. *Persécutions et sauvetages: juifs et français sous l'occupation et sous Vichy*. Paris: Cerf, 1993.

Cohen, Yolanda. *Les Jeunes, le socialisme et la guerre: histoire des mouvements de jeunesse en France*. Paris: Éditions l'Harmattan, 1989.

Coston, Henry. *Partis, journaux et hommes politiques d'hier et aujourd'hui*. Paris: Lectures Françaises, 1960.

Cross, Gary. *A Quest for Time: The Reduction of Work in Britain and France, 1840–1940*. Berkeley: University of California Press, 1989.

Curtis, Michael. *Three Against the Third Republic: Sorel, Barrès, and Maurras*. Princeton: Princeton University Press, 1959.

Datta, Venita. *Birth of a National Icon: The Literary Avant-Garde and the Origins of the Intellectual in Modern France*. Albany: SUNY Press, 1999.

De Grand, Alexander. *Italian Fascism: Its Origins and Development*. Lincoln: University of Nebraska Press, 1989.

De Grazia, Victoria. *How Fascism Ruled Women, Italy 1922–1945*. Berkeley: University of California Press, 1993.

Del Bayle, Jean-Louis Loubet. *Les non-conformistes des années 30: Une tentative de renouvellement de la pensée poltique française.* Paris: Seuil, 2001.

Dermenjian, Genevieve. *La Crise anti-juive oranaise, 1895–1905.* Paris, L'Harmattan, 1986.

Di Felice, Renzo. *Intervista sul Fascismo.* Roma: Arnoldo Mondadori Editore, 1992.

Douglas, Allen. *From Fascism to Libertarian Communism: Georges Valois Against the Third Republic.* Berkeley: University of California Press, 1992.

Du Réau, Élisabeth. *Édouard Daladier, 1884–1970.* Paris: Fayard, 1993.

Duval, Jean-Maurice. *Le Faisceau de Georges Valois.* Paris: La Librairie Française, 1979.

Elbow, Matthew. *French Corporative Theory, 1789–1948.* New York: Columbia University Press, 1953.

*La France et l'Allemagne, 1932–1936.* Paris: Éditions du Centre National de la Recherche Scientifique, 1980.

*La France et la question juive.* Paris: Éditions Sylvie Messinger, 1981.

Friedman, Elizabeth. *Colonialism and After: An Algerian Jewish Community.* South Hadley: Bergin & Garvey Publishers, 1988.

Giolitto, Pierre. *Histoire de la jeunesse sous Vichy.* Paris: Perrin, 1991.

Goodfellow, Samuel Huston. *Between the Swastika and the Cross of Lorraine.* Dekalb: Northern Illinois University Press, 1999.

Gosnell, Jonathan K. *The Politics of Frenchness in Colonial Algeria, 1930–1954.* Rochester: University of Rochester Press, 2002.

Guchet, Yves. *Georges Valois: l'Action française, le Faisceau, la République syndicale.* Paris: Éditions Albatros, 1975.

Halls, W.D. *The Youth of Vichy France.* Oxford: Clarendon Press, 1981.

Hamilton, Alastair. *The Appeal of Fascism.* London: Anthony Blond, 1971.

Hawthorn, Melanie and Golson, Richard, eds. *Gender and Fascism in Modern France.* Hanover: University Press of New England, 1997.

Hellman, John. *The Communitarian Third Way: Alexandre Marc and Ordre Nouveau, 1930–2000.* Montreal: McGill-Queen's University Press, 2002.

——. *The Knight-Monks of Vichy France.* Montréal: McGill-Queen's University Press, 1993.

——. *Emmanuel Mounier and the French Catholic Left.* Toronto: University of Toronto Press, 1981.

Herf, Jeffrey. *Reactionary Modernism: Technology, Culture, and Politics in Weimar and the Third Reich.* Cambridge: Cambridge University Press, 1984.

Hoffmann, Stanley. *Decline or Renewal: France Since the 1930s.* New York: Viking Press, 1974.

Hyman, Paula. *From Dreyfus to Vichy: The Remaking of French Jewry.* New York: Columbia University Press, 1979.

Irvine, William, D. *The Boulanger Affair Reconsidered: Royalism, Boulangism, and the Origins of the Radical Right in France.* Oxford: Oxford University Press, 1989.

——. *French Conservatism in Crisis: The Republican Federation of France in the 1930s.* Baton Rouge: University of Louisiana Press, 1979.

Jackson, Julian. *France: The Dark Years, 1940–44*. New York: Oxford University Press, 2001.

——. *The Popular Front in France: Defending Democracy, 1934–1938*. Cambridge: Cambridge University Press, 1990.

Jeanneney, Jean-Noël. *François de Wendel en République: l'argent et le pouvoir, 1914–1940*. Paris: Seuil, 1976.

Jenkins, Brian (ed.). *France in the Era of Fascism: Essays on the French Authoritarian Right*. New York: Berghahn Books, 2005.

Jennings, Jeremy. *Syndicalism in France: A Study of Ideas*. New York: St. Martin's Press, 1990.

Joly, Laurent. *Vichy dans la solution finale: Histoire du Commissariat générale aux Questions juives (1941–1944)*. Paris: Grasset: 2006.

——. *Xavier Vallat (1891–1972): Du nationalisme chrétien à l'antisémitisme d'État*. Paris: Grasset, 2001.

Judt, Tony. *The Burden of Responsibility: Blum, Camus, Aron and the French Twentieth Century*. Chicago: University of Chicago Press, 1998.

Kéchichian, Albert. *Les Croix de Feu à l'âge des fascismes*. Paris: Champ Vallon, 2006.

Kennedy, Sean. *Reconciling France Against Democracy: The Croix de Feu and the Parti social français, 1927–1945*. Kingston and Montréal: McGill-Queen's University Press, 2007.

Koon, Tracy H. *Believe, Obey, Fight: Political Socialization in Fascist Italy, 1922–1943*. Chapel Hill: University of North Carolina Press, 1985.

Koonz, Claudia. *Mothers in the Fatherland: Women, the Family, and Nazi Politics*. New York: St. Martin's Press, 1987.

Kuisel, Richard F. *Seducing the French: The Dilemma of Americanization*. Berkeley: University of California Press, 1993.

——. *Capitalism and the State in Modern France*. Cambridge: Cambridge University Press, 1983.

——. *Ernest Mercier: French Technocrat*. Berkeley: University of California Press, 1967.

Laborie, Pierre. *L'Opinion française sous Vichy*. Paris: Seuil, 1990.

Laloum, Jean. *La France antisémite de Darquier de Pellepoix*. Paris: Éditions Syros, 1979.

Landau, Lazare. *De l'aversion à l'estime: Juifs et Catholiques en France de 1919 à 1939*. Paris: Le Centurion, 1980.

Laneyrie, Philippe. *Les Scouts de France*. Paris: Éditions du Cerf, 1985.

Larkin, Maurice. *France Since the Popular Front*. Oxford: Clarendon Press, 1988.

La Rocque, Edith and Gilles. *La Rocque tels qu'il était*. Paris: Librairie Arthème Fayard, 1962.

*Le Corbusier: la ville, l'urbanisme*. Paris: Fondation Le Corbusier, 1995.

Le Naour, Jean-Yves. *La Famille doit voter: le suffrage familial contre le vote individuel*. Paris: Hachette, 2005.

Machefer, Philippe. *Ligues et fascismes en France*. Paris: Presses Universitaires de France, 1974.

Maier, Charles. *Recasting Bourgeois Europe*. Princeton: Princeton University Press, 1975.

Mangan, J.A., ed. *Shaping the Superman: Fascist Body as Political Icon*. London: Frank Cass, 1999.

Marrus, Michael and Paxton, Robert O. *Vichy France and the Jews*. Stanford: Stanford University Press, 1981.

Martin, Benjamin F. *Count Albert de Mun: Paladin of the Third Republic*. Chapel Hill: University of North Carolina Press, 1978.

Maugenest, Denis, ed. *Le Mouvement social Catholique en France au XXe siècle*. Paris: Cerf, 1990.

Mayeur, Jean-Marie. *Catholicisme social et démocratie chrétienne*. Paris: Éditions du Cerf, 1986.

Mazgaj, Paul. *The Action française and Revolutionary Syndicalism*. Chapel Hill: University of North Carolina Press, 1979.

Mazower, Mark. *Dark Continent: Europe's Twentieth Century*. New York: Vintage Books, 1998.

McMillan, James F. *Dreyfus to De Gaulle: Politics and Society in France, 1898–1969*. London: Edward Arnold, 1985.

——. *Housewife or Harlot: The Place of Women in French Society, 1870–1940*. New York: St. Martin's Press, 1981.

Millman, Richard. *La Question juive entre les deux guerres*. Paris: Armand Colin, 1992.

Milza, Pierre. *Fascismes français: passé et présent*. Paris: Flammarion, 1987.

Monnet, François. *Refaire la République*. Paris: Fayard, 1993.

Monnier, Gerald. *Le Corbusier*. Lyon: La Manufacture, 1986.

Muel-Dreyfus, Francine. *Vichy and the Eternal Feminine: A Contribution to the Political Sociology of Gender*. Durham: Duke University Press, 2001.

Nguyen, Victor. *Aux origines de l'Action française*. Paris: Fayard, 1991.

Nobecourt, Jacques. *Le Colonel de La Rocque 1885–1946, ou les pièges du nationalisme chrétien*. Paris: Fayard, 1996.

Noiriel, Gérard. *Les Origines républicaines de Vichy*. Paris: Hachette, 1999.

Nolte, Ernst. *Three Faces of Fascism*. London: Weidenfeld and Nicolsen, 1965.

Ory, Pascal. *La Belle illusion: culture et politique sous le signe du Front Populaire*. Paris: Plon, 1994.

Ostenc, Michel. *L'Education en Italie pendant le fascisme*. Paris: Publications de la Sorbonne, 1980.

Passmore, Kevin. *Women, Gender, and Fascism in Europe, 1919–1945*. New Brunswick: Rutgers University Press, 2003.

——. *From Liberalism to Fascism: The Right in a French Province*. Cambridge: Cambridge University Press, 1997.

Paxton, Robert O. *French Peasant Fascism: Henry Dorgère's Greenshirts and the Crises of French Agriculture, 1929–1939*. Oxford: Oxford University Press, 1997.

——. *Vichy France: Old Guard and New Order*. New York: Columbia University Press, 1972.

Payne, Stanley G. *A History of Fascism, 1914–1945.* Madison, University of Wisconsin Press, 1995.

Péan, Pierre. *Une jeunesse française: François Mitterrand, 1934–1947.* Paris: Fayard, 1994.

Pederson, Susan. *Family, Dependence, and the Origins of the Welfare State: Britain and France, 1914–1945.* Cambridge: Cambridge University Press, 1993.

Perfetti, Francesco. *Il Sindicalismo Fascista. Vol. 1: Dalle Origini dello Stato Corporativo (1919–1930).* Roma: Bonacci Editore, 1988.

Peschanski, Denis. *Vichy 1940–44: contrôle et exclusion.* Paris: Éditions Complexe, 1997.

Peukert, Detlev. *Inside Nazi Germany.* New Haven: Yale University Press, 1987.

Plumyène, J. and Lasierra R. *Fascismes français, 1923–1963.* Paris: Éditions du Seuil, 1963.

Pollard, Miranda. *Reign of Virtue: Mobilizing Gender in Vichy France.* Chicago: University of Chicago Press, 1998.

Popelin. Claude. *Arènes politiques.* Paris: Fayard, 1971.

Prost, Antoine. *Les Anciens combattants et la société française.* 3 Vols. Paris: Presses de la Fondation Nationale des Sciences Politiques, 1978.

———. *Les Anciens combattants.* Paris: Gallimard, 1977.

———. *Histoire de l'enseignement en France, 1800–1967.* Paris: Librairie Armand Colin, 1968.

Rémond, René. *The French Right: From 1815 to De Gaulle.* Philadelphia: University of Pennsylvania Press, 1971.

Rémond, René and Bourdin, Janine, ed. *La France et les français en 1938–1939.* Paris: Presses de la Fonds Nationale de Sciences Politiques, 1978.

Reynolds, Siân. *France Between the Wars: Gender and Politics.* New York: Routledge, 1996.

Roberts, David D. *The Syndicalist Tradition and Italian Fascism.* Chapel Hill: University of North Carolina Press, 1979.

Roberts, Mary Louise. *Disruptive Acts: The New Woman in Fin-de-Siècle France.* Chicago: University of Chicago Press, 2002.

———. *Civilization Without Sexes: Reconstructing Gender in Postwar France, 1917–1927.* Chicago: The University of Chicago Press, 1994.

Ross, Kristin. *Fast Cars, Clean Bodies: Decolonization and the Reordering of French Culture.* Cambridge: MIT Press, 1995.

Roth, Jack J. *The Cult of Violence: Sorel and the Sorelians.* Berkeley: University of California Press, 1980.

Rousso, Henry. *The Vichy Syndrome: History and Memory in France Since 1944.* Cambridge: Cambridge University Press, 1991.

Rudaux, Philippe. *Les Croix de Feu et le PSF.* Paris: Éditions Franc-Empire, 1967.

Ruedy, John. *Modern Algeria: The Origins and Development of a Nation.* Bloomington: Indiana University Press, 1992.

Sauvy, Alfred. *Histoire économique de la France entre les deux guerres.* Vols 1–2. Paris: Librairie Arthème-Fayard, 1967.

Schneider, William H. *Quality and Quantity: The Quest for Biological Regeneration in Twentieth-Century France.* Cambridge: Cambridge University Press, 1990.

Schor, Ralph. *Histoire de l'immigration en France de la fin du XIXe siècle à nos jours*. Paris: Armand Colin, 1996.

———. *L'Antisémitisme en France pendant les années trente*. Paris: Éditions Complexe, 1992.

———. *L'Opinion français et les étrangers*. Paris: Publications de la Sorbonne, 1985.

Schuker, Stephen A. *The End of French Predominance in Europe: The Financial Crisis of 1924 and the Coming of the Dawes Plan*. Chapel Hill: University of North Carolina Press, 1976.

Scott, Joan Wallach. *Gender and the Politics of History*. New York: Columbia University Press, 1999.

Sérant, Paul. *Les Dissidents de l'Action française*. Paris: Copernic, 1978.

Siegel, Mona. *The Moral Disarmament of France: Education, Pacifism, and Patriotism, 1914-1940*. Cambridge: Cambridge University Press, 2004.

Sirinelli, Jean-François, ed. *Histoire des droites en France*. 3 Vols. Paris: Gallimard, 1992.

Sirinelli, Jean-François and Ory, Pascal. *Les Intellectuels en France: de l'affaire Dreyfus à nos jours*. Paris: Armand Colin, 1986.

Sivan, Emanuel. 'Stéréotypes antijuifs dans la mentalité Pied-noir' in *Les Relations entre Juifs et Musulmans en Afrique du nord, XIXe–XXe siècles: actes du Colloque international de l'institut d'histoire des pays d'outre-mer*. Paris: Éditions du CNRS, 1980.

Soucy, Robert. *French Fascism: The Second Wave, 1933–1939*. New Haven: Yale University Press, 1995.

———. *French Fascism: The First Wave, 1924–1933*. New Haven: Yale University Press, 1986.

Spackman, Barbara. *Fascist Virilities: Rhetoric, Ideology, and Social Fantasy in Italy*. Minneapolis: University of Minnesota Press, 1996.

Stephenson, Jill. *Women in Nazi Germany*. London: Longman, 2001.

———. *The Nazi Organization of Women*. Barnes and Noble Books, 1981.

Sternhell, Zeev. *La Droite révolutionnaire, 1885–1914*. Paris: Gallimard, 1997.

———. *Antisemitism and the Right in France*. Jerusalem: Shazar Library/Institute of Contemporary Jewry, 1988.

———. *Neither Right Nor Left*. Princeton: Princeton University Press, 1986.

———. *Maurice Barrès et le nationalisme français*. Paris: Presses de la Fondation Nationale Scientifique, 1972.

Sweets, John F. *Choices in Vichy France*. Oxford: Oxford University Press, 1986.

Talbott, John. E. *The Politics of Educational Reform in France, 1918–1940*. Princeton: Princeton University Press, 1969.

Tannenbaum, Edward. *Action française*. New York: John Wiley and Sons, 1961.

Weber, Eugen. *Action française: Royalism and Reaction in Twentieth-Century France*. Stanford: Stanford University Press, 1963.

Wilson, Stephen. *Ideology and Experience: Antisemitism in France at the Time of the Dreyfus Affair*. East Rutherford: Fairleigh-Dickinson University Press, 1982.

Winock, Michel, ed. *Histoire de l'extrême droite en France*. Paris: Seuil, 1993.

———. *Nationalisme, antisémitisme et fascisme en France*. Paris: Éditions du Seuil, 1990.

——. *Edouard Drumont et Cie.* Paris: Seuil, 1982.

Wohl, Robert. *The Generation of 1914.* Cambridge: Harvard University Press, 1979.

Zeldin, Theodore. *France, 1848–1945.* Vol. 2, *Intellect, Taste, and Anxiety.* Oxford: Clarendon Press, 1977.

Zuccotti, Susan. *The Holocaust, The French, and the Jews.* New York: HarperCollins, 1993.


**Articles**


Arnal, Oscar. 'Shaping Young Proletarians into Militant Christians: The Pioneer Phase of the JOC in France and Québec.' *Journal of Contemporary History*, 32 (1997): 509–526.

——. 'Towards a Lay Apostelate of the Workers: Three Decades of Conflict for the French Jeunesse ouvrière chrétienne (1927–1956).' *Catholic Historical Review* LXXIII/2 (1987): 211–227.

Assouline, Pierre. 'Henry Coston: itinéraire d'un anti-Sémite,' *L'Histoire* 148 (1991): 56–60.

Berstein, Serge. 'La France des années trente allergiques au fascisme.' *Vingtième Siècle* no. 2 (1984): 83–94.

Blatt, Joel. 'Relatives and rivals: The Responses of the Action française to Italian Fascism, 1919–1926.' *European Studies Review* 2 (1981): 263–292.

Caron, Vicki. 'The Antisemitic Revival in France in the 1930s: The Socioeconomic Dimension Reconsidered.' *Journal of Modern History* 70 (1998): 24–73.

——. 'Prelude to Vichy: France and the Jewish Refugees in the Era of Appeasement.' *Journal of Contemporary History* 20 (1985): 157–176.

Chanet, Jean-François. 'La Fabrique des héros: Pédagogie républicaine et culte des grands homes de Sedan à Vichy.' *Vingtième siècle* 65 (2000): 13–34.

Clarke, Jackie. 'France, America, and the Metanarrative of Modernization: From Postwar Social Science to the New Culturalism.' *Contemporary France and Francophone Studies* 8 (2004): 365–377.

——. 'Imagined Productive Communities: Industrial Rationalisation and Cultural Crisis in 1930s France.' *Modern and Contemporary France* 8 (2000): 345–357.

Cohen, Paul. 'Heroes and Dilettantes: The Action Française, Le Sillon, and the Generation of 1905–14.' *French Historical Studies* 15 (1988): 673–687.

Cole, Joshua. '"There Are Only Good Mothers": The Ideological Work of Women's Fertility in France Before World War I.' *French Historical Studies* 19 (1996): 639–672.

Costa-Pinto, Antonio. 'Fascist Ideology Revisited: Zeev Sternhell and his Critics'. *European History Quarterly* 16 (1986): 465–483.

De Grand, Alexander. 'Curzio Malaparte: The Illusion of the Fascist Revolution.' *Journal of Contemporary History* 7 (1972): 73–89.

Del Bayle, Jean-Louis Loubet. 'Une tentative de renouvellement de la pensée politique française.' *Nouvelle Revue des Deux-Mondes* 5 (1975): 320–335.

Delaporte, Christian. 'Les Jeunesses socialistes dans l'entre-deux-guerres.' *Mouvement social* no. 157 (1991): 33–66.

Douglas, Allen. 'Violence and Fascism: The Case of the Faisceau.' *Journal of Contemporary History* 19 (1984): 689–712.

Eisler, Jerzy. 'Georges Valois et une idéologie des combattants.' *Acta Poloniae Historica* 48 (1983): 133–163.

Fabre, Remy. 'Les Mouvements de jeunesse dans la France de l'entre-deux-guerres.' *Mouvement social* no. 168 (1994): 9–30.

Fridenson, Patrick. 'L'Idéologie des grands constructeurs dans l'entre-deux-guerres.' *Mouvement social* no. 81 (1972): 53–68.

Gay-Lescot, Jean-Louis. 'La Politique sportive de Vichy.' *Cahiers de L'Institut d'histoire du temps present* 8 (1988): 55–75.

Godin, Emmanuel. 'La Fédération française des étudiants Catholiques (FFEC) de l'entre-deux-guerres au régime de Vichy.' *Revue historique de l'éducation français* no. 87 (2001): 87–111.

Gordon, Bertram. M. 'Radical Right Youth Between the Wars.' In *Proceedings of the Fifth Annual Meeting of the Western Society for French History*, 5 (1978): 313–321.

Green, Mary Jean. 'Gender, Fascism, and the Croix de Feu: The 'Women's Pages' of *Le Flambeau*', *French Cultural Studies* 8 (1997): 229–239.

Hanna, Martha. 'Iconology and Ideology: Images of Joan of Arc in the Idiom of the Action française.' *French Historical Studies* 14 (1985): 215–239.

Hillaire, Yves-Marie. 'L'Association catholique de la jeunesse française, les étapes d'un histoire (1886–1956).' *Revue du Nord* no. 261/262 (1984): 903–916.

Huss, Marie-Monique. 'Pronatalism in the Inter-war Period in France.' *Journal of Contemporary History* 25 (1990): 39–68.

Irvine, William D. 'Domestic Politics and the Fall of France in 1940.' *Historical Reflections/Réflexions historiques* 22 (1996): 77–90.

——. 'Fascism in France and the Strange Case of the Croix de Feu', Journal *of Modern History* 63 (1991): 271–295.

Julliard, Jacques. 'Sur une fascisme imaginaire: à propos d'un livre de Zeev Sternhell.' *Annales, E.S.C.* no. 4 (1984): 84–94.

Kaplan, Steven L. 'Un laboratoire de la doctrine corporatiste sous le régime de Vichy: l'Institut d'études corporatives et sociales.' *Mouvement social* no. 195 (2001): 35–77.

Kestel, Laurent. 'The Emergence of Anti-Semitism Within the Parti Populaire Français: Party Intellectuals, Peripheral Leaders and National Figures', *French History* 19 (2005): 364–384.

Koerner, Francis. 'L'Extrème-droite en Oranie (1936–1940).' *Revue d'Histoire Moderne et Contemporaine* 20 (1973): 568–594.

Koos, Cheryl A. 'Fascism, Fatherhood, and the Family in Interwar France: The Case of Antoine Rédier and the Légion.' *Journal of Family History* 24 (1999): 117–129.

——. 'Gender, Anti-individualism, and Nationalism: The Alliance nationale and the Pronatalist Backlash against the *Femme Moderne*, 1933–1940.' *French Historical Studies* 19/3 (1997): 699–723.

Kuisel, Richard F. 'Vichy et les origines de la planification économique (1940–1946).' *Mouvement social*, no. 98 (janvier–mars 1977): 77–101.

Kupferman, Fred and Machefer, Philippe. 'Presse et politique dans les années trente: le cas du *petit journal.*' *Revue d'histoire moderne et contemporaine* 23 (1975): 13–45.

Ledeen, Michael A. 'Italian Fascism and Youth.' *Journal of Contemporary History*, 4 (1969): 137–154.

Levillain, Philippe. '*Rerum Novarum* et *Quadragesimo Anno*: Une même question? Une même réponse?' *Revue du Nord* 290–91 (1991): 349–355.

Levey, Jules. 'Georges Valois and the Faisceau: The Making and Breaking of a Fascist.' *French Historical Studies* 8 (1973): 279–304.

Lottman, Herbert R. 'André Gide's Return: A Case Study in Left-Bank Politics', *Encounter*, 58 (1982): 18–27.

Machefer, Philippe. 'Les Syndicats professionnel français'. *Mouvement social* no. 119 (1982): 91–112.

——. 'L'Action française et le PSF.' *Études Maurassienes* 4 (1980): 125–133.

——. 'Tardieu et La Rocque.' *Bulletin de la Société d'histoire moderne* 15 (1973): 11–21.

——. 'Les Croix de Feu (1927–1936).' *L'Information historique* 34 (1972): 28–34.

——. 'Le Parti social français en 1936–1937.' *L'Information historique* 34 (1972): 74–80.

——. 'L'Union des droites: le PSF et le Front de la liberté.' *Revue d'histoire moderne et contemporaine* 17 (1970): 112–136.

——. 'Sur quelques aspects de l'activité de Colonel de La Rocque et du Progrès social français pendant la Seconde Guerre Mondiale.' *Revue d'histoire de la Deuxième Guerre Mondiale* 57 (1965): 35–56.

——. 'Autour du problème algérien en 1936–1938: la doctrine algérienne du PSF: le PSF et le projet Blum-Violette.' *Revue d'histoire moderne et contemporaine* 10 (1963): 147–156.

——. 'Le Parti social français et la petite entreprise', unpublished paper.

Mazgaj, Paul. 'The Young Sorelians and Decadence.' *Journal of Contemporary History* 17 (1982): 179–199.

Millman, Richard. 'Les Croix de Feu et l'antisémitisme.' *Vingtième siècle* no. 38 (1993): 47–61.

Müller, Klaus-Jürgen. 'French Fascism and Modernization.' *Journal of Contemporary History* 11 (1976): 75–107.

Nello, Paolo. 'Mussolini e Bottai: due modi diversi di concepire l'educazione fascista della gioventù.' *Storia Contemporanea*, 8 (1977): 335–366.

Ogden, Philip E. and Huss, Marie-Monique. 'Demography and Pronatalism in France in the Nineteenth and Twentieth Centuries.' *Journal of Historical Geography* 8 (1982): 283–298.

Passmore, Kevin. 'Planting the Tricolore in the Citadels of Communism: Women's Social Action in the Croix de Feu and Parti social français.' *Journal of Modern History* 71 (1999): 814–851.

——. 'The Croix de Feu: Bonapartism, National Populism, or Fascism?' *French History* 9 (1995): 93–123.

——. 'Boy Scouting for Grown-ups? Paramilitarism in the Croix de Feu/Parti social français.' *French Historical Studies* 19 (1995): 527–557.

——. 'The French Third Republic: Stalemate Society or Cradle of Fascism?' *French History* 7 (1993): 417–449.

Reggiani, Andrés Horacio. 'The Politics of Demography, 1919–1945.' *French Historical Studies* 19 (1996): 725–754.

Régnier, Jérôme. 'Diffusion et interprétation de *Quadragesimo Anno*.' *Revue du Nord* 73 (1991): 357–363.

Rémond, René. 'Pensée sociale de l'église et mouvements catholiques.' *Revue du Nord* 73 (1991): 469–476.

Roberts, Mary Louise. 'Rationalization, Vocational Guidance and the Reconstruction of Female Identity in Postwar France.' *Proceedings of the Fifth Annual Meeting of the Western Society for French History* 20 (1993): 367–387.

Salsano, Alfredo. 'Georges Valois e lo Stato Tecnico. Il Corporativismo Tecnocrato tra Fascismo e Antifascismo.' *Studi Storici* 34 (1993): 571–624.

Sarti, Roland. 'Fascist Modernization in Italy: Traditional or Revolutionary?' *American Historical Review* 75 (1970): 1029–1045.

Shaw, Lynette. 'The *Anciens combattants* and the Events of February 1934.' *European Studies Review* 5 (1975): 299–313.

Simard, Marc. 'Intellectuels, fascisme, et antimodernité dans la France des années trente.' *Vingtième Siècle* 18 (1988): 55–75.

Soucy, Robert. 'French Fascism and the Croix de Feu: A Dissenting Interpretation.' *Journal of Contemporary History* 26 (1991): 159–188.

Sternhell, Zeev. 'The 'Anti-Materialist' Revision of Marxism as an Aspect of the Rise of Fascist Ideology.' *Journal of Contemporary History* 22 (1987): 379–400.

——. 'Anatomie d'un mouvement fasciste: le Faisceau de Georges Valois.' *Revue française de science politique* 26 (1976): 5–40.

Talbott, John E. 'The French Left and the Ideology of Educational Reform.' *French Historical Studies* 5 (1968): 465–476.

Thébaud, Françoise. 'Le Mouvement nataliste dans la France de l'entre-deux-guerres: L'Alliance nationale pour l'accroissement de la population française.' *Revue d'histoire moderne et contemporaine* no. 32 (1985): 276–301.

Tingley, Clarence. 'Georges Valois and the Faisceau: Post-Apocalyptic Politics in Twentieth-Century France.' *Proceedings of the Fifth Annual Meeting of the Western Society for French History* 3 (1976): 382–390.

Watson, D.R. 'The Politics of Educational Reform in France During the Third Republic, 1900–1940.' *Past and Present* no. 34 (1966): 81–99.

Winock, Michel. 'Fascisme à la française ou fascisme introuvable.' *Le Debat* no. 25 (1983): 35–44.

Wohl, Robert. 'French Fascism, Both Right and Left: Reflections on the Sternhell Controversy.' *Journal of Modern History* 63 (1991): 91–98.

Wolff, Richard J. 'Fascistizing Italian Youth: The Limits of Mussolini's Educational System.' *History of Education* 13/4 (1984): 287–298.

Wolikow, Serge. 'Le PCF au temps du front populaire.' *Cahiers d'histoire de l'Institut des Recherches Marxistes*, 36 (1989): 5–15.

## Dissertations

Antipolis, Sophia. 'L'Extréme-droite au parlement sous le Premier Ministre Blum, juin 1936–juin 1937', Mémoire de maîtrise, Université de Nice, 1997.

Jaubertho, Christine. 'Des Croix de Feu au Parti social français, la dérive vers la République', Mémoire de maîtrise, Université de Toulouse, 1993.

Kennedy, Sean Michael. 'Reconciling the Nation Against Democracy: The Croix de Feu, the Parti social français and French Politics, 1927–1945', Ph.D. Dissertation, York University, 1998.

Kestel, Laurent, 'De la conversion en politique: gènese et institutionnalisation du Parti populaire français, 1936–1940', Ph.D. Dissertation, Université Paris-I (Sorbonne), 2006.

Levey, Jules. 'The Sorellian Syndicalists: Édouard Berth, Georges Valois, and Hubert Lagardelle', Ph.D. Dissertation, Columbia University, 1967.

Lung, Weng-Ting. 'L'Historique et la doctrine des Croix de Feu et du Parti social français', Thèse du Droit, Université de Nice, 1971.

Mislin, Claude. 'Les Croix de Feu et le Parti social français en Alsace (1930–1939)', Diplôme d'IED, Institut d'Études Politiques de Strasbourg, 1981–1982.

Sarnoff, Daniella. 'In the Cervix of the Nation: Women in French fascism, 1919–1939', Ph.D. Dissertation., Boston College, 2001.

Thomas, Jean-Paul. 'Un Droite nouvelle dans la République? Continuités et ruptures du PSF au RPF, 1936–1948', Mémoire pour le DEA d'histoire de la France contemporaine, 1991.

Tinghino, John. 'Edmundo Rossoni: Fascist Champion of Labour', Ph.D. Dissertation, New York University, 1982.

Whitney, Susan Brewer. 'The Politics of Youth: Communists and Catholics in Interwar France', Ph.D. Dissertation, Rutgers University, 1994.

# Index

*Volonté du Centre* 224
*Volontée Brétonne* 129, 205

Wendel, François de 44, 85
Winter, Pierre 37
Women—France
    education of 115, 122
    *femme nouvelle/moderne* 111–12, 120,
        122, 127
    female labour 111, 114, 116, 122–3
    feminism 127, 232
    and Great War 111, 114
    as housewives 122–3
    interwar male reaction to 111–12,
        114–15, 123
    Napoleonic Code and 114

X-Crise 62, 102–3
Xenophobia—France 3, 186–7, 189, 217–27

Ybarnégaray, Jean 174, 182, 238
Youth—France
    education 147, 154–6, 167–8, 172,
        179–80
    extreme right and 151–3
    movements 145–7, 232–3
    physical fitness of 173–4
Yvar, Colette 128

Zangeuil, Israël 191
Zay, Jean 167–71, 174, 199, 213
Ziegler, Gillette 170, 172